BLUEPRINT FOR ACTION

Also by Thomas P.M. Barnett

ROMANIAN AND EAST GERMAN POLICIES
IN THE THIRD WORLD

THE PENTAGON'S NEW MAP

BLUEPRINT FOR ACTION

A Future Worth Creating

THOMAS P. M. BARNETT

G. P. PUTNAM'S SONS
NEW YORK

G. P. PUTNAM'S SONS
Publishers Since 1838
Published by the Penguin Group
Penguin Group (USA) Inc., 375 Hudson Street, New York, New York 10014, USA •
Penguin Group (Canada), 90 Eglinton Avenue East, Suite 700, Toronto, Ontario M4P 2Y3,
Canada (a division of Pearson Penguin Canada Inc.) • Penguin Books Ltd, 80 Strand,
London WC2R 0RL, England • Penguin Ireland, 25 St Stephen's Green, Dublin 2, Ireland
(a division of Penguin Books Ltd) • Penguin Group (Australia), 250 Camberwell Road,
Camberwell, Victoria 3124, Australia (a division of Pearson Australia Group Pty Ltd) •
Penguin Books India Pvt Ltd, 11 Community Centre, Panchsheel Park, New Delhi–110 017,
India • Penguin Group (NZ), Cnr Airborne and Rosedale Roads, Albany, Auckland 1310,
New Zealand (a division of Pearson New Zealand Ltd) • Penguin Books (South Africa)
(Pty) Ltd, 24 Sturdee Avenue, Rosebank, Johannesburg 2196, South Africa

Penguin Books Ltd, Registered Offices: 80 Strand, London WC2R 0RL, England

LIBRARY OF CONGRESS CATALOGING-IN-PUBLICATION DATA

Barnett, Thomas P. M.
Blueprint for action : a future worth creating / Thomas P. M. Barnett.
p.   cm.
Includes bibliographical references and index.
ISBN 0-399-15312-8
1. United States—Foreign relations—2001–   2. Security, International—Forecasting.
3. Globalization.   4. United States—Military policy.   5. World politics—1989–
I. Title.
JZ1480.B36   2005   2005048715
327.73—dc22

Printed in the United States of America
1   3   5   7   9   10   8   6   4   2

This book is printed on acid-free paper. ∞

Book design by Lovedog Studio

While the author has made every effort to provide accurate telephone numbers and Internet addresses at the time of publication, neither the publisher nor the author assumes any responsibility for errors, or for changes that occur after publication. Further, the publisher does not have any control over and does not assume any responsibility for author or third-party websites or their content.

To Vonne Mary

For connecting me to a new past, present, and future

And to Emily Vonne, Kevin Clifford,
Jerome Edward, and Vonne Mei Ling

Ya vas lyubil tak iskrenno, tak nezhno,
Kak dai vam Bog lyubimoi byt' drugim

A. S. PUSHKIN (1829)

CONTENTS

PREFACE:
A FUTURE WORTH
CREATING

A GRAND STRATEGY REQUIRES a grand vision, and that is what I sought to provide in my first book, *The Pentagon's New Map: War and Peace in the Twenty-first Century.* The response to that book within the U.S. defense community was, and continues to be, overwhelming, but likewise challenging. Long-range planners at various regional commands, as well as at the Pentagon, have embraced its global perspective and the strategic requirements for change that it portends, but they, like so many other readers, quickly cracked the code of the first book: the implied blueprint for action is simply *so much larger than anything the Defense Department can manage.*

That was the book's great limitation: it explained the world's fundamental dynamics—or the rule sets that govern globalization—as viewed from the military outward, and many nonmilitary readers were left wondering how they and their communities could join this larger effort to reshape the international security environment upon which all economic activity and political stability ultimately depend. Some readers, too, had difficulties with points regarding the use of force, believing that no discussion of peace can ever admit rationales for war. In reality, of course, security is necessary but never sufficient for lasting peace.

That first volume related how globalization has spread to encompass two-thirds of the world's population, defined as the global economy's Functioning Core, and how one-third of humanity remains trapped outside this peaceful sphere in regions that are weakly connected to the global economy, or what I call the Non-Integrating Gap. Since the end of the Cold War, all the wars and civil wars and genocide have occurred within the Gap, and so my vision of ending war "as we know it" begins with shrinking this Gap and ends with making globalization truly global and eradicating the disconnectedness that defines danger in the world today.

This vision propels a strategy for the United States, one that makes the audacious demand that America equate its national security with that of globalization's continued survival and success. In so arguing, I reconnect America's national security strategy to a global peace strategy, much as it had been during the Cold War, when our defense of the West against threats from the East spoke not just to our own nation's survival but to that of freedom around the world as well.

America forgot that connection across the 1990s, enamored as we were with the notion that globalization's unstoppable march around the planet would solve all security problems lying in its path. We learned differently on September 11, 2001. We learned that globalization, and all the freedom it fosters through connectivity, requires a bodyguard, because there are still numerous forces throughout the Gap and even inside the Core working against it.

The goals are universal inclusiveness and global peace. As fantastic as those goals might seem in the early years of a global war on terrorism, they speak to a future worth creating, and so I have made the enunciation of this strategy my life's work. Readers throughout the U.S. defense establishment, as well as those serving in militaries the world over, made clear in their responses to the first book that they

desired more than an accurate description of today's security environment and a grand strategy for directing its ultimate improvement.
They wanted a description of the journey. They wanted an enunciation of the crucial tasks ahead: the rule sets to be forged, the institutions to be built, the peace to be won.

This second volume delivers them.

I do not offer this blueprint lightly, because I am both sobered by
the sacrifices already rendered in this conflict and deeply cognizant of
those lying ahead. I have spent my adult life living among, and working with, the U.S. military, a force for global good that I believe has no
equal, and I have watched loved ones depart our shores for service in
war zones, knowing that their sacrifices made them not *better* Americans but *true* Americans—generous to both their fellow citizens and
the world's citizens.

I believe America finds itself in such generosity, such sacrifice, such
love. There will always be enemies of connectedness and the freedom
it engenders, but this book is about not just the defeat of such enemies
but the victory of our ideals. Those ideals exist only to the extent that
we make them real in our words, deeds, and legacy. This blueprint is
not about *them* but *us*—what we stand for and what we believe in.

Since I wrote *The Pentagon's New Map*, I have come to believe ever
more deeply in America's fundamental purpose as source code for this
era's successful and far-reaching brand of globalization. We have set
in motion a powerful networking effect that encompasses economic
and technological connectivity of the highest order yet seen. But we
still have much to do. Yes, we must help the Gap join that existing connectivity. But we must likewise help the world as a whole—both Core
and Gap—create networks of political and security connectivity commensurate with the mutually assured dependence that now exists
among all states that are deeply integrated with the growing global
economy.

The world needs to play catch-up, so to speak. We need to make
sure our security rule sets match our growing network connectivity,
and that our political rule sets keep pace with our economic transactions. We need balance, pure and simple, not moving ahead any faster

than the slowest among us can manage, and not waging wars without waging peace—lest our victories prove illusory.

To state this great requirement and to achieve it are two vastly different things. But I don't simply believe that America *can make a difference;* I know that America *is the difference:* between success and failure, between stability and strife, between creating a better future for our children and expecting them to restore what we've let come undone.

None of what this book advocates will be easy, but all is feasible if we stop treating other great powers as rivals and start treating them as equals in desire, if not capability. America has created many new rules since 9/11, but the only ones that matter in the end are those recognized by other nations and taken up as their own. Globalization comes with rules but not a ruler. We may propose but never impose, because the difference between the leader and the led is not merely their competing visions of power but the power of their competing visions.

America is up to this task. I don't speak of possibilities here but inevitabilities. The work will eventually be done, if not by our leadership then by the leadership of others. I simply believe that if something is worth doing tomorrow, then it's worth doing today, and that if we know America can do it, then Americans should do it.

Let us begin.

T.P.M.B.

4 July 2005

GLOSSARY
OF KEY TERMS FROM
THE PENTAGON'S
NEW MAP

ASYMMETRICAL WARFARE A conflict between two foes of vastly different capabilities. After the Red Army dissolved in the 1990s, the U.S. military knew it was basically unbeatable, especially in a straight-up fight. But that meant that much smaller opponents would seek to negate its strengths by exploiting its weaknesses, by being clever and "dirty" in combat. On 9/11, America got a real dose of what asymmetrical warfare is going to be like in the twenty-first century.

CONNECTIVITY The enormous changes being brought on by the information revolution, including the emerging financial, technological, and logistical architecture of the global economy (i.e., the movement of money, services accompanied by content, and people and materials). During the boom times of the 1990s, many thought that advances in communications such as the Internet and mobile phones would trump all, erasing the business cycle, erasing national borders, erasing the very utility of the state in managing a global security order that seemed more virtual than real, but 9/11 proved differently. That connectivity, while a profoundly transforming force, could not by itself maintain global security, primarily because a substantial rise in connectivity between any nation and the outside world typically leads to a host of tumultuous reactions, including heightened nationalism.

DISCONNECTEDNESS In this century, it is disconnectedness that defines danger. Disconnectedness allows bad actors to flourish by keeping entire societies detached from the global community and under their dictatorial control, or in the case of failed states, it allows dangerous transnational actors to exploit the resulting chaos to their own dangerous ends. Eradicating disconnectedness is the defining security task of our age, as well as a supreme moral cause in the cases of those who suffer it against their will. Just as important, however, by expanding the connectivity of globalization, we increase peace and prosperity planet-wide.

FUNCTIONING CORE Those parts of the world that are actively integrating their national economies into a global economy and that adhere to globalization's emerging security rule set. The Functioning Core at present consists of North America, Europe both "old" and "new," Russia, Japan and South Korea, China (although the interior far less so), India (in a pockmarked sense), Australia and New Zealand, South Africa, and the ABCs of South America (Argentina, Brazil, and Chile). That is roughly four billion out of a global population of more than six billion. The Functioning Core can be subdivided into the Old Core, anchored by America, Europe, and Japan; and the New Core, whose leading pillars are China, India, Brazil, and Russia.

GLOBALIZATION The worldwide integration and increasing flows of trade, capital, ideas, and people. Until 9/11, the U.S. Government tended to identify globalization primarily as an economic rule set, but thanks to the global war on terrorism, we now understand that it likewise demands the clear enunciation and enforcement of a security rule set as well.

LEVIATHAN The U.S. military's warfighting capacity and the high-performance combat troops, weapon systems, aircraft, armor, and ships associated with all-out war against traditionally defined opponents (i.e., other militaries). This is the force America created to defend the West against the Soviet threat, now transformed from its industrial-era roots to its information-age capacity for high-speed, high-lethality, and high-precision major combat operations. The Leviathan force is without peer in the world today, and—as such—frequently finds itself fighting shorter and easier wars. This "overmatch" means, however, that current and future enemies in the global war on terrorism will largely seek to avoid triggering the Leviathan's employment, preferring to wage asymmetrical war against the United States, focusing on its economic interests and citizenry. The Leviathan rules the "first half" of war, but is often ill-suited, by design and temperament, to the "second half" of peace, to include postconflict stabilization and reconstruction operations. It is thus counterposed to the System Administrators force.

MILITARY-MARKET NEXUS The seam between war and peace, or the link between war and the "everything else" that is globalization. The nexus describes the underlying reality that the warrior culture of the military both supports and is supported by, the merchant culture of the business world. I express this interrelationship in the form of a "ten commandments for globalization": (1) Look for resources and ye shall find, but . . . (2) No stability, no markets; (3) No growth, no stability; (4) No resources, no growth; (5) No infrastructure, no resources; (6) No money, no infrastructure; (7) No rules, no money; (8) No security, no rules; (9) No Leviathan, no security; and (10) No (American) will, no Leviathan. Understanding the military-market link is not just good business, it is good national security strategy.

NON-INTEGRATING GAP Regions of the world that are largely disconnected from the global economy and the rule sets that define its stability. Today, the Non-Integrating Gap is made up of the Caribbean Rim, Andean South America, virtually all of Africa, portions of the Balkans, the Caucasus, Central Asia, the Middle East, and most of Southeast Asia. These regions constitute globalization's "ozone hole," where connectivity remains thin or absent in far too many cases. Of course, each region contains some countries that are very Core-like in their attributes (just as there are Gap-like pockets throughout the Core defined primarily by poverty), but these are like mansions in an otherwise seedy neighborhood, and as such are trapped by these larger Gap-defining circumstances.

RULE SETS A collection of rules (both formal and informal) that delineates how some activity normally unfolds. *The Pentagon's New Map* explored the new rule sets concerning conflict and violence in international affairs—or under what conditions governments decide it makes sense to switch from the rule set that defines peace to the rule set that defines war. The events of 9/11 shocked the Pentagon and the rest of the world into the realization that we needed a new rule set concerning war and peace, one that replaces the old rule set that governed America's Cold War with the Soviet Union. The book explained how the new rule set will actually work in the years ahead, not just from America's perspective but from an international one.

RULE-SET RESET When a crisis triggers your realization that your world is woefully lacking certain types of rules, you start making up those new rules with a vengeance (e.g., the Patriot Act and the doctrine of preemption following 9/11). Such a rule-set reset can be a very good thing. But it can also be a very dangerous time, because in your rush to fill in all the rule-set gaps, your cure may end up being worse than your disease.

SEAM STATES The countries that ring the Gap—such as Mexico, Brazil, South Africa, Morocco, Algeria, Greece, Turkey, Pakistan, Thailand, Malaysia, the Philippines, and Indonesia. Some are already members of the Core, and most others are serious candidates for joining the Core.

These states are important with regard to international security, because they provide terrorists geographic access to the Core. The U.S. security strategy regarding these states is simple: get them to increase their security practices as much as possible and to close whatever loopholes exist.

SYSTEM ADMINISTRATORS (SYSADMIN) The "second half" blended force that wages the peace after the Leviathan force has successfully waged war. Therefore, it is a force optimized for such categories of operations as "stability and support operations" (SASO), postconflict stabilization and reconstruction operations, "military operations other than war" (MOOTW), "humanitarian assistance/disaster relief" (HA/DR), and any and all operations associated with low-intensity conflict (LIC), counterinsurgency operations, and small-scale crisis response. Beyond such military-intensive activities, the SysAdmin force likewise provides civil security with its police component, as well as civilian personnel with expertise in rebuilding networks, infrastructure, and social and political institutions. While the core security and logistical capabilities are derived from uniformed military components, the SysAdmin force is fundamentally envisioned as a standing capacity for interagency (i.e., among various U.S. federal agencies) and international collaboration in nation building.

SYSTEM PERTURBATIONS A system-level definition of crisis and instability in the age of globalization; a new ordering principle that has already begun to transform the military and U.S. security policy; also a particular event that forces us to rethink everything. The terrorist attacks of 9/11 served as the first great "existence proof" for this concept, but there have and will be others over time (some are purposeful, like the Bush Administration's Big Bang strategy of fomenting political change in the Middle East by toppling Saddam Hussein's regime in 2003, but others will be accidents, like the SARS epidemic or the Asian tsunamis of December 2004). As a system perturbation, 9/11 placed the world's security rule set in flux and created a demand for new rules. Preemption is the big new rule. By creating that new rule, 9/11 changed America forever and through that process altered global history.

BLUEPRINT FOR ACTION

Chapter One

WHAT THE
WORLD
NEEDS NOW

I SUPPORTED THE DECISION to topple Saddam Hussein's regime in Iraq. I knew our awesome warfighting force, or what I call the Leviathan, was without peer on this planet, and would handle Iraq's military with relative ease. I also knew that this war would constitute merely the first half of Iraq's transformation from authoritarian nightmare to pluralistic, connected society, and that waging that second-half effort—that peace—would be immensely hard. This second-half force of peacekeepers, which I call the System Administrators, was an army I knew many leaders in our military simply didn't want to raise, much less employ, evoking as it does painful memories of past U.S. efforts at nation building during the Cold War (read, Vietnam). Like others, I knew our military wasn't ready for this difficult task, and that its initial failures would be both acute and costly—far more than the war, in fact.

But I also knew this: No public institution responds to failure better and more quickly than the U.S. military.

And it has.

Right now, throughout the U.S. military, but especially in its ground forces (Army and Marines), we are witnessing a new phase to the military modernization process known as "transformation." What was once just the high-tech waging of war now encompasses numerous levels of operations, from the highest forms of information sharing to the simplest rules of engagement used by our troops on the ground, all of which are now focused on the new challenge at hand: waging peace. The shift is so profound that the term itself (*transformation*) has largely fallen from favor because of its strong identification with certain high-tech programs. So instead of focusing on classified "black projects" to facilitate the Leviathan's lofty ambitions, the Pentagon conducts secret talks with allies on how they might better shoulder the SysAdmin's many burdens. Instead of sizing itself to fight two conventional regional wars simultaneously, the 2005 Quadrennial Defense Review proposed new definitions of both warfare and what constitutes victory. As so often is the case in military history, the occupation has transformed the occupier more than the occupied. The Iraq War will leave no lasting imprint on the U.S. military, but the Iraq Peace will redefine it from top to bottom, shifting transformation's center of gravity from the air to the ground, from major combat operations to postconflict stabilization operations, from the Leviathan to the SysAdmin.

And it won't be easy.

The struggles over budgetary priorities will be fierce in the coming years, as military transformation shifts from being capital-intensive (e.g., the Leviathan's hugely costly weapons systems) to labor-intensive (e.g., the SysAdmin's well-trained counterinsurgency forces and military police). The defense-industrial complex will be forced into wrenching change: from producing the few and the absurdly expensive to cranking out the many and the cheap—and increasingly the unmanned. Careers will be made and lost, industries will rise and fall, and waging peace will finally be prioritized over waging war. America will administer the system known as the global economy: policing its bad actors, engaging its failed states, and guiding the rise of its emerging pillars—

all the while rooting out threats to the homeland at their points of origin.

And no, I'm not talking about some distant, personal dream. I'm talking about the new national military strategy of the United States—the most significant revamping of our military in decades—recently enunciated by the Bush Administration. The current administration entered office in 2001 with an avowed disdain for everything this new strategy embodies, but it will leave office in 2009 having remade the Pentagon in the image of the post-9/11 international security environment: the Old Core of the West (North America, Europe, Industrialized Asia, Australia) that still needs to be defended; rising New Core powers in Asia (India, China, South Korea, Russia) and Latin America (Argentina, Brazil, Chile) that need to be deeply engaged; Seam States (e.g., Mexico, Algeria, Turkey, Indonesia), lying on the edge of the global economy, that need to be further integrated; and a Gap, full of disconnected regions (Caribbean Rim, Andean South America, Africa, Caucasus, Central Asia, Middle East, Southeast Asia), that needs to be shrunk one threat at a time.

I've worked with the Pentagon for enough years to know there's a huge difference between signing new doctrines into being and fielding the forces that will bring those strategies to life. There can be no illusions about the profound task ahead: generating a new global security order that not only extends the Core's peace but ends the Gap's wars. Yes, it all starts with America and yes, it all starts with security. So the recent changes within the Pentagon are quite necessary, even if they're nowhere close to being sufficient. But even more daunting tasks lie ahead, ones that will call upon not just the military but the entire American political system, meaning each of us in our capacity as informed citizens, vocal advocates, and discerning voters.

America stands at the tipping point of possibly the most peaceful period in human history, where war as we have known it for centuries is banished from the strategic landscape. But to achieve these lofty ends, we need even loftier means. We need to end the disconnectedness that defines danger in our world. We need to shrink the Gap and all its pain and suffering—right out of existence. We need to make global-ization truly global in a just manner.

And to do all these things, we need a military that will wage peace just as effectively as it now wages war. We need a new department that bridges the divide between our current departments of war (Defense) and peace (State). But most of all, we need a Core-wide capacity—an institutional capacity—to shrink the Gap one disconnected state at a time.

This is not a grand strategy that describes war strictly in the con-text of war, but one that seeks to place our thinking on *war in the context of everything else,* which today goes by the shorthand "glob-alization." This process of economic, political, and social integration among many of the world's states is the defining characteristic of our age, and as such, it defines conflict in this era, limited as it is to those regions still left on the outside of this historical integration process—or what I call the Non-Integrating Gap.

Many established security experts condemned *The Pentagon's New Map* for both its optimism and its ambition, believing it to be a com-plete rejection of the classic balance-of-power model and the "real-ism" they consider to be that model's essential underpinnings. They were right to do so, and they will be even more correct in viewing this *Blueprint for Action* as a further repudiation of all they hold dear. For in this book and especially in this first chapter, I aim to convince you that all the building blocks for this new global security order are at hand, awaiting only our commitment to bring them into being and employ them judiciously.

Let us begin to dispel the myths of ideology, disperse the fog of war mongering, and define the future worth creating.

UNDERSTANDING THE SEAM BETWEEN WAR AND PEACE

About a month before *The Pentagon's New Map* was published, I got a call from Greg Jaffe, Pulitzer Prize–winning defense reporter at the

Wall Street Journal. Greg wanted to do a front-page profile on me and what he later called a "new theory of war." In many ways, the article was less a profile of me than of the famous PowerPoint briefing I was delivering throughout the Defense Department on my grand strategy for the United States in the post-9/11 era. As Jaffe explained it to me, there have been four great briefs in the post-Vietnam era, or presentations that so shaped a generation of military strategic thinking that each was known as "the brief" in its day. Within these four presentations lies the essential explanation of the Pentagon's current struggle to define its preferred future vision of both war and peace.

Each of the briefs was associated with its own decade, starting in the 1970s.

The first was by Colonel John Boyd, the iconoclastic Air Force colonel most famous for his decision-cycle theory (the OODA loop of observe-orient-decide-act), whose many ideas subsequently shaped not only the Marine Corps's definition of maneuver warfare but also the enunciation of so-called Fourth-Generation Warfare (based on Mao Zedong's insurgency model) by William Lind and others. Beginning in the 1970s, the "mad colonel" became famous for convincing an entire generation of future military leaders that warfare was—first and foremost—more about destroying the enemy's morale than his physical assets or personnel. Articulate and profane, John Boyd gave his brilliant presentations well over a thousand times before various defense audiences. Despite his impressive intellectual reach, this renegade reformer never became a favorite of the generals, earning as many enemies as admirers.

In the 1980s, a second great brief sought to reconcile the seemingly insatiable desire of the Reagan Administration for high-tech weapons systems with the enduring dangers of deficit spending. This presentation, by legendary Pentagon budget analyst Chuck Spinney, pushed the contemporary military debates about the future of war into the halls of Congress, earning the previously anonymous bureaucrat the cover of *Time* magazine in 1983. Employing long-term economic data, Spinney forced the Pentagon to confront what he called the "plans/reality mismatch." In a nutshell, this is the tendency of defense planners to insert within the annual budget submitted by the White House to Congress new programs whose burgeoning "out-year" (referring to the time period beyond the current five-year planning cycle) requirements for spending would ultimately break the bank. In other words, if the program in question cost only a minor amount in research-and-development costs in year one, by year ten that amount—which would then encompasses actually building, fielding, and supporting the proposed weapon or platform (e.g., tank, ship, aircraft)—might be several orders of magnitude more expensive than the initial opening "wedge" price. As you might imagine, the generals *really* loved this bit of truth telling.

The third brief was delivered in a style far different from the first two by the man known as the "Yoda" or "rabbi" to today's high-tech military. Andrew Marshall, after a long career as a rather anonymous analyst at the RAND Corporation (where he left virtually no paper trail), became the first—and so far only—director of the Pentagon's Office of New Assessment in 1973. Beginning in the late 1980s and stretching across the nineties, this office became famous within the defense community for its enunciation of the concept that the rise of information technology was setting in motion an inevitable "revolution in military affairs." Much like Colonel Boyd, Marshall is credited with inspiring an entire generation of disciples—the so-called church of St. Andrew. One of his better-known followers is Vice Admiral Arthur K. Cebrowski, my mentor and the man known as the "father of network-centric warfare." Famous for his taciturn, almost delphic manner of speaking, Marshall nonetheless reshaped the Pentagon's entire lexicon of warfare, setting in motion the drive toward a high-tech, largely stand-off force that would overwhelm opponents by long-range arms and dominating airpower while not subjecting ground forces to retaliation.

In Jaffe's assessment, my "new map" presentation on the post-9/11 security environment had become "the brief" for this decade within the defense community. Why? Because I sought to create an overarching grand strategy that would logically reconcile "Genghis John" Boyd's down-and-dirty definition of future war with Andrew Marshall's seemingly bloodless high-tech one, while simultaneously seeking to relate their yin-and-yang-like interplay to the larger economic reality of globalization's emergence as the dominant characteristic of today's strategic environment. In short, my "new map" brief sought to end the plans/reality mismatch between the Pentagon's traditional definition of war and globalization's emerging definition of peace.

Contrary to popular imagination, the Pentagon is primarily in the business of preparing for war, not waging it, the latter being led by the combatant commanders in the field. The Pentagon is essentially a corporation, and what it does is think long and hard about what the future of war should be like, and then it directs vast research and acquisition programs to generate a force capable of waging war successfully in that domain—however defined. As such, the Pentagon's demands for intelligence tend to be future-oriented (as in, "Show me where the future bad guys are found!").

This system of planning is relatively secure from outside influences—to wit, the Pentagon's persistent ability across the 1990s to ignore the rise of globalization, along with the transnational, largely religious-inspired terrorism that accompanied it. Yes, I can find you lots of PowerPoint slides from planning briefs across the 1990s that contained the words *globalization* and *terrorism,* but frankly these remained complicating factors to be managed, not the focus of serious planning and acquisition. All such items were considered "lesser includeds," meaning situations and threats that the Pentagon assumed it could handle employing the force it fielded, even as that force was largely optimized for large-scale war against a large-scale enemy ("resurgent Russia" through the mid-1990s, "rising China" ever since).

It just so happens that the wars we have fought in this new century are not the wars the Pentagon planned and bought for a decade ago. Does this change the culture of The Building? Not easily. Bureaucratic torpor is its own force of nature.

Wars, of course, interrupt this long-range planning. They steal time, attention, energy, and resources from the process of building tomorrow's force. It may seem counterintuitive, but the defense budget accounts only for future wars, not today's. So whenever America actually engages in war, the Pentagon immediately goes over-budget, triggering the Pentagon's requests to Congress for "supplementals," or additional, above-budget funding to cover the excess costs. Of course, Congress never gives the Pentagon enough money to cover these operations, and so whenever any of these overseas interventions drags on, the Defense Department inevitably ends up cannibalizing its people, equipment, and infrastructure to make ends meet. That's why, in reality, the Pentagon hates waging war, because today's conflicts fundamentally wreak havoc with its true function: building the future force. An exercise in sublime illogic perhaps, but the truth all the same.

Today's wars also create tomorrow's generation of senior military leaders. What do most admirals and generals do? A huge number of them are found in the Pentagon tending to tomorrow's force, armed with their visions of future war that have been shaped by their experience in combat operations.

Right now there is a debate raging within the Pentagon and the military as a whole about what the war in Iraq, as well as the ongoing occupation, tells us about the future of war. This debate fundamentally pits the two dominant visions of future war against each other in what I consider to be a false dichotomy, meaning a choice that does not need to be made—and, frankly, should not be made.

As you might have guessed by now, the two sides in this debate are functionally derived: the air community (the flyboys) versus the infantry (the boots on the ground). Of course, such naked descriptions are not typically employed. The outlook of the air community (the Air Force plus the Navy's carrier-based aircraft) is widely known as Network-Centric Operations (NCO), the currently dominant phrase for describing how the "revolution in military affairs" has "transformed the force." In contrast, the ground-pounders of the Army and Marine Corps tend to subscribe to the seemingly opposite position, or Fourth-Generation Warfare (4GW), which naturally favors definitions of conflict far less driven by technological advances than by the enduring qualities of men in combat. This debate can be described as machines versus warriors.

The maritime community, by and large, doesn't have a dog in this fight, and thus it remains far too obsessed with China and the Taiwan Straits scenario (along with, to a certain extent, the Korea scenario, featuring, as it does, all that coastline). The fleet in particular feels somewhat left behind in both these visions. Why? Network-Centric Operations favors carrier-based aircraft above all, and the tyranny of their combined cost (carriers plus air wings) drains construction funds from the rest of the ship and submarine categories. Fourth-Generation Warfare obviously focuses on land operations, which at best speak to port control and riverine operations, as far as naval forces are concerned. But these two missions remind the Navy far too much of Vietnam, an operation it supported but for which it was not integral. So naturally, a debate about what Iraq means and how it shapes the future force makes Navy leaders rather nervous, because they can see only cuts ahead no matter which side wins.

Now, at first glance all these debates might seem like Pentagon insiders arguing about standards and practices, and so you might be tempted to plead, "Wake me up when we get to the good part!" But it's not as esoteric as all that, because if we in the national security community can't get our story straight on how we wage war, we'll never get to the good part of waging peace. If the military services do what they want to do—namely, split all the differences and give everyone their usual budget shares—then we'll continue to field four mini-versions of the Leviathan force without a coherent SysAdmin force among them. That tradition of giving every service its warfighting "due" has yielded an Army with its own navy, a Navy with its own army, a Marine Corps with its own air force, and an Air Force that's convinced it can win wars all by itself. That sort of belt-and-suspenders redundancy is all fine and good if you're still waiting on World War III, but if we're going to shrink the Gap, we'll need to rationalize this force quite a bit more. In short, we need to optimize for *both* war and peace.

Naturally, advocates on both sides of this debate are certain their vision encompasses that which is truly important and profound about the current era of globalization (technology proliferation for NCO,

chronic tribal wars for 4GW). Both are certain they see war within the
context of everything else, meaning they seek to relate their definitions of war to the wider, day-to-day world of peace—namely, the
globalization process. While it's true that either vision does a better
job than any previous iteration of capturing this larger reality, the
sheer fact of this doctrinal standoff demonstrates that neither can
yet see the forest for the trees. In effect, these two views of war are
essentially in violent agreement with each other. They just lack an
overarching construct to help them understand that they're really
describing two sides of the same coin.

In early 2005, I spent a week debating the future of conflict with
two great theorists of Fourth-Generation Warfare, Chet Richards
(self-professed keeper of the John Boyd "flame") and Colonel Thomas
Hammes of the Marine Corps (author of the 4GW standard *The Sling
and the Stone*). This debate took place at the Norwegian naval war
college in Bergen, Norway, in front of a slew of young officers assembled for this occasion. Now, going into this lengthy seminar, many of
the officers were of the opinion that they essentially had to choose
between Network-Centric Operations and Fourth-Generation Warfare as their future conflict paradigm, meaning it was either going to
be high-tech wars against traditional military opponents or low-tech
conflicts against insurgencies. Their obvious angst about the future,
quite frankly, stemmed from their sense that Norway's military would
have no important role in either conflict mode. Feeling too small to
join in any big wars and too peacekeeping-oriented to beat back any
bloody insurgencies, the Norwegians, like most of the Core's militaries, couldn't decide which way to jump in this ongoing debate. To
them, it seemed as though the U.S. military wasn't interested in their
help in either realm.

But a funny thing happened as our debate unfolded: what at first
seemed like a dichotomy began to look more like a continuum, with my
SysAdmin force concept being the crucial bridge. The rise of Network-
Centric Operations has given us the tremendous warfighting capacity
of America's Leviathan force, but in doing so, it's created a huge
"overmatch," a disparity between our warfighting force and any other

traditional force fielded by states. To use that Leviathan force is to encourage potential nonstate opponents to skip the war and head straight to the peace, where instead of waging traditional war they engage in insurgencies and guerrilla movements (aka, Fourth-Generation Warfare). What does this mean? It means that if you want to secure the victories your Leviathan force can generate, you have to be able to master the security environment lying just beyond that war and just short of the peace that's easily disrupted by 4GW opponents. In sum, you need to be able to generate security at the seam between war and peace, making possible the society's seamless transition from the former to the latter. If it's done right, you can preclude the rise of Fourth-Generation Warfare in most postwar situations, although you certainly need to be able to deal with 4GW no matter what.

When presented with the larger overarching concept of the Leviathan-SysAdmin construct, these young Norwegian officers immediately grasped where their own military could fit in: that seam between war and peace. The Americans might field the world's Leviathan force, and the SysAdmin will always need the U.S. military's capacity for Fourth-Generation Warfare (largely found in the Marine Corps, the SysAdmin's "Mini-Me Leviathan"). But unless the United States can integrate the contributions of smaller militaries like Norway into the larger SysAdmin effort, we'll be left with two types of forces, neither of which can really secure the victory on its own: a Leviathan force that can run up the "score" in the first half, and a colonial-style mopping-up force that can salvage a graceful exit strategy once the peace is lost to never-ending insurgencies—the same mix of forces that got us Vietnam.

Unilateral military superpower? Meet the post-9/11 world, where multilateralism means never having to say "quagmire." Yes, America can fundamentally go it alone in wars, but it can't go it alone in the peace. The Leviathan force may have little use for allies, but the SysAdmin force is made possible by their participation.

Before I describe how I see the Iraq debate unfolding in the years ahead, let me lay out the key concepts from both sides in this doctrinal debate. I don't pretend to be an expert in either Network-Centric

Operations or Fourth-Generation Warfare, and I'm sure as hell not a disciple of one versus the other, so my descriptions will definitely seem incomplete to the true believers in both camps (i.e., "He just doesn't understand!").

Network-Centric Operations is nothing less than a long-term effort by the military to understand how the rise of the Information Age alters the fundamental nature of war. In the jargon-heavy vernacular of NCO advocates, the past force was "platform-centric," meaning we organized ourselves around the major machines we created to wage war (aircraft, ships, tanks, etc.). The future, by contrast, is network-centric, meaning platforms are considered nothing more than nodes in a larger network, whose main attribute is not its massed fire power but its ability to wield that power with pinpoint accuracy and blinding speed. It's on the question of speed that NCO employs John Boyd's concept of getting inside the enemy's "decision loop," meaning we make two or more decisions for every one our opponent can manage— our silicon-based computers trumping their carbon-based brains every time.

If past wars were decided along the dictum of "He who moves the mostest the fastest wins" (i.e., logistics), then the future of war is all about moving bytes faster than bullets—sort of a "He who decides the fastest wins" definition of victory. The rise of "smart bombs" epito-mizes this evolution: instead of dropping tons of gravity bombs to destroy a target, we now use high-tech mapping, guidance systems, local target "illumination" (e.g., those special ops guys in Afghanistan with laser pointers), and cruise missiles to achieve the same effect with far fewer bombs, and likewise far less collateral damage. NCO advo-cates call this "trading mass for information."

NCO defines the twentieth century's long march toward the notion of "winning from above," or the strategy of bombing your way to victory. Starting in World War I, that vision was all about long-range, high-tech artillery. In World War II, it shifted to massive aerial bomb-ing campaigns. By the Cold War, it had been recast as strategic bombing with nukes. Still later, following the frustrations of Vietnam, where we carpet-bombed to no apparent effect, this strategy settled into its current form with *Operation Desert Storm* in 1991. Add to that the Kosovo bombing campaign and the seemingly easy devastation wrought upon the Taliban in Afghanistan, and, going into Iraq, it seemed as though NCO was not only the dominant mode of war strategizing, it had reached an apogee at which serious thought was given to radically slimming down the ground forces in a future, "transformed" force.

I used to joke about that a lot in my brief, noting to Army and Marine Corps audiences that I had seen the plan in Secretary Rumsfeld's Office of Force Transformation (whose staff was, quite naturally, dominated by Air Force and naval air officers) whereby we were plotting to get rid of the Army altogether. Right up to the Iraq invasion, you could get a big nervous laugh with that line.

And the Army and Marines were right to be nervous. The trajectory of combat across the 1990s hadn't served them well in Pentagon debates. While the Air Force was winning wars "all by itself" in Iraq, the Balkans, and—later—Afghanistan, the Army and Marines got left holding the bag in such crappy situations as Somalia and Haiti and, to a far lesser extent, in the Balkans. If you have either read the book or seen the movie *Black Hawk Down,* then you know what a losing argument Military Operations Other Than War (MOOTW) seemed to be. "Moot-wah," a Pentagon buzz phrase, was the Army's almost plaintive demand that it not be left behind in some Third World hellhole while the Air Force raced ahead to its next fabulous, pristine war-from-above. The strong perception within the Pentagon about MOOTW was—and frankly still remains in many quarters today— that it's a form of war the American public can't stomach in terms of the losses incurred (i.e., body bag syndrome), staying power required (America's strategic attention deficit disorder), morality tested (e.g., atrocities like Abu Ghraib and beheadings of hostages), and resources expended (Senator So-and-So: "We spend more money in Iraq by breakfast than we've spent all year on [name his/her favorite cause]!").

Thus, in this seemingly never-ending debate, the ground-pounder's blood-and-guts mentality is pitted against the flyboy's technocratic bias: the Marines accuse the Navy of forgetting what "real war" is like, while the Air Force derides the Army's inability to deal with the high-tech world of today. So it's bloody war versus bloodless war, or the warrior spirit of the knuckle-draggers versus the computer-brains of the Borg.

Right through President Bush's declaration of "mission accomplished" in Iraq (May 2003), the NCO crowd seemed invulnerable to attack. Defense Secretary Donald Rumsfeld had been right in both Afghanistan and Iraq: the small-footprint force, armed with technology, could network its way to relatively bloodless victories. Neither regime-toppling exercise cost the United States more than two hundred dead in just a few weeks of major combat ground operations against significant local forces defending their homelands. That isn't just impressive, in the history of modern warfare that's virtually unprecedented.

But in that growing hubris lay the seeds of NCO's current problems, plus the mounting backlash by the Fourth-Generation Warfare boots-on-the-ground crowd. The extremely spotty planning by the Pentagon for the postwar stabilization and occupation of Iraq obviously enabled the rise of the disastrously efficient insurgency we subsequently faced. Part of that bad planning stemmed from the planners' arrogance about what could be achieved by NCO, but far more seemingly came from the defensiveness of Secretary Rumsfeld and his assistants regarding the Army's charge that they willfully disregarded its warnings about how many grounds troops would ultimately be required.

You remember this alleged clash: Rumsfeld versus then–Army Chief of Staff General Eric Shinseki. Rumsfeld said we could win the war with a small, highly transformed force, whereas Shinseki argued for a massive number of ground forces (more than 200,000). In the press coverage of this "debate," the argument became known as the question of "How many troops are required to win the war?" As such, later accusations revolved around the question of whether or not Rumsfeld sought to fight this war with too few troops.

My problem with this mistaken description is that it conflates two very different missions, that of regime change and that of postconflict stabilization. I call the former the "war" and the latter the "peace." So in my more careful lexicon, I say that Rumsfeld was arguing, and arguing correctly, about how to win the war, while Shinseki was arguing, and arguing correctly, about how to win the peace. In the end, both were right. The real story is that Shinseki and Rumsfeld didn't clash over the war, since everyone involved in that planning understood it for what it was: *Operation Just Cause* on steroids. This wasn't a rerun of *Operation Desert Storm,* but a transformed version of the take-down approach we employed on General Manuel Noriega in Panama in 1989. "Light and agile" was the norm here, with some legitimate concerns all around on logistics. But the risks were considered accept-able, and there's little arguing with the outcome.

Now, here's the rub on the Army: more than a few inside the Pen-tagon will tell you that Shinseki's stance on the postwar situation was *both* principled *and* wrongheaded. In short, he didn't want the war because he knew the Army would get stuck with the peace, so he argued (quite accurately, it turned out) for a huge ground presence in order to raise the public's perception of long-term costs—almost a form of public emotional blackmail. This is a charge that has been leveled against the Army in the past (e.g., perceived foot-dragging responses to our involvement in the Balkans in the late 1990s), reflect-ing the Army's *Black Hawk Down* fear of being left holding the bag in some backward and savage landscape. In Iraq, this bureaucratic passive-aggressive response reached its apogee: as the Army's own his-torian later discovered, "no one produced an actual document laying out a strategy to consolidate the victory after major combat opera-tions ended." That's right! Our boots were put on the battlefield with-out any written comprehensive plan for the peace.

How bad was that? In June 2004 I delivered the keynote address to the annual worldwide convention of civil affairs officers in North Car-olina. The audience was full of these officers—the most SysAdmin officers we own—just back from Iraq. What they told me was this: we had close to half a year to feel the love in Iraq and we blew it. This was not some wild guess on the part of the neocons but a predictable phenomenon that you can hear about from anyone in the electrical industry or the domestic disaster-relief community. As I learned from many discussions with electrical companies during my work on the Year 2000 Problem, whenever there's a serious disruption of life-as-we-know-it, you can always count on the public to keep its cool for about the first five days. Why? Because "we're all in this together" and everyone knows, for example, that the electrical workers are doing their best working around the clock to get the grid back up. It's around day six that the guns come out. At some point in the process people's patience runs out, and it's no longer about "being in this together" and it's all about "take care of me now or else." Two perceptions drive the anger: a feeling that the powers-that-be aren't doing everything within their power to restore life-as-we-knew-it and the sense that the recovery is benefiting some disproportionately while harming others disproportionately. As always, it's the sense that "this is just not right" that fuels the average person's sense of anger.

Many civil affairs officers who were in Iraq at the start of the occupation will tell you there should have been more of them there, and not so thinly spread out but probably concentrated in certain key cities we should have known would become centers for any insurgency if things went sour. Most of these officers will tell you they were led down a garden path by prewar intelligence on the state of Iraq's infrastructure, left to believe it would be in a decent state of affairs when in reality it was tremendously decayed after years of damage and neglect. All will tell you that the looting that erupted in the days following Saddam's fall was an unmitigated disaster that doomed much of their initial efforts at rebuilding. What was the obvious solution? The same one we apply here in the States following some horrific disaster: lots of uniforms swarming the area and making clear to everyone on scene that such behavior is simply not tolerated. That's the first great function of the SysAdmin force: overwhelming presence on the ground to stifle any instincts toward chaos or looting. Iraq should have looked like Wall Street in Manhattan when New York swarms cops on the area. Instead, we were stretched thin across a country the size of California and we chose to chalk up looting to a "boys will be boys" mentality that no one could prevent from happening.

In the end, General Shinseki, the man many credit with coining the term *transformation,* was right in his estimates about needed troop strength. Ideally, we would have fielded a good quarter-million troops on the ground. Could we have done it on our own? Not without messing up our troops a whole lot in the process (the general's fear). The obvious alternative was that we should have had large contingencies of peacekeepers from a variety of fellow Core pillars. Ideally, we would have had 30,000 to 40,000 peacekeepers each from NATO, Russia, India, and China. Instead we got dribs and drabs from a host of smaller nations and a decent contingent of Brits, leaving the United States to provide roughly 90 percent of the troops compared with the far less than 20 percent we provided in the two Balkans stabilization scenarios earlier. Too much to ask of these countries? That was probably the case with NATO, which was pretty much tapped between ongoing responsibilities in both the Balkans and Afghanistan, but the New Core pillars of Russia, India, and China went completely untapped. We asked India for 17,000 peacekeepers but were eventually turned down by its parliament, our diplomatic sales job on the war not doing the trick. We asked, according to credible reports, Vladimir Putin to consider sending as many as 40,000 troops to Iraq, but that likewise never materialized. As I told my Chinese hosts when I lectured in Beijing in the summer of 2004, "You should have 50,000 troops in Iraq, because it's really going to end up being your oil in the end." They nodded their heads in agreement and replied, "In a perfect world, you'd be right. But we don't live in that perfect world, do we, Dr. Barnett? And your country's leadership is not moving us any closer to it."

Let me tell you what that huge, multinational SysAdmin force would have meant to Iraq: no chaos, no looting, no Iraqi Army disappearing into the woodwork with its weaponry, no missing caches of explosives, no Moqtada al-Sadr rising in response, no militias, no spontaneously swelling insurgency—nothing like that. All of that could have been prevented with an overwhelming presence that signaled, "We're here and we're not leaving anytime soon." Moreover, a force full of Slavs and Asians would have spoken volumes to any potential insurgency: "This is not just the Americans. This is not just the West that might pull out if you give it a good bloody nose or execute some hostages. This is a force both Occidental and Oriental, both West and East, and it's full of people who aren't squeamish about killing troublemakers to prevent an uprising."

Would such a situation have left us with a perfect postwar Iraq? Hardly. The Baathists would have still fought on, and some foreign terrorists like those led by Abu Musab al-Zarqawi still would have made their mark. The larger point is this: It was within our power to prevent as much as 90 percent of the Iraqi public from turning against us in this occupation, but instead of winning that vast majority by demonstrating serious commitment to Iraq's postwar stability and rapid reconstruction, we did just the opposite, effectively losing that goodwill in the process. Like the electrical recovery teams in any power outage, we had our chance to get the grid back up. Instead of five days it was five months, and then—to what should have been no one's surprise—the guns came out.

In the end, the Bush White House came up with a fabulously Orwellian phrase to describe what actually happened in Iraq: "catastrophic success." That's what happens when you plan to win the war with your Leviathan force but don't bother to mount a serious SysAdmin effort—a Pyrrhic victory. Simply put, this did not have to be.

Now, of course, many ground-pounders believe that the Army should look back on that debate with pride, for it made its usual Powell Doctrine–like arguments about "overwhelming force," and if those warnings were ignored, then the resulting quagmire only demonstrates—yet again!—that "real wars" are ones in which ground troops suffer almost all the casualties in a bloody irregular conflict against a feral warrior force whose blast-from-the-past combat tactics render irrelevant the entire NCO vision of future warfare. *Aha!* Not only is the

Army needed now, it is forced to recruit personnel exiting the Navy and Air Force just to fill ranks rapidly depleted by rotations into Iraq! If that isn't damning proof, then what is?

Enter the Fourth-Generation Warfare argument with a vengeance. Now, before I lose you in 4GW lingo, let me offer a quick-and-dirty rendition of the generations of war. The big thinker here is William Lind, who introduced the concept of Fourth-Generation Warfare in a seminal *Marine Corps Gazette* article he cowrote with four military officers (all Army and Marines) back in 1989 called "The Changing Face of War: Into the Fourth Generation." The First Generation is defined as extending from the Treaty of Westphalia (1648) to the American Civil War. This period's warfare was shaped by the rise of the smoothbore musket and the need to maintain order on the battlefield, so it was all about marching columns of men lining up and shooting one another with rifles and cannons in a very orderly manner. By the mid-nineteenth century, advances in technology had altered that calculus dramatically, which is why the American Civil War was so bloody. If you simply lined guys up like that, the improved rifles and cannons were simply going to shred them into pieces with great efficiency, so operations like Colonel Picket's charge at Gettysburg were tantamount to suicide runs.

The French military is credited with coming up with the Second Generation of warfare around the time of the First World War, which Lind shorthands by their dictum "The artillery conquers, the army occupies." Upon joining that conflict, the U.S. Army and Marine Corps picked up much of the operational mindset that persists inside our military today, except now it's the Air Force that conquers, not artillery. *Desert Storm,* for example, was very 2GW in its onset. Remember the forty consecutive days of bombing before we sent in the troops?

The German military invented the Third Generation in the period between the world wars and unveiled it as *blitzkrieg,* or "lightning war," in Poland in 1939. Here, maneuverability across the breadth and length of the battlefield was added, so speed progressively replaced firepower. If 2GW focused on attrition (i.e., killing as many enemy troops as possible), then 3GW was all about destroying your enemy's strategic rear—namely, his industrial capacity and supply networks.

At first glance, Fourth-Generation Warfare can seem quite orthogonal (i.e., going off on its own tangent) to those preceding definitions, in large part because it has a back-to-the-future sensibility regarding tools of the trade. 4GW is essentially guerrilla- or insurgency-based warfare that seeks to defeat an enemy not militarily but politically, and not on any one battlefield but over years and even decades of low-intensity conflict. China's Mao Zedong is considered the father of modern 4GW, which obviously has been around as long as the weak have encountered far superior foes. In his brilliant book *The Sling and the Stone,* Colonel Hammes runs through the history of this modern variant of guerrilla war: from Mao to the Vietcong, straight on through to the Sandinistas of Nicaragua and the intifadas of the Gaza Strip and West Bank. Naturally, al Qaeda is considered very 4GW, coming as it did out of the great victory that was the Islamic insurgency's defeat of the superpower Soviet Union in Afghanistan.

Now, in general, I like the concept of Fourth-Generation Warfare, because, far better than Network-Centric Operations, it incorporates the notion of *war within the context of everything else* by contextualizing it within the larger complexities of globalization. In 4GW, military tactics are always subordinated to a host of broader considerations, like the economic, political, and social pain inflicted upon the opponent. Instead of trying to destroy the enemy's ability to wage war logistically or operationally (a hopeless task against a far superior opponent), 4GW practitioners seek to destroy the enemy's societal will to wage war—one long "bloody nose" strategy of brutalizing your enemy's soul.

So what did we end up with in Iraq? What many defense experts will tell us is Fourth-Generation Warfare in which the enemy doesn't have to win, just prevent our victory. We may rack up impressive body counts, but our foes are targeting something completely different: our sense of will, morality, patience, and staying power. It's back to the West's "cowboys" versus indigenous "Indians." We're trying to create just enough stability for the settlers to take root and the railroads to be laid, while our enemies are performing high-tech scalpings in the form of ritualistic beheading of hostages. We seek to create facts on the ground, like a sewage treatment plant whose very existence must be kept secret lest the insurgency target it for destruction (a secret sewage plant!), while they seek to shock us into withdrawal by streaming their atrocities over the Internet for global consumption. We wage a war of connectedness, they wage a war of disconnectedness, and the race is on to see which side can exhaust the other into disengagement.

My problem with 4GW is that it revels a bit too much in its gore-without-end. If Network-Centric Operations tends to be too optimistic in its capacity to "lift the fog of war," then Fourth-Generation Warfare too often seems to advocate that America settle in for perpetual war with savages who are both unredeemable and inexhaustible in supply. This strategic outlook dovetails with journalist Robert D. Kaplan's popular vision of the future as one big African wasteland teeming with Mad Max–like warriors who rape, pillage, and murder while roaming the countryside in jeeps armed with bolted-on heavy machine guns (the archetypal image of Somalia's "technicals," or more recently Sudan's janjaweed). Also, prior to 9/11, the 4GW crowd was just as fixated on China as its preferred future opponent as was the NCO crowd. Why? China was the best hope of all camps prior to 9/11, especially since the incoming Bush Administration had signaled its complete unwillingness to do anything that smacked of "nation building," something that serious 4GW strategists readily admit is central to any victory over an insurgency-based opponent (the unserious ones see only counterinsurgency operations at work in Iraq today, and effectively beg off on the wider nation-building effort).

The fight right now between Network-Centric Operations and Fourth-Generation Warfare over who "lost" the war in Iraq is basically a repeat, then, of the Rumsfeld-Shinseki nondebate (note that Shinseki's arguments on peacekeeping troop levels became highly publicized only after the postwar situation began emerging in June 2004). The 4GWers accuse NCO advocates of blindly stumbling from a third-generation victory over Saddam into a fourth-generation stalemate with the insurgency. But again, this accusation tends to conflate two very different situations: a brilliantly waged war and a subsequently botched peace. Our Secretary of War did just fine in Iraq, but our missing Secretary of *Everything Else* has a lot to answer for . . . on "hillbilly armor," on Abu Ghraib, and on a host of other botched aspects to this occupation. You don't just "go to the war with the army you have," you go to the peace as well. And it's not just a question of the army you want, but the army you've been *wanting* for the past decade. Until the Army really starts *wanting* the SysAdmin force, America can't *have* the military it needs to secure the victories our Leviathan force achieves.

In the end, there is no need to choose between these two visions of future conflict. If we're going to shrink the Gap, one country at a time, we'll need both visions and the forces they logically generate, the Leviathan and the SysAdmin, to deal with rogue regimes *and* insurgencies. We'll need to be able to wage war *and* peace.

The good news is: that Army *is* being built, as *is* that Marine Corps. Senior leaders within all four services and the Office of Secretary of Defense (where a new assistant secretary of defense position was recently created for "stabilization operations") fervently believe that America's future security portfolio will be dominated not by concerns of a "rising near-peer" but by failed states that define the key battlegrounds in this global war on terrorism. They see the Gap and understand the Defense Department's crucial role in shrinking it.

How can I be so sure? In the winter of 2005, I was asked by *Esquire* magazine, where I'm now a contributing editor, to research and write a profile of Secretary of Defense Donald Rumsfeld, one that examined the non-warfighting side of his campaign to transform the U.S. military into a force able to better meet the challenges of the post-9/11 international security environment. As part of this story, I was given access to the senior-most civilian and military leaders of the Pentagon, including Secretary Rumsfeld himself. What became clear to me in writing this story ("Old Man in a Hurry," July 2005) was that Rumsfeld's transformation of the Pentagon has had far more to do with altering how we prepare for war than how we wage it and that the bulk of the Bush Administration's transformational changes to the U.S.

military will focus on how the Defense Department utilizes personnel rather than on the stuff it buys for future wars.

In essence, Rumsfeld's main legacy will be one of radically revamping the U.S. military's human equation, resulting in a new, far more agile force, or basically a frontier-style Army of the kind that America hasn't seen since the 1800s, one that is far more expeditionary than it was in the Cold War and far more organized to conduct SysAdmin-style operations. Two big attributes of this new system? The first is the Army's radical reformatting from its division structure to far smaller "brigade units of action" and the second is the emerging National Security Personnel System, by which the military services, instead of sending people to places they don't want to go, on a schedule that plays havoc with their home life, allow individual service men and women to—in effect—bid against one another for desired postings in an eBay-like online auction system. As then–Chief of Naval Operations Admiral Vern Clark told me, "They're going to negotiate on the Web for jobs. The decision's going to be made by the ship and the guy or gal. You know, we're going to create a whole new world here."

But this emerging vision is without illusions. The next transformation of the force begun inside the Pentagon will have implications far beyond its five walls, changing the very structure of the U.S. national security establishment in coming years. This revolution has been set in motion, but where it ends up taking this country is not a conversation you can have right now inside the E Ring, or the outermost Pentagon ring of offices, where the senior leaders are found, because that discussion is one only the President can have with the American public.

Anticipating the inevitability of that debate, let's explore it now. For therein lies a crucial missing link in this blueprint for action.

A DEPARTMENT FOR WHAT LIES BETWEEN WAR AND PEACE

One of the last sections I wrote for *The Pentagon's New Map* was about splitting the American military into two parts: a Leviathan-like force that focused on waging war and a System Administrator force that focused on the *everything else,* meaning all the military operations *other* than war (e.g., peacekeeping, crisis response, humanitarian/ disaster relief, training of foreign troops, postconflict stabilization and reconstruction, counter-insurgency). I wrote it so late because I kept going back and forth about whether I should include this concept in the book. In many ways, it felt like a bridge too far—just a bit too out there. The Bush Administration had just created a new Department of Homeland Security, and that pretty much took 9/11 *plus* the anthrax scare to happen. So what made me think that something big enough would come down the pike to force the bureaucratic bifurcation of the federal government's single largest agency?

Up until the time I wrote the book, I had made a few timid attempts in my various briefings to defense community audiences to bring up this concept of splitting the force. But frankly, the response I typically got went something like this: "Oh yeah! Our Leviathan force just kicked ass in both Afghanistan and Iraq, so tell me exactly why we should mess with that winning hand?" And through the summer of 2003, I didn't have much of a comeback to that. The "transformed" force *did* seem as though it could handle any truly important warfighting contingency you could name. Give the U.S. military an objective, and it would be achieved, because there really wasn't any traditional "battlespace," or environment of conventional military conflict, that our forces couldn't utterly dominate.

The problem, of course, is that dominating the battlespace only gets the U.S. military through the war, or what the Powell Doctrine prefers to call "mission accomplished" (bad guys out of power, captured, or killed), and if that's all you need to light up the victory cigars and strike up the band, then your duty is done. But if you're waging a global war on terrorism, then all you've done by conquering that battlespace is kill a bunch of bad guys and nothing else. You've stormed into the inner-city ghetto, shot the place up, maybe snatched the most wanted criminals if you're lucky, and left the situation more beat-up than you found it. To the innocent locals, you can't help but come off like a man-made disaster in the end, despite your good intentions, because what you leave behind is no more likely to produce good guys than before—in fact, it's more likely than ever to produce *even worse guys*. You may enter with surgical precision, but all you leave is an open wound in your wake—unless you make good on the peace.

In Iraq, that open wound was just coming into view in the fall of 2003. The Bush Administration had promised a rapid makeover of Iraq within twelve months, but after the first four months had passed, it was becoming clear to me that the Pentagon's planning effort had suffered a bad case of the "magic cloud" phenomenon. "Magic cloud" is my pet name for the simple cloud graphics that you often see on diagram maps of information networks. Very large networks, like the Internet itself, are often rendered in this simplistic way, because to try to draw anything truly representative would be a waste of time, or just too complex to capture on paper. So instead, the audience is offered a symbolic graphic, and the symbol that's often used for enormously complex systems is a simple cloud—as in, "Lots of data goes in, lots of data comes out, but how it exactly works is basically beyond our ability to show on this one PowerPoint slide."

In certain Pentagon planning briefings, the cloud graphic often takes on a rather magical quality, meaning it's used as shorthand for "At this time, we have no idea how this whole damn thing is going to work out, but if we end up needing to insert a miracle, it goes right here!" Now, the kind way to describe such a process is to call it "adaptive planning," meaning you can't tell what the answer or solution is going to be at this time (thus the fog) but you know that eventually you're going to reach the point where push comes to shove and you'd better be a whole lot smarter than you are right now. The unkind way to describe this process is to say you're making it up as you go along. The key difference between the two is whether or not you truly learn along the way, and thus come up with a solution in time. If you do, that's called "leadership." If you don't, that's called "a Senate investigation."

In U.S. military planning for major overseas interventions, such magic clouds aren't exactly passing the buck, because the officers involved know that nine times out of ten (no plan survives first contact with the enemy), our troops will get stuck paying that bill with their blood. Instead, these bouts of wishful thinking tend to reflect the great frustration the military feels whenever it's asked to accomplish goals that naturally extend beyond the war and into the *everything else*—where its ability to control the situation rapidly slips away. You can tell whenever the military hits such a "showstopper," as they like to call them, because you'll hear the generals start talking about how "there's no military solution to this political problem." That's the basic seam: When there are still military solutions, it's called war, but when the problems are political, then you're into the *everything else*.

Well, despite the bold predictions of future success in Iraq by the Administration, by the fall of 2003 my gut instinct was that the occupation in Iraq was going to head south over the subsequent months, meaning that when *The Pentagon's New Map* came out in the spring of 2004, it had better provide some answers, or at least some diagnosis, of the situation at hand.

Oddly enough, the very material I was most reluctant to include in the book has become its most popular attribute among many in the military. I got a huge preview of that when Greg Jaffe's profile of me appeared in the *Wall Street Journal* just a couple of weeks after the book hit the streets. To my amazement, I started getting e-mails from all over the world (but especially from Iraq), from U.S. servicemen and servicewomen who were both excited and gratified that someone seemingly with influence inside the Pentagon had finally come out and said what they had long known: we already have two militaries. Naturally, the ones who wrote me came overwhelming from the SysAdmin side of the force (e.g., civil affairs, medical, logistics, military police, construction), and the gist of what they said, in e-mail after e-mail, was, "Yes! Finally someone's willing to describe things as they truly are!" All these military personnel were immensely proud of the work they did, especially in Iraq. But most were also indignant about how they felt their specialties and communities were treated by a Defense Department that always viewed their activities as essentially inconsequential, meaning last in line in budgetary priorities. In the occupation of Iraq, that long-held bias against SysAdmin work would come back to haunt the Pentagon.

As with my briefings over the past decade and a half, what I had done in the book was the equivalent of what Vice Admiral Cebrowski (the original Director of the Pentagon's Office of Force Transformation) liked to call "data-free research." There's not enough operational data in the world that pushes you to make the leap from the Defense Department to the Leviathan-SysAdmin split. That's an idea you simply have to hang out there, because if you wait for the data to demand it somehow, you'll be waiting till kingdom come, given the nature of bureaucratic inertia. By enunciating the larger vision, what I did was trigger an avalanche of interest from across the global defense community regarding the concept, and likewise from ordinary citizens.

Why such a strong response? First, the creation of the Department of Homeland Security strikes so many Americans—not to mention most of the world—for what it is: a fantastic cop-out. It blames the victim for 9/11, and satisfies the knee-jerk desire within all Americans to withdraw from the world after something as horrific as those attacks. But of course that's the last thing the world needs from us. In our fear we reached for a new department as the answer and created the wrong one, whose very existence seems to scream out, "It's all about me, the United States," when in reality it's all about those regions in the world that are poorly connected to the global economy, or what I call the Non-Integrating Gap, and all the pain and suffering trapped inside there.

Within the U.S. military, the strength of the response grew exponentially the lower you went in the ranks, because the younger the officer, the more clear it was to him or her that the "other than war" stuff had crowded out the traditional definitions of armed conflict long ago. In fact, you can already talk to captains and colonels who've built entire careers around SysAdmin operations, especially if they've served extensive time in U.S. Southern Command, whose focus on the narcotics traffic within its area of responsibility makes it the purest SysAdmin of the four overseas regional commands. But in a broader sense, military personnel, no matter their specialty, *simply enjoy* engaging in SysAdmin operations more than in Leviathan operations. Given a choice between pulling a trigger in combat and pulling someone to safety in a disaster, they'll always choose the latter. There's no surprise in that. That's simply human nature, whether you put on the uniform or not.

For instance, since December 26, 2004, there has been a huge ongoing battle for hearts and minds in Asia that has nothing to do with a 4GW enemy and yet, if waged well, does much to prevent such an enemy's rise in the future or diminish the appeal of those already operating in the region. The Asian tsunamis generated right off the coast of Indonesia immediately led to the largest humanitarian-assistance/disaster-relief operation the world has ever seen—or that the U.S. military has ever addressed. An instant in the making, this is a System Perturbation, or a bolt-from-the-blue shock to the global community of states that will trap millions upon millions across Asia's littoral in recovery efforts that span years. A truly transformed U.S. military is one that can cover both the Leviathan and System Administrator functions effectively. This force yields a military that not only can process a politically bankrupt regime like Saddam Hussein's Iraq but likewise is ready to deal with once-in-a-lifetime opportunities to preemptively secure "peace victories" in situations like the catastrophe in Asia.

With foreign governments and militaries (e.g., United Kingdom, France, Norway, Denmark, Germany, Canada, Australia, China, Brazil), the SysAdmin force concept became the most popular part of my presentations and speeches. In fact, it's often triggered the best sort of responses: where audience members race up to you after the talk to declare this is "exactly" the sort of thing their agency, command, or think tank had long been proposing for their own military. They just hadn't been able to link it to some larger strategic argument that made it seem less like idealism and more like realism. It was as though by simply voicing the concept from the American side, I found myself taking applications for allies at the same time the Bush Administration seemed intent on alienating so many of them.

But there's nothing mysterious about the attraction: the SysAdmin force fundamentally speaks to the level and type of operations that most militaries in the world are not only optimized for, but to which, frankly, they're limited in sheer capability. Most foreign officers from

WHAT THE WORLD NEEDS NOW   29

Core militaries, especially NATO member states, see no shame in that whatsoever, but rather a positive evolution from a bloodier past. In fact, most of them argue that Europe's more consensual political style yielded militaries more naturally adept at the SysAdmin's peace-keeping functions than the U.S. military. As for representatives from Gap militaries (especially those from the Middle East, sub-Saharan Africa, and Southeast Asia), most tell me they dream of the day when a police model of force will be enough to deter mass violence in their regions, so they too see nothing demeaning in having their militaries work toward this ideal.

Now, given the painful experience of the U.S. military in the Iraq occupation, the Pentagon is moving in the direction of crafting the SysAdmin force with a vengeance, especially in the Marines and the Reserve Component (National Guard and Reserves). Numerous serious studies have been conducted in the last year and a half on the question of how best to strengthen the military's ability to conduct postconflict stabilization operations. Beyond the concept-development efforts, a host of new programs and initiatives have emerged throughout the defense research-and-development community, with the experimental center of gravity being Joint Forces Command in Norfolk, Virginia, the military command within the Defense Department most concerned with fielding tomorrow's most capable force. Within weeks of *The Pentagon's New Map*'s coming out, I was asked by the future-plans-and-experimentation division there to join their ongoing efforts as a Senior Concept Developer. This spontaneous networking of like-minded thinkers simply reflects a critical mass of understanding being reached within the Defense Department. That critical mass reflects three different dynamics all coming together at the same time: the continued push for institutional change by the Rumsfeld team, the return of the budgetary squeeze after the short-term boost provided by 9/11, and the fact that the Army and Marines are no longer putting up the same resistance to the SysAdmin function. This "perfect storm" will push the U.S. military to greater change in the next five years than it has seen in the previous fifteen.

But herein lies the political danger: The debacle of the postwar occupation of Iraq finally triggers the long-delayed reform process within the Pentagon. That much is good. But that debacle and the cost in human lives it incurs can likewise sour the American public on the long-term prospects of the U.S. military ever getting sufficiently good at this process to make it a politically feasible choice in future scenarios. In effect, we suffer a recurrence of the Vietnam Syndrome, meaning we're hesitant to engage a similar Gap situation out of fear of the resulting occupation. In the end, the biggest and most profound horizontal scenario coming out of the Big Bang we laid on the Middle East could well be felt in the United States, not in the Persian Gulf. The Core's greatest military power becomes self-deterred, and the forces of disconnectedness inside the Gap become far more emboldened. Why? Because those in the Gap who thrive most on diminished connectivity with the global economy know full well that when the United States disengages, there ends any hope of a coordinated Core-wide military response to whatever violent agenda they may wish to pursue.

That's why I think the truly visionary blueprint for action right now is to treat our failure in the Iraq occupation with even more political vigor and bureaucratic response than we did the attacks of 9/11. America needs to commit itself to the concept that getting countries from the Gap to the Core is not only a national security imperative, it's our overarching foreign policy objective for the next several decades. To that end, we need a new cabinet-level department that expresses and guides that long-term aspiration, something that bridges the gap between our current Department of War (Defense) and our de facto Department of Peace (State). We need a Department of Everything Else, a Department of Global Security that speaks to the world in terms of our shared responsibility, balancing the obvious selfishness embodied in our just-created Department of Homeland Security, and perhaps even cannibalizing it by putting all that SysAdmin talent trapped there to better use abroad (rather than assuming a new department would be needed), an intriguing idea Senator John Kerry of Massachusetts challenged me to consider when I briefed him recently. Again, we need to declare our intent to wage peace as effectively as we wage war.

Let me do my best to convince you of the wisdom and inevitability of this move, and, I hope, by doing so, enlist your support for making this happen sooner rather than later. Because if it's a good idea for twenty years from now, then it's a good idea for today, because the future worth creating must always be connectable to actions taken in the here and now. Otherwise, such a notion remains a pleasant but ultimately diverting abstraction. And as we have learned and forgotten repeatedly over history, inertia is not an acceptable course of action.

There is overwhelming historical evidence, I believe, alerting us to the reality that America will inevitably engage in frequent efforts at postconflict stabilization and nation building in coming decades. In *The Pentagon's New Map,* I described the fundamental downshifting of violence that we've witnessed in the last two decades: from the system-level threats of great-power war in the Cold War, to the challenges of interstate war posed by regional hegemons in the post–Cold War era, to the post-9/11 environment in which virtually all mass violence of significance will occur either within nation-states (e.g., civil strife, mass repression by authoritarian elites) or at the hands of dangerous transnational actors such as terrorists, often abetted by rogue regimes. If, as the advocates of Fourth-Generation Warfare note, we face a future security environment dominated by the Gap's tribal wars and the terrorism they spawn, then that is simply the result of our success in moving the planet away from both war among great powers inside the Core and conventional interstate wars inside the Gap. The journalist Robert D. Kaplan likes to describe the Gap's tribal environment, where civil strife within states still abounds, as "Indian territory," recalling the military challenges posed by the long-term settling of the American West. That such imagery speaks to our pre-Core past is not surprising. It just says that in terms of global violence, that's all that's left now that the Functioning Core of globalization encompasses the majority of the Western Hemisphere and the Eurasian landmass. Yes, it's true that we've come to the hard part, or the toughest nuts to crack, but that historical journey represents a huge shift in the world's correlation of forces.

What can we learn from that shift? The evidence is apparent from how we've employed U.S. military forces abroad since the end of the Cold War.

First, the relationship between war and peace operations has fundamentally changed. In effect, as we've transformed our military power into the high-tech Leviathan force that it is today, we've dramatically altered the historical model of our overseas interventions. As described in a recent report by the National Defense University (NDU), in the past our major wars naturally entailed both long-term buildups and executions, committing to the theater of operations large numbers of American troops, which in turn were far more readily available for any subsequent nation-building mission. To win wars in the past, we needed far larger numbers of troops, and that war effort naturally accommodated the follow-on peace commitment.

The problem we face today is like most of the challenges we encounter: a result of our historical success to which we've not yet adjusted our strategy. Today's Leviathan force can project power around the planet with great agility, conducting wars of ever-shorter duration while fielding a much smaller force that suffers far lower casualty rates. But our ability to field an effective nation-building response, which naturally remains manpower-intensive, has not kept pace, primarily because the Pentagon has long refused to invest in such capabilities. Thus, our current ability to wage war with great efficiency has created what the NDU calls a "mission gap": America can be in and out with its Leviathan force before the SysAdmin force can barely get its act together. Plus, because we stubbornly try to use the same personnel for both functions, the smaller footprint of the Leviathan force means we'll always have too few boots on the ground come the end of the war, thus shortchanging the follow-on peace effort.

What really needs to happen is this: The ethos of the Powell Doctrine's "overwhelming force" must shift from the war to the peace, because our transformed Leviathan is now capable of writing checks that our current SysAdmin force can't cash, unless it gets a lot more personnel. When we reshaped the U.S. military following Vietnam, we did so according to the Abrams Doctrine, so named for then–Army Chief of Staff General Creighton Abrams. The Abrams Doctrine said we should never be able to go to war without the approval of the American public, and so to achieve that buy-in, many of the key support units of the warfighting force were placed in the Reserve Component (Reserves and National Guard). The reality of the transformed Leviathan is, however, that the Pentagon *can* go to war quite effectively without asking buy-in from the public. What it can't do, because we've also stuffed most of our natural SysAdmin forces (e.g., military police, civil affairs, construction) in the Reserve Component, is go to peace without gaining the public's buy-in. Taking down Saddam didn't tap the Reserves and Guard, but occupying Iraq did big-time, meaning the Abrams Doctrine has been effectively turned on its head by our Leviathan's successful transformation, and new rules are required.

Now, the normal counter to that is to say, "Why not make the Leviathan force huge going in so as to accommodate the postconflict stabilization effort?" But rather than bog down this incredibly efficient Leviathan force with unnecessary numbers, logic would dictate that we simply optimize the follow-on SysAdmin force to take advantage of the Leviathan's core competency of winning wars quickly and decisively. That's basically the new rule the Pentagon has yet to adjust to: the shorter the warfighting, the longer the peacekeeping. The smaller the war force, the larger the peace force. The easier the war, the tougher the peace.

Tell me that doesn't sound like a positive trend that we should take advantage of rather than bemoan. The better the Leviathan force gets, the smaller it can get, and the wars become cheaper and faster and less bloody as a result. But if we don't adjust to that emerging reality, then all we end up with is serial failed occupations. So the smaller the Leviathan gets, the bigger the SysAdmin must become. The cheaper the Leviathan gets, the more money must flow to the SysAdmin's needs. The success of the Leviathan thus naturally fuels the rise of the SysAdmin force. The Pentagon's figures speak clearly to this dynamic. In terms of the additional costs imposed upon our defense budget by major overseas interventions since the end of the Cold War, stabilization and reconstruction costs have outpaced those of major combat operations by at least four to one, meaning we've spent more than four-fifths of our budget for operations inside the Gap on the peace and less than one-fifth on wars. Amazing, isn't it? Yet we still maintain the fiction that war is the U.S. military's primary function inside the Gap, thus the SysAdmin force is starved for lack of resources and disregard within Pentagon planning circles. This is what I mean when I say we've spent the past fifteen years buying one force (the Leviathan) while operating another (the SysAdmin).

Judging by those budget numbers, it's clearly not just the model of war and peace that has changed but the relative frequency of operations. During the Cold War, we took on nation-building exercises roughly once every ten years. Since then, we've picked up this challenge, on average, once every two years. And we're not alone in this process. Roughly 80 percent of all UN peacekeeping missions, going all the way back to the UN's founding, in 1945, have been launched since the end of the Cold War. This is not some imaginary demand we're addressing, nor does it reflect some fantasy about American empire in the post–Cold War era. This is the Gap self-immolating at a much higher frequency in the last decade and a half. The question is, How does America choose to adapt its use of military force to account for this change?

It's not an idle question, because it is clear that the forces of disconnectedness inside the Gap have already adjusted to this new pattern of war and peace, thus putting them in the driver's seat and the Pentagon far too often in the position of trying to catch up. As the recent definitive report from the Pentagon's Defense Science Board stated, our potential adversaries have learned how to game our likely response to any outbreak of mass violence. First, prior to our intervention, they work to discourage our mobilization by manipulating the global media, leveraging the usual anti-American sentiments found inside the UN, taking advantage of whatever economic bonds they have with key Core powers to dissuade them from action (and yes, those bonds typically involve energy exports), and doing their best to encourage political opposition within Core states to any military response. The purpose of all these acts is simply to delay the Core's response to whatever atrocities are occurring.

When a military intervention does occur, these adversaries simply do their best to lie low and wait out our mighty blow, knowing that they can do little about its impact but hoping that it will be short in duration. In this way, they conserve their resources for the real fight ahead: our subsequent halfhearted attempts to impose peace and civil order. Once America is into stabilization operations, then the forces of disconnectedness recast themselves as insurgents, and their preferred conflict venue begins in earnest: whatever social chaos they can engender. Their goal is simple: make the situation so bad that whatever Core coalition is involved, it will soon be divided against itself. Back home the fingers of blame will begin pointing, the voices of "moral reason" will call out, and their political victory will come within reach. The Core withdraws, the disconnect achieved, and the country can return to whatever hellhole status elicited the initial moral outrage from the Core—now long forgotten.

And it's easy for the Core to rationalize such withdrawals, not just in terms of the usual self-serving arguments (e.g., "Who are *we* to impose our morals on others?") but also because it relieves us of a tremendous burden and absolves us of our obligation to act. This points even more clearly to the need to institutionalize this capability more fully within our government. As our wars grow ever shorter and less costly, the manpower requirements associated with them remain flat or decrease with time. But as we take on new nation-building challenges with regularity, our manpower requirements for waging peace will skyrocket. The in-and-out Leviathan force can effectively reuse the same personnel time and time again, replenishing with ease as troops age out (war being overwhelmingly a young man's activity), but since postconflict stabilization and reconstruction efforts last—on average—just over five years, the cumulative demand for SysAdmin forces will be substantial. In other words, if we're going to be serious about shrinking the Gap and winning this global war on terrorism, then our SysAdmin force will eventually dwarf our Leviathan force in personnel. Again, the *better* the Leviathan, the *bigger* the SysAdmin must be (though it doesn't necessarily follow that the U.S. portion of a Core-wide SysAdmin capability must increase—hold that thought!).

That dictum captures the essential rule set for sizing our forces in the coming decades.

Are there strategic dangers in this approach? Only if America pretends it can take up this burden on its own, because only in that approach are we sure to alienate other great powers who, in their growing apprehension, will seek to balance our military power by growing their own. The employment of our SysAdmin force must represent the highest order of our military cooperation with the rest of the world's advanced militaries. Moreover, if structured correctly, whereby the United States provides "hub" to the rest of our coalition's "spokes," our unilateral ability to employ our portion of the larger, multilateral SysAdmin force will be effectively curtailed, meaning we will be unable to wage peace inside the Gap without effectively gaining at least the approval of the Core's other major pillars, such as Europe, Russia, India, China, and Brazil.

The same would not be true for our Leviathan force and its capacity to wage war. Yet for that employment of force to have any lasting meaning, it must be but rarely engaged without the concurrence of our fellow great powers. Otherwise, the cooperation required to maintain and employ the Core's collective SysAdmin force would dissolve, leaving America increasingly deterred by the realization that its Leviathan force would find no enemies it could deter inside the troubled regions of the Gap, knowing, as these potential adversaries would, that our warmaking capacity could do little to change permanently the landscape within which they operate. In short, our enemies can simply duck and cover during our aerial strike campaigns, certain of our subsequent unwillingness to put boots on the ground. So yes, a unilateral America can bomb any Gap country back to the Stone Age (for some, a very short trip), but what sort of permanent victory would the resulting fear and loathing represent in an age where disconnectedness defines danger? In effect, we'd just be beating the dog already made vicious by years of mistreatment.

There is, naturally, huge bureaucratic resistance within the defense community to seeing the force formally split into distinct Leviathan and SysAdmin functions, but most of this angst reflects the reality that the defense-industrial complex is far more comfortable cranking out the hugely expensive weapons systems and platforms (e.g., ships, aircraft) required by the Leviathan than it is in confronting the resource requirements of the SysAdmin force. But let me be even more honest: the Leviathan's main costs are in procurement, whereas the SysAdmin's are in operations and manpower. So don't expect this to be an easy sell to anyone inside the Pentagon or on Capitol Hill. Instead, expect all such natural opponents to argue that while the broad outlines of this vision are correct, "it fails to take into consideration the incredibly vital military capabilities provided by [insert favorite defense program here]." You want to magically transform a dove into a hawk? Just walk up to any member of Congress and explain why the huge defense project being funded in his or her state is completely irrelevant to the future global security environment. At that moment, no matter what your credentials, the power of your argument will drop in direct proportion to the member's rising indignation over the potential job losses the "people back home" will suffer. In fact, I know of no way to more quickly garner the label of being "weak on U.S. national security."

But of course this view is incredibly shortsighted. In actuality, the private sector will benefit tremendously from a shifting of resources from the Leviathan to the SysAdmin. First, the narrow confines of the defense-industrial base will be widened to include a much larger array of potential suppliers and contractors—especially for services provided in the field. Second, the information-networking challenges of the SysAdmin force actually dwarf those of the Leviathan force, coming as they do in the far more complicated peacetime environment. For the SysAdmin force, it's not just a matter of keeping track of "bad guy" targets, but keeping track of them while they're typically commingled with the everyday workings of a society experiencing post-conflict recovery. Fighting a conventional military opponent in the desert is one thing, but dealing with insurgents who blend into the dense fabric of urban life in a Gap megalopolis of 10 to 20 million inhabitants is quite another.

Finally, reflecting the blurring of the previously firm line between war and peace the world over, most of the technologies developed for the SysAdmin force package will have "dual-use," or clear private-sector applications, in the post-9/11 environment. This is especially true for nonlethal crowd-control and suspect-apprehension technologies, as well as unmanned monitoring systems that both are mobile and have a long "dwell" capacity (meaning they can persistently cover an area for a great length of time). If you think the Leviathan force promotes robotics, that'll be nothing compared with the SysAdmin's rising demand curve for such systems (especially on the ground). In sum, the defense sector will be presented with more challenges, more complicated mission objectives, and far more opportunities for heightened profitability in private-sector spin-offs as it shifts more and more from feeding the Leviathan to supplying the SysAdmin force. So it's not just true that peace has gotten more expensive than war, there's also a lot more money to be made in the peace than in the war.

There are better arguments to resist the splitting of the force, but they always arise from elements within the military that feel they already fit this bill—both Leviathan and SysAdmin. For example, the Marines have long maintained the operational concept of the "three-block war," in which any expeditionary Marine force must be prepared to fight high-end combat in one urban neighborhood, engage in peacekeeping operations in the next one over, and conduct humanitarian relief in a nearby third. But the fact that the Marines aspire to such ambidexterity doesn't prove that the logic would hold for the U.S. military as a whole. In reality, the Marines need to be that agile in their operations precisely because, as the smallest and most expeditionary of the four services, they represent the closest thing the Pentagon currently has to a SysAdmin force. But claiming that the Marines already have that function covered is disingenuous, because to consider them the new SysAdmin force, we'd need a Corps several times larger than the one we have today, and such a step would be a waste of resources, given the large concentrations of SysAdmin-type assets within the other three services—especially within the Army. Plus, the Marines would stop being Marines at that point. They'd just be Army, and yeah, we'd lose something very important there.

But of course it is the Army that is most resistant to the notion of the SysAdmin force, fearing that it will lose its warfighting ethos and be turned into a giant peacekeeping force (always the Army's supposition regarding the transformation "conspiracy"). In many ways, the modern distribution of warfighting capabilities across the four services reverses the historic role of the Army as the core of the Leviathan force (remembering that prior to 1947, the Department of War and the Department of the Army were effectively one and the same). Today, the core of the Leviathan force is concentrated within the Air Force and the carrier-based air of the Navy. Add to that the growing role of naval ships as platforms for missiles, and you basically have the vast majority of the Leviathan's force structure.

Meanwhile, it's now the Army and Marines who settle into the long-term SysAdmin function of keeping the peace. So, in a nutshell, the new rule set on war and peace effectively reverses the historical roles of the Army and the Navy, as the two experience a sort of Freaky Friday–like swap of functions. The Army, once the main force for war, now becomes the main force for peace. As far as the big-ship traditional Navy goes, it's assets are now far more defined by Leviathan functions than SysAdmin ones, and yet a certain portion of the fleet, dramatically downsized in ship size, will ultimately play "coast guard" to the world within the larger SysAdmin force.

Where will we find the civilians to join this SysAdmin force—this pistol-packin' Peace Corps? Where do we find the cops and firemen and emergency medical response people within our own society? Do they do it for the money? Not judging by relative wages. Heck, most firemen in this country are volunteers, meaning they do it for free, out of some larger sense of their defined community and shared responsibility to same. I don't think populating the SysAdmin force will be the problem. I think finding them the necessary budgetary support for this force will be the real issue, and that's what—in the end—drives my argument for a new cabinet-level department.

I seriously doubt that, absent a dedicated cabinet-level department, America's efforts to shrink the Gap will succeed over time. For while the Leviathan is necessary to keep the Core whole and the Gap from growing, it is not sufficient. So long as the SysAdmin's main assets remain buried and poorly prioritized inside the Defense Department, it will always be the unfunded mandate it is today. Moreover, the recent move to create a czar-like office in the State Department to oversee this function won't change anything, because it's basically just a title, a tiny bit of money, and really no budgetary authority to build dedicated capacity over time. We don't need another "coordinator," we need significant bureaucratic empowerment—someone with a real hammer and the authority to use it. All this new office will do is make it easier, following our next nation-building failure, to call the "responsible official" in front of a Senate committee. Why won't it work? Defense and State will always be at odds with each other in war and peace, befitting their "bad cop/good cop" roles in U.S. foreign policy debates, and the National Security Adviser, allegedly in control of the "interagency" process that forces the two departments to cooperate with each other, will remain focused on insulating the White House from any political fallout from recognized failures. No one will really own the postwar peace, any more than anyone currently owns the portfolio of getting Gap states into the Core.

No, the SysAdmin force must grow within, and eventually grow beyond, the confines of the Defense Department. It will grow like a cancer, eating up budget and manpower within the Pentagon, where, over time, the masters of the Leviathan force will grow resentful of its competitor's rising political and budgetary clout within the department. This process began in spades with the fiscal year 2006 defense budget, the first to feel the brunt of the Iraq occupation's impact: big cuts in "big-ticket" procurement programs and major shifts to the SysAdmin's manpower needs. At some point, the SysAdmin function will have grown so large and seemingly so at odds with the department's core warfighting function that the Pentagon will have no choice but to spin it off like a subsidiary that's become too burdensome for the parent company. This is what has happened with Halliburton, the giant oil-field services company, and its SysAdmin-like subsidiary Kellogg Brown & Root, which has grown dramatically in size (not to mention political controversy) in relation to the Pentagon's burgeoning SysAdmin portfolio. Eventually, Halliburton decides the subsidiary isn't worth the hassle, and that it is pushing the parent company too far from its historic roots, and so in 2005, Halliburton actively debates whether to sell KBR, spin it off, or take it public on its own. Whatever decision ensues, I think Halliburton's instinct to distance itself is reflective of the same sort of bureaucratic dynamics we'll eventually see between the Pentagon and its own SysAdmin force, for there too I expect the Defense Department to eventually "sell off" this "subsidiary" at some point in the not-too-distant future.

Will such a development represent yet another "scary" grab for global power by the U.S. federal government? Is this yet a new "frightening" move toward eventual "one-world government"? Slow down a bit before you start hearing the black helicopters buzzing in your head. This isn't some conspiratorial move toward global domination but simply the U.S. Government finally adapting itself to the end of war as we have known it.

Understanding the utility of the separation of powers and the desire of our Founding Fathers to make war a last resort, ask yourself this: When was the last time the United States formally declared war on an enemy identified as an imminent threat to U.S. national security? Well, the last time we actually declared war against another state was against Romania in 1942, once it was viewed as joining the Nazi axis of power in Europe during World War II. Since then? No one. Despite all the wars, military interventions, and Cold War crises in the decades since, America has never formally declared war on anything or anybody. I realize that there are some in our country who view this state of affairs with apoplexy, believing that the executive branch has run amok, constitutionally speaking, but I have a simpler explanation: we haven't faced an imminent threat to our fundamental national security since World War II.

What America has done in the decades since is to play sometime Leviathan and full-time System Administrator. During the Cold War we stood up to the Soviet threat and kept the peace in the West, occasionally meddling in the Third World (along with the Soviets) to little good effect. Since the Cold War, we've had no real security role across the Core, and we've come to understand our growing security role inside the Gap.

The problem with our intermittent and always stingy funding of both war and peace inside the Gap is that while the White House can use the power of the presidency to compel Congress to fund war, that same power is rarely used—and never used effectively—with regard to the peace. Foreign aid programs are currently distributed across a half-dozen cabinet departments, and they are—each and every one of them—the poor stepchild of their respective agency, to include the U.S. Agency for International Development's singularly weak status within the State Department. As such, the U.S. lags behind virtually every other industrialized state in terms of foreign aid as a percentage of GDP. Of course, if we chose to count the roughly quarter-trillion dollars (and counting) that we've spent in postconflict stabilization and reconstruction operations since the Cold War, our ranking would most certainly improve dramatically (especially if combined with all the hundreds of humanitarian assistance/disaster relief operations we've conducted over those years), because here we'd be talking about a sum of money that's more than triple or even quadruple what the Core as a whole has tended to offer the Gap on an annual basis in recent years.

But there's a more specific problem. While Congress can readily be counted on to "support the troops on the ground" in any intervention, our nation's willingness to follow through on the peace doesn't match our record on war. We'll pay through the nose to dismember some Gap rogue regime, but almost nothing to move the battered country in the direction of the Core, which means that the state will likely continue to fail. Why do we allow this failure to continue? For a member of Congress, there's real danger in not supporting "the war" (see John Kerry's problems in the 2004 election over just one vote), but not much in blowing off the peace. In many ways, this phenomenon mirrors the Core's overall tendency on major disasters that occur inside the Gap: a huge show of support right after the disaster, segueing to a lot of incomplete aid projects years later. In sum, we have a tendency to "photo-op" the Gap: we all love to have our pictures taken with the troops during the war, but no one's around to take any pictures of the resulting failed peace.

But that has to change if there's going to be serious, long-term progress in this global war on terrorism. Investment follows the flag, and the flag that counts the most is that of the United States, because where our troops go, there too is found the enduring commitment of our government to ensure a region's lasting stability. It's that stability, guaranteed over the long haul by U.S. military presence and alliances, that's enabled both Europe to integrate successfully and Asia to emerge economically rather than lapse back into self-destructive conflicts and self-limiting arms races. For the Gap to be shrunk effectively over time, America must inevitably move beyond those past successes to new long-term efforts in the Middle East (already begun) and Africa (still waiting). We'll have to put in the same 24/7/365 effort that's marked our multi-decade commitments inside the now stable Functioning Core of globalization.

We are in one of those great historical periods when the world demands more from its most experienced multinational political and economic union than just a singular voice. It demands a singular vision of a future worth creating for the planet as a whole. I believe that vision will find best expression within the U.S. Government by the establishment of a Department of Everything Else, or a Department of Global Security, or whatever you want to call it—just something that says we're committed over the long term to shrinking the Gap and making globalization truly global.

But even that step is just the opening bid for the far more ambitious Core-wide rule set that inevitably lies beyond.

BARNETT'S A-TO-Z RULE SET ON PROCESSING POLITICALLY BANKRUPT STATES

The National Intelligence Council is sort of the "Supreme Court" of the intelligence community, which is spread across fifteen individual agencies, including the well-known CIA. The Council, or NIC, as most people in the business call it, is made up of a collection of National Intelligence Officers (or NIOs), each of whom is the government's top expert on some particular subject, such as "economics and global issues" or "East Asia." Collectively, this organization issues significant reports known as National Intelligence Estimates, which guide senior decision makers throughout the national security establishment in matters of war and peace. But to the public (and especially the Web community), the NIC is probably best known for its "global futures" reports that regularly project the future of the planet ahead a good fifteen years or more. These reports are by far the best examples of futurology to be found within the national security community, in large part because the authors eschew the usual doom-and-gloom of the Pentagon's futurism, which always portrays the world going to hell in a handbasket. Why? Because that's just good for business.

Over the course of my career I have participated on several occasions in the NIC's long process of consulting with "outside experts" as they build these "mapping the global future" reports, and National Intelligence Officers came to virtually every workshop I ever put on at the Naval War College. I came to respect the NIC's institutional process of looking ahead, because of its willingness to listen to alternative viewpoints, meaning those that posited hopeful or at least benign developments lying ahead and not just the negatives. Soon after *The Pentagon's New Map* came out, I was asked by the Intelligence Council to participate in one of these gatherings, a workshop focused on the future of war. I was given the question "Does the United States face a never-ending future of subnational and transnational violence?" I answered yes, and that this was a good thing compared with the Cold War's far higher levels of interstate warfare and the threat of global nuclear clashes between superpowers.

But I didn't stop there. I said that future was benign enough *only* if the United States took it upon itself to try and fashion new rules and new international organizations designed to focus on these particular problem sets. Absent this effort, our tacit acceptance of heightened worldwide levels of such civil strife and terrorism certainly would be bad, in large part because if we didn't deal with these problems, inevitably some other great powers would feel compelled to do so on their own, possibly triggering intra-Core arms races or—worse—the return of great-power rivalries inside the Gap (i.e., wars by proxy).

Well, the resulting NIC report, *Mapping the Global Future: Report of the National Intelligence Council's 2020 Project,* lived up to the Council's usual fine standards. It lacked the typical hyping of the threat and presented future scenarios in highly imaginative ways. Naturally, when it came out in early 2005, a lot of my Weblog readers pressed me for comments, knowing I had been involved in the process. The blogosphere, the universe of bloggers, was discussing the report at length when it came out, and the judgment of this crowd, full of both amateurs and professionals, was rather uniform: "a very sobering and disturbing view of the future."

My take was a little different. All the NIC really said in its projection of the world in 2020 was the following: the United States wouldn't dominate global affairs as it does today; China and India would be far more powerful players; Russia and the Central Asian republics might take several steps backwards politically; the Middle East could experience some serious democratic reform—or not; terrorism would still exist but would be expressed in different, probably more challenging forms, especially as proliferation of weapons of mass destruction continued; and the UN would probably be far more marginalized as new political realities emerged in the global security order as a result of all this change. That's it. That's the "very sobering and disturbing" future the blogosphere was gobbling up and digesting as a source for pessimism about the world in 2020.

In my view the report was basically a careful, realistic, straightforward projection of today's trends over the next decade and a half—*absent any sort of imaginative response from the global community as a whole.* It was like a warning from a physician to his middle-aged male patient: "If you don't change your lifestyle whatsoever, this is what you're going to look like in fifteen years: older, flabbier, and generally less healthy." Surprise, surprise.

By its very nature, the intelligence community feels that it must never engage in advocacy of any particular policy, meaning it defines its job as "just projecting the trends, ma'am," as it avoids telling the U.S. Government what it should or should not do in response to such projections. That's their code: Analysts don't have opinions, just analysis. So what happens when the NIC projects a global future is that the authors feel compelled to describe what every other country in the world will do in response to this unfolding series of events while essentially keeping the United States itself static, meaning the whole world's experiences change while the United States does not—at least not in any proactive way. Sure, we're allowed to "age" like everyone else in the scenarios, but the maturation process of other states is dynamic, whereas ours is not.

The problem with this approach, of course, is that in its zeal to avoid policy advocacy, the NIC comes up with future global scenarios that essentially ignore the ability of the play's leading protagonist to develop further as a character across the unfolding plotline. This is not only ahistoric—meaning it doesn't jibe well with America's long-standing role as a generator and purveyor of new rules for the global system—it also sends all the wrong signals to unsophisticated readers about what's truly possible. By its very character, the NIC can describe only the future "floor," not the "ceiling." It can only give us a sense of the natural decay of international order, not its potential for positive regeneration. In short, reports such as these can only describe how bad it *would* get if America basically did nothing, not how good it *could* get if we chose to do something about it.

The problem is that most people read these reports and take them as the gospel truth ("After all, these guys know all the secret stuff, right?"), but instead of motivating them toward action, these scenarios drive readers toward fatalism and passivity. Most futurology has this effect: after you put the book down and contemplate its depressing description of what lies ahead, you either want to get the frightening image immediately out of your head or—as so often is the case now—go online and Chicken Little it to death. Frankly, that's why my blog readers tend to be so loyal: I am a shining beacon of counterintuitive analysis, which in this environment means I am a cockeyed optimist.

Why is that? Aren't we all working off the same trends? Sure we are. We just choose to view those trends differently. Whereas most national security analysts define their professional environment as "futures to be avoided," I focus on a future worth creating. They see trends that are inescapable, and so their goals tend to involve finding ways that America can shield itself from dangerous outcomes. I see trends that determine reasonably identifiable incentives among major players, incentives that can be structured in ways that turn potential flash points into opportunities for new rules, new relationships, and safer outcomes. In sum, your average security analyst doesn't want to engage the future but escape its inevitable grasp ("America will be less powerful!"). What I want to do is embrace that future and shape it from within. So my advice is always, When you see fear, start running *toward* it.

I can't write a global future with the lead protagonist stuck forever in some Hamlet-like pose of "To shape the security environment or not to shape, that is the question." My America has always shaped the future, typically arriving there years before anyone else. As history goes, we're not the kid in the backseat asking incessantly, "Are we there yet?" Hell, we're the teenager at the wheel going way over the speed limit, assuming we'll live forever because we'll be forever young. And you know what? That spirit is what I like best about this country, and deep down, it's what the rest of the world likes best about America. We are an insanely optimistic people, and because we are, our brand of leadership tends to scare more than soothe. Because every time the world thinks it's got the current rule set down in its head, those "damn Americans" try to come up with a new one, always describing it as some "revolution" or something. It's the "sexual revolution," or "women's liberation," or the "information revolution," or the "cyberrevolution." Whatever the rule set, it's always cast as some damnably unstable impact on global order—and, of course, that's what it usually is.

This is especially true when matters of war and peace are involved. Our long-term effort to transform the U.S. military from its industrial-era roots to its current capacity for network-centric operations is—

quite literally—a revolution in military affairs. It has created a Leviathan in the global security environment whose demonstrated power is beyond doubt, at least as far as conventional state-based threats are concerned—which gets me back to the paper I wrote for the NIC's conference on the future of war.

When I got into this business fifteen years ago, I did strategic nuclear planning in anticipation of global war against the Soviet bloc. By the middle of my career, or the late 1990s, I had downshifted, along with the rest of the defense community, to a focus on defeating and deterring regional hegemons, or rogue regimes like Iraq and North Korea. Now, like most of my community, I focus on the questions of how to deal with bad actors operating inside the Gap, be they the "evil leader" of a politically bankrupt state or dangerous transnational terrorists. In my short career, then, I have watched the community leave behind almost all the questions of system-level war between great powers and most issues of interstate wars, leaving us what's left over: bad individuals who do bad things and must be stopped.

Now, many analysts see only a cumulative effect here, as in bad actors *plus* bad regimes *plus* global nuclear dangers. But I see that perspective as fundamentally flawed because it refuses to acknowledge two great victories: (1) the end of the Cold War ended the dynamic of nuclear standoff between great powers; and (2) the willingness of the United States to serve as Leviathan, or proxy for the global community in defeating and deterring rogue regimes, has effectively killed interstate war. Those two historic victories, if simply grasped, reveal to us the unprecedented opportunity we now have to end war as we know it, because we now have the means—if not yet the will—to shrink the Gap progressively by effectively and efficiently processing politically bankrupt states. By doing so, we can tame this Wild West known as the Gap. We can take out the bad guys and help the "settlers"—who are already there and just awaiting our recognition—join the global economy in a just manner.

What do I mean by *process politically bankrupt states?* I mean, take those states from their current state of dysfunctionality to some future condition of reasonable functionality.

How is a state "dysfunctional"? Let's keep it simple. Either the state tries to do too much and it succeeds, making it authoritarian or a dictatorship, or it simply cannot do what it needs to do to keep its society secure, happy, and able to connect up with the outside world in a beneficial manner—that is, a failed state. In either case, it's politically bankrupt in terms of legitimacy, meaning it just doesn't provide what the public needs, either in terms of proper freedom or proper security—or both. "Processing" such a state, therefore, becomes a matter of moving that regime from its dysfunctional Point A to some desired Point Z, admitting, as we must always, that the journey from A to Z is unique for any state and cannot simply be dictated. Yet make that journey it must, otherwise the state remains a source of danger or instability not just for itself but for the larger region it inhabits as well.

Add up all of these politically bankrupt states and you basically come up with my definition of the Gap. This doesn't imply that every state in the Gap is clearly politically bankrupt, because that's certainly not the case. But it does mean that enough of these politically bankrupt states do exist inside the Gap to perpetuate those regions' relatively disconnected status vis-à-vis globalization. In effect, these states are bad for property values and investment climates and other forms of global connectivity, like tourism and trade flows. Processing them toward the conditions of greater functionality, then, is the main task of the Core in developmental aid, trade policies, and security strategies.

This definition of a Core-wide grand strategy for the twenty-first century would have made sense absent 9/11 and the resulting global war on terrorism. It just makes compelling sense now. Why? Politically bankrupt regimes tend to have one of two relationships with transnational terrorism: either they support such activities or they engender and attract such activities. State sponsors of transnational terrorism, like Iran and North Korea, make such trouble possible across big chunks of the world. Conversely, decrepitly authoritarian regimes such as Saudi Arabia and Egypt have historically fueled the rise of violent transnational terrorist groups that wish to see those dysfunctional governments overthrown and replaced by their preferred version, which, unfortunately, would clearly involve even more disconnectedness between those societies and the outside world (as witnessed by the successful imposition of such rule under the Taliban in Afghanistan). This is why recent movement toward even the most rudimentary forms of pluralism (e.g., local elections in Saudi Arabia and multiparty national elections in Egypt) is so important. It attacks al Qaeda, which means "the base," *at its base*.

Failed states also attract terrorist networks simply because they present a loose security rule set within which terrorists, criminals, and anybody else looking to escape scrutiny tend to hang out and do their thing. I once had a veteran of the U.S. Agency for International Development (USAID) tell me he could easily predict future combat zones inside the Gap regarding transnational terrorism. All you need to do, he said, was look where the United States had pulled out a USAID mission, and five years later terrorist networks would be thriving there. What did he mean by that? When USAID gives up on a Gap state, that means it's just about as disconnected and failed as it can get, with America's consummate withdrawal effectively serving as a "for sale" sign to international terrorist groups looking for weak regimes upon which to prey. So to me, there is a real historical confluence here between winning a global war on terrorism, a pool of politically bankrupt (and therefore disconnected) states within the Gap, and this unprecedented, Leviathan-like power the United States now possesses to topple regimes.

Yes, America has this tremendous military capacity, but it's not contextualized within any larger global rule set on how to employ it. The United States has proposed such a rule set, the clumsily titled global war on terrorism, but in its application (Afghanistan, Iraq), we've managed to alienate a lot of allies—both old and potentially new ones. Our Core allies are interested in avoiding conflict over this, and genuinely wish to see transnational terrorism defeated. So what we're looking for is a rule set that makes the application of the solution to this problem *transparent* to all interested parties (eliminating the sense of zero-sum competition among great powers), *judicious* in its application (the Leviathan does not generate more work than the SysAdmin can handle), *consistent* in its use (a sense of due process), and *just* in its outcome (the guilty suffer, but the innocent are reconnected to the larger global community in a manner respectful of local needs and desires).

Hell, I know I'm reaching here, because I haven't exactly been nominated King of the World (and no, nominations from among my blog readers don't count). But frankly, I'm tired of hoping that the UN might someday reform itself enough to take on this role, and I'm not interested in waiting on war between great powers to finally force this much-needed rule set into being. So forgive my graduate-term-paper earnestness here, as I run you through my argument on several different levels. It's just that I want to argue this point—*Rashomon*-style—from a variety of perspectives.

I'll start off by noting that this seemingly fantastic rule set already exists in embryonic form and that it's been used with some success from A to Z, meaning from logical starting point to logical finish.

Hold that thought in your mind for a minute: *We've already done this!*

Having planted that seed of curiosity to sustain you in the pages ahead, here's my plan of explanation: Let me describe this rule set in its sum total first, and then give you an example of how it has worked in the past and how it hasn't worked with Iraq. Next, I want to walk you slowly through the process, right from A to Z, to give you a sense of the key aspects of each link in the chain. Finally, I'll reveal how I think the process of constructing this rule set will probably unfold in the coming years.

Here's the A-to-Z rule set that I define as logically encompassing the successful processing of politically bankrupt states inside the Gap. It consists of the following six pieces:

1. The existing UN Security Council functions primarily as a global "grand jury" that is able to indict parties within the global community for acts of egregious behavior connected to a regime's political dysfunctionality.
2. When a critical mass of such indictments is achieved, a Functioning Executive Body, made up of the Core's biggest economies, steps in—on the basis of consensus—to issue "warrants" for the arrest of the offending party.

3. At that point of agreement, a United States–led warfighting coalition engages in whatever variation of force-on-force effort is required to defeat the targeted regime's traditional military capabilities, continuing such operations until such time as the indicted parties are apprehended.

4. Following right on the heels of this Leviathan-like force is a Core-wide SysAdmin force, whose core warfighting capabilities (optimized for counterinsurgency operations) will come from the U.S. military (Army, Marines) but the bulk of whose force will nonetheless be both civilian and multinational in origin. In its mature form, the SysAdmin force will be roughly one-half military, one-quarter civilian uniformed police, and one-quarter civilian government workers with expertise in disaster relief, nation building, and economic development. U.S. participation in all three aspects should hover in the 10 to 20 percent range of total personnel. The SysAdmin force will initially flood the country in question with military personnel, segueing with all deliberate speed to the second wave of civilian uniformed police, followed quickly by the third wave of primarily civilian relief and reconstruction officials.

5. Once stabilization operations yield to civilian security schemes, reconstruction operations begin, overseen by a Core-funded—or, more specifically, a Functioning Executive Body–funded—international organization dedicated specifically to such nation-building projects, or what *Washington Post* columnist Sebastian Mallaby has described as an International Reconstruction Fund (IRF), modeled on the structure and functioning of both the International Monetary Fund (IMF) and the World Bank. This IRF would serve as the Core's initial occupational authority and the instrument by which both an interim and subsequently elected permanent national government would be constituted and given, over some period of time, political authority over the resulting new state (or states, if some breakup of the original state occurs).

6. The final step in the process would involve the criminal prosecution of the indicted/apprehended parties in the International Criminal Court (ICC) located in The Hague, Netherlands.

That's it, from A to Z. Bad states go in, better states come out.

In many ways, what this system tries to do is provide the political-military equivalent of what the International Monetary Fund and the World Bank provide for economically bankrupt states, or governments that suffer default on their sovereign debt. Crude and seemingly inchoate as it may often appear, there is an essential A-to-Z rule set on how an economically bankrupt state can be processed back into good standing in the global community. As the IMF endeavors over time to codify this process as much as possible, there is naturally great debate about the specific rules throughout the process, but hey, at least we *have* a process! So if you're Argentina and you default on your country's debts, there is a recognized process, with recognized authorities and standards of transparency and conduct to which adherence is not so much required as expected. Does this process work perfectly? Hardly. Do we adjust this process seemingly every time we employ it? Certainly, for its complexity is not a minor point, meaning every time we engage the process we can expect to fill in the blanks all the more. Is the processed state without power? Not exactly, because in these cases, you're talking about a state that may well be functioning politically despite the economic crisis, so you can expect some genuine push and pull between the international authorities and the political leadership of the country. As Argentina itself recently demonstrated, you don't have to follow the A-to-Z rule set exactly; even if you don't, you can still largely earn the same credit (pun intended) for the desired end point of currency stabilization and financial reconstruction.

So all I'm really talking about here is an equivalent to this financial process that deals specifically with politically bankrupt states. You can say, "But it's so much easier when you're talking about something as fungible as money, and so much harder when you're talking matters of war and peace." This is true, but the difficulty of the process simply reflects both the higher stakes involved (human lives at immediate risk on both sides) and the greater need for a consistent and transparent rule set that can be applied both judiciously and with a tangible sense of fairness.

I ginned up this six-part model in my brief following the publication of *The Pentagon's New Map*, because in the concluding chapter I made such a proposal for an A-to-Z process but did so without mentioning anything beyond Sebastian Mallaby's embryonic concept of an International Reconstruction Fund, first mentioned in a *Washington Post* op-ed. As I fielded more and more questions from blog readers and briefing-audience members, I was forced to elaborate on what I meant. I was forced to provide a blueprint for this process, and a description of its functioning. Once I had presented the six-part model numerous times in various formats and venues, various thinkers came to me with descriptions and data points suggesting that, indeed, this model already existed in a rudimentary form, one that had been slapped together haphazardly by the United States and others in response to events—first in Bosnia-Herzegovina and later in Kosovo—in the former Republic of Yugoslavia in the 1990s.

Think back to this process and you will see what they meant:

1. The UN Security Council had indicted Slobodan Milosevic and the government of Serbia on numerous occasions across the early part of the decade, but as so often happens with the Security Council, it was all talk and no action.

2. Action on these indictments came only when a Functioning Executive Body came into being in the form of NATO, which took it upon itself to intervene in the resulting wars between Serbia and the other republics. In both instances, the UN Security Council effectively subcontracted the use of force to NATO *after* the decision to act militarily had been reached.

3. In both Bosnia and Kosovo, the United States, with an assist by NATO member states, provided the Leviathan in the form of airpower, which enabled combat events on the ground overwhelmingly conducted by indigenous, anti-Serbian forces.

4. The SysAdmin force that subsequently entered both theaters was overwhelmingly NATO/European in character (the Implementation Force, or IFOR in Bosnia, and the NATO-led Kosovo Force, or KFOR, in conjunction with the UN Mission in Kosovo force, or UNMIK), meaning the U.S. ground force component was but a small fraction of the total boots on the ground.

5. Specifically in the case of Bosnia, a Peace Implementation Conference in London, which was run effectively by NATO members in their role as a Functioning Executive Body, appointed a High Representative to conduct the framework agreement by which both the stabilization and reconstruction efforts would be achieved. In Kosovo, a quartet of international organizations (European Union, UN High Commissioner for Refugees, Organization for Security and Cooperation in Europe, and the UN) performed a similar function, with obviously greater challenges in unity of command.

6. Slobodan Milosevic was later tried, ultimately to be joined by others from his government, by the UN War Crimes Tribunal in The Hague. This tribunal, created by the Security Council in 1993, serves as effective precursor to, and model for, the International Criminal Court.

So yes, a complex system, but one that logically springs into being to process a politically bankrupt state such as the former Republic of Yugoslavia became across the 1990s. As a result of this effort, it's reasonable to describe the Balkans as effectively joining the Core in the years since. The neatest example? Croatian and Macedonian peace-keepers working alongside NATO troops in Southwest Asia. The more important example? Croatia in talks to join the European Union.

All I'm talking about is replicating that system and making it a permanent feature of the Core's political-military landscape. In aggregate, this acknowledged rule set becomes the key supranational mechanism for the Core to shrink the Gap. By regularizing and codifying such a rule set, the Core will be able to deal systematically with politically bankrupt states inside the Gap in such a way as to avoid major differences of both opinion and approach on individual cases, as occurred in the long-running situation with Iraq:

1. With Saddam Hussein's Iraq, we were talking about a regime that no one really wished to see continue, except for obvious, implicit villains within the Core who had grown rich in the illegal trade conducted with Saddam's regime over the many years Iraq was

subject to UN sanctions. But at least that initial point in the process was clear: Iraq had been "indicted" by the UN Security Council on many occasions. On that basis alone, it was illogical to argue that unless we actually caught Saddam in the act of transgressing Security Council resolutions, we had no right to enforce them. That's like saying you can only arrest a mass murderer when you specifically catch him in the act of killing someone.

2. In the first Persian Gulf war, the UN Security Council effectively subcontracted the execution of punitive acts against Iraq to a United States–led military coalition. In the second war, the UN Security Council's imprimatur was a subject of significant debate, with the United States and its allies claiming they had all the authority they needed based on past resolutions, but with many in the Council and the Secretary-General himself, Kofi Annan, disagreeing with that position. In the absence of that clear agreement, the United States effectively declared itself the Functioning Executive Body with regard to Iraq, leading to charges of "unilateral" war. Lacking a sense of international agreement, the Bush White House was forced by events to try to sell the war to the public on the basis of "imminent threat" (i.e., prewar intelligence indicating Saddam's regime had weapons of mass destruction) and by doing so seek its ultimate authority directly from the American people, as well as whatever allies we could talk into joining our effort.

3. With the country greatly divided over the war, the Bush White House did the equivalent of cops yelling, "He's got a gun!" as we stormed into Iraq on a military timetable of our own choosing. Our Leviathan force performed admirably, and Saddam's military forces were easily defeated.

4. As part of the Bush White House's sale to the American public on the war, however, all efforts were made to conduct the follow-on SysAdmin function with the smallest number of troops possible. This decision, along with several other key mistakes, allowed an insurgency to form inside Iraq and begin a low-intensity conflict with the United States–led occupational forces that has occasion-

ally flared into high-intensity sieges of major cities occupied by various insurgency forces.

5. Similarly, the Coalition Provisional Authority (CPA) ended up being a rather lowball, fly-by-the-seat-of-our-pants effort in which—at many points in the process—it was unclear both who was effectively in charge of the country and what exactly our top priorities were in reconstruction. This external authority was eventually replaced by an interim government that was appointed—for all practical purposes—by the White House.

6. The United States has chosen to pursue trials of Saddam Hussein and his senior leaders within a reconstituted Iraqi legal system, rather than in any international setting such as the International Criminal Court. As such, huge legal questions surround the proceedings, and their perceived international legitimacy is seriously in doubt, much like the United States's original decision to invade.

The Balkans cases showed how an A-to-Z system can logically spring into being, given the right circumstances and agreement among—or at least abstention from opposition by—the Core's major powers. The second Iraq war led by the United States demonstrated, and continues to demonstrate, the converse perils of failing to string together that entire six-part process. Taking the sum of those and other similar experiences into account, let me now argue for what this A-to-Z rule set would look like in its best possible form.

There is the natural temptation to say that the UN Security Council could and should constitute the entirety of the decision-making process, absent the concluding role logically deferred to the International Criminal Court, but such hope would be completely unfounded. The UN did nothing to stop the wars and genocide that ravaged Central Africa across the 1990s, and its role in the Balkans was completely spurred by the actions undertaken by NATO. Three other disturbing situations in the international community over the past several years (North Korea, Sudan, Zimbabwe) have all likewise received no effective measures from the UN Security Council. Where the UN has engaged in economic sanctions, the results have typically been either wholly ineffective or completely counterproductive and quite deadly. The sanctions employed against Iraq across the 1990s prove both points quite effectively. Between the obvious corruption of the Oil-for-Food Program and the UN's own estimates that as many as half a million Iraqi children suffered premature deaths as a result of sanctions, there is very good cause to question the utility of relying on these measures to force regime behavior change inside the Gap.

In contrast to sanctions, UN interventions most associated with success have all involved subcontracting out the executive decision making regarding the employment of military power to member states, such as the United States–led coalition in the first Iraq war, NATO in the Balkans conflicts, the Economic Community of West African States in Liberia and Sierra Leone, and an Australia-led multinational group in East Timor. This pattern is well established and suggests the obvious logic of some permanent, non-UN body to serve as a Functioning Executive Body for the process as a whole.

As for the SysAdmin function, here we need to be very realistic: what the UN provides is not a stabilization capability but a pure peacekeeping capacity that only works well after conflict resolution has been achieved. Finally, rather than attack the nation-building process with a plethora of UN agencies, it seems more logical, given the historical record of the United States in this type of endeavor, to seek something with far more unity of command and purpose. As many critics point out with regard to the Balkans, the UN relief and development agencies have a demonstrated tendency to make themselves a permanent part of the landscape and, in doing so, retard local development of similar talent and organizational capacity. In short, the UN tends to be the social worker who can never quite give up the client.

Having said all that, I do see continued utility in having the UN Security Council function as the effective "grand jury" that starts the process. Why? Two reasons. First, the UN is the logical place where any state can legitimately bring charges against another state or the actors located therein. Second, the UN's technical and regulatory agencies, such as the International Atomic Energy Agency, act as de facto "special prosecutors" who have both the authority and expertise to bring to light nefarious activity by regimes and nonstate actors. All such agencies tend to concentrate the vast bulk of their day-to-day activities inside the Gap, so here we're simply taking advantage of existing capabilities and accepted rule sets.

Turning to the question of the Functioning Executive Body, here I see a clear front-runner for the role: the Group of Eight countries, or G-8. This body originally came into being in 1975 around the notion that the world's major economies needed to cooperate in steering the operation of the global economy in light of the tumultuous events of the preceding years (e.g., end of the gold standard, oil price shocks). Over time, this group has likewise sought to shape globalization's progressive expansion and to reach out to the Gap on development issues. The G-8 reached its current membership with the accession of Russia in 1998, and in 1999 a larger G-20 was also created. For now, the G-8 remains the central body, or the one that meets at the level of national leaders, whereas the G-20 meets only at the ministerial level and is considered the informal companion of the smaller formal body. The G-20 is basically the Functioning Core of globalization (Argentina, Australia, Brazil, Canada, China, European Union, France, Germany, India, Italy, Japan, Mexico, Russia, South Africa, South Korea, United Kingdom, United States), plus two key Seam States (Indonesia, Turkey) and one Gap energy pillar (Saudi Arabia). Taken together, these twenty entities capture roughly two-thirds of the world's population and over 90 percent of global GDP.

In my vision, the G-8, as it slowly expands to include the rest of the G-20 membership in its formal inner body (China being next), is the logical place to start in creating a Functioning Executive Body to translate the global community's will regarding politically bankrupt states inside the Gap into genuine and consistent action. The G-8's main goal today is essentially the same as what I preach: making globalization truly global. Although the G-8 is seen as primarily an economic-oriented organization, it's agenda has tilted dramatically toward security issues since 9/11—to wit, the 2004 Sea Island summit hosted by George Bush was essentially the what-are-we-going-to-do-with-Iraq-now? summit.

Why? The G-8 has simply evolved into the Core's preeminent summit of political leaders, so rather than the UN Security Council, with its rule-bound and often pointless meetings, the G-8 is the natural venue in which individual Core pillars seek a hearing on important Core-wide security issues. For example, when the Bush Administration sought to put its vision for a Greater Middle East Initiative on the table, it did so at the G-8, seeking that group's leadership role in steering the process of dialogue with Middle Eastern governments regarding the goal of political reform there. This only makes sense, for in effecting any region's transition from Gap to Core, the G-8 will logically play a huge role in setting the agenda on trade and investments. Likewise, with over 90 percent of global GDP in their hands, the constituents of the G-20 are the logical source of funds for any post-conflict International Reconstruction Fund activities (and yes, the IRF should be limited to postwar situations; otherwise it just becomes another IMF).

The G-8 should serve as the institutional link between the Security Council's "grand jury" indictments and the unleashing of the combined Leviathan-SysAdmin forces and—beyond that—the follow-on efforts of the proposed International Reconstruction Fund. By utilizing the G-8 in this manner, we effectively bind the world's richest countries to the overall decision-making process, forcing them to decide, in a consensual fashion, which politically bankrupt Gap states should be targeted for rehabilitation in any shrink-the-Gap strategy. By doing so, we internationalize the rule set from A to Z, thus relieving the United States of the burden of having to argue each intervention using the outmoded language of "imminent threat" with the American people.

Would such a military-market nexus create the undue demands of a so-called global test? To an extent, yes. But this is a good thing, because it means America's arguments for regime change must make sense to those fellow Core pillars that will inevitably be called upon to finance the resulting nation building. Does such an arrangement preclude the ability of the United States to wage war unilaterally in extremis? Hardly. It just means we'll either get stuck with the total bill on the far side or we'll be forced to leave some god-awful mess in our wake. Sound familiar? Sounds like Iraq to me. Want to do better? This body is the right place to make any truly needed sale. Sell the need for a regime change to the ever-expanding G-8 and you've just created a set of transparent expectations about how this whole process must come about both militarily and monetarily. It's more than just a matter of not planning a war if you're not willing to plan the peace: don't do it unless you've got the money lined up beforehand. Moreover, make the level of upfront funding a key decision factor—as in, "Do it up right or don't do it at all."

The U.S. military has an expression, "You want it bad, you get it bad." Bush Administration officials wanted the toppling of Saddam Hussein's regime and they wanted it bad. And because they didn't follow the logic of this A-to-Z rule set on gaining widespread Core buy-in, they got it bad. They didn't need the Core's buy-in to unleash our Leviathan force, so the war went well. But the Bush Administration certainly could have used tens of thousands more peacekeeping troops for the SysAdmin function, and so the peace has gone badly, and will continue to go badly if we—as a result—end up wearing out the Marines, the Army, its Reserves, and the National Guard. But it's not just that the United States ends up providing the overwhelming majority of the troops, we end up with the overwhelming majority of the bill for reconstruction and very little sense of international legitimacy for either the subsequent trials of Saddam and his henchmen or the follow-on regime (however duly elected) that's trapped into a long-term struggle with a vicious insurgency. But clearly, it didn't have to be this way, and it certainly doesn't have to be this way in the future. To that end, the conversation must start—in my opinion—within the G-8, for therein lies the Core's best hope for a Functioning Executive Body to propel this A-to-Z process.

Moving on to the Leviathan, that's basically the U.S. military, largely in the form of airpower. This is the transformed force envisioned by the advocates of Network-Centric Operations. It is real, and it works, but its utility is clearly limited primarily to conventionally arrayed opponents. Still, having this Leviathan means the Core already has at its disposal the capability for the relatively successful dispatch of any rogue regime you can name inside the Gap. For the United States in particular, this force means we have an effective hedge against any fellow Core pillar turning against us militarily down the road. This is not a difficult advantage for the Pentagon to maintain, and the Leviathan's recent record should give the Defense Department the confidence to move forward in investing in the SysAdmin force that we don't currently have but very clearly need.

How do I judge that need? I examine the facts on the ground. In Afghanistan, for example, the U.S. forces operating there in *Operation Enduring Freedom* have focused their activities overwhelmingly on combat against suspected militants and terrorists along the southeastern border with Pakistan. In contrast, the United States has pressured our NATO allies in the International Security and Assistance Force, or ISAF, to concentrate on peacekeeping and reconstruction efforts in other sections of the country. So, stretched as our meager forces are in their Leviathan role, our NATO allies are naturally pushed into SysAdmin work. Why does this bifurcation emerge? Because it simply meets the needs of the tasks at hand by efficiently utilizing the capabilities each side brings to the table.

The same splitting of the force has occurred in Iraq, where the United States–led coalition command was bifurcated into a Multinational Corps Iraq and a Multinational Force Iraq, with the former focused on battling the insurgency city by city in major shoot-outs, and the latter focused on training the indigenous security forces that we hope someday effectively replace our own troops on scene. As *U.S. News & World Report*'s Michael Barone stated, "To me that sounds an awful lot like leviathan and sys admin. And it sounds as if [Secretary of Defense Donald] Rumsfeld and [Chairman of the Joint Chiefs of Staff General Richard] Myers, together with Bush, have decided to adopt Barnett's ideas on restructuring our military forces." Do such moves reflect the logic of *The Pentagon's New Map*? Or does this vision simply reflect quite accurately the world within which this global war on terrorism unfolds? My humble vote is for the latter.

If we take as inevitable the splitting of the force, then it is crucial that the way in which America builds its own SysAdmin force sets the hub-and-spokes standard for the rest of the Core, as in *our* hub matches up to *everybody else's* spokes. Because most of the world's militaries are built primarily to remain at home and defend the country from external attack, the disparity between the U.S. military and the rest of the Core's militaries is substantial in power-projection capabilities. In short, there is the force that can actually fight, and then there is the force that is primarily about moving that first force to some distant locale and keeping it replenished with supplies and all other manner of combat support, such as command and control, communications, medical, intelligence, and computing needs. America has both forces, but most countries have only the first force, and even that force is closer—in the vast majority of cases—to a peacemaking force in its firepower and overall combat capabilities than a true warfighting force that's capable of decisively defeating well-armed and well-defended opponents.

The point being, for America's military to marry up well with the rest of the Core's military contributions to a coalition SysAdmin force, our portion needs to concentrate its capabilities in high-end combat and those logistical and specialized support functions I described above. In sum, the U.S. SysAdmin force won't look that different from the one we have today, because if we play our cards right, the bulk of the low-end, boots-on-the-ground peacekeepers should come from other nations, leaving our troops to specialize in high-end counterinsurgency operations and logistical support to both our own troops and those of other nations. A third area where our force capabilities might logically overlap with those of our best and most able allies (e.g., Brits, Aussies, French) is in the training of indigenous security forces, especially in counterinsurgency tactics.

Having said all that, I want to be clear that the U.S. military still has a long way to go toward effectively fielding its own core capabilities in SysAdmin forces. I often describe this leap in capabilities in the manner once suggested to me by an Army colonel who had seen my brief. This senior officer, who had participated in the Iraq occupation, compared that nation-building mission to a screw that needs to be driven into a wall. "Right now all we've got is a hammer and we are driving that screw into the wall with our hammer as best we can. But it won't set right. What we really need is a screwdriver." So when the Bush Administration announced in October 2004 that it was going to rebalance its ground forces over the next seven years "to create 100,000 military police, civil affairs, intelligence and other positions needed for stabilizing war-torn countries," that's a serious commitment in the right direction.

There will always be the temptation, in trying to create a global SysAdmin function, to pretend that we can somehow outsource that function to Gap nations themselves. This is especially true in Africa. But frankly, this goal is a chimera. There will never be any serious situations of instability inside the Gap that will be solved totally by our training local forces to do all the dirty work themselves. In these chronic conflict environments, there's definitely no shortage of hardened warriors. That's not the issue. The issue is one of follow-on process. Killing an insurgency starts with the military defeat of the rebel forces, but it never ends there. You either dry up the sources of insurgency recruiting by offering the target population a better life and a better deal or you better plan on just killing rebels for the long haul. Better warfighting is not the answer; better peacemaking and nation building is.

The other great temptation is to outsource the vast bulk of the SysAdmin function to private military contractors, and a great deal of such outsourcing has happened in Iraq. But this is dangerous on multiple levels. First, there is the question of oversight, as we've seen time and time again in Iraq but most saliently in the prison abuse scandals at Abu Ghraib. Second, there is the morale problem associated with mixing moderately paid military forces with de facto mercenaries and bodyguards who draw salaries that are sometimes several times what ordinary grunts earn. Third, there are a host of legal questions regarding the actions of civilian security in war zones. Especially in postconflict stabilization environments, where the legal rule set of the local country is either nonexistent or emerging at best, private contractors can sometimes not only transgress local or international laws but likewise become our country's worst possible diplomats. Finally, as we've seen in Iraq, where at one point local military commanders were ordered to stop awarding military citations to civilian security personnel, the blending of military and private-sector disciplines can yield unintended consequences. By and large, while I advocate that as much as one-half of any coalition SysAdmin force be civilian, I would like to see all security forces be uniformed as either military police or in the manner of civilian police personnel.

As for Sebastian Mallaby's brilliant proposal for an International Reconstruction Fund, his original ideas encompass much of what I describe as the SysAdmin function:

> The best hope of grappling with failed states lies in institutionalizing this mix of U.S. leadership and international legitimacy. Fortunately, one does not have to look far to see how this could be accomplished. The World Bank and the International Monetary Fund (IMF) already embody the same hybrid formula: both institutions reflect American thinking and priorities yet are simultaneously multinational. The mixed record of both institutions—notably the World Bank's failure on failed states—should not obscure their organizational strengths: they are more professional and less driven by national patronage than are U.N. agencies.
>
> A new international body with the same governing structure could be set up to deal with nation building. It would be subject neither to the frustrations of the U.N. Security Council, with its Chinese and Russian vetoes, nor to those of the U.N. General Assembly, with its gridlocked one-country-one-vote system. A new international reconstruction fund might be financed by the rich countries belonging to the Organization for Economic Cooperation and Development and the other countries that currently contribute to the World Bank's subsidized lending program to the poorest nations. It would assemble nation-building muscle and expertise and could be deployed wherever its American-led board decided, thus replacing the ad hoc begging and arm-twisting characteristic of current peacekeeping efforts. Its creation would not amount to an imperial revival. But it would fill the security void that empires left—much as the system of mandates did after World War I ended the Ottoman Empire.

The new fund would need money, troops, and a new kind of commitment from the rich powers—and it could be established only with strong U.S. leadership. Summoning such leadership is immensely difficult, but America and its allies have no easy options in confronting failed states. They cannot wish away the problem that chaotic power vacuums can pose. They cannot fix it with international institutions as they currently exist. And they cannot sensibly wish for a unilateral American imperium. They must either mold the international machinery to address the problems of their times, as their predecessors did in creating the U.N., the World Bank, and the IMF after World War II. Or they can muddle along until some future collection of leaders rises to the challenge.

What's most important about Mallaby's idea is that it pre-loads the notion of an international organization overseeing the occupation of a Gap state almost immediately upon the cessation of the Leviathan's major combat operations. What's so attractive about that? Such a hand-in-glove operation would allow the U.S. Leviathan force to depart the scene with both the speed and the sense of a clean break forever desired by the adherents of the Powell Doctrine. In effect, that force could leave the scene as soon as there weren't any more targets to blow up, and what would step into the authority void created by the departure of the U.S. four-star commanding general would be an international authority armed with both boots-on-the-ground muscle (the international SysAdmin force), plus reconstruction funds and the mandate to spend it.

But even in this proposal for an International Reconstruction Fund, the U.S. Government would need to develop far more significantly its relevant intellectual capital. As Francis Fukuyama argues:

> The Americans who presided over the successful reconstruction of postwar Europe and Japan were for the most part New Dealers who had just lived through a period of intense state-building in Washington. No similar cadre exists now. If there is any lesson to be drawn from our haphazard reconstruction of Iraq, it is that we need to reor-

ganize all of our soft-power agencies (State, USAID, the civil affairs units of the military and the broadcasting agencies) to be better able to do both reconstruction and development. In the place of ad hoc planning, we need to provide a permanent institutional home for people with experience in prior efforts. Difficult and contradictory as these functions are, they will be as much a key to overall American power and influence in the coming years as the technological prowess of our armed forces.

When you encounter such arguments, made from the angle of economic development, you begin to realize that the SysAdmin concept isn't just something I dreamed up from inside the Pentagon. A lot of expert observers are calling for exactly this type of force, and they're doing so from the perspectives of the State Department, the World Bank—even the UN. The question isn't *if* we're going to build this force, but *when*. Too many players across the global system want it for it not to happen eventually.

And again, don't think fuzzy-headed internationalism will drive this process, because it won't. Continued failure will drive this process of creation. America will build the SysAdmin force not out of idealism but out of desperation.

Moving on to the last of the six pieces in this A-to-Z system, I personally place a strong emphasis on funneling any "suspects" we pick up in this process toward the International Criminal Court, an institution that is both free and independent of the UN system and was recently set up specifically to target individuals for prosecution of genocide, crimes against humanity, and related war crimes. This court is fundamentally a creature of the Core, and its primary purpose is to make sure that individuals who perpetrate such crimes inside the Gap do not go unpunished because the legal system of the country in question simply isn't up to the challenge. The ICC is designed to operate complementarily with a nation's functioning legal system, meaning that if that legal system engages in either suitable investigation and/or prosecution of such crimes, the ICC considers itself to have no effective purview. It is only in such cases where the country's legal system is effectively negligent that the ICC's prosecutorial powers come into play.

The problem with the ICC's establishing treaty is that it leaves open the possibility of prosecutions of American political officials and military personnel as a result of military interventions inside the Gap. This fear began with the Clinton Administration and continues with the Bush White House, which has aggressively sought to insulate the United States from such charges by concluding a great number of so-called Article 98 "bilateral immunity agreements" with countries throughout the Gap. These treaties effectively provide such protection in advance of any future military intervention by the United States. We've set up close to a hundred such treaties, and virtually all of them are with Gap countries—which just so happen to number around a hundred states, so no surprise there. But equally unsurprising, this course of action has greatly disturbed the international human rights community and has led to America's deep alienation from the court.

My prediction is this: While the U.S. Leviathan force will never come under the purview of the ICC—because it will remain deeply embedded in military law—the far more internationalized SysAdmin force, including its U.S. components, must reach some blanket-clause protection regarding its activities inside the Gap. The reality is that the ICC was not set up to prosecute the "crimes" of peacekeepers and Core military personnel intervening inside the Gap, but rather to extend the Core's principles of war crimes into the Gap and, in this way, provide some sense of international consequence for what goes on in these chronic civil wars, long-running terrorist campaigns, and brutal dictatorships.

I've given you a lot of reasons for why I think the A-to-Z system should come into being. Now let me spell out how I think this process will actually emerge over time:

1. It all starts with the Pentagon's recognizing its role as key enabler and hub for a globally derived SysAdmin force.
2. The Pentagon seeds that capability within its own forces to the

point where it is conceivable that the United States alone could pull off a significant SysAdmin effort inside the Gap.

3. When other states see the "sure thing" in this capability and the commitment of the United States to employ it in conjunction with other Leviathan-engineered regime changes, and when they see our willingness to let them join either the front-half warfighting coalition or the back-half peacemaking coalition with no prejudice exhibited regarding commercial access to the economy in question (yes, the reconstruction contracts), then these potential allies will seek new and expanded levels of bilateral cooperation with the United States in all such measures.

4. When that Core-wide asset pool is married to the U.S. capability, we have the A-to-Z military tool kit in place.

5. When that combined Leviathan-SysAdmin capability is successfully employed in a Gap country, the new rules generated by that process result in a Core-wide understanding of, essentially, "This is how you take down a Gap dictator successfully."

6. As that rule set becomes apparent, the United States should seek its informal codification in the G-8 venue, with the goal of formally establishing the International Reconstruction Fund for oversight of the second-half process of postconflict stabilization by the SysAdmin force and subsequent nation building.

7. Once that international organization is set up, the processing of politically bankrupt states begins in earnest.

8. Once the "list" becomes known, you will see those placed on it alter their behavior immediately in most instances, making actual military takedowns not necessary. For every Saddam Hussein we have to topple militarily, we're likely to get two or three Charles Taylors, or the Liberian strongman who left his country once he was indicted for war crimes by a UN-sponsored tribunal.

9. As these bad actors vacate the Gap of their own free will (typically, with the bulk of their stolen loot) or are pulled down violently by the Leviathan-SysAdmin combo, regional security situations inside the Gap will improve dramatically.

10. As those security situations improve, just watch the international financial and business community step up to take advantage of the opportunities for new connectivity.

This is how we—not just America but also the Core as a whole—can harness the tremendous power and influence that the United States currently possesses because of its military prowess. And I do not mean this merely in terms of America's ability to employ that warfighting capability around the planet but also in terms of how its sheer existence empowers us to construct a Core-wide rule set on its successful and focused employment throughout the Gap. No other nation in the world can actualize the long-term scenario I've laid out in this chapter—none. Just realizing the unique opportunity history has provided should strike us as thrilling, not because of the difficult tasks that lie ahead but because the payoff is clearly the end of dictators as we have suffered them, the end of wars as we have known them, and the end of futures as we have feared them.

The blueprint I have described here is not some pie-in-the-sky fantasy. Its main actions are well within our grasp, yielding a future easily within our imagination. If you really want to win a global war on terrorism in your lifetime, then this is not a question of *if* but of *when*—not *why* but *why not*. Agreeing that the Core needs to agree on such a solution is more than half the battle, for once we make the decision, the blueprint is made real.

Chapter Two

WINNING THE WAR THROUGH CONNECTEDNESS

I HAD TO GO ALL THE WAY to Beijing last year to gain some perspective on the wide array of reviews I received on *The Pentagon's New Map*. Reviewers either loved or hated the book. I was either a naïve idealist or the cruelest sort of realist, a wide-eyed prophet of global peace or the most chilling, warmongering neocon they had ever seen. No one seemed indifferent, and I had a hard time believing these reviewers had all read the same book!

During the several weeks my wife and I spent in China adopting our fourth child, I managed to carve out a couple days of lectures and meetings with various government officials and academics who had helped me secure a local publisher (Beijing University) for the Chinese edition. Over a lavish lunch following one of my presentations in the capital, a Chinese official surprised me by remarking that my book would never be well understood in America, because there "everyone likes to choose one interpretation" instead of seeing the mix or balance that naturally attracted Chinese readers to the text. He said, "We think you are both a great idealist *and* very much a realist," with the former defining my long-term strategy and the latter my short-term pragmatism. Americans will never accept that mix, this official noted, because "in America you are forced to define yourself as one or the other—idealist *or* realist." If you try to balance both, I was warned, "everyone will assume that one is your false face and the other is your real one."

That simple observation explained basically every review I've received on the book, including the rare ones that replicated the official's basic premise: that the vision's main value came in its attempt to reconcile today's difficult choices with tomorrow's best hopes. That's a balance any good grand strategy must achieve, otherwise current sacrifice becomes disconnected from perceived future gains. Once that happens, you don't have a grand strategy anymore, just scary current events plus your natural desire to distance yourself from their effects. Unfortunately, most of what passes for grand strategic thinking in the United States today seeks to answer exactly that reflexive need for a "way out" that's simply defined and easily achieved—as in, "It's all America's fault, and if only we'd change our bad policies, all these dangers would disappear!"

However tempting such an approach may seem, it does not constitute a grand strategy that seeks to shape a world for the better. Instead, it seeks nothing more than to insulate America from globalization's nastiest short-term effects, which right now most people would define as transnational terrorism with a catastrophic bent (i.e., our fear of weapons of mass destruction). In a world where 20,000 people die every day from extreme poverty, we need to ask if our grand strategy should aspire toward a global future worth creating or focus merely on preventing bad things from happening to America this year, this month, this week. No matter how many reviewers sought to paint it as such, *The Pentagon's New Map* didn't offer a grand strategy for the summer of 2004, or even through—what I then suspected would be—the second Bush Administration.

No, the grand strategy I'm pitching is one for the next several decades, and the reason why so many U.S. Government agencies are attracted to it is precisely that it seeks to contextualize—or connect— a global war on terrorism with larger, longer-term goals that more naturally reflect this country's cherished ideals of who we are and what our nation represents to the world. Maintaining that sense of collective identity is what gets us through the hard times. It helps us visualize a finishing line, which in turn enables our ability to make difficult choices in the short run.

The global war on terrorism marks the ruthless realism by which we'll deal with our enemies—day in and day out—over the coming years. But the goal of making globalization truly global by shrinking the Gap speaks to something larger and far more long-term: not individual scenarios to be prevented but a global future to be created. Winning the war will be zero-sum: *some* must die so *others* can remain safe. But securing the peace will be far more inclusive: *they* must be connected so *all* can participate. There is no logical choice between these two pathways, just a balance to be maintained.

In Chapter 1, I presented a trio of balanced compromises that I believe are essential for any credible blueprint for action: a merger of seemingly opposing visions of future war, an institutional bridge between our current departments of war and peace, and a global rule set for connecting the world community's will to great-power action on the pressing matter of politically bankrupt states. Each proposal represents a complex mixture of idealism and realism, a balancing of high expectations with difficult but much-needed tasks. In this chapter, I'll need to convince you that the global war on terrorism is not an end unto itself, but merely today's brutal means to a future worth creating: a Middle East that's reconnected to the world. Not subjugated, not colonized, and not pacified, but reconnected on terms both sides come to respect.

The Bush Administration's decision to lay a Big Bang on the Middle East (my preferred term for the purposeful shock applied to that region's calcified system of authoritarian rule) began quite ruthlessly with the toppling of Saddam Hussein's terrible regime and then segued into our own terrible mismanagement of the occupation. But as the world has witnessed since the Iraqi elections in January 2005, the powerful demonstration effect of growing political freedom in Iraq, however brutally achieved by force, triggers an undeniable ripple effect throughout the region as a whole. America needs to own the consequences of both its short-term actions and their long-term effects. We need to connect ourselves to each and—by doing so—embrace the grand strategy that has been there all along, awaiting first our recognition and then our commitment to see it through.

The grand strategist doesn't "get it" alone, he just gets there first, conceptualizing and enunciating that which we all come to realize as both worthy and true. When long-range planners from U.S. Central Command asked for my help in translating *The Pentagon's New Map* into an actionable long-term strategy for the Middle East, they weren't taking any cues from me, just a shortcut to arguments they knew instinctively would prevail in U.S. Government policy debates about where this whole war on terrorism must inevitably head. Across the street from Central Command's headquarters in Florida, U.S. Special Operations Command came to a similar decision, asking for my participation in their own long-term strategizing against transnational terrorist networks. If Central Command needed the high idealism, then Special Operations Command wanted the brutal realism, for as the former sought to connect the Middle East to the world at large, the latter set about disconnecting certain bad actors from the scene altogether. Each needed a bridge to the other side, a vision that balanced today's compromises with tomorrow's promise. *The Pentagon's New Map* could provide those strategic connections *precisely* because its vision refused to choose between realism and idealism.

Refusing to believe in the no-win scenario is not hubris, it just reflects my optimistic faith in America's ability to adapt itself to any future challenges that globalization might throw at us. We have approached similar crossroads in our own past, when we were forced to realize that "a house divided against itself can not stand." All 9/11 and the resulting global war on terrorism have done is to remind us of this essential truth on a grander scale. As such, our response has grown equally grand in scope and ambition: the Gap must be shrunk, and the Middle East is the logical place to start.

CONNECTING THE MIDDLE EAST TO THE WORLD

One thing I've learned in my years as a strategist working for the military is that, as Dirty Harry once said, "A man's got to know his limitations."

I'm a practicing strategist, but that'll never make me a general—armchair or otherwise. So I stick to vision and focus on ends, leaving the details and means to those who've spent their adult lives mastering a very difficult business. I get the same respect from senior officers that I offer them: I honor their experience and judgment, while remembering my limitations. When I lay out a vision or strategy, I don't tell them what's so great about it from their perspective, because if they can't see it on their own, then it probably doesn't exist for them. Conversely, I don't spend a lot of time telling officers how a strategy should impact their decisions, or what they should do next in their jobs as a result of hearing it. Those who really get it typically know instantly what needs to be done, and those who don't, well, they won't be around in uniform much longer if I'm right. So I never spend any time trying to "convert" anyone; I simply go where the vision takes me, interacting with the reformers, or "change agents," willing to act on it. When you achieve a breakout on the front line, you just run with it.

I'm not talking humility here, because nobody likes a wishy-washy futurist ("Well, it *might* be sort of like this . . . or . . ."). Military officers like their visionaries like their coffee: very strong and tending to leave a bad taste in their mouths. But you'll lose them the instant you start bullshitting your way through their core business. This is an important principle for civilians seeking to influence military thinking: you never try to tell anybody in the military how to "suck eggs," which is a particularly odd phrase within the culture that refers to telling someone how to do a job they already understand well. Military officers often use this phrase when they feel that their civilian masters are telling them to do things they know they must do but don't know *why* they should, primarily because the civilian leadership hasn't explained its larger goals very well. So if you hear something like this: "If the White House tells us to suck eggs, we suck eggs," what the officer is really saying is (1) "We do what we're told," and (2) "This makes no sense to me whatsoever."

By and large, what a national grand strategy should do is impart sense to everything the military does, and that's why the military loves grand strategy: it gives them a guide to determine which activities fit in and which are a waste of time. Why is that so important? What the military often hears from its civilian leadership, not to mention the White House, is a flurry of contradictory signals regarding, say, a military intervention overseas, such as "do A, but also try to do B, C, and D at the same time, while not jeopardizing E, F, G, H, and I as pursued by the State Department, but also making sure that J, K, L, and M remain possible options for the President, while ruling out N, O, P, Q, and R for our enemy, and making damn certain no one in the system comes back to us complaining about S, T, U, and V or—under any circumstances—demanding W, X, Y, or Z!" Typically, in any one scenario, that sort of guidance from above will conflict with the military's long-established policies in some particular arena (e.g., how to conduct a certain operation under preferred logistical conditions) or region (e.g., long-term relationships with local militaries built up through years of dedicated cooperation).

How were those "long-standing requirements" originally defined? In the same way that they're typically changed by any one scenario: the new word comes down from above, and that's what the new policy ends up being from then on—until the next time the political masters decide to change it. So one year America might have no expressed interest whatsoever in Iraq's long-standing beef with Kuwait as its "lost province," but if Iraq decides to invade Kuwait in 1990 and America decides to kick it out, then all of a sudden the military has a new "requirement" to protect Kuwait from Iraq over the long term. That's how our "national interests" are created over time: just add up all these situations the world over, racking and stacking them with some sense of priority or hierarchy, which naturally can change quite dramatically with each new presidential administration.

From the military's perspective, though, it all just gets layered one on top of the other over the years, as today's "requests" become tomorrow's "requirements" and consistency in policy just means that nothing's come down the pike lately to trump that particular activity. If a particular "requirement" survives for a very long time, then you're talking about a "national interest," which is just code for "It's been that way so long we just can't imagine changing it." America's defense guarantee on Taiwan vis-à-vis China is like that. It's just been around for so long that the military assumes it's carved in stone, when of course nothing is carved in stone when it comes to national security—except America's survival.

What a national grand strategy offers the military as it seeks to balance all these competing demands is a simple set of rules that are transferable to any situation. That's why the Core-Gap vision sticks to some very basic and flexible concepts, such as: connectivity is always preferred to disconnectedness, and shrinking the Gap should always trump a Cold War–like stance of holding the line. The utility of a simple rule set is that it allows local commanders to define "connectivity" and "shrinking the Gap" in whatever way most makes sense to them, in terms of both their capabilities and the particulars of the environment. So while the civilian political leadership might speak of spreading democracy and free markets, what military commands in the field can focus on over the longer term is fostering connectivity and letting the pundits and politicians decide whether or not to call it a "democracy" or a "free market." Again, I don't tell the military how to suck eggs. I just try to give them a simple set of rules for deciding which eggs are worth sucking and why.

Of course, if you get this right, the vision becomes equally useful for the civilian leadership. One of the best compliments I've ever received on the brief and book came from Congressman Mac Thornberry of Texas, who said that now, whenever he is asked to judge a particular piece of legislation with foreign policy implications, he asks himself, "Will this help shrink the Gap or make it worse?" Could I possibly tell a veteran lawmaker of Thornberry's caliber how to go about rendering that judgment—how to suck those eggs? Of course not, because that's an experience base I can't touch from my perch as a generalist. But by giving the lawmaker the strategic concept, I can help link him to like-minded people with similar goals inside the defense community, and that's the essential value of a grand strategy: the horizontal linkages established among participants that promote unity of purpose and, one hopes, coordinated action.

In the spring of 2004, about a month after *The Pentagon's New Map* came out, I was contacted by long-term planners in the policy and plans division (J-5) of Central Command down in Tampa. Central Command is the U.S. combatant command responsible for the Middle East. The J-5 people said they were revamping their long-range political-military planning for the region as a whole in light of the unfolding global war on terrorism and were using my volume as a sourcebook for concepts, language, and rules.

Now, you might think these "action officers," or those middling-rank officers given the actual task of writing up the plan to be approved by the command's senior admirals and generals, would approach me like some "great mind" whose blessing is needed for their particular employment of his ideas. And yeah, they're quite respectful in their interactions with you. But it's not like you have a veto or editorial control over anything. They're just asking for your "roger this" and "check that" and "you might want to consider using this term instead of that one"—that's all. In the end, these guys know fundamentally what their bosses are looking for, because their bosses know what their political masters are looking for. If a command picks up your material, it's because it seems *accurate* in the opinion of its senior officers, not because it's visionary or cool or way "out of the box." It has to fit the world within which they find themselves working.

So it starts with a phone call, then a slew of e-mails, and then you're reviewing documents and offering advice, here and there at the margins. You play Oracle to their Neo from the *Matrix* movie series. They've already made their decision. Your job is simply to help them understand *why* they've made this decision. So the strategist's role is not one of power, or really even influence, but one of *informing*. You don't make decisions, and you don't influence them directly, because—

remember—they choose you, not the other way around. But once you've laid out your vision and these officers decide it's accurate for their particular purposes, then you get to shape their employment of your lexicon and concepts, albeit only in the most initial sense. Because you're working with the "worker bees" at the commander and lieutenant colonel levels, and in the end, the policy will be enunciated, day in and day out, by the admirals and generals located far above them in rank. So at times, this "informing" process can seem like Telephone, that children's game where you whisper a phrase into the first kid's ear and by the time that act is repeated throughout the long chain of friends it comes out sounding quite different at the end.

Then again, sometimes it comes out sounding just fine.

So, after a drawn-out series of virtual interactions over the Web, I finally made an in-person office call to the senior flags in charge of the whole process. This is basically the culminating point in the process, and not surprisingly, it's still you—the "great strategist"—who's getting blessed, not the other way around. So I eventually stopped by at the J-5 office at Central Command's headquarters in Tampa while I was down there on Special Operations Command's dime for some other strategizing business. This meeting was a big deal for the younger officers, who were—in effect—showing me off to the two-star admiral in charge of J-5, as well as his one-star Marine deputy. It was their chance to present their source to their bosses, and their bosses' chance to thank me for my "contribution to national security"—as that old saw goes.

Now, it was a big deal for me, too, because these flags are incredibly busy, so getting a chance to just hang out and chat with them for an hour is a real opportunity to try out your thinking directly with those who sit—so to speak—on the pointy end of the policy pen. I mean, all I had to do was look out the window at the dozens of flagpoles standing in the compound, signifying all the allied nations' liaison offices literally plunked down there like so many little vacation cabins, to realize how complicated these guys' workdays tended to be. So if I wanted to plant any seeds in their minds regarding long-term strategic issues worth anticipating, now was the time.

I love moments like these, because in just a few minutes you can generate and/or test strategic observations of real use, meaning messages you can take back from one command and use again and again as you later explain their strategic predicaments to policymakers and politicians in D.C. and elsewhere. So you don't just chat about the weather or how much they like your book. Hell, you dive right in like your pants are on fire.

So what I did was start waxing strategic about CENTCOM's area of responsibility, or AOR, proposing my rudimentary theories of how its boundaries to the south (sub-Saharan Africa), to the north (Europe and Russia), and to the east (East Asia) all posed very different sets of problems to the command. Mind you, these were just my pet theories at the time, but I figured, What the hell, they might as well get shot down here so I can be done with them if they're wrong. Remember, nobody likes a wishy-washy visionary.

Well, they're weren't wrong or right so much as they were reasonably accurate, but they naturally needed some real-world fine-tuning— as in, as soon as I presented them, these senior officers started spitting back all sorts of personal anecdotes confirming the basic outline of my ideas. So while it starts out with just me standing up in front of the giant wall map, within a few minutes we're all on our feet making sweeping gestures with our arms, trading theories and concepts and anecdotes. A quick half hour later, I have a new PowerPoint slide in my mind, one that I've used ever since to great effect with senior audiences all over Washington and in several overseas capitals.

Thanks to this intense exchange (often called a "group grope"), I developed a way of explaining what I thought were the key tactical, operational, and strategic challenges facing the command as it sought to actualize the Bush Administration's goal of transforming the Middle East. Again, I didn't come up with any of these on my own but rather developed them based on what the CENTCOM planners described to me as the Command's experiences—both good and bad—in pursuing the war on terrorism in their particular corner of the Gap.

CENTCOM's AOR encompasses the Persian Gulf area extending from Israel all the way to Pakistan, the Central Asian republics formerly associated with the Soviet Union, and the horn of Africa (from Egypt down to Somalia). This is clearly the center of the universe as far as the global war on terrorism is concerned, and yet viewing that war solely in the context of that region alone is a big mistake, one that could easily foul up America's larger grand strategic goals of defeating terrorism worldwide and making globalization truly global. Here's why: CENTCOM's area of responsibility features three key seams, or boundaries, between that collection of regions and the world outside. Each seam speaks to both opportunities and dangers that lie ahead, as well as to how crucial it is that Central Command's version of the war on terrorism stays in sync with the rest of the U.S. foreign policy establishment.

The first seam lies to the south, or sub-Saharan Africa. This is the tactical seam, meaning that in day-to-day terms, there's an awful lot of connectivity between that region and CENTCOM's AOR. That connectivity comes in the form of transnational terrorist networks that extend from the Middle East increasingly into sub-Saharan Africa, making that region sort of the strategic retreat of al Qaeda and its subsidiaries. As Central Command progressively squeezes those networks within its area of responsibility, the Middle East's terrorists increasingly establish interior lines of communication between themselves and other cells in Africa, as Africa becomes the place where supplies, funds (especially in terms of gold), and people are stashed for future use. Africa risks becoming Cambodia to the Middle East's Vietnam, a place where the enemy finds respite when it gets too hot inside the main theater of combat. Central Asia presents the same basic possibility, but that's something that CENTCOM can access more readily because it lies within its area of responsibility, while sub-Saharan Africa does not. Instead, distant European Command owns that territory in our Unified Command Plan, a system constructed in another era for another enemy. Those vertical, north-south slices of geographic commands were lines to be held in an East-West struggle, but today our enemies tend to roam horizontally across the global map, turning the original logic of that command plan on its head.

Central Command's challenge, then, is to figure out how to connect these two regions in such a way as to avoid having Africa become the off-grid hideout for al Qaeda and others committed to destabilizing the Middle East. By definition, such a goal is beyond CENTCOM's pay grade, or rank, because it's a high-level political decision to engage sub-Saharan Africa on this issue—in effect, widening the war. And yet solving this boundary condition is essential to winning the struggle in the Middle East. What the Core-Gap model provides Central Command is a way of describing the problem by noting that transnational terrorism's resistance to globalization's creeping embrace of the Middle East won't simply end with our successful transformation of the region. No, that struggle will inevitably retreat deeper inside the Gap, or to sub-Saharan Africa.

Why is this observation important? It's important because it alerts the military to the reality that success in this war won't be defined by less terrorism but by a shifting of its operational center of gravity southward, from the Middle East to Africa. That's the key measure of effectiveness. Achieving this geographic shift will mark our success in the Middle East, but it will also buy us the follow-on effort in Africa. You want America to care more about security in Africa? Then push for a stronger counterterrorism strategy in the Middle East, because that's the shortest route between those two points.

Ultimately, you're faced with the larger, inescapable requirement of having to connect Africa to the Core to run this problem to ground, otherwise today's problem for CENTCOM simply becomes tomorrow's distant problem for EUCOM. When you make that leap of logic, the next decision gets a whole lot easier: America needs to stand up an African Command. Now, I know that sounds like a huge expansion of our strategic "requirements," but when you consider the boundary conditions in this way, the discussion shifts from *if* to *when*.

The second boundary of note for Central Command lies to its north. Because the Core, and especially the United States, has gone on the offensive regarding al Qaeda and other Middle East terrorist groups since 9/11, much of the ability of these groups to mount long-distance operations has been disrupted. This is why we haven't seen any major attacks on the United States but instead have seen a resumption of such attacks along the southern rim of Europe and Russia. In effect, by boxing these groups in, we've restricted their reach to the same pattern we saw across the 1970s and 1980s: they can blow things up at will in the Persian Gulf region, but they can stretch themselves northward only to a certain limited extent. Of course, the extent of that reach still matters, because, as we saw in the case of the March 11, 2004, backpack bombings in Madrid, such attacks can accomplish the goal of picking off Old Core allies from our coalition. Likewise, as in the case of the Beslan school massacre in southern Russia, such attacks may be pursued so as to trigger harsh responses from Core members that, in turn, serve to create divides within the Core (e.g., the West's alarm that Russia is becoming frighteningly authoritarian as a result of the ongoing Chechen conflict). As with the tactical seam issue, the same problem exists here: How does CENTCOM seek to firewall the Core off from such violence while simultaneously promoting the Middle East's ultimate connectivity to those same Core regions?

The final seam lies to the east, and it is the strategic seam defined by Developing Asia's burgeoning demand for Middle Eastern and Central Asian energy supplies. Here, my strategic outlook is expressed more as warning: India, China, Korea, and Japan are all coming to the Persian Gulf militarily in future years. They'll come either to join the fabulous "transformation" process set in motion by our remaking of Iraq, or they'll come out of desperation to salvage what they can on their own in securing energy relationships with individual suppliers in an otherwise strife-torn region. Either way, these nations will come militarily to the region. They have no choice; that's the inescapable logic of economic connectivity as globalization continues to unfold.

So when China and India, for example, signed major new oil and gas deals with Iran recently, did this represent those countries' seeking to undermine our military goals in the region? Or is this economic connectivity something to be welcomed and taken advantage of? That all depends on what role Iran ends up playing in a transformed Middle East, now, doesn't it? Iran's the 800-pound gorilla here. You can work around it and you can try to isolate it over its pursuit of the nuclear option, but let's not kid ourselves here: we're not going to establish a stable endstate in this strategic security environment without Iran's participation. It's as simple as that.

Ultimately, of course, stability in the Gulf region also depends on what kind of security relationships the United States has with India and China (Yes! Get used to hearing that!). Do we recognize joint regional interests, or do we cast their new ties with oil producers there—especially ones we don't like—as a "dangerous competition for resources" or, worse, as reflecting their "obstructionism"? To answer those questions, you really need to step back even farther and look at the growing economic interdependency of India and China with U.S. markets and investment flows.

As soon as you get to that point, your head is swimming with all sorts of factors to juggle as you consider what it is exactly you're trying to accomplish with Iran in the Persian Gulf. But again, if you're not taking into consideration these larger connections, then your strategies vis-à-vis Tehran are likely to be counterproductive to your strategies elsewhere in the world. Making those connections is what my grand strategy does for you, and that's why Central Command has ended up using it so extensively. So when *Washington Post* columnist David Ignatius spent a week in late 2004 with General John Abizaid, head of Central Command, he drew the following connection back to *The Pentagon's New Map:*

> [Barnett's] concepts have spread so fast among the military brass that when I was in Bahrain two weeks ago, I heard a Barnett-style briefing from the commander of U.S. naval forces in the Persian Gulf, Vice Adm. David Nichols. He outlined a strategy of encouraging countries in the Middle East to move toward "connected" economies, orderly "rule sets" and democratic political reform.

My definition of America's grand strategy appeals to U.S. military commands because it seems to describe quite accurately the world as they find it. So yes, the short term is all about hunting down and killing terrorists, and the mid-term is all about trying to transform the Middle East's political environment, but the long-term goal involves connecting the Middle East to the world at large, especially to the global economy, in ways far broader than simply the energy transaction it currently conducts. Because if our interest in the region remains about oil, then the Middle East will remain a global ghetto, and the consequent age-old problems of that disconnected state will also remain. So as with Representative Thornberry, my vision gives Central Command's leadership a rule of thumb that constantly prompts the simple question, "Does this activity help connect the Middle East to the outside world in a good way or not?" In other words, "Are we shrinking the Gap or making it worse?"

This global war on terrorism is all about connectivity because the terrorists themselves arise in response to such emerging networks, taking advantage of them wherever possible while simultaneously seeking to destroy them as part of their strategy to disconnect the Middle East and other Gap regions from the larger, corrupt world exemplified by globalization and restore what they believe is the Islamic world's natural unity. In effect, what radical Islamic fundamentalists such as Osama bin Laden seek is not merely a disconnect from globalization's creeping embrace of the region's more traditional societies, but a reconnect to an idealized past they believe offers a better alternative— an Islamic definition of globalization that contrasts itself with the Western one. Radical Islamic fundamentalism is a response to globalization first and foremost, and not merely a function of U.S. foreign policy in the region—no matter how their rhetoric may dwell on us. As defined by leading terrorism expert Marc Sageman:

> The global Salafi jihad is a worldwide religious revivalist movement with the goal of reestablishing past Muslim glory in a great Islamist state stretching from Morocco to the Philippines, eliminating present national boundaries. It preaches *salafiyyah* (from *salaf,* the Arabic word for "ancient one," referring to the Prophet Mohammed), the restoration of authentic Islam, and advocates a strategy of violent jihad, resulting in an explosion of terror to wipe out what it regards as local political heresy. The global version of this movement advocates the defeat of the Western powers that prevent the establishment

of a true Islamist state. Al-Qaeda is the vanguard of this movement, which includes many other terrorist groups that collaborate in their operations and share a large support base.

There is no single U.S. policy that will meet the demands of this movement other than our complete political, economic, and military withdrawal from roughly the upper geographic half of the Gap at first, but ultimately from it entirely. That is because, in the end, what Osama bin Laden and the movement offer the Core is a civilizational apartheid, where—in effect—each side defines itself as the rule-defined, stable "Core" and the other side as the violent, corrupt "Gap."

Saudi Arabia is clearly the focus of the Salafi jihadists, because the kingdom encompasses Islam's two most holy sites, Mecca and Medina, but other than that particular geographic focus (and a third one regarding Jerusalem), this movement's focus is less territorially defined than it is identity defined. The focus of the religious revivalism is, in many ways, an attempt to define what it means to be a good Muslim in a globalized world. Until globalization began to encroach on the Middle East more directly in recent years, to include the large-scale emigration of Muslims to non-Muslim regions like Europe, the effort to contrast that religious identification with the world at large was more muted, as local tribal identities and divisions trumped any larger definition of the whole of Islam.

But as globalization progressively infiltrated the Islamic world in recent decades, especially since the end of the Cold War, a choice was forced: connect and thus assimilate over time (e.g., increasingly secular and democratic Turkey looking for EU membership in addition to its NATO affiliation) or remain largely disconnected (or narrowly connected) and attempt to retain unique identity (e.g., increasingly fundamental Saudi Arabia, which prefers to limit its connections to the Core to selling only energy). A third model could be described as trying to have it both ways (connected and uniquely Muslim), and the best regional example of that approach would be Pakistan's authoritarianism. Additional, far softer forms of authoritarianism can be found in Southeast Asia (Singapore, Malaysia, Indonesia), where the increasingly successful commingling of capitalism and democracy with distinct Muslim social values gives the lie to the notion that accommodation between the West and Islam is impossible and that a clash of civilizations is the only logical long-term standoff.

So it is essentially wrong to cast this conflict as a clash of either civilizations or religions. As noted Islamic expert Olivier Roy points out, al Qaeda did not choose to attack the Vatican on 9/11, but rather symbols of globalization and its perceived power structure—the World Trade Center and the Pentagon. Most of Islam is not at war with globalization, although much of Islam is in conflict with itself over how best to join that globalized economy while retaining a distinct cultural and religious identity. In that way, it's correct to think of the Salafi jihadist movement as simply the strongest and therefore most violent response to that challenge. Most Salafi adherents, which are drawn exclusively from the Sunni branch of Islam, view their revivalist movement less as a call to arms than as guide to a separatist social order, not unlike the Amish within Christianity. So their definition of disconnectedness is both voluntary and nonviolent in form, whereas the Salafi jihadists are an extreme and fairly small subset of that movement who advocate violence to achieve strict disconnectedness with the outside world and would enforce such disconnectedness through rigid application of religious law, the Islamic *sharia*. The Salafi jihadists resemble a mix of political totalitarianism and a violent, apocalyptic religious cult.

Beyond those inner circles of nonassimilation lies the bulk of the Islamic world, which seeks some balance between integration with the outside world and retention of unique cultural and religious identity. This more moderate view is often described as Islamist, or an outlook that views Islam as fundamental to defining a country's social and political order but not in such a way as to impede logically beneficial integration with the outside world. In this way, Islamists can be compared to those in our country who cite the Judeo-Christian values that define our political and economic systems, such as the motto "In God

We Trust" that adorns our money. This kind of religious-cultural outlook naturally seeks to determine the form and shape of a predominantly Muslim society's connectivity with the outside world, just as it
does here in the United States, where religion frequently imposes upon
domestic policy debates such as those surrounding abortion, stem-cell
research, or human cloning.

Beyond all that, we can also cite a still larger population of Muslims the world over who are unhappy with how they feel they and their
brethren are treated by either the global economy or the international
political order, and it is here that we locate the vast majority of the
anti-American animus regarding our support to both Israel and corrupt, repressive Islamic regimes inside the Gap. But again, we need to
be clear that while significant changes in those policies might assuage
the anger of these discontented Muslims the world over, no accommodation could meet the demands of the Salafi jihadists and their dream
of an alternative Islamic political transnational union that would
stand both disconnected from, and in violent opposition to, globalization's Functioning Core.

Fourth-Generation Warfare adherents like to cite al Qaeda as the
quintessential 4GW movement because it thinks in decades, not years,
and believes that time is on its side. And, of course, the 4GW thinkers
tend to agree with this strategic assessment, citing the West's and especially America's inability to remain on a war footing for an extended
period of time, except in a Cold War–like standoff where we would
accept bin Laden's offer of civilizational apartheid at the "silk curtain" that would presumably forever separate the two "incompatible"
cultures. So it is the argument of the 4GW crowd, especially through
the voice of gung-ho journalist Robert D. Kaplan, that the only way
we can defeat such a committed foe over the long haul is to reacquire
our own warrior-like spirit and commit ourselves—much as we did in
the settling of the West—to a long-drawn-out replay of cowboys and
Indians.

My problem with this harsh perspective is that it tends to mirror-
image the Salafi jihadists by dismissing the possibility that either the

Core can be grown or the Gap effectively shrunk. In this very dark take on the future, the Gap is capable only of further decay and descent into primordial lawlessness, but never of economic or social integration with the larger world. So the visionaries of this future-worth-avoiding, such as Martin van Creveld and Robert D. Kaplan, tend to write off the entire Gap as one gigantic West Bank, forever ablaze with nihilistic and cannibalistic violence, and ruled over by mobs of drug-crazed male adolescents, suggesting a far nastier Gap version of the American suburban nightmare of African-American "gangstas." Except, of course, in this future dystopia, there are no cops, just robbers, and the railroads never quite make it into the Gap, so the settlers never settle and the savages run rampant. In short, this is the same old post-apocalypse vision from the Cold War, except now these dark visionaries typically substitute environmental degradation for nuclear Armageddon as the trigger. Instead of mad generals who send us all to hell, it'll now be greedy corporations that will accomplish the same feat, just over a longer time frame. And there is little, if anything, we can do to change things for the better.

Geez! No wonder most of these guys remember the Cold War as a simpler, better time!

The problem with this logic is that it does not stand the test of time, but rather simply defines the passage of time. Yesterday's grand Fourth-Generation Warfare struggles (e.g., civil wars in China and Vietnam) had absolutely no lasting impact on the global security environment, beyond the temporary damage inflicted on the United States through its lengthy bout of Vietnam Syndrome. Yes, Mao Zedong and his Pol Pot killed millions of their own citizens in China and Cambodia, respectively (Mao, many times more), but ultimately, all these Asian countries moved to embrace the very economic system they once spent decades (allegedly) fighting. What are we to take from the great 4GW victories of Mao and Ho Chi Minh if these countries end up integrated into globalization's Core (something China is rapidly achieving and which Vietnam and Cambodia show all indications of doing in China's enormous wake)? That the "poor warriors" of the Gap will fight on for decades just so they can establish authoritarian governments that ultimately adopt export-driven capitalist growth strategies to integrate their states with the global economy?

Ah, but we are told that the Islamic Middle East and Africa are the worst examples yet, and that these savage cultures' resistance to modernization, Westernization, and globalization will dwarf anything we may have endured or still endure in Asia or Latin America. As this dark view argues, these people simply *love* war. It defines who they are and what they hope to become. The flaccid West has no idea how bad this will get or how long it will drag on. Time is on *their* side, not ours, especially since those tricky Chinese are only mimicking our development to lull us into thinking they're nice when what they're really going to do is unleash some incredible high-tech version of Fourth-Generation Warfare down the road! *See! Those people never give up!*

Indeed.

But looking at the Middle East, not only do I see more settlers than Indians, I see a number of trends that say not only is time on *our* side but also that it's running out for the bin Ladens and al-Zarqawis. I know that may sound counterintuitive, because most of what you've been hearing about our invasion and occupation of Iraq is that it handed al Qaeda the perfect recruitment venue as well as a golden opportunity to bog down the United States in a quagmire that will ultimately trigger its military retreat from the region. But again, what I see in this action is a real tipping point for U.S. strategic interest in the region, and that, all by itself, sets the region on another pathway altogether.

First, while the region as a whole is enduring a massive youth bulge, fertility rates have dropped considerably in recent years, meaning the pressure will decrease significantly in coming decades while still remaining high relative to the Core. It is true that most Middle Eastern economies are very poorly equipped to provide jobs to this huge flood of youth, but there's no reason to assume that the only outcomes to such pressures are either increased authoritarianism or failed states leading to large-scale instability.

In the wealthier oil states like Saudi Arabia, the youth bulges are going to put an end to the state's heavy reliance on foreign workers, and we're already seeing this sort of long-term response from the government to swap out jobs from foreigners to the native youth. Why? Again, here is the impact of the U.S. invasion and occupation of Iraq: the response of the insurgency has been to target foreign workers as a way of scaring their national governments away from participating in the rebuilding of the country. The most famous example of this was when the kidnapping of a single Filipino truck driver was enough to blackmail the Philippines into pulling out its small military contingent. Don't think for a moment that Saudi Arabia didn't take notice. While the House of Saud has long bragged about reducing its oil industry's dependence on Western managers (they now account for less than 2 percent of all foreign workers in the kingdom), it's no secret that their economy depends greatly on a large number of Asian laborers (roughly six million).

In June 2004, Saudi Arabia suffered its worst terrorist attack in over a year. The terrorists targeted oil workers at a residential complex, killing 22. Three Saudis died in the attack, as did five Westerners. The other 14 were guest workers, 13 of whom were Asians. So with terrorists kidnapping and beheading Asian guest workers in Iraq, it doesn't take a lot of imagination to see the spillover effect, especially as the same young Saudis who were heading to Iraq to fight the infidels could just as easily come back and perform similar acts at home, something they've already started to do. So if you're the House of Saud and you see this huge youth bulge coming at you, do you just wait for the inevitable or do you do something about the fact that your own citizens make up less than 15 percent of your private-sector workforce?

Another logical response to the Middle Eastern youth bulge is actually facilitated by the U.S. decision to invade and occupy Iraq: job creation. Perhaps surprisingly, foreign direct investment flows into the region since the invasion are close to doubling in volume, and a significant inflow of previously expatriated capital has begun. Stock markets grew significantly across the region in 2004, rising over 30 percent and adding almost half a trillion dollars in capitalization. Why have not only regional but also global investors become so suddenly bullish on the Middle East? Investors are willing to take risks so long as they see major powers such as the United States being committed to regional security—and despite the difficulties of the insurgency in the Sunni-dominated portions of Iraq, America's firm commitment to following through on its takedown of Saddam Hussein's regime sent exactly that signal.

The region as a whole has long been a woeful economic underperformer, despite having a reasonably skilled labor pool, and the main reason has been local entrepreneurs' lack of access to capital. What about all that oil money? Too much tends to go overseas for its investment opportunities, so meanwhile local businesses are forced to rely on a small number of regional banks instead of stock markets, bonds, and venture capital—all of which remain fairly embryonic across the region compared with those of advanced economies. My point is this: the Middle East has plenty of "settlers" in the making, and the quickest way to turn them on is to increase the region's financial connectivity with the Core.

Second, for most Muslims in the region, the rise in religious fundamentalism is more a modernizing phenomenon than it is an attempted retreat into the past. It reflects a vibrant debate over what's acceptable and unacceptable, for example, as women gain more access to higher education, join the workforce, and delay marriage (all contributing factors to the declining fertility rates). It also reflects a mammoth youth culture that's not only attracted to the West's culture and values but has far more access to it, thanks to the rise of global media. The Islamist conservatives in countries such as Saudi Arabia can seek to deny the youth such connectivity through censorship and interdiction, but by and large, it's going to be a losing battle as time wears on.

Regimes in the region have a difficult choice: either open up economically to provide the jobs necessary to process the youth bulge or try to contain all that ambition through political repression. If they choose the former, the resulting connectivity will render their attempts at social conservatism all the more difficult, but if they choose repression, they run the risk of social explosion. One thing is certain: the slimmer your economic connectivity to the outside world, the easier it is for terrorists to disrupt that trade flow and destabilize your regime. Shutting down the U.S. economy would be a gargantuan undertaking, but shutting down Saudi Arabia's entire energy exports would take only a handful of well-placed attacks.

Again, the specter of America's long-term occupation of Iraq only speeds up these processes by making the threat of youth-driven political instability seem all the more real and increasing the sense of urgency among governments that they had better act as quickly as possible. As King Abdullah II of Jordan stated, the U.S. military campaign in Iraq "allowed some of us to say that if we don't come up with our own initiative, something will be forced on us. And once you say you are going to reform, you trigger a process that you can't turn back." This sense of reformist urgency is being reflected in other ways—for example, the unprecedented amount of public debate among Muslim intellectuals in the region on the Koran's meaning regarding violence perpetrated in the name of Allah against infidels, a discussion driven largely by the stream of hellish images that came out of Iraq, whether it was American Marines attacking mosques or terrorists beheading civilians.

Those images likewise propelled the international peace and human rights community to focus more of their attention and activities on the region, beyond just the usual fixation on the Palestinian-Israeli conflict. In Saudi Arabia, as militants emboldened by their experiences in Iraq come back to the kingdom and start attacking symbols of regal authority, all those citizens who've longed cheered on native son Osama bin Laden from afar are coming to realize that if Iraq becomes the new center of al Qaeda activity, their own country will suffer great instability as a result.

All these citizens and officials are right to be worried, because the Big Bang strategy was never about decreasing international terrorism but about localizing it right where it belongs. Thus bringing to a head a long-standing, seemingly interminable problem. In the end, it was almost impossible for the Iraq occupation to go too badly, because the worse it became, the more it transformed the region. Osama bin Laden wanted the American public to feel the Middle East's pain on

9/11, but what he got in reply was a Bush Administration committed to redirecting all that violence back to its source. In many ways, the two sides are running the same race: seeing which can destabilize the region's regimes more quickly and force the desired change.

As the events of early 2005 indicated, George Bush seems to be winning this race. Elections in Iraq and Palestine triggered a "why not here?" mentality that's proved a powerful popular sentiment in countries like Lebanon, which began agitating for the withdrawal of Syria's long-standing military presence, and Egypt, where longtime strongman Hosni Mubarak suddenly felt the need to allow somebody else's name on the presidential ballot for the first time in over two decades of "emergency rule." Factor in Saudi Arabia's first local elections in over seven decades (however restricted they were), and we're talking a host of hopeful political developments that no regional "experts" were predicting would follow in the wake of Saddam Hussein's fall at the hands of the United States–led coalition.

Does the region still have a long way to go? Absolutely. Will there be plenty of setbacks and retrenchments along the way? You bet. But make no mistake about what's been the key driver here: America's demonstrated commitment. The Bush Administration has sent a very clear signal throughout the region: we're not leaving the Middle East until the Middle East rejoins the world. It's as simple as that. Pundits who whine that these positive political developments are occurring *despite* our invasion of Iraq just don't get it. The demonstration effect works both ways: the Iraqi elections generate the positive example ("Want some of this?"), and the insurgency generates the negative example ("Want some of this?"). What America's commitment to seeing the effort through in Iraq does is simply add the air of inevitability (". . . because *eventually* you're gonna get some of this—one way or the other").

Experts who think George Bush was history's gift to bin Laden have it backwards: bin Laden was history's gift to American grand strategy. Al Qaeda's attacks on 9/11 erased the strategic ambiguity that we—for far too long—dubbed "the post–Cold War era." Bin Laden reconnected America's grand strategy to the world, reminding us all, despite our knee-jerk reach for a Department of Homeland Security, that there is no such thing as a "home game" (security over here) and an "away game" (stability over there). Understanding that the two environments are one in the same is what moves us toward a grand strategy for this era of globalization, *if* we have the courage and foresight to take up that challenge and not pretend we can withdraw from the world and expect it to get better on its own.

The outlines of this direct struggle are now clear: al Qaeda will seek to disconnect the region faster from the global economy than the United States and its allies can work to stabilize the region militarily and encourage subsequent broadband economic connectivity. Both sides will fight over the same pool of young men, one side hoping to enlist their ambition and the other hoping to enlist their anger. The rest of the Core may view the Bush White House as myopically focused on this struggle while the rest of the planet's main concerns revolve around the global economy, but shrinking the Gap is as important as growing the Core. The goals of winning the war on terrorism and expanding globalization are two sides of the same coin.

As I've learned from the world of information technology, connectivity drives code. If you want political reform in the Middle East, your fastest route to this outcome is to foster economic connectivity between the Core and the region, letting the dynamics of those transactions force the desired political changes naturally, much as we've done in Asia for the last three decades. As one Arab prime minister recently complained to President Bush during a discussion on the need for political reform in the region, "I have two trains—the political train and the economic train. And the political train cannot run ahead of the other." Pretending political change will come about under the threat of economic isolation is just plain wrong. Governments don't reform out of desperation but out of hope for the future. When they're really isolated in this manner they lash out either at their neighbors or at their own citizens.

This is why, for example, calls for America to radically reduce its dependency on foreign oil are misguided in the extreme, because working to reduce our economic leverage in the region rather than increase it will only force us to rely all the more on military solutions over the long haul. That's because Asia's rising dependency on the Persian Gulf as a source for energy, which already dwarfs ours, will spike in coming years. Osama bin Laden's best hope for getting the West to abandon the Middle East is for the American public to realize that we're really not dependent on the Persian Gulf for energy: If it's not our oil, then why our blood? The problem with this scenario is that it will force Asia to assume military responsibility over the Middle East in our absence: their oil becomes their blood. Why not let this happen? After all, the economic interests of these Asian states will naturally drive them to the region militarily in the coming years anyway. Why not simply acquiesce to this and let them pick up the tab?

Of course, this is something we want and need to see happen, but guiding that process or simply abandoning it to fate are two vastly different things. We need Asia to come to the region militarily in a spirit of joint ownership of the security issues there. If we let this process unfold in a highly competitive way, what will we buy as a result? My fear is that we'll end up with a Yalta-like divide between those portions of the Middle East that look to the West and those that look to the East, and I see no good reason for such a split to occur yet again. We've been down this path before, where an East-versus-West rule set impedes the spread of the global economy by cleaving the globe.

In the Middle East, such a split would center on Iran, with the Shiite-defined crescent stretching from Beirut to Islamabad, plus East Asia's Muslim societies, moving in the direction of a China-centric economic order, and the Sunni Arab populations, moving more in the direction of transatlantic economic order, with Russia (natural gas king) and Saudi Arabia (oil king) as key swing players seeking to play both sides off the middle. In this long-term scenario, though, an al Qaeda or Salafi jihadist movement still fixated on capturing Saudi Arabia by revolution from below would remain far too much in the driver's seat regarding regional security, meaning it would be likewise able to play East and West against each other with the kingdom as the prize.

Bin Laden and the leadership of the Salafi jihadist movement are smart to realize, much as the House of Saud already knows, that the region's importance to the global economy will diminish greatly over the next two to three decades. Why? As the Core as a whole moves progressively off oil and into a hydrogen-based economy that derives that fundamental element primarily from natural gas or as a by-product of nuclear power, leaving oil the odd man out as we collectively move to decarbonize our energy profile further (continuing a long historical trend), OPEC will lose its now central place in the global economy. The Persian Gulf especially will stop representing the future (all those known oil reserves) and start representing the past. Logically, the long-term strategy of the Salafi jihadists must be to destabilize the region so profoundly as to push the Core more quickly down this pathway toward the emerging hydrogen economy, thus reducing our national security interest in the Gulf. If, in the meantime, the current instabilities of the region serve to pit a "greedy" West against an increasingly "needy" East, then so much the better from bin Laden's perspective, because that dynamic simply adds more grist to the mill, accelerating the hoped-for decision point by the West to abandon the region.

So what we have in the Middle East is essentially a series of overlapping historical races. Al Qaeda is racing against time with globalization, hoping to capture a youth bulge before it is lost to Westoxification. The House of Saud is racing against al Qaeda, hoping to put that youth bulge to work, while likewise not losing control over their hearts and minds as the economy is thereby opened up to further Western influences. The United States is racing against time, trying to transform a Middle East before the global shift to hydrogen threatens to turn the region into a historical backwater. Asia is racing against time, trying to achieve a doubling of its energy requirements while not entangling itself too dramatically in the volatile Middle East, a region it is largely loath to engage out of fear of security confrontations with the West. All these races suggest that the next two decades will see the Middle East either rapidly integrate with the Core or become a new battlefield between a West that grows weary of trying to impose stability on the region and a rising East that has no choice but to deal with that continued instability if the West won't. And that, my friends, is a recipe for splitting up the Core, pitting a vigorous New Core led by India and China against a tiring Old Core that's sinking under the weight of its staggering "imperial" indebtedness (America) and its rapid demographic decline (Europe, Japan).

You may have noticed how long I've gone in this argument without touching upon the Palestinian-Israeli conflict to any meaningful degree. This is not an oversight. I truly do think that in the grand scheme of things, this conflict is more a distraction than a driver of change. In my mind, the truly central independent variable, the country whose future sets in motion a host of other dependent outcomes, is neither Israel nor Saudi Arabia, but Iran.

Now, at first glance, that choice may seem odd. After all, we're talking about the Arab Middle East, which is overwhelming Sunni, while Iran is neither Arab nor Sunni, but Persian and overwhelming Shiite. But these distinctions are a big part of why Iran stands out in the region as the crucial security partner for any external power, including the United States, which is interested in achieving lasting stability there. Iran's outlook is not only unique, it is less easily swayed by a sense of pan-Arabism, which over the decades has become an ideology whose main function is to excuse the lack of political reform in the region by blaming Israel's existence for just about everything the region suffers. Iran is also the one country in the Gulf that naturally combines an ambition for political influence with a position of military power. With Saddam's Iraq out of the way, Iran now stands as the only Gulf power that can effectively veto regional efforts at peace through either its explicit support of transnational terrorist groups or the employment of its military power—especially as it achieves status as a nuclear power.

There is no other state in the region that combines the same assets and ambition in terms of politics, economics, and security. Saudi Arabia has no effective security profile, nor does Egypt for that matter, and the House of Saud's political ambitions are more limited in scope, concentrated as they are primarily on keeping the monarchy in power at all costs. Pakistan possesses a far larger population, but its largely uncontrollable domestic situation consumes whatever ambition the political leadership there has for a larger regional role.

It is Iran that can effectively veto movement toward peace and stability in either Jerusalem or Baghdad, through its effective support to, and manipulation of, the political agendas of regional terrorist groups such as Hezbollah and Hamas. It is Iran that has the capacity to destabilize the flow of oil out of the Gulf. It is Iran that determines how much of the energy coming out of the Caspian Basin may be safely accessed by both India and China. And it is Iran, which, by virtue of being a top-five player in both oil and natural gas *and* a longtime diplomatic pariah as far as the United States is concerned, offers Asia the best possibilities for locking in long-term bilateral energy ties, a process already begun by India and China.

And yet, oddly enough, for all the same reasons why the Shah of Iran was once the preferred security partner of the United States in the region, today's Iran still retains many of those same attributes. Iran is not a source for, or a supporter of, the Salafi jihadist movement embodied by al Qaeda. As a Shiite state, its definition of "revolution" differs from that track altogether. Iran's Islamist regime results in a sort of tired authoritarianism, never truly aspiring to the sort of totalitarianism pursued by the Salafis, who can be thought of as the over-the-top Maoists (or Trotskyites) to Iran's rather pedantic post-Stalin Soviet Union. Iran is a nation-state first and foremost, not some transnational religious-inspired movement. Yes, like Brezhnev's Soviet Union, Iran is more than willing to exploit transnational terrorist movements to its own ends, but this is a cynical pursuit of national power, not a millenarian fantasy of regional, much less global, revolution. Iran is not interested in overthrowing the West's political and economic order, it just wants to receive its due place in those corridors of power.

In many ways, the Shiite revolutionary spirit died a long time ago in Iran, leaving behind a cynical political order where the mullahs pretend to rule, the citizens pretend to obey, and the government pretends to reform. Iran is a frightfully young society, full of ambition for a better life and chafing under what the majority of the population consider to be the rather idiotic rule of the religious fundamentalists, one that offers them no future worth pursuing in an increasingly globalized world that demands far more rational rule sets.

Iran most resembles the late-Brezhnevian period of the Soviet Union: a bankrupt ideology, a vastly underperforming economy and workforce, a sullen majority detached from political life as well as economic ambition, and an out-of-touch political leadership (the mullahs) increasingly at odds with the technocratic leanings of its government's bureaucratic elite. However, as the presidential election of 2005 proved, most Iranians will nonetheless vote for a hard-liner as president if he promises a reduction in the political regime's pervasive corruption—such is the state's perpetual failure in Iran.

Like the late Soviet Union, Iran doesn't wield military power so much as security vetoes. It can prevent security from arising but it cannot deliver security effectively anywhere beyond its borders. Because Iran lacks any true client states, its regional security influence is derived primarily from its support of transnational terrorist groups and its persistent quest of weapons of mass destruction. But even in its quest for the bomb, Tehran displays a calculated cynicism throughout, demonstrating all too well that it understands that nukes are for having, not for using.

Iran will get the bomb, no matter how the United States or the rest of the Core seek to prevent that outcome, and who can blame them for the effort? After the Bush Administration easily toppled the Taliban on its eastern border and Saddam Hussein's regime to its west, Iran was incentivized not only to reach for the bomb but to do so quickly, while the U.S. military was effectively tied down by those two efforts and thus self-deterred from military action against Tehran. Having said that, let me also note that Tehran was the regional power most pleased by seeing both the Taliban and Saddam deposed. In many ways, the United States' global war on terrorism has inadvertently made Iran the greatest beneficiary so far in the region in terms of security obstacles removed, begging the question "Wouldn't it be nice to get something in return from Iran for all that effort?"

So if Tehran is going to get the bomb no matter what, the question shifts from "What can the United States do to prevent it?" to "What does the United States get out of it?" If Iran was our natural security partner in the past for a lot of good reasons, then most of those reasons remain today, simply obscured by the continuing dictatorship of the mullahs (of which we have some very bad memories). Our natural goal with Iran, then, is to marginalize that religious leadership while recapturing the same security partnership we once enjoyed.

Inconceivable? No more than having Russia acquiesce to our growing military domination of both the Persian Gulf and Central Asia, not to mention Eastern Europe's merging with both NATO and the EU. After all, we once pursued détente with a very similarly "evil" regime in the Soviet Union in the early 1970s (e.g., tired authoritarianism, bankrupt ideology, enabler of transnational terrorism, finger on the nuclear button), only to effectively kill that regime with connectivity over the subsequent years, yielding a compliant security ally in the process.

Why not pursue the same pathway with Iran? Iran is the one country in the region where it's the rulers who hate the United States and the public that loves us. Yes, the Iranian hostage crisis was a hugely embarrassing experience for us a quarter-century ago, but typically the passage of that much time allows us to move beyond such humiliations as a new generation of political leadership ensues.

Our grand bargain with Iran is not hard to imagine. Iran gets the bomb, diplomatic recognition, the lifting of sanctions and the opening of trade, and its removal from the axis of evil. In return, what Iran must offer the United States is long-term support for both the two-state solution in Palestine and a stable Iraq dominated by a Shiite majority, the cessation of its support for terrorist groups in the region, joint pressure on Syria for an end to its hegemony over Lebanon (removing their troops is only a nice start), and—most symbolically—its recognition of Israel diplomatically and its formal declaration of that country's right to exist.

Is this bargain too much to hope for? Ask yourself this: Can you imagine a future Middle East peace where these steps have not been achieved? I cannot, and so I choose to see Iran's reach for the bomb as possibly the best thing that's happened to the Middle East peace process in decades. Why? Because a huge hang-up in the Palestinian-Israeli struggle has been the Muslim world's sense of military inferiority, which was first proven in a series of wars across the latter half of the twentieth century and which remains codified in the popular imagination by Israel's possession of both the bomb and a nuclear superpower sponsor willing to wage war on its behalf—two things the Middle East's Muslim states have always lacked. Iran's possession of nuclear weapons levels that playing field in a proximate sense, by finally allowing the Muslim Middle East to sit one player at the negotiating table as Israel's nuclear equal. This is not just opportune, it is crucial. As for the fears that Iran's possession of the bomb will destabilize the region, there is no good historical evidence for that. Rather, the historical record is quite clear: two relative equals with nuclear weapons is a far better equation than one that features a permanent imbalance.

Would Iran give terrorists the bomb? Only if terrorists could get Iran something that it could not otherwise achieve directly with the West. Tell me, since Iran is getting the bomb anyway eventually, would you feel less comfortable about this possible scenario if Iran were to open up to the West or if it remained isolated and surrounded by hostile American troops? In which scenario do you think Tehran might risk it all by sponsoring a terrorist WMD strike against Israel or the West—when it has something to lose or nothing to lose? If America wants Iran to act responsibly in the region, it needs to give Iran some responsibility for regional security. Meanwhile, offering Tehran's government-reform elements economic carrots in exchange for denying the hard-line mullahs their self-perceived nuclear security blanket remains an unworkable approach.

In sum, this scenario pathway presents wins for all sides. The United States finally gets a Muslim security partner in the region worth having (as opposed to, say, the "sick man of the Arab world," Egypt, or even the let-them-eat-cake royal mafia in Saudi Arabia). Israel finally gets enough buy-in from the Islamic world for the two-state solution to proceed. Iran gets to return to its rightful place as regional-power-of-note, and its public experiences growing economic connectivity with the outside world, which in turn will inevitably restart a political reform process that rapidly marginalizes the mullahs' religious-based political rule.

As far as Iraq goes, this scenario offers us the hope that Iran will emerge as regional patron to a Shiite-dominated government there. If, in the short run, the prospect of both a nuclear-armed Iran and a Shiite-dominated Iraq frightens the House of Saud into faster pursuit of political reform, then so much the better. The United States, for its own sake, needs to get out of the business of keeping the House of Saud comfortable in its rancid authoritarianism. Naturally, a full solution on Iraq will involve encouraging Turkey's beneficent oversight and mentorship of the Kurdish portion of the country, if only to secure its own border's long-term stability vis-à-vis that emerging state-within-a-state. Ideally, the Sunni portion of Iraq will receive the same sort of patronage from an interested Saudi Arabia, but I see that positive situation emerging only over the long run, as the House of Saud's short-term response will probably be to seal itself off from any ongoing intifada-like chronic insurgency there.

Over time, the United States should encourage Iran's role as gateway for the New Core's growing security interest in the region. India, for example, has long seen itself as both an unrecognized and under-utilized Persian Gulf security pillar and Iran's natural mentor. The growth of that relationship, to include the planned gas pipeline that connects them through Pakistan, can only dampen the potential for conflict between Islamabad and New Delhi. China's emerging strategic partnership with Iran, in addition to its long-standing one with Pakistan, should likewise be encouraged as a way of assuaging Beijing's strategic nervousness regarding its long-term access to energy in the Gulf and Central Asia. Moreover, with the confluence of the security interests of these four states (Iran, India, Pakistan, China), the United States would then have an effective regional quorum for pursuing far more ambitious regional security-enhancing measures for Central Asia as a whole.

In the end, I foresee this pathway of engaging Iran yielding a security solution for the Persian Gulf as a whole that binds both Old and New Core in a series of interlocking relationships of mutual advantage: the United States gaining access through traditional allies Egypt, Israel, Jordan, and Saudi Arabia; Europe's growing interests being expressed through its ties with Turkey, Syria, Lebanon, and Palestine; Russia entering the equation through its need to have both the Caucasus and Central Asia remain stable (its so-called Near Abroad); India's influence coming through its rising economic connectivity with Iran and the Gulf states; and China's strategic interests winding their way into the region through relationships with Pakistan and Iran. Naturally, the short-term focal point of all this activity will be Iraq's settling into some definition of a normal state that is reasonably pluralistic and integrating economically with the outside world. But this larger security puzzle wouldn't be dependent on that process so much as a driver of that process, with the key opening trigger being the rapprochement between Iran and the United States.

How difficult is this pathway? Certainly no harder than what we pulled off with the Soviets between 1973 and 1989—in fact, probably far easier, given our current disproportionate strength as the world's sole military superpower.

In the end, we'll defeat transnational terrorism by connecting the Middle East to the globalizing world faster than the terrorists can disconnect it and thus hijack these societies from history. In this quest, Iran becomes the key connection and thus the main focus of our diplomatic efforts in coming years.

CREATING THE NEW RULE SET ON GLOBAL TERRORISM

Let me be clear right from the get-go: I'm talking about an entirely different rule set here from the one I defined in Chapter 1, or the A-to-Z rule set on processing politically bankrupt states. Here I'm talking about processing individual terrorists, so the ideal model we want to work toward comes closer to the familiar police paradigm than a UN-like process of adjudicating rogue or failed states. Nonetheless, the goals behind building the two different rule sets are fundamentally similar: create transparency, reduce uncertainty, generate non-zero-sum outcomes, and foster a sense that everyone needs to play by the Core's emerging rules (lest you be perceived as excessively "unilateral").

We need two different rule sets (one for rogue/failed regimes and one for bad actors), because, in many ways, we fight this global war on terrorism on two different levels: (1) replacing bad or weak states with good ones (i.e., shrinking the Gap) corresponds to the broader goal of constricting the permissive operating environment of the terrorist networks we target; and (2) disabling and dismantling the terrorist networks themselves corresponds to direct military action (i.e., killing or apprehending their members) inside the Gap. And yes, in the latter instance, we also need to keep in mind the effort of law enforcement agencies working throughout the Core to battle terrorist networks.

But in this section, I really want to focus on the special problems associated with waging warfare against individuals operating as terrorists inside the Gap. Ultimately, we'll need a Core-wide rule set not just for coordinating the activities of national police systems pursuing counterterrorist strategies throughout the Core, but likewise for coordinating the activities of national militaries pursuing counterterrorist strategies throughout the Gap. In both situations, all our Dirty Harrys will need to know *their* limitations, because in neither case will this war be waged in an unrestricted fashion on our part. Otherwise, the Abu Ghraib–like scandals will continue to pile up, killing our moral authority in the process.

And yeah, that's worth a lot.

In the summer of 2004 I was asked by Special Operations Command (SOCOM) in Tampa to come down and spend a week on a panel of strategists that would advise the senior leadership regarding the future of the global war on terrorism. True to form, we weren't being brought in to tell them how to suck eggs (here, kill terrorists), because they had other panels of "graybeards" (retired flags) and "young Turks" (junior officers) to brainstorm that sort of stuff. No, we were brought in to help them strategize the *everything else,* which in this context inevitably centers on the so-called struggle for hearts and minds.

It was an eclectic group of thinkers who had been brought together: a psychiatrist who specialized in interrogating terrorists and other mass murderers, a noted futurist from the business world, a best-selling author of science-fiction novels popular with military officers, an expert on the online activities of youth . . . you get the drift. It was a collection of unorthodox, or out-of-the-box, thinkers with almost nothing in common, which was the entire point as far as SOCOM was concerned. Its leaders simply wanted to get us all together in a single room for several days, throw a lot of PowerPoint briefs at us describing their current strategies, and see what we'd make of them as a group. So we're talking about a serious "fishbowl" effect here, with the eggheads in the bowl and the officers sitting around the walls of the room, writing down everything we said.

Naturally, the intellectual competition within the panel was fierce. All of us assembled were used to being the smartest person in the room (at least, in our estimation), and here we were staring across the table at a number of similarly self-regarding "big-picture" thinkers. So the first day was mostly what facilitation experts call the "butt-sniffing exercise," where all the big dogs check one another out rather warily. By day two, we were pretty much hard at it, with the synergists among us trying to keep the peace ("What I think I hear the group saying is . . . !") and the hardest-charging types typically intervening with the admonition "What I think everyone here seems to be missing, if I may be so bold, is that none of what we're talking about here matters one bit unless we factor in the obvious importance of . . . [insert speaker's pet theory here]."

By day three (thank God!), the discussion finally began to jell, as the egos wore down a bit and the overlapping ideas began to be recognized by all as having merit. And so we began putting together sort of a rough-sketch plan of action for SOCOM's hearts-and-minds effort. It was all very good, and all very reasonable, but in the end, I found myself fundamentally disagreeing with the thrust of the entire effort, and here's why: Special Operations Command is basically divided between the "trigger pullers," or high-end warriors you put in the field to hunt and kill down bad guys, and the Civil Affairs crowd of experts who can enter any country and engage in ground-floor training and reconstruction activities designed to get a political and legal system up and working—at least better than it was before. The Civil Affairs (CA) specialties also include all the mass media experts who work the hearts-and-minds stuff the military likes to call "psychological operations."

So, in sum, SOCOM is basically divided between the warriors and the geeks. That doesn't mean the warriors aren't smart, because they are, and it doesn't mean the geeks can't fight, because they know how to all right, but it does mean that you can pretty much tell whom you're talking to (warrior or geek) within an instant of laying eyes on the person. The Civil Affairs guys (and gals) tend to be a lot taller and typically fairly bulky, as though they spend a lot of time at their computers, whereas the trigger pullers (no gals) all tend to look suspiciously like ultra-marathoners: 5 feet 8 inches tall, maybe 160 pounds, wiry as hell, built for throwing out of aircraft moving at high speeds. Stand next to a CA geek, and you can almost hear the gears moving in his head. Stand next to a trigger puller, and you can almost feel his engine's vibration—even when it's on Idle.

Now, these two SOCOM cultures get along all right, because the trigger pullers know how valuable the Civil Affairs people are when it comes to "securing the victory"—the motto of Civil Affairs units. And yet there's a natural distance between the two, because the trigger pullers want to be first in and first out, whereas the CA personnel tend to take the longer view necessary for winning hearts and minds. Before the global war on terrorism, that tension was easy enough to manage, because the Pentagon's tendency was to never get bogged down anywhere, thus it tended to use SOCOM in small doses. But once we declared a global war on terrorism and Secretary Rumsfeld anointed Special Operations Command as the lead agency in waging this struggle against transnational terrorist networks, then all of a sudden SOCOM was thrust into a limelight it had never experienced before.

That's why SOCOM's commander set up these expert panels in the first place: to think through some of the tough choices the command faces thanks to its new popularity. The special ops guys, in general, don't like attention, preferring to be the "silent service" that doesn't generate headlines, and yet the war was putting them at the forefront of a debate: Should America be toppling regimes that aid transnational terrorism or focusing more on "hunting down and killing" those terrorists, to use a popular phrase from the presidential election? If you favor regime change, then the Civil Affairs portion of SOCOM gets stretched to its maximum workload capacity awfully quickly, as we discovered with Afghanistan and Iraq. Moreover, your trigger pullers tend to get bogged down in that location as well, being sucked into all sorts of seemingly menial security tasks, like bodyguarding local political leaders. If you're not careful, pretty soon SOCOM is tied down in just a few locations on the map and can't mount the same fluid surge responses when the trigger pullers might be needed elsewhere at a moment's notice.

So you can imagine the natural tension that arises between the trigger pullers and the CA geeks: the former want to disengage from interventions as quickly as possible, while the latter want to stick around as long as needed to "secure the victory." As the demand curve rises and resource constraints inevitably emerge, the trigger pullers want SOCOM to stay true to its warrior spirit and prioritize their needs, while the Civil Affairs officers argue just as vehemently for their share of the pie, making all the usual cases for winning hearts and minds and not just pretending that killing bad guys will win the war. Both sides are right in this argument, with the real question being, Should Civil Affairs remain with SOCOM and grow in response to the rising demand curve? Because if it does, won't SOCOM lose its original focus (special warfare) in the expansion?

To put it in a larger context, we can pose the question as this: Should the United States put more of its resources behind "draining the swamp" of the Gap and thereby shrinking the operating domain of the terrorists (i.e., where they run wild and free compared to in the Core), or should we cowboy-up our best killers and send them into the Gap to deal with these bad actors on their own terms?

Of course, it's a false dichotomy, because you need to do both: take down the worst gangsters while trying to deny them both new recruits and regional sanctuaries. But the question of resourcing is not a small one, because while regime toppling improves the long-term prospects for security, in the short run it's both expensive and risky compared with the strategy of limited regret one pursues with special ops teams, where both failures and successes tend never to appear in newspapers. Plus, let's be honest, regime change doesn't exactly reduce your terrorist pool in the short run. If anything, it tends to excite the process in the near term, trapping America into lengthy and complicated nation-building efforts.

But just killing terrorists can seem sort of pointless after a while as well, because the Gap's ability to supply them seems rather endless. We've watched Israel pursue this hard-core approach for years, but the Palestinians don't appear to be running out of suicide bombers anytime soon. So what do you do? Where is the balance? How much of this dirty war do you wage in the shadows versus on the evening news?

During the presidential election campaign of 2004, I was attracted to John Kerry's message that our goal in the global war on terrorism was to render such threats a "nuisance." Understanding we wouldn't be able to use that word seriously for quite some time, the goal is dead-on: When we grow the Core, we grow the number of states with effective police systems and legal rule sets, and in those states the problem of terrorism is essentially one for law enforcement officials, not the military. After all, terrorism is rare and typically associated with loner wackos like Timothy McVeigh and UNABOMBER, right? And that's our view of terrorists in the Core: they're someone we see shuffling by in orange jumpsuits and chains, with a burly U.S. marshal on both arms, on their way to a court appearance. That's what you do with terrorists in the Core. That's how they become a social nuisance instead of a political storm.

Inside the Gap, though, you don't typically see terrorists in that pose. Instead you tend to see them in three venues, all of which are disconcerting: (1) celebrating their victories, killing their hostages, or issuing their threats on videotape; (2) prostrate on morgue slabs after the bloody shoot-out; or (3) staring at you from grainy mug shots advertising their at-large status. There is definitely a "wild frontier" feeling to all these images, which is what gets you the cowboys-versus-Indians analogies often employed by our troops sent into the Gap to do battle with these groups. It's like our special ops guys are stepping into time machines to fight enemies from our past—and in many ways, that's exactly what's happening. They're bringing the Core's justice to the lawless Gap.

It's thankless work, by and large, because when our Men with No Names (special ops trigger pullers) battle the Men with No States (the transnational terrorists), we don't so much extend the Core as simply beat down the Gap. What I mean by that is, we're not exactly promoting the rule of law here, just sending our toughest hombres into the Gap's worst ghettos to rub out their nastiest inhabitants. While that keeps the Core safe (or at least safer), it doesn't exactly improve the Gap's situation much. So on a strategic level, it's "once upon a time in the Gap," and in this premodern western, there's not really any character development, just a series of violent plotlines ending and beginning over again—like a bad Quentin Tarantino movie. To have some lasting success, we need to leave some grateful "settlers" in our wake, not just bodies riddled with smoking holes.

So how do we secure the victory? How do we make it stick? How do we permanently shrink the Gap? Again, the motto of Civil Affairs units in the U.S. military is just that: *Secure the victory*. So even in the Pentagon there's no illusion that killing bad guys solves the problem. When military officers talk about there being "no military solution to this political problem," that's when they send in their best hope under the circumstances: the Civil Affairs guys, or the specialists in trying to erect new rule sets in the wake of war. Civil Affairs personnel tend to be cops a lot of the time, and since the vast majority are reservists, they sort of constitute America's mobile police force, meaning we pull them out of their day jobs as police officers and sheriff's deputies across America and send them into the Gap in fleeting attempts to generate a sense of law and order in the wake of our military operations. When the boys come home, these are the last guys off the plane.

So you can see why there's such a struggle going on inside the Pentagon over who should own the Civil Affairs units. Going back to their origins, the Civil Affairs personnel belonged to the Army proper. When the Army invaded, as when we landed in France on D-Day (June 6, 1944) in World War II, it was the Civil Affairs units that followed the amphibious landing, right on the tail of that first wave of troops. Later, as the Cold War unfolded and that paradigm shifted from large-scale invasions to the sort of low-intensity warfare that defined most of our interventions in Third World locales, Civil Affairs units came to be regarded by the regular Army as a negative symbol of the nation-building task it viewed as perverting the warfighting mission in Vietnam. Following that war, Civil Affairs units were effectively disowned by the Army, eventually being sent away to a sort of foster parent: the Special Operations Command that sprang into being in the early 1980s.

The contentious debate over sending Civil Affairs back to the Army was really driven by resourcing issues on both ends of that equation, as well as by the defining matter of warrior ethos. When the Army divested itself of CA units following Vietnam, it signaled its strong desire to avoid postconflict stabilization and reconstruction duties. Thanks to the subsequent Weinberger and Powell Doctrines, over the 1980s the Army would become a predominantly first-half team, meaning one that entered any war zone with overwhelming force and a clear "exit strategy"—which is code for "we don't build nations after wars," or what I call the second-half effort. So for the Army to take back Civil Affairs means it has to admit it's primarily responsible for that second-half effort, and just as in the case of SOCOM's trigger pullers, the Army fears losing its warfighting ethos in that evolution. And yeah, that's a big deal, because there are no four-star Civil Affairs generals. You want to rise up Army ranks and wear a lot of stars on your shoulder boards, then you fight wars, buddy! You stick to the first-half game and leave that second-half "babysitting" to others.

Safely embedded down in SOCOM, Civil Affairs became a largely forgotten career backwater for officers. By relying so extensively on reservists, the function was effectively outsourced to the domestic public sector, or local police departments around America in a sort of backdoor draft (as in, "When we need them, you—local police departments—need to give them up on demand, no matter how much it hurts"). While there's a good logic for that approach if you're only going to use Civil Affairs here and there (e.g., better they keep their skills up in the civilian sector during their long stretches of nonuse), that model essentially broke down across the 1990s, as the Pentagon was pulled into nation-building efforts galore. As a result, Civil Affairs officers that were allegedly reservists became de facto active-duty, meaning they were in their khakis far more than in their civvies.

Along comes a global war on terrorism, and guess which resource we run out of almost immediately? Civil Affairs personnel. So when the presidential election campaign of 2004 kicked in and John Kerry was looking to establish his profile on defense, he pushed what seemed to be a logical proposal to double the number of personnel in Special Operations Command. Now, you might think that when confronted with that windfall, the commander of SOCOM would be licking his chops to plus-up the number of trigger pullers under him, but just the opposite was true. What SOCOM's leadership really wanted was more Civil Affairs personnel, not more trigger pullers. They wanted more Civil Affairs because, in having more of the "left behind" personnel, the trigger pullers would be freed up to move on to whatever their next target or mission was. If they ran short of such personnel, what typically happened was that the trigger pullers got bogged down doing work better left to the reservist cops or private security, like bodyguarding or training local police forces.

Now, what's been odd about my interactions with Special Operations Command is that while I was brought down to advise its leadership primarily on the basis of my advocacy of the SysAdmin force concept (it was the Civil Affairs elements of SOCOM that pushed for my participation), my advice to both SOCOM and to the Pentagon on this subject probably didn't end up being what the Command expected. For when it comes to the question of investing more heavily in Civil Affairs, I don't think that money should really go to SOCOM, but to the U.S. Army, along with all those Civil Affairs units that SOCOM currently owns. In short, I believe the child (Civil Affairs) should be returned to its birth parents (the Army).

Why? I agree with Secretary Rumsfeld that what SOCOM should be focused on is "direct action," or the "kinetic stuff"—two euphemisms for killing bad guys. Using the Civil Affairs units here and there in the trigger pullers' wake, sometimes perhaps too cynically in an attempt to cover their tracks, is not a long-term strategy for winning. In my mind, special ops forces are purely a Leviathan force and should stay that way. They may operate in allegedly peacetime environments, but frankly, the places we send them inside the Gap are anything but peacetime environments. In short, I want to see my trigger pullers trigger-happy. I want them to have the loosest rule sets possible, not bogged down in never-ending bodyguard jobs. They should be able to disappear into the Gap, do what needs to be done in killing or snatching bodies, and then leave no paper trail behind. They should be optimized for this function and left to maintain their warfighting ethos to the maximum.

The "social workers" should therefore be sent back to the Army, which finally needs to admit that it no longer has the preeminent warfighting role in today's transformed U.S. military, which, when required, destroys foreign militaries overwhelmingly with airpower. What the Army does in this global war on terrorism are all those babysitting jobs it has constantly sought to avoid since Vietnam: it occupies, it stabilizes, it reconstructs, it builds nations. To the extent the SysAdmin force needs high-end combat capabilities, again, that's what the Marines are primarily for: small wars, quick actions, and lots of dead bodies in their wake. To the extent terrorists need dispatching quietly, that's what the trigger pullers of SOCOM are for—in and out with no lasting responsibilities.

In short, I want war and peace to be very distinct instruments of America's ongoing struggle against transnational terrorism, with the Leviathan's special operations trigger pullers offering no apologies for their secrecy and stealth, and the SysAdmin's Civil Affairs units committed to transparency in all their operations. I'm never looking to set up our Leviathan forces for "fair fights." I want those operations to be as unfair as possible, because in that asymmetry, our personnel find their best odds at survival in warfare. But with the SysAdmin force, unless that function is embedded within a larger, Core-wide rule set regarding its employment, we greatly lower our chances for success in permanently shrinking the Gap. Civil affairs isn't about covering tracks but laying them.

SOCOM shouldn't be burdened with the Civil Affairs portfolio of nation building and the far subtler task of winning of hearts and minds. Those missions, right down to mastering counterinsurgency and being able to teach it to others, should belong to the Army primarily, but certainly not exclusively. The Army should be optimized for the complete spectrum of Fourth-Generation Warfare, while the Marine Corps should remain a mini-Leviathan within the SysAdmin force, capable of waging war right up to its highest intensity. In combination, the Army and Marines need to become the big force that follows in the wake of the largely air-defined Leviathan. Their troops are the ones who do not come home at the war's end, but who keep building the outposts that settle the Gap. If we are truly committed to winning this war, that is what it will take.

We don't really fight regimes anymore, and we can't find armies willing to take on the might of our Leviathan force. What we engage in today is primarily warfare against individuals: either killing them or rounding them up for prosecution in onesies and twosies. In fact, the U.S. military has progressively specialized in warfare against individuals across the entirety of the post–Cold War period. Consider this trajectory of our major interventions: We went into Panama in 1989 looking for one guy (Manuel Noriega); after entering Somalia in 1992, we subsequently became fixated on toppling a single warlord (Mohamed Farrah Aidid) and his top leadership; in the Balkans across the 1990s, we settled on a strategy of targeting the leadership clique of Slobodan Milosevic with very specific sanctions and a bombing campaign that ultimately put him in the docket of the International Criminal Court in The Hague; in Afghanistan we entered with specific goals of killing or capturing al Qaeda's senior leaders; and in Iraq we went in looking for a "deck of cards." Think of the big successes of this war so far: assassinations of individual al Qaeda leaders, arrests of small terrorist cells, capturing Saddam. Think of our most gnawing failure to date: our inability to capture or kill Osama bin Laden. Think about our likely targets in years to come—individuals all.

We have left the era of mass war and entered the era of customized warfare. There are no interstate wars of note in the global security system today, but there are a host of bad actors inside the Gap that the Core would prefer to see disappear—violently, if necessary. The questions are how, and under what circumstances. If the Core can't come to some explicit consensus on the rule set needed to dispatch these bad actors, then not only are the Core's powers likely to work at cross-purposes but ultimately their shared perception that this is a zero-sum process will foster a dangerous sense of competition. When that happens, the Core risks dividing itself into conflicting rule sets, where the United States is viewed by other Core pillars of having a "hit list" that advances our security interests inside the Gap while damaging their own.

The question of the "most wanted" or "hit list" is not a trivial one, because it says to the world that these are the essential rule breakers in the system, meaning the transnational terrorist networks, such as al Qaeda, who've declared war on globalization's creeping advance and all the integrating dynamics that historical process triggers. Identified as such, we send strong signals to both Core and Gap about the implied rules we seek to uphold: transparency, free markets and trade, collective security, and individual freedom. Moreover, the identification of such a list is a rallying point for domestic support for the global war on terrorism. It says, this is the face of the enemy and this is what he represents. America has always personalized its wars, whether it was King George or Adolf Hitler, and we have and will continue to personalize this war in much the same way. For the retribution of 9/11, the face of the enemy is Osama bin Laden, and for the next generation of Iraq-fueled terrorists, that face is now Abu Musab al-Zarqawi—a Kaiser Soze–like figure if ever there was one.

Okay, that Dennis Miller–like reference requires some explanation.

The character Kaiser Soze appeared in the 1995 crime film *The Usual Suspects*. More myth than reality, Soze was described to police by a captured criminal as everyone's worst nightmare, or an almost fairy-tale figure of grotesquely evil proportions. His feats of barbarity were legendary and were clearly passed along by his subordinates in an attempt to buttress his unchallenged standing within the criminal organization atop which he allegedly reigned as kingpin. At the end of the movie, the audience discovers that Kaiser Soze is a complete fiction, created by the captured criminal to convince the police holding him that he could be released as a trivial underling in the crime syndicate they were seeking to dismantle, when in reality this self-professed snitch was the very character that he successfully mythologized with his diversionary tale of the make-believe Soze.

Throughout this global war on terrorism, you will witness time and time again this tendency for our side to elevate individual representatives of our enemy to similarly legendary status. We will create many Kaiser Sozes along the way, in part to give our enemy a defined face and in part because such figures focus our attention on the evil of our foes. Is either bin Laden or al-Zarqawi the all-powerful figure that we consistently make him out to be in our popular imagination? In the end, it doesn't matter, for if they did not exist, we would have to create them, and indeed, we will have to replace them whenever they are caught or killed. Because, as with any war, we need to provide the larger pool of real and potential enemies with an escape route toward peace, so personalizing this war allows us discretion not only in whom we choose to kill but in whom we offer the option of peace as well. As we have shown repeatedly in our post–Cold War interventions, as well as in this war on terrorism, our conflict is never with the affected nations themselves but merely with the bad actors found within. We are not at war with the Middle East or with Islam, but with a particular strain of religious totalitarianism that we seek to extinguish so that Muslims worldwide and the region itself can migrate toward peaceful integration with the Core. So these bogeymen are not only useful in this struggle, they define it.

The Kaiser Sozes define this war in the same way that grotesquely exaggerating depictions of globalization as a "Jewish-American plot to rule the world" serve to embody the fears of many inside the Gap that the global economy's advance is both overwhelming and in-escapable. Anything powerful enough to elicit the response of suicide bombers and willing martyrs must—by definition—be a transforma-tional experience of stunning proportions, otherwise why the mind-less sacrifice? Again, international terrorism associated with the Salafi jihadist movement is fundamentally a function of globalization's pro-gressive unfolding as a historical process. Yes, the grievances of this movement are local, as are the actual wars to be waged, but the millenarian-tinged, willingly apocalyptic vision that it offers demon-strates the profound sense of fatalism with which these quixotic adherents wage their struggle. They have no hope of victory but merely the chance to deny us the future we know is ours.

And so, as that future unfolds in our favor, the efforts of our ene-mies to thwart it will become all the more desperate, all the more fan-tastic, and all the more pointless. In return, our descriptions of their motivations will grow commensurately more absolute in our sense of moral purpose. We will exhibit this growing certitude because it will be many years before the threat posed by transnational terrorism will be reduced to the status of simple criminality or social nuisance, even though this is obviously our long-term goal in shrinking the Gap and extending the Core's legal rule sets around the planet. What we need to remember in this struggle, however, is that we *do not* offer any truces to the determined forces of disconnectedness, for they have no future in our shared world, our global community. These individuals are indeed slated for extinction, and so we must expect them to fight to the bitter end, triggering more and not less violence as globaliza-tion effectively penetrates their relatively isolated worlds.

The strategy of the Big Bang in the Middle East was never about instant peace or democracies-in-a-box, but about speeding the killing to its logical conclusion. The integration of globalization's frontier areas will always engender violent resistance by young males who feel disenfranchised, disempowered, or emasculated by the resulting new order, which inevitably involves more universal freedom unencumbered by restrictive culture or tradition. Denied the promise of their presumed authority in social hierarchies defined by brute force and gender, these angry young men will unleash their fury in mindless violence that's only too easily organized and packaged by cynical elites who will like- wise lose power and authority if their preferred definition of the status quo crumbles. So let us be clear and realistic in our purpose: to actual- ize our definition of a future worth creating, one defined by universal freedoms enabled by connectivity and the rule sets that engenders, we are effectively killing our foes' definition of a future worth preserving. For every dream of individual freedom we enable, competing dreams of collective oppression are destroyed.

Our success in this long-term struggle will be met with alternating responses from our enemies. Often they will threaten us with com- plete and utter destruction, but they will likewise regularly surprise us with offers of truce and cease-fires. As we naturally experience bouts of fatigue, we will be sorely tempted to accept these offers, but we should not, because they will always represent calculated attempts by our enemies to achieve breathing spaces and strategic pauses designed to facilitate their regaining of strength, or often to diminish their growing alienation among the very populations whose hearts and minds they seek to win.

We see this phenomenon at work with the steady stream of mes- sages we have received personally from Osama bin Laden in the years since 9/11, as he has alternated between gleeful predictions of our future suffering at the hands of his followers and explicit quid pro quo offers for our retreat from the field of battle. Clearly, he seeks to divide the Core with such messages: separating East from West, Europe from the United States, and red states from blue inside America. But these offers reflect the movement's growing weakness and desperation. By going on the offensive against al Qaeda, the United States has de- flected its violence back inward toward the region. The danger in this for al Qaeda is that when it switches focus from the "far enemy" (America) to the "near enemy" (House of Saud), its terrorist strikes can easily arouse feelings of nationalism from the very populations bin Laden seeks to win over, a backlash we're already seeing in Saudi society. As a result, not only has bin Laden switched tactics within the kingdom (avoiding domestic targets and focusing on Western ones), he's also toned down his act vis-à-vis the West, affecting the pose of "an elder statesman from a borderless Muslim nation." Again, this is bin Laden bargaining from a position not of strength but of profound weakness.

Al Qaeda, far from enjoying a winning streak, has instead sustained its movement largely by accepting defeat time and time again and shifting its center of gravity to some new locale. Bin Laden and his lieutenants have long perpetuated the myth of the foreign fighter being instrumental in defeating the Soviet Union in Afghanistan, proving—yet again in the minds of the Fourth-Generation Warfare adherents—that the only force capable of beating a military super-power is a 4GW-like insurgency. But in reality, al Qaeda, and foreign fighters in general, were not instrumental in defeating the Soviets. It really was the indigenous mujahideen, supplied by the Pentagon, that won that guerrilla war. The foreign-fighter contribution was negligible to the victory, although the experience of joining in combat did much to define the terrorist network's growing sense of identity.

But the larger point is this: al Qaeda and the Salafi jihadist movement have won no battles over the years. Instead, they lived as parasites within either ongoing civil wars or easily corrupted failed states. Their history has been one long series of evacuations under duress. Like cockroaches in an apartment building, they are forced to flee to the next unit over every time the exterminator steps in to spray the current nesting place. Attempts to romanticize this long series of evictions are grossly misleading, because al Qaeda has not been able to sustain itself in any host body for any length of time, only burrowing in during times of raging conflict. Its one safe exile, in Taliban Afghanistan in the late 1990s, lasted only so long as its efforts at transnational terrorism stayed in the category of pinpricks against expected targets (e.g., U.S. military and diplomatic installations overseas). Once bin Laden sought to take the fight directly to the "distant enemy" on 9/11, he and his senior leadership were forced to scatter and stay in hiding.

Listen to al-Zarqawi himself in the summer of 2004 on the outcome he feared most in Iraq:

> America is being bloodied in Iraq but has no intention of leaving, no matter the bloodletting among its own soldiers. It is looking to a near future, when it remains safe in its bases, while handing over control to a bastard government with an army and a police force. . . . There is no doubt that our field of movement is shrinking, and our future looks more forbidding by the day.

Al-Zarqawi's worst nightmares presage our winning strategy in this war: we replace bad state with good, dispelling the chaos upon which al Qaeda thrives with functioning states and their instruments of self-control. By doing so, we constrict the terrorists' operating domain. So what can al-Zarqawi do in the face of the SysAdmin's relentless push to install order? He can wage his terrorist campaign with as much ferocity and perversity as possible, because he knows that the alternative is to continue the losing streak that has defined al Qaeda's nomadic journey.

Another al Qaeda myth we need to dispel is the notion that it somehow grows more coherent as an ideological force, when, in reality, it grows more incoherent with each new "franchise" it takes under its wing. In this process, al Qaeda gains more enemies than adherents, with each new enemy adding more substantial assets to the Core's overall efforts. I know terrorism experts like to portray this global struggle as a 360-degree battlefield for us, but that image is far more true for al Qaeda than for America.

By setting itself up as the great "base" of anti-American, anti-Western, and antiglobalization warriors from all over the Gap, al Qaeda has moved into the same peculiar position that ultimately bankrupted the Soviet Union's revolutionary ideology in the Third World. Al Qaeda now feels the need to adopt every anti-Core rebel or terrorist group as its own, so long as it mimics the bare minimum of jihadist rhetoric. By doing so, it pulls under its wing a host of disparate opportunists who will effect their "conversion" to Islam simply to elevate their movement's status as part of the grand "global struggle" against Western imperialism. As one front-page *Wall Street Journal* story noted:

> Beneath the changing slogans is a broader shift set in motion by the end of the Cold War. Radical Islam has mutated into something akin to communism in the past—a convenient, off-the-shelf ideology that can clothe complex local conflicts that few would care about otherwise. These include separatist struggles in Aceh in Indonesia, Indian-controlled Kashmir and Russian-ruled Chechnya. In a host of other countries from Morocco to Malaysia, Islamists have replaced communists as the principal source of opposition to established ruling orders. By donning Islamist garb, leaders of these widely different causes can open the door to foreign funds, particularly from wealthy Gulf states, and also to manpower from a pool of footloose militants looking for work.

A good example of this phenomenon is seen in the Chechen warlord Shamil Basayev, he of Beslan massacre fame. Prior to 9/11, Basayev was known for worshipping at the altar of Che Guevera, but after 9/11 he became "Allah's slave," despite never having shown any prior inkling toward religious faith. Sure, Basayev cynically used his newfound faith to tap external funding sources in the Middle East, but al Qaeda was likewise forced to be associated with Basayev's "courageous" act of taking several hundred schoolchildren hostage in southern Russia and then executing them en masse. Al Qaeda got a new franchise all right, but America gained another big believer in the strategy of preemptive war inside the Kremlin. Guess which side picked up more resources—not to mention more moral authority—in that transaction?

According to our best estimates, al Qaeda's "central staff" currently oversees, in a loose, coordinating fashion, three clustered "small-world" networks (i.e., networks marked by a relatively small number of connecting players whose relationships with nearly everyone else in the group define its essential structure) within the global Salafi jihad: a cluster of "Core Arabs," another group of Maghreb (North African) Arabs, and a smaller network of Southeast Asian groups. Among those three clusters, the most direct interconnections lie between the Core Arab and Southeast Asian networks, which originally evolved from founding jihadist movements in Egypt and Indonesia, respectively. The Core Arab group, now dominated by Saudis, was responsible for the terrorist strikes of 9/11, as overseen and supported by the al Qaeda's central staff network.

In terms of our tactics in this global war against a global movement, our immediate tasks seem rather obvious: we seek to disrupt what network connectivity exists between these clusters, targeting those individuals who provide the greatest degrees of connectivity. Picking up the essential doctrine of Colonel John Boyd's counterinsurgency approach, we seek to isolate the enemy in ever smaller numbers, because in that isolation the enemy loses vitality. That's the essential task of the trigger pullers in Special Operations Command, and it's fundamentally the same strategy pursued by U.S. law enforcement against crime syndicates, except here we're going to shoot to kill whenever we have them in our sights.

When we can't bag them, then we'll seek to tag them, which means that a future high-priority task for the U.S. defense community involves generating technologies that allow us to identify, locate, and track "targets of interest," even as they move in very complex environments chock-full of civilians. A simple analogy would be a LoJack for terrorists that allows us to track them surreptitiously as they move among civilian populations (much like stolen vehicles), typically in large urban environments. Maybe these tiny transmitters or other tags would be planted on their physical persons (or even in their bodies), or maybe they would be attached to their vehicles or simply built into certain signature items, such as guns or explosive materials, during manufacturing, allowing for their later detection and tracking by counterterrorism sensor networks.

So long as we are fighting this global war on terrorism inside the Core, we're mostly talking about law enforcement agencies taking the lead. It's only inside the Gap where you'll see the U.S. military engaging in this SWAT-like activity of assassinating and snatching terrorist targets with relative impunity, meaning we often won't be asking the local governments' approval for our actions up front, in large part because most of these operations will occur in states without well-functioning governments. There is obviously a certain amount of potential blow-back from such activity, not just from the Gap nations whose sovereignty we impinge upon, but likewise from fellow Core powers who might well be tempted to view our activities in a highly negative light. So no matter where you go in this global war on terrorism, and no matter whom you're hunting, all warfare against individuals occurs within the context of everything else. Inside the military, the "everything else" usually falls into the bailiwick of the J-5 office, or the unit in every major command that deals with allies, like the CENTCOM J-5 group I interacted with down in Tampa.

But there's also a J-5 office that sits in the Pentagon, in the Joint Staff headquarters that unites all four services into a single integrated "back office" sort of command, meaning the Joint Staff doesn't command the troops in field (that authority sits with the Combatant Commands like Central Command) but it does oversee the long-term plans and policies for the military as a whole. The Joint Staff's J-5 division likewise called me in for a discussion the summer after *The Pentagon's New Map* came out, asking for my general impressions of how America's pursuit of a global war on terrorism would impact our overall relations with allies and their militaries.

Like everybody else in the military, the Joint Staff's J-5 officers were attracted to the book's arguments about the need to identify and/or generate the new rule sets associated with this new form of war—warfare against individuals. J-5's concerns were on target: It is worried about how the United States would bring along key allies in this process of enunciating new rules, making sure the process strengthened such relationships and ultimately brought new allies into the fold. Essentially, the Joint Staff was intuiting—quite correctly, in my view—that the United States was fast reaching the point where its own declarations of new rules (the most prominent one being preemptive war) either had to find broad acceptance across the rest of the Core or risk permanently isolating us, not so much in a military sense, because most of the world's militaries are instinctively on-board with these new rules, but in a diplomatic sense, meaning we risked losing the battle for hearts and minds among the Core's domestic political constituencies.

All you have to do is read the papers to see how both the Pentagon and the intelligence community are still scrambling, four years after 9/11, to propose new rules for the global war on terrorism. Quite frankly, we are making it up as we go along, and there's nothing wrong with that so long as this process ultimately leads to formal codification of new rules that our allies can subsequently buy into over time. Good examples of this process can be seen in the Pentagon's ongoing attempts to expand its role in counterterrorist intelligence collection and analysis, arenas historically the near-exclusive purview of the CIA outside the United States, as well as the CIA's own attempts to redirect its long-standing focus on terrorist groups operating inside the Core to those more obviously centered inside the Gap.

In both instances, the Pentagon and the CIA are forced to come up with new rules, like those for Special Operations and CIA agents operating clandestinely inside the Gap. *Clandestine* here refers to activities where our personnel seek to conduct themselves not only in a stealthy, or covert, fashion, but in a manner that denies our official involvement. This is the real undercover work. For CIA agents, it means not operating under "official cover" out of U.S. embassies. Why? Often America won't have embassies with the truly disconnected Gap states where these agents must operate if they're going to infiltrate terrorist networks. For the Special Operations forces, the need is even more obvious, for in certain instances we'll use them to kill individuals within Gap states without asking those governments for permission.

But this is clearly where it gets tricky, because in promulgating these new rules for our clandestine activities inside the Gap, we're effectively admitting what I've maintained all along: the Core is defined by the existence of codified rules on security, whereas the Gap is defined by the lack of such rule sets. And as soon as you get that notion out in the open, you're essentially admitting that in this global war on terrorism, state sovereignty inside the Gap is legitimately transgressed by Core states as required. As soon as you cross that line, which I believe is an essential one to cross, then you're no longer pretending that this is something the UN is going to solve on the system's behalf, because the UN's fatal flaw is that it pretends that all states have equal sovereignty, when in reality there's the Core of "adult" states that deserve such rights fully and a Gap that features plenty of "minors" who come nowhere near meeting that threshold or deserving such respect.

By promulgating our own rule set (often secret) regarding how we conduct this war inside the Gap, we leave ourselves open to the charge of unilateralism or even imperialism. So what we need to do, as we work our way through enunciating this new rule set and testing it, is progressively open up this rule-codification process to the rest of the Core, starting—quite logically—with those we trust most.

Inside the Core, terrorists are handled by law enforcement agencies, so each state has its own internal rules for detecting, capturing, and processing terrorist suspects, as well as, in most instances, fairly well-defined rules for those circumstances when terrorists commit acts in one Core state but are caught in another—namely, the issue of extradition. So I'm not talking about coming up with a host of new rules for countries inside the Core, because those are fairly well established.

What I'm talking about is the vital need for a rule set across the Core, not only regarding how Core states increase cooperation with one another on defeating global terrorism but also concerning how, and under what conditions, it's okay for any Core state's military to engage in the killing or capturing of terrorists inside the Gap and, beyond that, our formal processing of those captured suspects, meaning explicitly defined rules for prisoner handling, detention, interrogation, adjudication, and imprisonment. This is a vitally important rule set to create in conjunction with allies, because left to its own devices and political pressures, any presidential administration is going to cut corners where it can, getting us scandals like the CIA's secret "rendition" program.

This is clearly an emergent rule set that needs to be rationalized to our allies' content. Suspects can't simply disappear on chartered jets to destinations (wink, wink) we know could be very detrimental to their health (and you just know these places are always found inside the Gap). We need to render justice, not just bodies, and we need to account for their fair treatment throughout the judicial process. Not every enemy of my enemy constitutes a friend to the process of extending this essential rule set, which cannot include torture.

Why is this so crucial? Why not just let individual Core states do what they must inside the Gap, and—in aggregate—slowly but surely clean it up and thus enable the Core's integration of these states? The problem with that approach is threefold: First, enunciating that common rule set is a good way to strengthen Core unity. Second, unless we codify such rules openly over time, the Core misses the opportunity to signal to states in the Gap how they might improve themselves in the direction of eventual Core membership by adopting similar rule sets internally that would over time obviate the Core's requirement to intervene in the first place. Third, and most important, by enunciating such a Core-wide rule set, we avoid the danger of this collective effort devolving into a perceived zero-sum competition among the Core's great power inside the Gap—in short, a return to great-power rivalries there or even proxy wars.

Over the long term, the greatest danger in any such competition would be the possibility that some rising Core power might delude itself into thinking that if its support for such activity could be kept anonymous, it might be possible to wage destabilizing war against other Core states *through* the Gap, either through action directed there (e.g., supporting terrorist networks hostile to our economic interests) or through proxy actors acquired there for destabilizing actions inside the Core (e.g., what if another Core state decided to back an al Qaeda secretly in its war against the United States?). Would this be war as we have known it? Probably not, although some kinetic aspects (e.g., stuff or people getting blown up) would probably be part of it. The larger portions would be acts designed primarily for disruption and the sowing of panic or simple confusion. For example, a two-man

sniper team came close to paralyzing the operations of many government agencies in Washington, D.C., for weeks on end in 2002. Imagine
a foreign entity backing an effort in which twenty such teams were set
in motion across twenty major metropolitan areas at once, with each
unit being given the same simple instructions: shoot one victim a day
for ten days and then move on randomly to another city. Or imagine a
foreign state spreading hoof-and-mouth disease throughout our cattle
supply in order to gain a competitive advantage in global beef exports.
Again, would you call this war or something else?

I compare this sort of broadband warfare, or what some Fourth-
Generation Warfare theorists consider the epitome of that concept, to
the notion of the "yellow flag" in a NASCAR race. In that situation,
the caution flag, raised as a result of some accident on the track,
requires all drivers to maintain their position vis-à-vis one another
until the debris is cleared. In this form of 4GW, the purpose of creating anonymous disruption of networks would be to generate a perceived "yellow flag" situation so as to take advantage of the resulting
confusion to improve one's position in the "race," either absolutely
(leaping places ahead, so to speak) or just relatively (closing the gap
with competitors). The purpose of the anonymity would therefore be
to alter one's position in any competition without being identified as
the cause of events that triggered the change.

Can this be imagined? Well, look at it this way: China's relationship
with the United States, compared with the rest of the Core, was
greatly improved by 9/11. Prior to those events, the Bush Administration had China firmly locked in its sights as both a fairly bad actor and
a clearly rising threat. As far as long-range planning went in the Pentagon, China was by far the preferred conflict scenario. All that changed
radically following the initiation of the global war on terrorism, as
China was effectively removed from the top of the "plan against" list
and began to be viewed as a potential security partner, as did Russia
and to a lesser extent India. If such advantage is possible as the result
of a 9/11-like event, could such attacks be engineered by a Core power
through untraceable proxy agents so as to achieve these advantages

time and time again as part of a larger, long-term strategy? I mean, an America that's constantly prodded by terrorist acts to topple Gap regimes cannot offer the same long-term attention to a rising China, now, can it?

The natural counter to such fears is that, in our increasingly networked world, it gets harder and harder to foresee the zero-sum payoffs in these imagined venues of Fourth-Generation Warfare inside the Core. I mean, how would China destabilize parts of the U.S. economy in such a way as to trigger our subsequent interventions inside the Gap without simultaneously damaging our ability to remain a leading consumer of its exports, not to mention the dollar's capacity to remain its favorite (meaning, stable) reserve currency? How would any state hope to disaggregate such a complex web of economic, political, and security relationships with a power like the United States? And yet, as the kinetic dimension of this potential strategy grows smaller (disruption doesn't require destruction), or as the growing interdependency among states means that such a disruptive attack upon a competitor could be achieved without traditional military means, then the potential for such warlike activity logically grows—in effect, becoming virtualized (as in, "like war but not war"). I mean, a power outage caused or a computer/biological virus unleashed ("accidentally," of course) wouldn't exactly meet most people's definition of war, and yet the same "yellow flag" dynamic could possibly be achieved, meaning some states might improve their international standing in this manner, at costs seemingly acceptable to themselves.

This is why I worry about a possible long-term divergence between America's definition of what is acceptable or unacceptable in waging a war against terrorism and those of other Core pillars—especially China. If such conflicting perceptions can arise with regard to regime change, such as in Iraq, then similar divergence is possible over warfare waged against individual terrorist networks. So long as the United States maintains a cloak of secrecy over how it has chosen to wage its own, very particular brand of a global war on terrorism, it runs the risk of encouraging other Core pillars to think ahead and imagine the day they, too, will wage their own particular brands of "preventive" war throughout the Gap, perhaps with an eye to improving their position vis-à-vis Core competitors. In sum, the Core needs a common definition not only of what is being prevented but also of the acceptable routes for achieving that prevention.

This isn't a path reflexively chosen by America, because while the United States was founded on individual rights and the rule of law, Americans also love the rule breakers and lone riders. The Dirty Harry icon who dispatches evildoers without remorse, going outside the law when necessary, is a literary and cinematic staple in our country. The Man with No Name doesn't explain, he simply acts, and we love him for it. George W. Bush embraced this archetype early on in the war. "I want justice," he said a few days after 9/11, referring to Osama bin Laden. "There's an old poster out West, as I recall, that said WANTED: DEAD OR ALIVE."

We're all familiar with the feeling of wanting revenge, so when the United States claims the right to assassinate terrorist leaders at will, the Bush Administration is playing to something other than our better angels. And yet someday soon a cinematic version of the Predator drone will corner the evil terrorist and ask, "Do you feel lucky, punk?" just before firing off one of those Hellfire missiles that turn the target vehicle into a fiery ball of righteous retribution—Clint Eastwood–style.

I know it's tempting to shoot first and ask questions later, but is it okay to imprison indefinitely and seek evidence later?

Yes, yes. So many suspects, so little time. So it's little wonder that we bend the rule here and there, declaring—as the Bush White House did—terrorists unworthy of protection under the Geneva Conventions. Such an approach can work for a while, but then the photos from Abu Ghraib are posted on the Web, and you have to explain to your kids why that sort of stuff is okay when it's the bad guys who are *really* bad. And if you're the president? Well, maybe the doubts creep in when your own White House counsel warns you about possible war-crimes charges over Guantánamo, your oversight-free mini-gulag down in Cuba.

The Geneva Conventions, as it turns out, served a few very good purposes. They created an international rule set, separating the rule-abiding states from the rogues and outlaw regimes, and protected many an American along the way. But the 1949 Conventions were designed to prevent a rerun of the atrocities of the last great global war (World War II)—a struggle between sovereign states. Today this is not the problem set we face. This is a new type of war (for us, at least) against a new type of enemy (the Man with No State). Unless we want to spend the rest of this long struggle trying to defend ourselves against charges of police brutality and torture, the United States needs to acknowledge that (1) we're not above the law; and (2) the Core needs a new set of rules for capturing, processing, detaining, and prosecuting such nonstate actors as transnational terrorists. In short, we need Dirty Harry to come clean. Frontier justice must be replaced by a real Core-wide judicial system. And no, there's nothing wrong with figuring this out as we go along. It has worked in past periods of rule-set resets, and it can work this time, too, so long as we stick to the principle of transparency wherever possible.

There's no mystery about who should write the rules. It should start inside the Core, and it should start first with our oldest and closest military allies, such as the United Kingdom, Japan, Korea, France, Germany, Italy, Spain, Canada, Australia, and New Zealand—to name the most obvious ones. The new rules need to define how this Core-within-the-Core group cooperates to suppress terrorist activity within their states using police methods (and yes, using CIA agents to snatch suspects from fellow Core states is a big no-no, as America recently found out with Italy), but they'll also lay out how and under what conditions it's okay for those same states' militaries to go into the Gap to snatch or kill suspected terrorists.

This is not a job for the UN, which only recently got around to passing a resolution outlawing the attempts of terrorist networks to obtain weapons of mass destruction (gosh, thanks, UN!). In a global body where Libya gets to chair the Human Rights Commission (who's next, Sudan?), some punks really have gotten lucky.

Ultimately this Old Core–heavy group would need to expand its membership to include the Core as a whole, with the ultimate goal being the creation of a World Trade Organization–like entity for global counterterrorism. A body such as this would set the operating standard for both intra-Core police networking (like building that fabled terrorist database in the sky) and the rules of engagement (to include prisoner handling, detention, and interrogation) for whenever the member states' militaries venture into the Gap looking for bad guys.

This envisioned World Counterterrorism Organization would operate by invitation only, unlike the sloppy Interpol. States like Pakistan wouldn't just flash a badge on their way into the meeting. No, if Osama bin Laden could hide out inside your territory at will, you'd probably be told to try again next year. Starting this way doesn't make it bad or unacceptably elitist, just realistic and standards-bound. Remember, the WTO was once just the General Agreement on Tariffs and Trade, which resulted from a few developed nations colluding behind closed doors.

It won't be pretty at first, and it will strike many as closer to a Star Chamber proceeding than anything the UN might stomach, but it's better to start something real with someone you trust than to pretend we're all in this together when we're not. Along the way, mistakes will be made and more than a few nasty investigations will result, but also along the way terrorists will be killed and we'll be doing that much more to make sure that WMD device doesn't go off in Chicago someday, killing a million people and forever corrupting our political process. You may stay up nights worrying about the John-Ashcroft-after-next, but let me tell you, the guy we really need to fear is the Osama-bin-Laden-after-next, or the terrorist leader who cracks the code on how to use WMD and get away with it.

On this particular battlefield, it will smack of paternalism to let big ol' Core militaries simply walk into the Gap and do what they must. But show me a Gap state with a solid police system and I'll show you a place we won't be slipping into in the dead of night. In the end, I'm referring only to the most feeble or nonexistent Gap governments, or ones without effective control over major portions of their own national territories, like an Afghanistan, a Colombia, or a Democratic

Republic of Congo. We definitely want Gap states to age out of their condition and, by doing so, integrate themselves into the Core's police and military networks. But that will be a serious fitness test to pass, just as it takes some real effort to join the WTO or NATO. Until then, the Core nations owe the citizens of the Gap some adult supervision.

The first order of business for the WCTO, which might logically be sponsored by the G-8 (as it expands into a real G-20), should be to establish legal guidelines and physical infrastructure for the handling and disposition of those who aren't considered legal combatants under the standard rules of war. So it'll need its own Alcatraz, and no, it can't be at some remote U.S. naval base.

As for the trials, prisoners will need to be funneled toward the International Criminal Court, which is perfect for this sort of thing. But again, the United States, plus the Core group as a whole, would need to reach some direct *modus vivendi* with the court, and if that didn't work, the group would simply need to set up its own. But my guess is that the ICC would jump at the chance to be accredited in this additional manner, because so long as the United States considers it more of a threat to its rule making than a venue for rule sharing with the rest of the Core, the ICC will remain vastly underutilized. And no, that wouldn't get us in bed uncomfortably with the UN, because the ICC is independent of the UN.

All this will sound risky at first, but either we can wait on some UN universal declaration full of noble nouns and awe-inspiring adjectives or we can let the troops who walk the beat inside the Gap get started building the case law that, eventually, some upstanding ICC Perry Mason can throw at the bin Ladens and al-Zarqawis when they stand in the docket at The Hague. Until then, I will continue to advocate letting our Dirty Harry (Special Operations Command) do its thing inside the Gap with minimal international supervision, knowing as I do what risks are entailed in that process.

The global war on terrorism will either divide the Core or unite the Core further and enable its orderly expansion. There's just too much at stake here for America to win or lose this conflict on its own terms without that resolution having some lasting impact on Core unity. For if we succeed or fail too much in this endeavor, the outcome will be the same: the rest of the Core will be spooked. While most of the Core's powers appear to have leaders who understand the nonzero outcome of a war against terrorism (namely, we all win), plenty of them still seem to believe that it's still largely a zero-sum competition among Core powers inside the Gap: a race for power, a race for energy, a race for markets, and so forth.

In sum, I don't believe this war's outcome can be neutral regarding the Core's future evolution. Help it or hurt it, there will inevitably be some turning point created. That's why I believe it's imperative for the future of globalization that America make the necessary effort to expand the definition of this war from that which most people in the world view as our singular obsession to something closer to a unifying security principle for the Core as a whole. Making globalization truly global is the only peace dividend worth considering in our long-term calculations of what will define a finishing line in this conflict. By starting this war, the United States set in motion a rule-set reset that cannot be reversed and certainly must not be abandoned by us—the system's sole military superpower—before its completion.

The rest of the Core is naturally looking to us for this road map, this blueprint. We now have no choice but to put it into action.

Chapter Three

GROWING THE CORE
BY SECURING
THE EAST

MORE THAN A FEW NEGATIVE reviews of *The Pentagon's New Map* complained that the map wasn't new—as in, "American military power has been involved in these Gap regions (especially the Middle East) for quite some time." It was an odd sort of critique, because, of course, my entire concept of the map began with the notion that this was a historical reality to which the Pentagon had adjusted poorly. The Defense Department spent the 1990s buying forces for the Big One against a "near-peer competitor," when 95 percent of our military activity around the world was concentrated in the Gap, where no legitimate near-peer would ever be found. So yes, the Gap portion of my map wasn't "new" (based as it was on historical data), just my admonition to the Pentagon that our strategic vision should center on the goal of shrinking it.

What *was* stunningly new about my Core-Gap map was those countries I included in the Core—namely, most of the former Soviet bloc (to include Russia) and the rising pillars known on Wall Street as "emerging markets" (most notably, China, India, Brazil). That wasn't just new, that was anathema to many strategic thinkers and force planners throughout the Defense Department. Why? So long as they could prioritize China as the big threat worth considering, each military service's plans for big-ticket items (e.g., aircraft, ships, weapons systems) could continue to be justified. But if the United States really committed itself to shrinking the Gap—say, by trying to transform the Middle East in one fell swoop—then the obligations of such an immense commitment would make it far harder for those arguing for expensive programs in budget battles to maintain that their preferred vision of future war (major conflict with China) should rule long-term planning inside the Pentagon, which exists—I remind you—almost solely to build tomorrow's force.

So what was both new and scary about the Core-Gap map was its potential to serve as a strategic rationale for altering the Pentagon's dominant vision of future war—to change *who owns the future*. In effect, this map shifts the military's planning focus from the much-fabled near-peer competitor to the so-called Arc of Instability, a widely used strategic concept whose original focus on the Muslim Middle East has now been expanded to the point of including the entire Gap. How do I know this? I get e-mails every week from officers all over the U.S. military who now employ the Core-Gap terminology openly in their scholarly articles and policy-planning documents (always attached for my perusal and comments).

This paradigm shift is crucial in two ways: (1) it facilitates the "transformation of transformation" by emphasizing the needs of the underfunded and undermanned SysAdmin force over that of the Leviathan; and (2) it moves China (and Developing Asia in general) from the category of future great-power war to logical strategic alliance. Mind you, there are still plenty of Cold Warriors in the Pentagon who want their China and want her bad, and their arguments will resonate so long as America is unable to view "rising Asia" for what it really is: our fundamental Cold War peace dividend. Not some threat, not some competitor out to "get us" (we need each other economically more than ever), but our most important future strategic alliance, one that will define the global security order of the twenty-first century. You want to shrink the Gap? You want to end war as we know it? Then hold this thought in your head: The most important strategic security goal of the next decade is to create an Asian equivalent of NATO that locks America into long-term military alliances with not just Japan and a united Korea, but even more so with China and India (not one or the other but both!).

So far I've described the Pentagon worth creating, a U.S. national security establishment worth imagining, and much-needed, Core-wide rule sets on shrinking the Gap—both one-bad-state-at-a-time and one-bad-actor-at-a-time. I've also described the wars worth waging and how we must fight them better. Now comes the good part: the wars we will never have to fight *if we meet our moment,* demonstrating the courage and strategic foresight that history now demands from America.

Will it be easy? No. Several tough choices lie ahead, including one possibly catastrophic war on the Korean peninsula. But if we are up to this challenge, we will close a door on our bloody past that will never be opened again.

LOCKING IN CHINA AT TODAY'S PRICES

As we planned the first week of our lengthy adoption trip to China, my wife Vonne made a strong pitch for going a couple of days early so we could spend as much time as possible just *being there* before our official program began. In her mind, we weren't just tourists, we were pilgrims exploring our new homeland, and she wanted as much time as we could afford to explore this newly shared cultural heritage. From the moment we took baby Vonne Mei Ling Barnett into our arms on August 15, 2004, we became a hybrid Chinese-American family. Whether we wanted it or not, that is how we'd be viewed back in the States—a transracial family.

I personally welcomed this challenge on many levels. Sure, there'd be the challenge of the fourth child, the second daughter, and just plain going back to diapers. Then there would be the enormous challenges of adoption itself, and the reality that this child would never know her birth parents from Jiangxi, a largely agrarian province deep in China's interior. But what intrigued me most was simply having my definitions of *mine* and *theirs* so radically altered. *Mine* is fair-skinned, blue-eyed, and big-nosed, but *theirs* is none of those things, meaning this brown-eyed girl would never quite fit in our family on appearances alone.

No, we'd need to make a choice. We'd need to commit ourselves to a new, bigger definition of *us*. We'd need to discard some ancient fears and locate some new hopes, understanding that our pathway would change no less than hers.

And we'd need to understand that there was no going back on this decision, that once forged, this clasp of civilizations would be made permanent. Embrace the child, embrace the culture, embrace the future—all in one fell swoop.

Sounds frightening, doesn't it?

Well, it is, but in the best sort of way, and in the *same* sort of way that America has always challenged itself in the past, building its multihued society through the progressive embrace of cultures the world over. Now when I look into the faces of my children, I see my future, I see their future, I see the world's future.

And I will admit, this makes for a different strategist and a different *me,* but the vision remains the same: connectivity challenges and connectivity changes, but *connectivity rules!*

Having already established a contact at Beijing University with a professor who was eager to see my book published there, I e-mailed him about the possibility of giving a lecture or two at various venues. The professor, Niu Ke, jumped at the chance and set them up through a superior of his, Yu Keping, the director of the university's Center for Chinese Government Innovations, but someone better known within senior circles as a leading thinker on China's future evolution. I ended up lecturing at both Beijing University and the China Reform Forum, the think tank of the Central Party School in Beijing. Both talks were warmly received and elicited a lot of spirited discussion regarding China's "rise."

Our hosts entertained us lavishly in return for the two talks, grateful as they were that I would take time out on this very important personal trip to address their groups. I was in turn very grateful for their interest in my work, which they described as unique in its progressive call for bilateral security cooperation between China and the United States. What did they mean by that? Other U.S. experts had called for strategic partnership with China in the past, but always as part of some argument for a larger danger to be prevented, such as growing Soviet influence in Asia during the Cold War. What the Beijing reformist researchers liked about my vision was that it naturally assumed a confluence of strategic interests between China and the United States regarding a future worth creating, not one that needed avoiding. As many of them had been educated in the United States, this made perfect sense to them, for they now saw China rapidly covering the same developmental territory the United States had covered in decades past, and were wary that so many security experts in America could see only danger in this pathway and not the opportunity for cooperation.

Along these lines, several of my hosts declared my vision too optimistic for the U.S. defense establishment, which, like their own military's culture, preferred to concentrate on worst-case scenarios. It's true. By focusing on the next peace instead of the last war, my Core-Gap vision is an easier sell in boardrooms than in command posts. It's just that I see a natural link between these two worlds, a military-market nexus that cannot be ignored in either China's rise or globalization's historic advance.

One Chinese professor went so far as to say that since my work could never be received very well in America but would naturally be understood in China, I should quit my job with the U.S. Government and come there to engage in the formulation of grand strategy for the Chinese, who, he noted, had more than enough grand strategic issues to deal with right now! I had to laugh, but he was right. There isn't a country on the planet right now with more strategic dilemmas than

China, which, through the person of President and Communist Party Chairman Hu Jintao, has tried to allay global fears regarding the same by proposing the Theory of Peacefully Rising China. The theory states simply that China's emergence as a real great power on the global scene need not lead to tension or antagonism with the West but rather should generate new and unprecedented possibilities for multilateral cooperation among the world's major powers.

My reply to this intriguing offer was to say that if these reformers felt they had their hands full explaining the Theory of Peacefully Rising China to the world, imagine how busy I was trying to explain my own Theory of Benevolently Warring America! That got a big laugh, but a knowing one as well. China's entire history is a strange mix of integrating wars and divisive periods of peace, so the Chinese are no strangers to the competing dynamics that globalization forces upon the planet as a whole. In many ways, the Chinese feel that they've undergone many Core-Gap wars over the years, as empire after empire sought to impose a larger, unifying vision for their vast civilization—this great but rather uneven collection of nations. I like to describe the United States as the world's longest-running successful multinational economic and political union, but I could likewise describe China as the world's longest-running unsuccessful multinational economic and political union. Whereas the United States enjoys one of the world's highest standards of living and serves as the source code for this era's spreading globalization, China is just now beginning to reclaim some of the economic power it once wielded, as it finds itself having to adjust to an American-defined model of international economic and political relations.

It is no secret that in a generation's time China's influence over the global economy will rival America's, so it requires no great leap of logic for any strategist to realize that China and America are destined to enjoy a deep strategic partnership if globalization is to continue its historical expansion across the twenty-first century. This is not a choice but a reality, for to avoid this outcome is to prevent a future in which all of humanity would benefit from globalization's promise. Few historic ends will ever come close to justifying such a wide array of means as the strategic partnership of the United States and China in coming decades. In this century, this partnership will define global stability just as much as the U.S.-British strategic partnership of the twentieth century did. It will be that important in its execution, that precious in its bond, that profound in its reach. The blueprint for global peace will be a joint Sino-American document. There is no alternative.

China will become as important to the East as America is to the West. Its values will come to define the East much as America's have come—for both good and ill—to define the West. America achieved its current stature by learning to fight way above its weight class and maintain that capacity for decades on end. China, in contrast, will achieve similar influence simply by finally fighting at its weight class, after several centuries of severe underperformance as an economic power. The sight of such rising power has and will naturally generate much fear in the West, but this fear is misguided. We face an unprecedented historical opportunity here to *raise* China peacefully within globalization's Functioning Core, primarily in response to the country's own clear desire to rise peacefully.

Absent 9/11, it's quite likely the United States would have gone down a far different path with China, especially with a Bush Administration committed to countering what it saw as its rising threat. But with 9/11 and the resulting global war on terrorism, that inevitable conflict was temporarily called off, a profound strategic pause of perhaps a decade or more, and that is more than enough time to lock in a strategic partnership between these two great powers and, by doing so, secure globalization's long-term stability in a way that nothing else can. This is probably the most compelling argument for viewing 9/11 as a gift from history.

It is hard for most Americans to comprehend just how big China really is: similar landmass to our own, but more than four times the population. Imagine a United States in which everyone from the entire Western Hemisphere (close to 900 million), *plus* the entire European Union (approaching 400 million), was crowded together in much the same pattern we have today, with the bulk of our population clustered on the two coasts and the middle sparsely populated. That is what 1.3 billion people would feel like in our *nation-state,* a term that often feels too small for what China encompasses. And it really is.

Travel around China and you'll quickly discover, as my wife Vonne and I did, that it's an aggregation of something far larger than what most people would readily identify as a mere nation-state. It's really closer to a vast collection of cultures in the same way you can talk about European civilization, the Slavic peoples, or the Arab world. There really is no such thing as "Chinese," whether you're talking a specific language or a specific culture. There are a host of languages, cultures, and distinct peoples all united under the concept of "China." That reality has long been both China's promise and its peril, for its entire political history has been defined by the pervasive fear among its leadership—as well as its people—that China's potential disintegration is always right around the corner.

America suffered a similarly disorienting fear in the decades running up to its one great civil war (1861–65), but most of China's history has been one long repeating cycle of such violently disintegrating and integrating forces. Following our Civil War, *these* United States became *the* United States, but China never quite managed that sense of unitary purpose despite regularly achieving a unitary state, as it did most recently under Communist rule. Even today, China's impressively globalizing economy is divided between an outwardly integrating collection of highly populated coastal provinces and an inwardly disintegrating collection of sparsely populated interior provinces. In many ways, China's emergence is not a threat *to* globalization as much as exemplifying the threat *of* globalization, or the danger of conflict between a Core that races ahead and a Gap that is left behind.

What we need to remember with China is that its past experiences of opening up to the world outside have not been particularly pleasant (China has endured its share of European colonialism) and that it has enjoyed its greatest periods of integrating peace when it withdrew from the world in a most profound fashion (e.g., Ming and Qing dynasties). So for China to modernize while opening up to the global economy pretty much goes against its entire history. The Theory of

Peacefully Rising China is less the country's promise to the world that it will refrain from the aggressive use of power as it is a request that the rest of the world do the same. In short, the government that is most intimidated by China's emergence sits in Beijing.

Then why, you might ask, does China's leadership cling so stubbornly to authoritarian rule and encourage—none too subtly—the growth of Chinese nationalism among the young? In both instances, these are not the strategies of a confident ruling elite but of a rather nervous one. China's leaders want the population to keep a bit of a chip on their shoulder concerning the world, because in steering their ambitions and demands in the direction of "what the world owes China" in matters of trade and security (especially with Taiwan), they hope to delay for as long as possible the inevitable conversation regarding "what China owes its own people" in political reforms. Is this a fantasy of self-delusion on the part of China's ruling Communist Party? Sure. But remember, governments facing huge agendas of internal economic development and integration naturally put off difficult and potentially divisive political issues. If you don't believe me, then just reread the history of the United States prior to the Civil War.

China's agenda regarding internal economic development and integration is so vast that it's almost impossible to get your arms around it mentally. In the last quarter-century (1980–2005), China has covered much of the same ground of industrial revolution as the United States took close to three-quarters of a century to cover (1875–1950), including the massive urbanization of the country and all that process entails. This is why China, while accounting for roughly 20 percent of the world's population, somehow demands 40 percent of the world's cement and close to 30 percent of the world's steel production. Visit any of China's major cities and you will see skylines that not only rival Manhattan's but routinely surpass it in both sheer size and architectural variety. Guangzhou's skyline in southern China, for example, is as big as any you will find in America, and virtually all of it was built in the past fifteen years.

China's internal integration process, meaning how its many provinces come together economically and politically over time, will *dwarf* its external integration process, meaning how it links up with the global economy, for quite some time still. In terms of America's own history of internal integration, China is logically located in the latter years of our nineteenth century, when rapid advances in transportation networks and communications knit our country together as it had never been before. Moving through history as fast as it is, China is rapidly approaching the same tipping point that America reached in the early years of the twentieth century, when we chose to break out our "big stick," even as we sought to "speak softly."

This is a hard notion to convey, because in many sectors, China seems so much closer in time to today's America. For example, its space program places it somewhere in the mid-1960s, whereas its lushly romantic film industry reminds one of Hollywood's classic 1930s period. In sports, China's emergence on the Olympic stage comes closer to America in the 1950s, but in terms of a burgeoning sexual revolution, China's youth approach American sensibilities of the 1970s. China's construction and stock market booms look suspiciously like America in the 1920s, while its push for high-tech industry places it closer to our 1980s. The country's often brutal labor conditions are reminiscent of our 1910s, right down to the routinely violent protests, whereas the huge social changes associated with the massive influx of female labor into industry recalls 1940s America. China's go-go capitalism is as frantic as our own was in the 1990s, but the monopolistic nature of so much of that activity is right out of turn-of-the-nineteenth-century America, with its robber barons and pervasive corruption.

And it is precisely this temporal incoherence that makes China so dynamic and a little scary right now. Like any mature society, life in China is organized around rules, both explicit (what passes for laws) and implicit (an ancient culture). But as in any country undergoing a whole lot of change at once, China's rule sets—meaning those collections of rules by which both current activities *and* popular expectations of the future are managed—are significantly out of whack with one another, as in, "too many of some rules and not enough of others." In sum, China's wildly proliferating economic rule sets have raced ahead of the political system's ability to manage them, while the country's technological rule sets have leapfrogged its corresponding ones in security. China is simply integrating internally at an economic pace that's unmatched by a similar political process, while it's wiring itself up to the global economy to a degree far beyond the country's military cooperation with the world at large—especially superpower America. It's those disparities, or rule-set gaps, that really scare experts the world over. It's not so much the opacity of China's leadership process that's disturbing as the sense of its general impotence—that feeling that no one's in charge in a country that's run under the assumption that someone really is.

China's Communist Party is not really in control of much that matters inside the country today. By maintaining significant control over political expression, it pretends that it's actually running China's economic development, which, quite frankly, is so vast that it's beyond anyone's capacity to manage at this point. Imagine a basketball game where the referees' only authority is to prevent players from cursing at one another but virtually anything else is fair play. That's about as close as the Communist Party comes to running this nonstop game called modernization. So to call China's current political system authoritarian gets to be awfully misleading, because so much of economic life there is brutally rapacious and freewheeling. It is a single-party state and, like many states that pursue rapid economic development under these political conditions, this, too, will eventually pass into something more pluralistic, first within the Communist Party itself and then beyond it. And this will happen by 2025.

The world has reached a similar moment with China in terms of its skyrocketing external integration with global markets; we've long since passed the time in which anyone can really steer this process. This is why current descriptions of China's emergence, economy, and so forth evoke a runaway locomotive: it's no longer a question of stopping anything but rather simply trying to slow things down to a more manageable pace. The danger, of course, is that the mismatch of connectivity and security rule sets can easily lead military leaders on both sides to contemplate visions of future confrontation and even conflict that would have the same sort of disastrous impact on the global economy as World War I did on the European-dominated globalization of a century ago, possibly even triggering globalization's temporary demise. Experts back then such as Norman Angell who described great-power war as unthinkably self-destructive given all that economic interdependency *weren't wrong,* they were simply ignored, and vast economic empires collapsed as a result. Are we capable of such myopic vision and strategic stupidity today? Based on my years of working with the Pentagon and my readings of Chinese military thought, I'd have to say: Absolutely. America finds no shorter pathway to second-tier-power status than to engage China in war. For China's Communist Party, there is no surer method of committing political suicide.

China is essentially running a series of races with itself, hoping that nothing too important breaks or drops off this runaway engine. The country's many simultaneous revolutions mirror the process of globalization's tumultuous advance into any underdeveloped country or region.

First, there's the revolutionary shift from agricultural to industrial, which tears up traditional rural social structures and replaces them with the isolating and disorienting uniformity of urban life. Right now one of the greatest migrations in human history is occurring *within* China, as millions upon millions of youth leave the countryside and head for the city. How much pressure will that bring for political change over time? By latest estimates, China will become a majority urban population in a little over a decade, roughly a century after the United States hit the same tipping point. Did America witness dramatic political change in the subsequent years? You bet. Most of what we know today as our government's modern regulatory infrastructure arose in the 1920s and 1930s, as our system of governance experienced a virtual revolution in both its scope and its power.

Second, there's the revolution of moving from centralized economic planning (the "dead hand") to free markets (the "hidden hand"), which naturally favors the more aggressive portions of society over the more passive. As such, China is currently awash in corruption and counterfeiting of all sorts. For example, when Vonne and I traveled to China to adopt Vonne Mei, we were required to bring all our fee and donation money (several thousand dollars) in brand-new, noncirculated U.S. bills. Why? There is so much counterfeit paper money in China today (there are reliable estimates of one-third) that anything less will be rejected by banks and currency exchanges.

Over time, such gross inefficiencies will be rooted out by the system as new rules and legal institutions arise to squash these negative activities. For now, the Party allows a certain amount of muckraking journalism and popular literature to push this agenda, but eventually the public will demand something far more organized and transparent, if only because China's development will make people there more concerned with protecting their newfound wealth from fraud. But so long as China features several hundred million people living in real poverty, expect the economy to play fast and loose with such rules. How far back do you have to go in American history to find a similar disregard for legalities? To roughly the "rising America" period following the Civil War, when a big chunk of our paper money was likewise counterfeit and American "inventors" routinely stole new technologies from European rivals.

The third great revolution going on involves moving from top-down political authoritarianism to the first stirrings of bottom-up pluralism and grassroots activism. The boom areas of local political activism in China tend to focus on the most prosaic, everyday concerns, such as the rights of homeowners, medical patients (especially those who are HIV-positive), laid-off workers, and peasants forced off their lands by developers. Probably the most impressive change has occurred in grassroots environmentalism, where activists have mobilized to the point where the government has actually shut down or halted certain large-scale power-generation projects (including some connected with the Three Gorges Dam) largely in response to these protests.

Fourth, there's the unprecedented shift from central political control in Beijing to stronger forms of provincial government, to include the rise of a regional trade bloc (again) *within* China (there are, population-wise, potentially several EUs *inside* China). How could this occur in a political system so obsessed with central control? In the early 1990s, China overhauled its tax code, giving these provinces more control over their own finances while simultaneously increasing Beijing's confidence that it would get its cut of the take. This rule-set reset has allowed provincial governments to pursue economic integration with one another that, in the words of one Chinese economist, "was unimaginable 10 years ago, both in the terms of the politics and economics."

Fifth, there's the revolutionary passage from being a society largely disconnected from the outside world to one that is rapidly networking with the global economy and encountering all the influences such connectivity brings. What's so odd about all this is how the outside world tends to be so critical about China not changing itself fast enough! For example, China goes from having virtually no one on the Internet ten years ago to having more than 100 million today, but many experts in the West only want to highlight how the government seeks to censor certain politically sensitive sites. Tell me, which process seems more profound: the growth in connectivity or the government's pathetic fear-threat reaction? Which one would you care to bet on winning over the long haul? And if Western information technology companies implicitly collude in these censorship efforts by selling such technology to the government, does that seem a reasonable price to pay for the resulting connectivity? Or must such connectivity only come about under the same conditions of freedom of speech that we enjoy in the West?

My favorite recent example of this futile censorship phenomenon was when American pop star Britney Spears began a concert tour in China. Yes, the Chinese Ministry of Culture approved her tour, but only on the condition that it could inspect all her stage outfits beforehand to make sure none were excessively revealing of her anatomy. Again, guess which side will win that censorship struggle in the end?

Finally, China is experiencing a demographic revolution more rapid than anything ever experienced in the history of mankind. No single society has ever aged more quickly than China will in the coming decades, thanks in no small measure to its one-child policy, designed to restrict population growth. This policy has been enormously successful, trimming probably 400 million (again, an entire EU in size) from China's current population total of 1.3 billion. Of course, this policy has led to a stunning gender imbalance within society, as families expressing a strong preference for males have led, through international adoptions and widespread sex selection by abortion, to a youth population that is abnormally skewed in sex ratio. The notion that China will be awash in males unable to find mates (upwards of 40 million) has led some demographers in the West to posit great social instability in coming years, possibly tilting the country toward military confrontation with the West as China seeks to burn off all those "excess males."

The problem with this theory, however, is that it tends to ignore the rapid aging of the population, or what ordinary Chinese call the "4-2-1 problem," as in, *one* child to support *two* aging parents and *four* elderly grandparents. Get the feeling all those elders are going to casually send off their sole meal ticket to die in combat? And as for being unable to marry, let's get real on that one. With China opening up so much in terms of overseas tourism, both inward and outward (as many as 100 million Chinese are expected to travel abroad each year by 2020), I think it's fair to say that these "little emperors," as single-child sons are often derisively known, can certainly find *someone* to marry. Sure, the bride may not be Chinese (or maybe just not China-born), but that'll just be the choice these young men must make, now, won't it? After all, think of all the tens of thousands of Chinese females growing up in the West thanks to all those overseas adoptions. They too will be making similar choices, one way or the other.

And as the father of a future Chinese-American woman who may well someday hope to marry, I guess I'd like to think that globalization could likewise accommodate her desired choice without triggering great-power war. As for *my* desired choice . . . no promises!

All these revolutions propel China through history at a pace no other country has ever achieved. Inside the Pentagon, strategists view this process with alarm, asking, Will China get rich before it gets threatening? When the real question is the obverse: Will China get old before it gets rich? Guess which one of those three possibilities (rich, threatening, old) is predetermined? The aging, of course. The only way China can get rich before it gets old is to conduct an ambitious transaction strategy with the outside world: hoping all that trade and foreign investment will keep the economy flush enough to tamp down social unrest (especially among the rural poor and urban labor who remain underemployed in state-run enterprises) while building up private-sector industries that will be competitive abroad but ultimately sustained by a huge domestic market of consumers brought along by the development process. What does China offer the global economy in return? Besides the increasingly friendly investment climate, it offers a seemingly unlimited supply of cheap labor that has a deflationary impact on global prices, plus that rising pool of consumers. Anything that kills that economic connectivity threatens China's ambitious development process while simultaneously damaging the global economy.

China's long-term gamble is that it can keep all these trade and investment transactions going at an ever-increasing rate, in effect getting the Old Core to fund its development on the backs of all that cheap labor. But it's an amazing experiment, historically speaking, because China must progressively sync up its internal economic rule sets with that of the global economy, otherwise it could just as easily lose its status as the world's number-one target for foreign direct investment, a title it just snatched away from the United States. China clearly attracts the world's investments based on a sense of its potential for long-term growth, but its track record remains a short one, and the gaps between its various rule sets remain profound. It is hard to imagine a greater disparity: the world's biggest target of foreign direct investment (economic rule set) and one of the world's least pluralistic political systems in terms of elite decision making (political rule set). But here's the scarier one: the global economy's most connected manufacturing powerhouse (technology rule set) and the great power most likely to go to war with the world's dominant military superpower (security rule set).

It's hard to imagine, in many ways, a period in which the global economy has been more dependent on the stability of a single country so potentially at risk of great instability. Economists like to argue that the most important individual player in the global economy is the aggressive American consumer, but I think it's actually the passive Chinese peasant. In short, what's good for the Chinese peasant (i.e., keeping him or her politically quiet) is good for the American economy, and what's good for the American economy is good for globalization. Can it get any more connected than that?

China's rising influence in the global economy is often described as "the China price," otherwise known as the "three scariest words" in global manufacturing. It basically refers to the notion that anything you can build, China can build cheaper—or roughly one-third off your best price. And I'm talking damn near anything, from furniture to computers, textiles to animated films. If there's a substantial amount of labor costs factored into the final price, China's going to beat your number hands down and there's nothing you can do about it.

The China price has been an eye-opener for some American economists who have long asserted that globalization was always a good thing for our economy. But the surging protectionist sentiment of some of these experts strikes me as rather disingenuous. After all, our position throughout the Cold War was that the East should eventually abandon Communism and join our capitalist world economy. Well, the East did, and by doing so it effectively doubled the global labor supply—seemingly overnight. To say that this turn of events puts the American economy at a "dangerous" disadvantage overshoots the strategic mark. Sure, American workers were better off when they didn't have to compete against the Chinese, but who wants to go back to some Cold War–like standoff to achieve that sort of "security"?

I mean, come on! You're reading a book by a former expert on the former Soviet Union! And yeah, eventually I got over it and found another career.

As globalization unfolds, workers everywhere simply have to accept a modicum of economic *insecurity* (otherwise known as competition) in exchange for heightened global security. There ain't no such thing as a free lunch!

Whenever the United States starts making arguments about globalization's harmful effects, I am reminded of how we got to the point where we can't automatically win the gold medal in basketball at the Olympics anymore. Remember how we used to field our best college players against the state-sponsored teams put out by the Soviets and other socialist-bloc countries, and we'd complain that it was our "true amateurs" against their "professionals"? So in the late 1980s we decided to let professional players from the National Basketball Association participate in the Olympics and—at first—we reestablished our dominance with ease. The problem was that globalization was changing the makeup of the NBA at roughly the same time, leading to a huge influx of foreign players, especially from formerly socialist-bloc nations. Over time, the NBA became effectively globalized, meaning those professional players could go back and play on their home countries' Olympic teams. As a result, it once again became hard for the United States to win a gold medal. My point is a simple one: once the other teams agree to play by roughly the same rules, you can't start complaining about the competition.

The reality is, of course, that China's rock-bottom labor prices will eventually rise, as they have in every other economy that has developed throughout history. No economy has an endless supply of cheap labor, meaning workers who don't expect their standard of living to get better over time. If that were the case, then Karl Marx's criticisms of capitalism would have been correct. But already we're seeing the unbelievable emerge in China: pockets of labor shortages for key factory demographics—namely, young females just off the farm and willing to work for almost nothing in terrible labor conditions. China's rapid development has meant that, even for this labor category, better work options already exist within the Chinese economy, forcing one of two outcomes on Chinese manufacturing businesses: either raise wages to attract the labor or move the production out of the country to some cheaper locale. We're already seeing the latter occur, as certain automobile assembly factories have left China for neighboring Malaysia. Instances of the former are likewise only a matter of time.

Having noted that long-term inevitability, the near-term reality remains that manufacturing superpower China's rising demand for raw materials is reshaping commodity markets the world over, or what some economists call the "China Syndrome." So while China might replace much of Southeast Asia's economic capacity in manufacturing within the global economy, the upside is that these same economies' exports of raw materials and other manufacturing inputs are automatically redirected toward China's insatiable demand for imports. In this spillover effect, China's reach is both long and varied. For example, China's demand for minerals has boosted not only South Africa's mining industry but also its entire related transportation infrastructure as a result. Likewise, it's not just commodity producers that gain, but high-end industrial exporters like Japan, which owed roughly 80 percent of its export growth in 2003 to China's market alone. China's demand for metal is so strong that it's actually helping to clean up the old Soviet Union, as scrap metal exports from former Soviet states are helping those countries dismantle and clean up rusting factories still sitting around from the socialist past.

Naturally, when China revives a country's key industry—say, like Brazil's steel industry—you can expect warmer political and security relations between the two states. Does that make China a military threat to the United States? No, it makes China a strong economic competitor of the United States', and that competition naturally reshapes the political-military landscape across the world. Hey, it works for them just as it's always worked for us. Again, unless you absolutely want a return to the antagonistic ideologies of the Cold War, stop complaining! Anyway, the old-line manufacturing sector in the United States is hardly missing out on this deal, as companies like Alcoa, the world's largest aluminum manufacturer, and General Motors, one of the world's largest automakers, are likewise seeing more and more of their profits emanate from Asia—China in particular. GM, for example, expects to make more money in Asia in 2005 than in North America. So apparently, what's good for China is good for GM, and what's good for . . . oh, you know the rest.

What's most amazing about China's rise from its socialist ashes is how it is affecting a sort of reverse domino effect throughout Asia.

You remember the original version: China goes Communist in 1949 and we subsequently fight long and hard in Vietnam to make sure that "loss" doesn't set off a domino effect throughout the region, turning every regime there into a Communist knockoff of the original. Well, today China is having exactly the opposite impact: turning everyone in Asia more capitalistic. As running dogs of capitalism go, China's a greyhound. The members of the Association of Southeast Asian Nations are contemplating an aggressive shift toward deeper economic integration largely out of fear that if they don't, each will be sucked up individually by China's powerful undertow. China's insatiable demand for raw materials is pulling previously isolated and largely socialist economies such as Mongolia and Laos out of their economic doldrums, while pushing Communist mainstay Vietnam to pursue both outsourcing and membership in the World Trade Organization vigorously, lest it suffer too much competition from China. How's that for reversing the flow of history?

But that reversing effect extends most of all to China itself: the more it seeks connectivity with the capitalist global economy, the more capitalist it must become to increase that transaction rate (i.e., the sheer volume of trade and technology transfer). So if China wants lots of foreign investment flows, it also has to be able to withstand business accounting scandals, stock market shocks, and the regulatory spotlight of the global investment community in general. Moreover, if a private-sector company is big enough so that its financial collapse could hurt the overall investment climate, then China has to be ready to offer a bailout package (something it just did for the first time in its history). Sure, I bet that's enough to send Chairman Mao spinning in his crystal sarcophagus, but that's "the globalization price," three of the scariest words in the Chinese Communist Party.

For every sliver of economic connectivity with the outside world, China is forced to accept more externally imposed rule sets, and over time this process significantly limits what the Party controls while expanding that which the Party only *wishes* it could control. If China wants to gain "market status" in the WTO because its current non-market status means it keeps losing rulings there, then it has to allow a host of profound changes, such as letting global retailers such as Wal-Mart and direct marketers like Avon enter its marketplace. If China wants help in reducing its roughly half a trillion dollars of nonperforming bank loans, then it has to let foreign players enter its market and purchase ownership in local financial institutions (something Goldman Sachs just did). And if China wants to continue enjoying a large trade deficit with the United States, then once it has filled up its currency reserves and flooded both the U.S. Treasury market and the U.S. secondary mortgage market with the excess flow, it invariably needs to start purchasing U.S. companies. This acquisition strategy, in turn, vastly benefits a Chinese private sector that faces a shortfall of seventy-five thousand capable senior executives over the next ten to fifteen years, because what China really needs, almost as much as the companies' material assets, is their senior managerial talent. And so America needs to ask itself, when Chinese companies, abetted by their government, seek to acquire such U.S. icons as Maytag and UNOCAL, whether or not we achieve more security vis-à-vis China by encouraging this flow of human capital or by blocking these attempts and, by doing so, triggering a protectionist response from China at this point in its rapid embrace of both capitalism and globalization. So while not everyone is ready to call China a market economy, it's getting awfully hard to find anyone who will call it a Communist one, and that's the globalization price.

If those are the prices paid for China's economic integration into the Core, then what are the prices to be paid for China's political-military integration? If the Old Core isn't working this deal vigorously, then we will have no one to blame but ourselves if those huge gaps in China's rule sets ultimately send it—and the global economy—down some scary pathway toward disintegration. I get asked a lot by American audiences what I consider to be the scariest security scenario out there in the global economy today, and my answer is always the same: something that causes China to withdraw from the world in ways similar to America's disastrous bout of isolationism in the 1920s and 1930s. We don't just need China to behave well in coming years (meaning *not* doing something stupid), we need China to emerge as a sophisticated administrator of global security—in all its forms—just as the United States has been in the decades since World War II, when we managed to resurrect globalization from the ashes of two great global conflagrations and guide its survival through half a century of catastrophic threat (World War III).

When foreign policy experts say America "can't go it alone," they're right. But when they assert that the West's unity alone guarantees global stability, they're kidding themselves. China's leaders are already smart enough to realize how much they depend on America to secure global stability—and thus their economic and political well-being. What's missing right now is similar understanding among our leaders that America depends equally on China for the same. Even more scary is how dimly aware China's leaders appear to be of this burgeoning strategic codependency.

Simply put, China's political connectivity with the outside world has not kept pace with its economic connectivity, and its security connectivity is—quite frankly—virtually nonexistent compared with its growing technological connectivity. China takes from the world but does not yet know what it should give back to that larger community. The Old Core grows ever more interdependent with China in both economics and technology, and yet we remain fundamentally disconnected in both diplomacy and security. America's relationship with China is schizophrenic at best—as in, "China, can't live with her (security), can't live without her (economics)."

If the United States is committed to winning a global war on terrorism by defending globalization's progressive envelopment of the planet, then our blueprint for action must obviously list somewhere near the top the following task: locking China in at today's prices. By that I mean securing a long-term strategic partnership with China on security affairs *now*, while Beijing's prices remain relatively low, rather than putting off the inevitable for another twenty years only to pay through the nose at some later date. Right now we know what China's price is: our defense guarantee on Taiwan and our acceptance of their growing security clout in the region. If Taiwan chooses to force the issue of independence, it could easily torpedo the most important strategic relationship America has right now. The straits remains the one potential military flash point that can still ignite East Asia and send this whole global economy up in flames in a heartbeat. China is the baby we can't throw out with the bathwater dubbed the global war on terrorism. If we *lose* China (again), we might just kill globalization, and if that happens, it won't just be a matter of what historians write a hundred years from now—we'll spend the rest of our days wondering whether we destroyed the planet's best hope for ending war as we know it.

To understand China's position on Taiwan today, you have to remember what it was like for the United States back in the early years of the twentieth century: Here we were, this burgeoning economic powerhouse with a rising-yet-still-relatively-small military package (you remember Teddy Roosevelt's "Speak softly and carry a big stick"), and all the old-school powers worried about us as an up-and-coming threat. While the European-defined form of globalization predominated at that time, our upstart version ("We don't need no stinkin' empire!") would come to dominate the landscape by the century's midpoint, primarily because Europe decided to self-destruct all their empires via two world wars that now—in retrospect—look like the European Union's versions of the American Civil War.

China is the United States of the early twenty-first century: rising like crazy but not really a threat to anyone except small island nations off its coast (think T.R. and his Rough Riders). China's so-called fourth-generation leaders have tried to calm global fears by emphasizing the Peacefully Rising China concept, but frankly, few of the Republican right wing are buying this. Why? The Far Right is still gunning for China ("Once a Commie, always a Commie!"), and precious Taiwan is China's San Juan Hill. Richard Nixon burned Taiwan's ass back in the early seventies when he effectively switched official recognition to the mainland, so the price the island demanded was the continued "defense guarantee" that said we'd always arm Taiwan to the teeth and rush to its rescue whenever China unleashed its million-man-swim of an invasion.

That promise is still on the books (yes, it's actually written down), like some blue law from a bygone era. Does anyone seriously think we'd sacrifice tens of thousands of American troops to stop China from reabsorbing Taiwan? Britain signed Hong Kong away, as Portugal did with Macao, but somehow America is going to the mattresses on Taiwan in this day and age? Tell me what we get with this principled stand? To say we're standing up to a "Communist" threat with China gets awfully far-fetched as time passes, as does the claim that Taiwan is a lone bastion of democracy in Asia. So even though the rest of Asia, including Japan, is being rapidly sucked into China's economic orbit, somehow the sacredness of Taiwan's self-perceived "independence" from China is worth torching the global economy over? To me, that's the Old Core cutting off its nose to spite its face.

Here's the weirdest part of that potential conflict scenario: China's been clearly signaling for years that it's perfectly willing to accept the status quo—*just so long as Taiwan makes no moves to rule out permanently the possibility of reunification!* That's it! China has basically guaranteed Taiwan's continued existence so long as Taipei's government maintains the appearance of remaining open to the possibility of rejoining the mainland someday. You may ask, Is it fair of the United States to renege on this promise after so many years? Clearly, the international environment has changed, so China's desire to reunite with Taiwan no longer carries with it the stench of either Communist aggression or a "loss" for the West. In reality, China wouldn't treat Taiwan any differently from the way it has treated Hong Kong, because China's long-term economic agenda is more important than the useless political symbolism of cracking down on what would be yet another golden goose for attracting foreign direct investment to the mainland (something Taiwan is already doing). But again, China's not even demanding Taiwan's return, just its continued abstinence from any act that suggests it is unwilling to consider political reunification at some point in the future. China is willing to let this issue ride so long as no one makes a move that seems to close the door on this scenario.

Think back to the U.S. Civil War. Imagine if Jefferson Davis and the leftovers of the Confederacy had slipped away to Cuba in 1865 to set up their alternative, nose-thumbing version of America on that island.

Then fast-forward to, say, 1905, and imagine how much the United States would have tolerated some distant imperial power like England telling us what we could or could not do vis-à-vis this "loser" sitting just off our shore. Imagine where Teddy Roosevelt would have told the Brits they could shove their advice—much less any defense guarantee.

That's the situation we face with China today. The Chinese have always considered Taiwan part of mainland China, and like much of China it was subject to periods of colonial rule, including half a century under the Japanese. Taiwan's status as the Republic of China was declared out of thin air by General Chiang Kai-shek, leader of the nationalist movement known as the Kuomintang, to mark that military force's last and final stand in its desperate retreat from the mainland following its defeat at the hands of Mao Zedong's Communist national liberation movement in the Chinese Civil War (1945–49). The United States supported the Kuomintang (just barely) in that war and long debated who was responsible inside our government for "losing" China to the Communist menace. As part of that guilt complex and our commitment to containing Communism's spread during the hottest part of the Cold War, we installed Taiwan in what would have been China's permanent seat on the UN Security Council. Later, when President Nixon switched our diplomatic recognition to China, Beijing was given Taiwan's seat, and America bought itself an even longer guilt trip regarding Taiwan's defense guarantee.

Did China complicate things with its in-Taiwan's-face "antisecession law" in the March 2005 National People's Congress session? Sure. But let's be clear on the motivations for that one, which involved internal politics far more than national security. Hu Jintao was simply buttressing his standing as the new head of the Central Military Commission, the crucial third "hat" he needed to add to his standing as both President of China and Chairman of the Chinese Communist Party to solidify his rule as others had before him. Hu had a hard time wringing that position from third-generation hard-liner Jiang Zemin, who held on to the post—in part—by starting a whispering campaign that said Hu was weak on Taiwan. So Hu throws down his marker first chance he gets in the March session, reminding us that even though China's a one-party state, there's no shortage of political infighting there.

Sure, I'd like to be able to tell you that America should defend Taiwan at all costs and use that issue to force good behavior from China over time, but frankly, that's not a tenable strategy for the long haul. That would be about as realistic as our having chosen Ireland over the United Kingdom on the issue of Northern Ireland. In a generation's time China will dominate the global economy just as much as the United States does today. The only way to stop that is to kill this era's version of globalization, and Taiwan is simply not worth that outcome. If Taipei is committed to starting a war with China, then it should do so on its own dime and on its own time, not by pulling America along for the ride or destroying globalization's Functioning Core in the process.

As Robert Wright has said, the first rule of trying to run the world is, Don't fight the inevitable. Taiwan will someday join China in a larger economic and—ultimately—political union, as will most of the smaller nations in Southeast Asia. Our strategic goal cannot be to stem such long-term integration in the region but must be to steer it. Taiwan shouldn't have to move in this direction any sooner than anyone else, but likewise it shouldn't possess the ability to throw a monkey wrench into the process in such a way as to make the United States the odd man out in the region, which is exactly what such a conflict with China would be likely to achieve. Remember my first (and only) rule of globalization: Connectivity rules!

This is not a back burner issue we can hope will eventually disappear on its own without any action of our part. Taiwan's increasingly nationalist government could easily shove this issue to the top of our president's in-box any day now. In the run-up to the December 2004 national elections, there was credible talk that if the nationalist party of President Chen Shui-bian had obtained a majority in the Taiwanese parliament, he would have pushed the legislature into doing something provocative like adding the word *Taiwan* in parentheses behind its official name, the Republic of China. That may not seem like much to us, but Beijing's reluctant hand might have been forced by this act.

Doesn't it seem crazy to leave the United States exposed on this issue while we're trying to transform the Middle East and fight a global war on terrorism? Again, how much of the global economy—much less our soldiers' lives—are we prepared to sacrifice just so Taiwan can rejoice in this moment of self-actualization? I think the answer should be none.

America needs to take its defense guarantee to Taiwan off the table, and do it now before some irrational politician in Taipei decides he's ready to start a war between two nuclear powers. Trust me, we'd be doing Taiwan a favor, because it's my guess that our defense guarantee would evaporate the moment any Taiwan Straits crisis actually boiled over, leaving Taipei severely embarrassed and Beijing feeling excessively emboldened. I say, let's lock in a strategic alliance with rising China at today's price, because that cost has nowhere to go but up over the coming years. Buying into this relationship now is like stealing Alaska from the czars for pennies on the dollar—it'll never be this cheap again.

China's rising nationalism is only natural, given its rising economic power. We can either assuage that powerful emotion, centered as it is on Taiwan (and occasionally Japan) or we can stoke it for all it's worth, keeping the possibility of great-power war in Asia on the agenda for the foreseeable future. We are not going to talk China out of this demand over time, and to try to do so would be a waste of time. The coming fifth and sixth generations of Chinese leadership were both educated—for the most part—in the United States (and if you think that doesn't matter, just wait a couple of decades and see what we'll lose by scaring away so many of the world's future leaders from our colleges in our post-9/11 paranoia). These coming generations of leaders, which will rule China from 2010 through roughly 2025, represent a serious strategic opportunity for the United States, perhaps our best opportunity for cementing a permanent transpacific bond such as we developed with Europe over the twentieth century. To sacrifice all that possibility over Taiwan's quest for permanent detachment from a feared Greater China would be a huge mistake.

Greater China is already well in the works in the economic realm. Nothing short of great-power war is going to stop that. Ultimately, the equivalent of Greater China will come into being in both the security and political realms, although it is likely to be described as an Asian Union, in the manner of the European Union. But make no mistake, these states will all be united at some point in the next several decades, and for that process to unfold in the best possible fashion, it needs a confident China able to describe a future Asian identity worth building. Beijing is already learning to speak such a language through its reabsorption of Hong Kong, and that process will ultimately change China more than it will Hong Kong. Taiwan could play a similarly positive role in the future integration of Asia, or a disastrously negative one.

Any shrink-the-Gap strategy, to be effective, must balance the long-term idealism of the goal with the short-term realism concerning its blueprint for action. There is no good reason why America should "lose" China for the second time, and there is little hope for a united Core shrinking the Gap if China is not a mainstay of that growing security alliance. On the question of Taiwan, the needs of the Core must outweigh the needs of the one. America needs military alliance with China that precludes any possibility of war between our two nations. There is no global future worth creating that does not feature this alliance as its centerpiece.

IN THE FUTURE, AMERICA'S MOST IMPORTANT ALLIES WILL BE NEW CORE STATES

One of the Bush Administration's major responses to the operational challenges of the global war on terrorism is its long-term plan to realign U.S. military bases around the world. As I noted in *The Pentagon's New Map,* the administration's plan basically corresponds to the geographic outline of the Gap—namely, it's all about moving bases closer to, and inside of, the Gap. When the book came out, I noticed that I immediately got a lot of requests for interviews on this subject from Asian journalists but none from European media.

I wasn't surprised, because the difference in the strategic security environment in the two regions is profound: Europe's massive "civil war" (stretching from 1914 to 1945) basically burned out that region on great-power war, yielding NATO and the EU as the long-term institutional expressions of that continent-wide desire to move beyond such warfare. When the Berlin Wall came down in 1989, both of these institutions headed east to consolidate the implied victory of the Cold War struggle and, as such, Old Europe is politically ready for America to move its military bases eastward.

But the same is not true for Asia, hence the many questions from the media there about "What does this all mean regarding America's future commitment to security in Asia?" The strategic sense of unease captured in that question is profound. No one in Europe is worried about anyone rising, but in Asia, not only do we find a "rising China" but a "rising India" to boot. Both countries feature major militaries of a million-plus troops, and both have a number of unresolved regional security issues. India, for example, almost went to war with Pakistan following the bombing on December 13, 2001, of the New Delhi parliament by Muslim Kashmiri separatists, while China went so far as firing off several missiles over Taiwan as recently as 1996 and has kept up the rhetorical heat on that issue ever since. Toss in the long-standing North Korean threat, separatist flare-ups in Indonesia, conflicting territorial claims by several players in the South China Sea, and an Islamic rebel force in the Philippines, and you have a mix that doesn't exactly scream out for a major reduction of U.S. ground troops in the region. And yet such a reduction is clearly in the works, as the global basing realignment process inevitably steals from Peter (East Asia) to pay Paul (Southwest Asia).

I don't disagree with the Bush Administration's push to realign bases from the Core to the Gap. In fact, I think it's a must if we're seriously going to pursue both the global war on terrorism and a shrink-the-Gap strategy over the long haul. When asked by a congressional commission on overseas basing to testify to that effect, I did so in late 2004. But I qualified my support for the Bush Administration's design by noting that decision makers in either Taipei or Pyongyang had it within their power to disrupt these plans, and that until the region found some permanent resolution on these security issues, this long-term realignment would remain at serious strategic risk.

The Achilles' heel of this strategic decision is a large one: we don't have a NATO in Asia, thus we need one to move beyond the regional security deficits inherited from the Cold War and toward the better future worth creating in this era. Absent such an institutional development, America will have a hard time disengaging militarily from East Asia and refocusing far more of its attention on Southwest Asia or the Middle East. That's why one of the most important items in any blueprint for action must be doing whatever it takes to get the New Core powers of Asia into a long-term security alliance with the United States.

A lot of Pentagon strategists continue to dismiss my labeling of Russia, India, and China as new allies, preferring to keep them all in the box labeled: KEEP A CLOSE EYE ON. Most of that is just habit from the Cold War, and some of it is sheer reluctance to make the effort, especially when so many long-range acquisitions plans would be better served by casting these nations—especially China—as a direct threat. Sticking with the Big One scenario would allow those Pentagon strategists who are reluctant to focus on postconflict stabilization and reconstruction operations to beg off any "lessons learned" from the Iraq occupation and stick to their preferred planning paradigm of big-time war with a big-time opponent. In fact, the most exciting prospect for hard-line geostrategists today is the notion that China and Russia—joined perhaps by India—will come together in a sort of anti-American military alliance. If we could just get that package, the Pentagon could simply write off the global war on terrorism (subcontracting it completely to Special Operations Command) and swear off regime change and nation building inside the Gap, and then we could all get back to what we know and love: World War III.

A comforting thought, no?

The logic of the balance-of-power enthusiasts (e.g., Zbigniew Brzezinski, Charles Krauthammer, Robert Kagan, William Kristol) on this score is odd indeed: expressing great reluctance to pursue strategic partnership with New Core powers (whose motives are always distrusted), they nonetheless express shocked amazement whenever there's the slightest evidence that these powers might—gasp!—actually go ahead and cooperate with one another *without* American permission, much less involvement. I mean, really! But quickly recovering, these same experts will argue that this was all so inevitable because the system simply can't have a sole military superpower without that unipolar situation eventually engendering a balancing response from other great powers.

The have-your-cake-and-eat-it-too mentality on that one always stuns me: America acts too unilaterally with its military, eschewing the opportunity to build stronger ties with potential rivals in the New Core, and then we express a sort of fatalistic acceptance of this "balancing" outcome. In many ways, this is indicative of the Pentagon's passive-aggressive response to the global war on terrorism and the shrink-the-Gap vision that it implies. So when a George W. Bush sounds all those expansive chords in his second inaugural address (opposing tyrants and dictators the world over) and the White House emphasizes its newfound friends in Moscow, Beijing, and New Delhi, this sort of institutional resistance from the Pentagon and the services begins to border on open bureaucratic insubordination.

You want to know why Secretary Rumsfeld has found himself under such consistent fire from the defense establishment throughout his tour? That's basically why. He saw the need for systematic change within the Pentagon to deal with the altered strategic landscape around the world, but many in the department found his price unacceptably high: a small-footprint Leviathan force based mostly on airpower; ground forces optimized for counterinsurgencies and post-conflict stabilization and reconstruction operations; and Special Operations Command given the freest possible hand in dealing with transnational terrorists. Since the military faces budgetary pressures from here on out (the post-9/11 windfall has ended already), meeting those requirements will entail a lot more security partnerships with New Core powers. Why?

The new long-term military strategy of the United States, developed by Rumsfeld and his senior staff and first leaked to the press in late summer 2004, posits that our most likely operations will involve either high-end catastrophic threats from terrorists or low-end, low-intensity operations against insurgencies, rebels, and other forms of civil strife within failed states. The least likely form of threat we face, the new strategy documents argue, is midrange conventional military threats from other nation-states. It doesn't get much clearer than that. The military services are being told that the type of war they prefer to prepare for is now viewed as the least likely threat we'll face in the future, whereas the types of conflict the services like least to prepare for (transnational terrorists and subnational insurgencies) are the threats we're most likely to face in the future. Neither terrorists nor rebels provide the Pentagon's acquisition community with the type of big-ticket threat scenarios that yield big-ticket weapon systems or platforms—like a two-billion-dollar attack sub. So here's the devil's bargain this new military strategy forces upon Pentagon planners: if you want to preserve those conventional warfighting assets as much as possible (likewise buying as many as possible in coming years), then your only choice for meeting those high- and low-end threats is to internationalize or subcontract those efforts as much as possible to allied nations. This is the essence of the SysAdmin model.

Inside the Pentagon, this sort of choice can be described as putting a gun to someone's head and asking them how they'd like to proceed. That's because the budgetary "hammer" is the most fearsome weapon known inside The Building. And it is really a devil's bargain as far as many strategists in the Pentagon are concerned: to preserve the conventional military hedge against potential great-power rivals, the military is basically being forced to seek more security partnerships with those very countries. That's why the Pentagon's planning documents have shifted from predominantly describing China as the future foe we need to deter to calling it the emerging power whose rise we need to influence.

The good news is, there are a lot of solid strategic reasons why the United States should pursue expanded security partnerships with New Core powers—besides escaping the always approaching "budgetary train wreck" on acquisitions.

First, the New Core is where the action is on new technology. That's because so much of that research-and-development function has been outsourced to the New Core's seemingly endless pool of engineers, increasingly centered in India and China. When the German industrial giant Siemens AG starts tapping design engineers in Beijing for its next-generation cell phone development, as it did recently, you know the worm has turned. During the Cold War missile race with the Soviets, we used to brag, "Our Germans are better than your Germans," meaning we had spirited away more of Nazi Germany's rocketeering talent than had the Soviets following World War II. Well, in coming years, we'll see German companies bragging, "Our Chinese are better than your Chinese," with many American firms probably countering, "Our Indians are better than your Indians."

Second, the New Core will be the dominant sales market for high technology over the coming decades. The Old Core is somewhat saturated with many of these new technologies, so high-tech companies must look to cell phone and computing markets in places like Brazil, Russia, India, and China. The first half century of the information age saw about one billion people in the Old Core come to use computers and related technologies in their everyday lives—and the same goes for the Internet. The next billion customers will come overwhelmingly from the New Core. The New Core is joining our network, and that means network security is going to become quite naturally a shared vision as well as a shared responsibility. The New Core is wiring itself up to the Old Core—we just need to catch up on the security rule sets to keep that process of integration as safe (and profitable) as possible for everyone involved.

Third, there will be natural economic competition among New Core powers, and while that's a good thing that encourages a "race to the top" to integrate themselves more fully inside the Core (especially between dueling China and India), such competitiveness shouldn't be allowed to spill over into the security realm. Rising China, for example, should be viewed as an opportunity to foster both economic and security integration in East Asia, and not as a precursor to some new containment strategy for us to pursue, because you know what? We'll lose in any attempt to isolate China militarily. In the end, China will become the center of economic integration in Asia, so that if the United States were to go overboard in depicting China as a rising security challenger to its power in the region, we'd probably find ourselves shut out first in the region's economic integration process and later in its security alliance-building process as well. And I'm not just talking small Asian states that have no choice, but longtime U.S. security partners like Australia and New Zealand, who simply cannot afford to choose between rising-China-the-economic-opportunity and rising-China-the-American-defined-security-threat. In the era of globalization, the flag is going to follow trade more than the other way around. Bet on it.

Fourth, when we're talking New Core powers that are more dependent on commodity exports, like Brazil on agriculture and Russia on energy, we'll need to be a little more patient with not just their domestic politics (too left in Brazil, too right in Russia), but their natural defensive tendency to ally themselves with fellow New Core powers against a United States that often seems both indifferent to their economic struggles and overly critical of their political choices. Both Brazil and Russia have a far longer route toward deep integration with the Old Core than do China and India, armed as they are with their rising high-tech capabilities, and yet both states offer much the same promise over the long haul. Right now both Brazil and Russia tend to see themselves as "body" states, meaning economies whose main offerings are commodities or raw materials such as energy. As such, both states can often display rather Gap-like behavior in their politics, such as Putin's imitation of the House of Saud in his none-too-subtle takeover of the Yukos oil company or Brazil's recent loose talk about—in effect—creating a New Core political alliance on trade and patent issues (with Russia, China, India) against a United States–dominated Old Core. Over time, we want Russia and Brazil to shed their inferiority complexes and begin to see themselves also as "head" states, meaning economies whose prowess includes high-tech industries and research and development. This is a crucial step for any rising power, and Brazil's current push to make itself an open-source software giant is a very good sign in this regard. This upward progression marked

America's emergence in the latter portion of the nineteenth century, and it must mark Brazil's and Russia's in the early part of the twenty-first. The key thing for us to remember is to avoid giving either state the impression that somehow it needs to "capture" India or China as an ally before we do, and that it's a zero-sum competition, with the loser left out of the club.

It is only natural that the Old Core fears the rising New Core powers, because their emergence pushes us beyond our current core competencies to those that must inevitably lie beyond as we extend the ladder of development and create and conquer new fields of endeavor. Rather than face that challenge head-on, the temptation is always to "hold that line" against *them* (now called "cheap labor," as if that's an unfair advantage!) and keep America where it belongs. But men and nations are not static, and those who pretend otherwise have much in common with the Flat Earth Society. In reality, of course, where America belongs is precisely at the bleeding edge of whatever constitutes those new fields of endeavor today (e.g., biotechnology, nanotechnology, hydrogen-age energy).

It is only natural for the New Core powers to want to band together, feeling stronger in that collective bargaining position—to wit, the New Core–dominated "G-22" negotiating bloc in the Doha Development Round of the WTO. That's because the Old Core powers tend to view every challenge to their perceived privileged position within the global economic hierarchy as a zero-sum threat—as in, a New Core power can only move up if an Old Core power loses stature or influence. It's this sort of fear that pushes Japan to announce it's joining America's defense guarantee on Taiwan (a former colony of Imperial Japan, no less). Tokyo's afraid of China's growing economic influence with the United States, and so it seeks to bolster its military alliance with Washington. It's also what pushes Washington to pressure the European Union not to lift its arms-trade embargo on China.

A more realistic way to look at it is to say that with the addition of each New Core power to the inner halls of great-power membership, it's not the case that each seat there is somehow devalued but rather that the reach of the entire group is commensurately extended. An

Old Core alliance that seeks to transform the Middle East, as it does today, is made that much more powerful by the addition of Russia, China, and India to its ranks, in part because of the sheer assets each can bring to the table, but likewise because of the additional avenues of influence opened, such as the growing Indian and Chinese ties with Iran. Every such connection is an opportunity for manipulation, not simply some challenge to America's attempts to isolate bad actors. China, for example, is not on the wrong side with regard to North Korea, it simply represents another way in to the outcome we collectively seek. The key is defining that collectively sought outcome.

This Old Core tendency to assume competition at every turn from New Core powers is seen most obviously in the issue of energy. The New Core, especially China and India, will clearly have rising energy requirements in coming years. This is part and parcel of their emergence and integration into the Core. As such, the Old Core must welcome this rising demand as an opportunity for influence and cooperation: we want the New Core to have safe and stable access to energy. Knowing something a potential ally really wants is a huge advantage, because it allows us to extract a price for whatever aid we might offer that potential ally in achieving its desired goal. There is no doubt that the New Core is highly desirous of stability in the Middle East. Naturally, it would be nice, from their perspective, if the United States did all the heavy lifting in this regard. Yet it's crucial that these emerging economic powers be seen and welcomed as natural partners in the process. For if they are not, they will be forced to carve out such roles on their own, and in doing so, they will naturally gravitate toward those states currently out of favor with the Old Core, such as Iran, Sudan, or even Venezuela.

China's significant push into Africa in recent years is simply a large-scale version of this obvious "hit 'em where they ain't" strategy: the West, and especially the United States, ignores resource-rich but highly troubled sub-Saharan Africa, but China cannot afford to be so picky in its trade choices, and so it leaps into the region with development and investment packages galore. In this effort, does China frequently get into bed with unsavory dictators merely to gain secure access to energy and raw materials? Sure, but let's not be too quick to throw the first stone on that charge. We can choose to try to steer China's growing presence in Africa into positive directions, but then we'd actually have to mount a more serious effort there ourselves, now, wouldn't we? In the meantime, decrying China's growing interest in a region we've long shortchanged gets to be awfully hypocritical. Frankly, we should view China's rising strategic interests there as a blessing and something to be leveraged, not something to be feared, because they represent sprouts of economic connectivity emerging throughout the single most disconnected portion of the Gap. As always, the question that naturally arises should be "How to take advantage of this?" instead of "How do we counter this?"

China is not the next Soviet Union. The Chinese Communist Party's ruling legitimacy is based almost solely on delivering economic growth— to the tune of 25 million new nonfarm jobs each year—under increasingly marketized conditions. It has no aspirations for setting up its own, competing world system, and instead has challenged America economically *precisely* because of its rapid embrace of a most rapacious style of capitalism that recalls our own rise as a global power in the late nineteenth and early twentieth centuries. You want to understand Chinese capitalism today? Watch HBO's series *Deadwood*, which depicts a "teeming outlaw camp" on the outskirts of frontier America in 1877, a veritable free-for-all of rapid economic development ruled over by a ruthless capitalist strongman. A small army of Chinese Al Swearengens, not the Communist Party, is running the Middle Kingdom today.

What should scare America most is how much like us China is becoming, suggesting that—far from the predictions of the "realists"— our long-term strategic relationship with the Middle Kingdom is likely to be highly cooperative instead of highly conflicted.

My consulting company, The New Rule Sets Project, collaborated with the unorthodox Rhode Island–based wargaming firm Alidade in June 2005 to conduct a seminar-style strategic exercise that examined the long-term competitive relationship between the United States (representing the Old Core), China (New Core), Brazil (Seam States), and

Iran (Gap). In this wargame, which projected through the year 2018, several dozen futurists and defense experts populated the four country teams in a multidisciplinary game design that placed no more emphasis on the security assets of each team than it did on each country's human capital, financial capital, or raw material assets, corresponding to the "four flows" model of globalization that I outlined in *The Pentagon's New Map.*

The results of "The New Map Game," as it was dubbed, were more than encouraging on the question of America's "inevitable" conflict with China. In this four-sided "co-evolutionary" wargame, in which each team constituted a "thinking and learning" competitor to the other three, our Control Group, headed by me, went out of its way to toss a number of nasty scenarios at our assembled China Team (e.g., North Korean regime collapse, Islamic insurgency in western China, Japan acquiring naval basing rights in the Philippines, the Chinese financial "bubble" bursting). What the game play suggested was that China's continuing economic rise will give it more than enough diplomatic muscle to counter any American attempts to impose its will on the international security order, unless the United States itself were to start a war with China.

The China team, led by an annoyingly clever U.S. Air Force general named Rich Hassan, quietly avoided conflict with America throughout the exercise simply by working to keep any common security issues from becoming a primarily U.S.-defined situation. As a result, the game never quite became a U.S.-versus-China showdown on anything, with the outcome of each round being that Washington slowly but surely learned to accommodate Beijing's increasingly central role in Asian regional security affairs. The American team had the biggest gun, all right, but the Chinese team consistently—and quite deftly— avoided giving the Americans a good opportunity to pull the trigger, leaving one player on the U.S. team muttering, "When are we ever going to get the chance to go to war with China?"

Well, it all depends on whom you ask. But be certain of this: The U.S. Navy's intelligence and submarine communities, the Air Force's space community, and U.S. Pacific Command will continue to hype the

Chinese military threat to the fullest extent possible, doing their best to co-opt journalists and mass media outlets into sounding the drumbeat of "inevitable war." And then there's the defense-industrial complex, which has at risk almost a trillion and a half dollars' worth of long-term Pentagon weapons and platform programs, most of which are intimately tied to the type of high-end, "near-peer competitor threat" that China represents. Without the China threat, that gravy train might just grind to a halt, and let me tell you, that kind of money buys you a lot of China hawks on Capitol Hill.

Now more than ever, the question of U.S.-Chinese security relations depends on how the president of the United States *chooses* to define the global future worth creating. George W. Bush has declared that future to be one of globalization's expanding pie and growing spread, both of which are envisioned to constitute avenues for successfully diminishing the incidence of and dangers posed by transnational terrorism and political and religious extremism of all kinds. China's continued emergence as a pillar of the global economy is crucial to that vision, whether the Pentagon's China hawks realize it or not.

Here's hoping the man in the Oval Office always does. Because, in the end, it's the president's job—not the military's—to declare which threats are really America's enemies. The military gets to decide *how* we go to war, but never *why* or under what conditions. In our system of governance, that's the essence of civilian control of the military, so whenever you see admirals and generals acting like they know better than the American public about who our *real* enemies are, pay close attention, because it's the U.S. Constitution that's really being threatened.

In sum, we force the New Core into a zero-sum mentality when we don't make sufficient effort to attract its partnership in our security efforts inside the Gap. When we later view New Core efforts to lock in long-term access to energy with states we currently disfavor, it is beyond disingenuous to claim this is an example of its "rising competition" with us in matters of energy security. Indeed, it is nothing more than a self-fulfilling prophecy—again, passive aggression masquerading as grand strategy.

The Bush White House blew it in Iraq by inflicting upon itself a timeline that maximized the mobilization of our Leviathan force while restricting our ability to mount a Core-wide SysAdmin effort in the postwar environment, yielding that self-confessed "catastrophic success." By doing so, America missed a perfectly good opportunity to demonstrate to both established Old Core allies and potential New Core ones that our shrink-the-Gap strategy's first great expression, the so-called Big Bang strategy in the Persian Gulf, would prove a win-win outcome for all involved. Almost more damaging than that willful display of strategic myopia was our subsequent bungling of the occupation, proving that we were both conniving in our bargaining and incompetent in our execution, rendering the United States the least attractive sort of strategic partner *possible* for New Core powers nervous over their long-term access to Persian Gulf energy—sort of a Machiavellianism without the brains. Tell me, if you're Beijing or New Delhi watching this tumultuous drama unfold in Iraq, are you saying to yourself, "Man, this is a superpower I really want to work with in the future! Who better to entrust my long-term energy security to than these guys?"

So when China pushes hard for long-term energy deals with Russia, our "realists" see a nefarious plot unfolding. When China and India sign long-term oil and gas deals with Iran, our "clear-eyed" strategists recognize obstructionism. When China "builds strategic relationships along the sea lanes from the Middle East to the South China Sea," the Pentagon's long-range forecasters predict "China will use its power to project force and undermine U.S. and regional security." And when China asks Russia to join it in their first joint military exercise ever, something they apparently never managed to accomplish during all those years as Communist allies, the unrepentant Cold Warriors finally find their conspiracy for global domination!

Again, tell me we couldn't have done better. Tell me we couldn't have been more strategic in our thinking. Tell me there isn't a better future worth creating than some pathetic defaulting to familiar foes and tired story lines.

Then put yourself in Beijing's shoes: Imagine a United States facing a doubling of its oil requirements over the next two decades, with the Persian Gulf being the only source it can readily turn to for that level of volume increase. Then imagine China, despite our concerns and even our protestations, invading a Gulf state that holds the world's second-largest oil reserves, declaring it wants to "transform" the entire region politically. Would you then consider the decision of a "rising United States" to build up its naval power along the sea lanes between America and the Persian Gulf an obvious attempt to undermine Chinese security in the region? Or would you consider that a reasonable hedge against the willful display of power by a disturbingly unilateral military superpower?

Probably the worst sort of these self-projecting fears comes in the form of the Japanese, Chinese, and U.S. navies. Hard-liners in all three seemed convinced that some form of naval showdown will occur in the next couple of years (a favorite bet is that China must strike well before the 2008 Olympics in Beijing), whether their respective governments—much less business communities—want it or not. China and the United States will *inevitably* clash over Taiwan, while Japan and China will *inevitably* spar over sea lanes that link both to overseas energy suppliers. Why? Because submarine experts—plus gung-ho journalists—on all sides say it is *inevitable!* China *must* build up its submarine fleet to defend its ability to threaten Taiwan, and the United States *must* counter that threat with its own naval forces, as well as with arms sales to Taiwan. China's buildup means Japan *must* counter with similar capabilities of its own, lest it be left behind in any naval arms race, thus it joins in the U.S. defense guarantee on Taiwan. And of course all three sides *must* regularly engage one another in various probing actions designed to reveal the other side's constantly improving capabilities.

Is any other direction possible but this dangerous path? Sadly, submarine experts on all sides say no. Historians may point out that both the Americans and the Soviets made similar arguments throughout the Cold War, only to abandon all such confrontations when it ended abruptly, but this is considered a bad analogy. After all, the Soviet Union engaged in minimal trade with the United States back then, whereas today China is Japan's biggest trading partner and the biggest source of America's trade deficit. Surely a realist can see where all that economic connectivity will lead us—*inevitably to naval war!*

Ah, to be a realist and to see the world as it truly is rather than as we might hope it to be! After all these years of working with the military, sometimes my naïveté still shames me.

The New Core is the swing vote for this era's version of globalization: If New Core countries buy into it and stick with the Old Core over the long run, globalization cannot fail. But if these emerging powers decide to opt out of the Core's security rule set—perhaps because they were never adequately invited to join that rule set and make it their own through progressive adjustments on both sides—then we are likely to see the renewal of spheres of influence across the Gap, as various Core powers strike out on their own in a zero-sum fashion. This is a completely believable future, in my mind, because the Core seems full of political and military leaders who see the Gap as the last refuge of such pointless competitions, and so long as they do, it does not matter much that business leaders know better because, absent sufficient security inside the Gap, those private-sector investments simply will not flow, thus fulfilling the prophecy of "realists" on both sides that such great-power struggles were indeed inevitable.

The danger of this potential pathway makes it clear to me that any blueprint for action must include comprehensive efforts by the United States to "deconflict" the security strategies of Old and New Core military powers. The original definition of *deconfliction* was, "Hey, stop shooting at me! I'm on your side!" If you don't deconflict, you end up with fratricide, meaning you kill your own troops by mistake. Obviously, I worry a lot about strategic fratricide inside the Core, because I fear that in America's attempts to do the right thing and shrink the Gap, we'll eventually trigger misdirected fire from other Core pillars, which—for the most part—will believe they are acting in similarly beneficent ways, even as all sides remain convinced this is clearly a zero-sum competition, meaning "I better get mine before you get yours."

Strategic deconfliction across the Core mostly has to do with transparency, but likewise with the timing of actions and the need to avoid ultimatums, such as the one the Bush White House offered the world during the run-up to the Iraq invasion—namely, "Show up for the war or forget about the peace (and the contracts too)!" It also has to do with telling good stories, meaning explaining exactly where you hope this whole thing will end up once you commit yourself and others to this pathway. So it's not about offering dozens of different rationales for the decision to go to war, but rather offering one compelling rationale for the decision to go to a new peace *after* the war. A happy ending. Finally, deconfliction means moving beyond old-think regarding the "injustice" of "free riders."

Free riding is the notion that while you do all the heavy lifting, somebody else gets to clean up on the easier stuff, leaving you rather tired and feeling uncompensated for your efforts. It is a notion often used to explain why America typically gets fed up with its European allies in NATO: the sense that we do most of the spending *and* most of the fighting, while occasionally we can talk the Europeans into showing up for a modest peacekeeping effort after the shooting has stopped. If there is one thing that modern globalization should make clear to us, it is that there ain't no such thing as free riding anymore. Everything is connected, so in the end, everyone pays a price—no matter who makes war or who maintains peace.

Our invasion and occupation of Iraq is a telling example in this regard. America believes it has borne the brunt of this burden because of the lives we've lost and the treasure we've expended. And yet it is the rest of the world that must deal with the resulting instabilities and downstream costs. When oil prices rise, America's economy may continue to roll along quite nicely, but many economies in Latin America will not, as we've seen in other historical periods. America may blithely scare away Muslim immigrants from our shores, but Europe couldn't even if it tried, and so it will bear costs unseen to us. Going on the offensive may keep al Qaeda from striking again in the United States, but it may well mean that al Qaeda makes greater efforts in the Caucasus or Central Asia, which Russia will end up dealing with. America topples the Taliban in Afghanistan, and Pakistan is forced to deal with its remnants operating from within its borders. America may well set off a Big Bang in the Middle East that not only destabilizes governments throughout that region but also pushes rising powers in Asia to invest more heavily in their military capabilities to ensure their own access to the region's oil. America may drive Salafi jihadists out of the Middle East, and Africa might find itself the new center of our global war on terrorism.

No one gets off free in this conflict, because this war, like the global terrorist movement we seek to defeat, is essentially a function of globalization's progressive advance around the planet. Globalization affects everyone in this world, whether or not they enjoy strong connectivity to the global economy, and so a war waged essentially on its behalf will likewise engender both costs and benefits for everyone in this world. Globalization has been and always will be primarily a domestic political issue.

The saddest aspect of our current inability to move more forcefully toward a security alliance with New Core powers is our lack of self-awareness of how much the United States obviously resembles the New Core and vice versa. I know that sounds counterintuitive from a political perspective, but from an economic perspective, it makes perfect sense. Why? Let's keep it real: Economics determines politics far more than the other way around, and if there's one thing capitalists and anticapitalists can agree upon, that's it! We may share plenty of past political history with Old Core Europe and Japan, but we'll share far closer definitions of capitalism's future with New Core pillars in the decades ahead.

These shifting alliances will be hard for most Americans over the age of forty to comprehend, much less accept. But it'll be far easier for younger generations to warm up to the notion that, in the globalization still to come, America will have far more in common with Brazil than with Canada, with India than with the United Kingdom, with Russia than with Germany, with China than with Japan—and, yes, even with Iran than with France.

Okay, so maybe that last one's not so hard to imagine, even if you're over forty.

This is why I don't spend any time in this book arguing that America needs to win over either Europe or Japan with some grand strategic vision of shrinking the Gap. Frankly, in both instances, I think it would be a complete waste of time. Instead, America should spend all its time and resources trying to win over China, India, Russia, Brazil, and a host of smaller New Core states in South America, Eastern Europe, and East Asia. The "West" is dead as a historically useful concept, much less a rallying cry in a global war on terrorism, so let's not spend any more diplomatic capital trying to resurrect a dead horse that wouldn't drink the water even if we dragged its hefty carcass to the shore.

I get this vibe all the time when I brief international audiences full of citizens from both Old and New Core states: typically the New Core people nod their heads vigorously throughout the talk whereas the Old Core people tend to frown throughout, occasionally sniffing in disgust at all the "imperialism" and "white man's burden" that's allegedly implied by my vision of shrinking the Gap. What I find so hilarious in this is the assumption of the Old Core types that their rejection of these ideas represents their death knell, when nothing's further from the truth.

Here's a good example why: While Old Core Europe and Japan are more than a little bit tempted by Osama bin Laden's offer of civilizational apartheid, both the United States and the New Core pillars understand what a false promise this truly is. America instinctively rejects the offer because, as citizens of the world's freest multinational economic and political union, we simply can't accept the notion of a world thus divided. As a society blended from all civilizations, the very notion of such separatism is simply repulsive to our citizenry. For if such cultural apartheid really made sense, most of American history would have unfolded in vain—the Civil War, the suffragist movement, organized labor, civil rights, gay rights, and so on.

With New Core powers, the offer is similarly rejected, but for different motivations. Since the major New Core powers all border the Islamic world, there are few illusions about "containing" this conflict once begun. The Gap is not some distant strategic abstraction to these governments but a very intimate sort of operational reality, in the same way that Arizona tends to view illegal Latino immigrants differently from the way Maine does.

But there are other similarities. Like the United States, New Core powers are the most willing to wage war to protect the global economy, because they have the most to lose by its collapse. Europe perceives its own economic union to constitute a universe unto itself, or a mini-globalization process of endless—not to mention "unprecedented"—integration. But China, India, and Russia all desperately need access to the global economy, because each is making up for a lot of past disconnectedness. As such, all are more attracted to America's relatively brutal definitions of capitalism and are willing to defend what they've earned.

Second, New Core powers show a real passion for doing what it takes to further globalization's advance. Brazil, for example, doesn't just rhetorically champion the right of Gap states to better trade deals with the Core, it actually goes out of its way to sue Old Core states in the WTO on behalf of Gap states. And you know what? It tends to win those cases, like its unprecedented victory against the United States on cotton last year with colitigants Chad and Benin, marking the first time any African states have successfully taken a Core member to court over its agricultural subsidies. Then there's Brazil's impassioned leadership of the so-called G-22 states, virtually all New Core, which have taken to bargaining with the Old Core on the Gap's behalf on a host of trade issues in the Doha Development Round. Again, when you're talking about things like low-priced pharmaceuticals for the Gap's raging AIDS crisis, which has likewise spread to several New Core pillars (Russia, India, China) at epidemic levels, globalization's advance seems less about McDonald's franchises "dirtying" French cuisine than a life-and-death struggle involving millions upon millions of lives.

Third, as many New Core states emerge slowly from long bouts of authoritarianism, these nations feel a far stronger connection to the goals of promoting liberty and freedom inside the Gap, as well as opposing tyranny and oppression. In the fall of 2004, when most Old Core coalition members were planning their troop withdrawals from

Iraq, little Seam State and aspiring Core member Georgia upped its military contingent there from 159 to 850. Why? As the Georgian ambassador to Washington said, "Georgians have felt the pain of terrorism, so we truly understand the importance of this global effort. Our young democracy is proud to help the Iraqis taste true freedom." What's in this effort for little old Georgia? Only a global future worth defending.

Fourth, primarily because their rapidly growing economies are the most dependent on future access to the energy resources of the Middle East and Central Asia, the New Core states of Developing Asia will clearly be most interested in making sure that those regions do not lapse into the sort of extreme disconnectedness desired by the bin Ladens of the global Salafi jihadist movement.

Finally, when the United States enlists the active support of China, India, or Russia in the global war on terrorism, it gains military partners who won't run at the first sight of blood, argue incessantly over the constitutional rights of "enemy combatants," or see their governments collapse every time the terrorists land a lucky strike back home. Yes, we will occasionally have to hold our noses over China's human rights record, Vladimir Putin's cynical manipulation of the Russian legal system, or New Delhi's tendency to look the other way on certain forms of internal sectarian violence. But favoring order over justice makes sense at this point in history, at least when it comes to picking strategic partners. Such support will clearly have costs. But we won't know what they are until we make a serious effort to find out what these nations would need from such a grand alliance.

More to the point, military alliances tend to arise out of military victories. If we want to pull the East's New Core powers into a long-term alliance devoted to shrinking the Gap, we should forge that partnership with a war worth winning, or perhaps just a regional rogue worth toppling. This blueprint for action already includes preemptively declaring a permanent truce in the Taiwan Straits, which is the *quid* we offer for Beijing's *quo* for the solution set that really matters in East Asia today: the reunification of Korea following Kim Jong Il's removal from power.

The Korean issue is the tailbone of the Cold War: completely use-less, but it can still plunge the Core into a world of pain if up-and-coming Asia slips and falls on it. North Korea is the evil twin, separated at birth, and yet, because it's still joined at the hip with its sibling, its better half grows ever more irrationally distraught—as time passes—contemplating the inevitably invasive surgery that lies ahead. But everyone knows that difficult event must someday arrive. North Korea is not part of anybody's future worth creating, and so long as it exists in Northeast Asia, key players (Russia, China, Japan, South Korea, and the United States) all possess valid excuses for not moving ahead to something better—as in, more mature security rela-tionships with one another.

Worse than that, North Korea becomes an excuse for the United States and Japan to erect a missile defense shield in East Asia that's ostensibly designed to protect both countries from Pyongyang's mis-siles but will ultimately get used to dissuade China from thinking that its own missiles make it a regional power without peer. As I said ear-lier, China will become a regional power without peer on the basis of its economic strength and its sheer connectivity throughout Asia, so what we have here is basically a rule-set gap between China's maturing economic profile and its adolescent political-military one. American strategists seem to think we can block China's military rise while allowing its economic emergence.

But you have to ask yourself if maintaining that unnatural mis-match ad infinitum is really desirable. We don't gain anything by keep-ing China always feeling vulnerable militarily, even on Taiwan, because that will simply encourage Beijing to seek regional political and eco-nomic alliances designed to shut America out of Asia's long-term inte-gration process, something we're already seeing in its negotiations with the Association of Southeast Asian Nations (ASEAN). And when push comes to shove on those deals, we'd better not expect India or South Korea or Japan or even Australia to line up automatically on our side. Given the choice, none of these potential balancers is going to choose America to the exclusion of China over the long haul, although all will work mightily to choose both whenever possible.

No, America needs to kill these dangerous scenarios in their infancy, smothering them by bold strategic action designed to keep our country a key pillar in Asia's political-military *and* economic future. We need to come to the obvious strategic conclusion that our long-term security alliance with China will be the cornerstone of the twenty-first century's global strategic order, for once we lock in China, tell me which of the remaining Core powers is going to want to remain on the outside of that by-invitation-only club?

I know I'm talking a serious leap ahead here, but that's what this whole book is supposed to be about. Remember, the economic destinies of China and the United States are inextricably intertwined, so please forgive my flip tone as I describe how this should all go down.

If North Korea's missiles are the great rationale for a joint U.S.-Japanese missile shield in East Asia that puts China on the receiving end, then I say it's time for North Korea to go away, just as East Germany did. Kim Jong Il has checked all the boxes: He'll sell or buy any weapons of mass destruction he can get his hands on, he's engaged in bizarre acts of terrorism against South Korea, and he maintains his amazingly cruel regime through the wholesale export of both narcotics and counterfeit American currency. Is he crazy? He once kidnapped two of South Korea's biggest movie stars and held them hostage in his own personal DreamWorks studio for years on end, forcing them to star in his own pathetic films. Sound nutty enough to you? But if that doesn't do it for you, then try this one on for size: the self-induced famine Kim oversaw in the late 1990s killed upwards of two million North Koreans (that's the lowest credible estimate; the highest ones are double that, but why quibble with statistics?). If that doesn't get you a war-crimes trial in this day and age, then what in God's name will?

Here's the squad we need to assemble: China, Japan, South Korea, Australia, and New Zealand, plus Russia. Forget about the United Nations. Just put the mask over the UN's nose and mouth and ask it to start counting backwards from 100.

We just shook hands with China over Taiwan. Japan's there because both China and America are on the team, and because they've got the most cash to finance the reconstruction. The Aussies and Kiwis are invited out of respect for their long-standing security role in Asia, and the Russians are in because they might just run a pipeline to Japan through the Korean peninsula when all is said and done. As for South Korea, we can expect them to go all wobbly at some point in the process, so we had better be prepared to just smack 'em upside the head when the time comes, telling them it's strictly business, nothing personal.

That's the coalition that walks into Kim Jong Il's palace and offers him three alternative endings to his uniformly disastrous rule. I'll call these three scenarios the Good, the Bad, and the Ugly.

- Scenario #1 (the Good) is the Baby Doc Duvalier package, in honor of the golden-parachute deal we offered another idiot-son dictator: We tell Kim, "Keep your money, keep your women, keep your entourage, keep it all . . . just somewhere else." Over the years, we've seen this scenario unfold—both happily and unhappily from our perspective—in the Middle East (Iran's Shah), Africa (Uganda, Liberia, and most recently Togo), and Latin America (do Haiti's leaders leave any other way?). China can offer Kim a fabulous forbidden city somewhere in Inner Mongolia. Hell, promise Cecil B. DeMented a five-picture deal and tell him Steven Spielberg wants to do lunch.

- If he doesn't bite on that one, then show him Scenario #2 (the Bad): We come after him and only him, like we did with Manuel Noriega in Panama, and once we've snatched him, he goes on trial in The Hague for years on end (just like Slobodan Milosevic), paraded around like the freak job he is, and once he's thoroughly stripped of what passes for his "majesty," we'll let him rot in a jail cell for the rest of his days.

- Version #3 (the Ugly) is delivered sotto voce: We just have our emissary show Kim the "six-month reconstruction plan" the Pentagon neocons drew up for the postwar occupation—I'm talking both PowerPoint slides! If he thinks we're bluffing, our man just leans over the table and slips him some of those morgue shots of Uday and Qusay Hussein looking all stitched up like a pair of Frankensteins. Kim will get the hint: If there's one thing the Bush Administration has accomplished, it's demonstrated that the U.S. Government is willing to wage war with almost no concern for the resulting VIP body count, the subsequently incompetent occupation, or the inevitable political uproar back home. I say, when we've got it, flaunt it.

If it comes to trigger pulling, can we pull it off? I believe we can, and even here we've got a choice between the stripped-down package (i.e., just kill Kim) and the more complex efforts (e.g., smash and grab WMD, decapitating command and control, pounding ground forces). North Korea's million-man army will prove less brittle than Saddam's Republican Guards but hardly invulnerable to our takedown techniques. Plus, on this one the local players (South Korea, China) will provide plenty of boots on the ground and humanitarian aid (Japan), just to prevent refugees from flooding across their borders. Moreover, Kim's power base sits atop a thin, mafia-like criminal empire that features the usual honor among thieves, so bribing his fellow kleptocrats is quite feasible. Finally, unlike in Iraq, the postconflict investment flows will be heavy on this one, because there will be no insurgency, no jihad, no nothing, just a gulag's worth of political prisoners to set free and a generation of developmentally delayed children needing three hots and special ed.

But the truth is, it probably won't come to full-blown war, simply because the neocons have given the United States such a scary reputation right now that we can probably stare down the Dear Leader—so long as we've got China glaring at him disapprovingly over our shoulder. Everyone knows China would just as soon jettison Kim, because he's outlived his usefulness. So what we really need to offer Beijing on the far side is something truly useful to replace him, and that something is an Asian NATO. That's right, Kim's tombstone should mark the spot where a NATO-like security alliance for Asia is born.

If we terminate Taiwan's defense guarantee in order to bring Beijing to Kim's table, then we offer to kill all our plans for missile defense (both at home and in Asia) to get the Chinese to pull the chair out from under him. Star Wars has probably been the single worst boondoggle in the history of the Pentagon—well over $100 billion wasted and not even Tang to show for it. By getting rid of it and securing America's military alliance with China, Japan, and United Korea, America not only kills the concept of great-power war in Asia for good, we've just extinguished Osama bin Laden's bid to pit East against West.

I know President Bush is committed to following through on what he's set in motion in the Middle East, and I know he's hell-bent to prove all the eggheads and regional experts wrong about the possibility of real democracy taking root in the region—and I like his certitude on both points. Bush is the "blink president." He reacts instinctively from his gut more than either his heart or his brain, and you know what? He's as big a gift from history as 9/11's wake-up call turned out to be—and almost equally hard for many Americans to swallow. But if Bush is truly committed to transforming the Middle East and shrinking that much of the Gap in one fell swoop, he should do everything in his power to secure the East during his watch, because serious instability there or—God forbid—actual war is the one great extraregional scenario that could suck the U.S. military out of the Gulf in a dangerous way that's ultimately destabilizing for globalization's long-term prospects.

I think the second Bush Administration's blueprint for action in Asia should zero in on these three tasks, all accomplishable by the time Bush-Cheney leave office in 2009: (1) lock down East Asia by putting a leash on Taiwan; (2) secure the New Core's long-term partnership by inviting China into globalization's copilot seat (don't worry, we'll pull India along in the process); and (3) put an end to the Cold War's last story in Northeast Asia by shoving Kim Jong Il underground—one way or another. If President Bush can manage this during his second term, not only will he have freed America's military resources for more urgent tasks in the Middle East, his administration will have succeeded in creating a sense of strategic despair in the minds of bin Laden and al-Zarqawi that they'll never be able to overcome. Their dream is to split up the advancing Core of globalization and stop its creeping embrace of their idealized Islamic world, which they know will be forever altered by that integration process. Their best strategic hope in this conflict is that some hostile great power will rise in the East to challenge the American-led West.

So if we lock in China today, we will corner and kill transnational terrorism tomorrow. Better yet, get that East Asian NATO and say goodbye to great-power war *forever.*

All right, time to breathe again.

And while you're catching your breath, let me leave you with this one thought before moving on: *The New Core sets the new rules.*

That's right. The New Core sets the new rules, and making sure America's part of that new rule set isn't just some Machiavellian daydream. No, it's the strategic imperative of our age.

THE TRAIN'S ENGINE CAN TRAVEL NO FASTER THAN ITS CABOOSE

As soon as our newly adopted daughter Vonne Mei joined our family last fall, I noticed a distinct change in the behavior of my three oldest kids: Emily, then twelve, Kevin, nine, and Jerry, four. Suddenly, Kevin stopped being the middle child and became part of the "older kids" with Emily, while Jerry suddenly stopped being the baby of the family and was immediately thrust into the unfamiliar role of middle child. As always happens with a new baby, not just positions but perspectives changed dramatically, and a rule-set reset rapidly ensued. That was hard for everyone but quite instructive to me as I thought about the differences in perspectives on globalization within the Core—namely, among the United States, the rest of the Old Core (Europe and Japan), and the rising New Core pillars of Brazil, Russia, India, and China.

The first thing that happened to our family following Vonne Mei's arrival was, of course, that everything slowed down to "baby speed," meaning we couldn't go anywhere or do anything faster than it took us to get the baby ready and rolling. But once that natural adjustment was made and we got good at performing that function on the fly, the family decision-making process regarding events, choice of entertainment, and excursions in general got a lot more complex. Basically, it came down to two positions: (1) that of the older two kids, Emily and Kevin, who always wanted to go as fast as possible at every opportunity; and (2) that of my wife Vonne on behalf of baby Vonne Mei, who always advocated going as slow as possible at every opportunity. Now, when I say "fast" or "slow," I'm really collapsing a host of disparate arguments or descriptions into that one word, so "fast" means aggressive, ambitious, mature, and complicated, whereas "slow" tends to mean careful, modest, beginner's level, and simple. So no matter what we were discussing (e.g., the hike we'd take, the DVD we'd watch, the restaurant we'd choose), there was always a clash between the Go Fast and the Go Slow positions.

The odd man out in all this was naturally our new middle child, Jerry, who constantly struggled with wanting to join his elder siblings in their Go Fast approach (rarely keeping up with them, of course) and being tempted to default to the Go Slow mode that spoke to his new baby sister's needs (i.e., the natural regression any young child feels when a baby joins the family). Not surprisingly, Jerry became the most vocal family member in these debates, basically because he served as the swing vote, but also because his choice presented him with the widest possible array of outcomes, so his sense of uncertainty and angst was naturally highest. It was always a big deal to Jerry because, no matter what the outcome, he'd need to adjust rather significantly, either suffering the anxiety and pressure of trying something new and difficult or risking the boredom and lesser sense of accomplishment associated with the safer path. For the rest of us, it was simply a question of whether we'd get our way or not on this particular issue, but to our four-year-old it always seemed like some life-or-death issue worth anguishing over at length.

What about me, you ask? For the most part I tend toward the Go Slow, not so much out of deference to Vonne Mei (my wife's natural instinct) but simply because I've spent so much of my adult life going fast that I'm ready to slow down wherever possible and learn how to smell the roses along the way. I could tell I reached this point around age forty, because it was roughly then that I realized (1) that I can't do upside-down roller coasters all day long anymore with Emily and Kevin at Six Flags; and (2) that it was about time I finally fulfilled my lifelong dream to play the piano.

What do I take from all of this? Things naturally tend to slow down at the extremes, meaning when you're just starting out in life or when you've basically "gotten there" as an adult and want to start enjoying things more. It's in between those two shoulders that you find the hump of the bell curve on this question, with most people wanting to go as fast as possible. But therein lies the rub.

There's a lot of discussion right now in intellectual circles concerning America's standing in the world with respect to both globalization in general (i.e., our model of economic development) and the new security issues surrounding transnational terrorism (i.e., the nature of our rather vigorous national security response). If you remember back to the 1990s, there was a strong global sense that America not only represented the future but did so in a way that was both admired and widely emulated by emerging economies. The United States, with its "new economy," seemed to be on the cutting edge of that new world order associated with modern globalization: transparency, free markets, and collective security. We were identified with a decidedly Go Fast ideology of embracing connectivity in all forms, figuring out the rules as we went along, but believing—quite frankly—that such rules were rather obvious and would reveal themselves with time as being very minimal in nature.

Naturally, our tendency to favor as few rules as possible gave our social and economic model a decidedly hard edge, leading to derisive descriptions of American capitalism as being "hypercompetitive" and thus brutally unfair to those who did not succeed or were left behind for various reasons. With the United States moving so aggressively to connect itself to the world at large, while Europe seemed so deliberate in its careful integration of the newly independent countries of Eastern Europe, a growing sense of divide emerged between these long-time allies that called into question the future of our security bonds, otherwise known as the transatlantic alliance. We seemed to be going not only at different speeds (our Go Fast to Europe's decidedly Go Slow) but also in different rule-set directions (our very minimal rule set compared with Europe's quite expansive one). Where the United States was cutting back regulations and the role of the state while urging rising New Core powers to do the same, Europe took much the opposite approach of adding new regulations and expanding the role of public oversight and urging the rest of the Core to meet its new, higher standards.

So, over time, America became identified as being the country that was always in a hurry to "get there," while Europe became known as the region more concerned with enjoying the ride without really caring if they "got there" or not. We were known for working lunches and career burnout, while the Europeans were famous for dinners that lasted deep into the evening and summers that were more vacation than work. The clichés became that American lives were harried and unfulfilling, while European lives were relaxed and enriching.

Then along came 9/11 and America seemed to storm off with a vengeance toward the Middle East, telling allies to either jump on the bandwagon or get the hell out of the way. Suddenly, the United States became one of the hardest countries to get into, seemingly no matter what your intentions. Plus, our political climate seemed to polarize to the point of paranoia: you were either with America or against America, but you most definitely had to choose. In response to the fundamentalist challenge of Salafi jihadists, America itself seemed to retreat into its own brand of extremism or a vigorous new identification with those aspects of our character that most people associate with our growth from a weak collection of thirteen former British colonies to the world's undisputed superpower: feelings of exceptionalism, a strong belief in our ability to reshape the environment around us, and a profound sense of historical duty to spread our values around the world. Naturally, this reinvigorated sense of American identity thrilled most of our citizens while scaring most of the outside world. As both sides adjust to the notion that 9/11 really did seem to change everything for the long haul, there arises this undeniable sense of growing conflict within the Old Core as to whether or not globalization should be sped up or significantly slowed down.

The Bush Administration is clearly identified with the Go Fast ideology of accelerating globalization's advance, because of its promise of connectivity leading to greater freedom and liberty, developments considered essential prerequisites for the ultimate defeat of transnational terrorism and tyranny in general. But that alone doesn't mark President Bush as dangerous in the eyes of Go Slow Europe; it's also his willingness—even his eagerness—to employ military power in pursuit of that larger goal. What Bush is saying in his self-declared global war on terrorism is that America simply can't wait for globalization's creeping advance to envelop the Gap on its own, because in that long process the Core will suffer too many threats to its economic and political stability while the Gap simply suffers too much mass violence and oppression for far too long. Go Slow Europe highlights an entirely different package of fears, arguing that Go Fast America's aggressive strategy of furthering globalization's advance will cause too much unrest and violence in the Gap in the short run and thus endanger the Core's very existence over the long run.

In many ways, 9/11 hasn't changed this long-running debate over the speed of globalization's unfolding, it has just reasserted the military-market nexus that underpins globalization's fundamental promise that connectivity enables peace. The Go Slow position wants the Core to preserve that promise, while the Go Fast crowd (to include myself) argues that because disconnectedness defines danger, the safest path to long-term stability lies in aggressively attacking the problem rather than allowing it to fester and grow.

Obviously, wisdom can be found in both approaches, suggesting that a balance between the two is in order.

I know, I know. In the last section I just said that we shouldn't bother trying to salvage the West as a political force. If that's true, then why admit any need for "balance" here? Why not just go for it?

Well, here's where the notion that the "New Core sets the new rules" comes in handy: It's not a matter of choosing Europe's yin over America's yang but of finding a path between the two, a path I think is most easily located with the unfolding development experiences of the New Core states. If America sticks with trying to win over the New

Core pillars, the cost of that victory will include having to see the world more from their perspective. Meanwhile, Old Core Europe and Japan will get pulled along for the ride, fundamentally out of their own fear of being left behind in the increasingly successful cooperation between the U.S. and the New Core in shrinking the Gap. In short, with the New Core, learn from the process, and get the rest of the Old Core in the bargain.

The key to such balance between the Go Fast and the Go Slow visions is, of course, to avoid engaging in excessively black-and-white descriptions of either the promise or the peril provided by globalization's advance, while admitting that the differences between Core and Gap are ones of both degree and kind. For example, the Core suffers its own internal pockets of Gap-dom—namely, significant pockets of inner-city and rural disconnectedness that are similarly defined by higher rates of poverty and social oppression (expressed as either violent crime or the systematic abuse of the weak). Likewise, the Gap is sprinkled with plenty of connectivity-friendly countries whose main misfortune seems to be their choice of neighbors: Costa Rica in Central America, Israel in the Middle East, Ghana in West Africa, Uganda in East Africa, Botswana in Southern Africa, and Singapore and Malaysia in Southeast Asia. In sum, no state is totally connected and no state is absolutely disconnected. Rather, as historian Mark Safranski writes, it's a question of any society's "degree of acceptance of globalization's many effects and the ability of a nation's individuals to access choices for themselves."

But just as clearly there are differences in kind between the Core and the Gap. In the Core, dealing with transnational terrorism is essentially a peacetime law enforcement function, whereas in the Gap, where national police systems tend to be far weaker and less efficient, the Core's response—when taken—will often involve military force and thus involve definitions of war. So there's a critical-mass argument that separates the two communities, with the Core basically meeting the definition of stable political community whereas the regions of the Gap by and large do not.

The Core may feature occasionally brutal crackdowns by state police organs, but these acts of state repression don't rise to the level of warfare. In the Gap, however, such acts can often trigger significant civil strife or even civil wars. Peacekeeping may thus be required inside the Gap, but you will not see this in the Core (though such efforts may mark the beginning of a Seam State's ultimate integration into the Core, as in the dissolution of the former Republic of Yugoslavia). Almost by definition, a functioning state inside the Core cannot allow foreign peacekeepers on its soil, because that would be a sign of diminished sovereignty stemming from state failure.

So the Core tends to feature states' sins of commission (e.g., going overboard in a police response), whereas the Gap tends to feature states' sins of omission (e.g., lack of sufficient police capacity, leading to civil strife and the resort to military force). A region essentially joins the Core, then, when its respective domestic state capabilities reach the point where it would seem inconceivable that the rest of the world would have to do anything about strife there, the regional security rule set being so strong that uncertainty is removed.

It is only when you reach that level of security rule-set maturity that serious social discussion can begin as to how globalization might be collectively managed in its pervasiveness and speed of connection. That's true because until certain basic needs of individual populations are met, most governments will view the question of connectivity with the outside world as a matter of inviolable national security, as in, "We need this connectivity to trade/resources, and any attempt to deny us these connections will be considered tantamount to an act of war." Conversely, there are authoritarian regimes that argue the opposite position, as in, "We deny the outside world such connectivity to our people and resources, and any attempt to gain such connections will be considered tantamount to an act of war." In both instances, claims will be made on the basis of "state sovereignty," either in terms of territorial access (i.e., the demand for connectivity to be granted) or the sanctity of borders (i.e., the demand that enforced disconnectedness remain unchallenged).

Inside the Gap, if a state is reasonably representative of its population's needs, it will seek greater connectivity with the outside world on the best terms it can get, pursuing that course in a Go Fast approach until such time as the majority of the population can be said to enjoy the essential fruits of broadband access to the global economy. So, for example, as long as the bulk of a Gap nation's population is living in serious poverty, it basically has no other option but to pursue globalization's connectivity as fast as possible. Conversely, if a Gap nation's government is unrepresentative of its population's needs and seeks to exploit that society for gains that accrue only to the elite, maintaining a certain level of disconnectedness with the outside world is a logical strategy for monopolizing those gains to the fullest extent possible.

Inside the Core, by definition, that critical mass of connectivity with the outside world has been achieved (buttressed first and foremost by the stable connectivity afforded by explicit security rule sets that define interstate peace), so the political debate on speed, whether it's conducted by a ruling elite or a representative government, shifts from connectivity-at-all-reasonable-cost to balancing achieved connectivity with the perceived need to mitigate the social impact of that connectivity within the population. So long as we're not talking a significant portion of the population being trapped in poverty, the debate becomes one of fairly balancing the benefits and costs of the connectivity across various sectors of the population (the winners and losers). So when a country has achieved a fairly broadband economic connectivity for its population, the discussion shifts from the quantity of connectivity (How much globalization?) to the quality of that connectivity (What mix of globalization?).

Just as in the case of my family, within the global community the question of speed only seems obvious at the extreme ends of the spectrum. If a Gap state simply hasn't developed to the point where it can handle the onslaught of connectivity that globalization provides, a Go Slow ideology makes sense; otherwise we're talking about the high likelihood that outside forces will take advantage of the lack of sufficient rule sets within a society to lock in unfair transactions (i.e., the charge that multinational corporations exploit weak Gap states, leading to persistent underdevelopment and trashed environments). But once a state has developed its capacity for self-rule sufficiently that connectivity can be imported in a reasonably controlled fashion, then there's a natural proclivity to ratchet up the speed as much as possible. If you are China and you still have several hundred million in poverty today, then going any slower than a 7 percent GDP annual growth rate would seem almost cruel to those still left behind in the country's white-hot development process. Does this mean China tends to abuse both a lot of rules and a good chunk of its labor in the process? Sure. But frankly, that's an age-old story for emerging economies, the bottom-line logic being "Hey, I'll fine-tune things later, but right now I've got to put food on the table and pay the bills."

Along those lines, emerging markets such as New Core pillar China tend to favor order over efficiency, meaning they often feature fairly authoritarian political systems or single-party states where the "pluralism," such as it exists, lies wholly within the ruling party. Such states often take on the air of a technocracy, as in, "We're the smartest and have the most information, so we get to make all the key decisions." So long as they deliver and the Go Fast ideology prevails, single-party states can do quite well. In fact, that's how most formerly Gap nations have achieved New Core status. It's only when the bulk of a society's economic development reaches a certain plateau, typically between $5,000 and $10,000 per capita GDP, that you begin to see the public start becoming more demanding of pluralism and openness from its government.

What does the Go Fast approach tend to yield in globalization policies? First, there's a big focus on increased connectivity with the outside world, so you tend to see export-driven strategies of growth coupled with an influx of outside economic expertise and investment flows. This modernization strategy, as it is often called, features significant legal and economic rule-set reforms (e.g., synchronizing internal rules with the global rule set), along with a publicly funded strategy to develop infrastructure of all types (e.g., communications, transportation, energy, educational). All this connectivity is self-reinforcing: the more the country produces for export, the more it attracts foreign direct investment and accumulates foreign currency, both of which dramatically increase the amount of capital available to local entrepreneurs, who then take advantage of that opportunity to develop goods and services both for export and for a growing domestic market. Again, so long as there are significant amounts of underemployed or impoverished people within the economy who are willing to work for low rates of pay, the Go Fast approach makes good sense.

Do workers tend to get abused along the way? By our standards, sure, but typically less than they were in their previous condition of massive underdevelopment. For example, compared with the brutal conditions of the sex industry, where young women represent the ultimate in disposable labor, most "sweatshops," however defined, are a significant step up. In general, *some money* beats *no money,* and *just enough money* tends to mean kids will have increased opportunity for education. Nothing is more crucial for improving a family's fortune over time—especially with girls (the dictum being, educate a male and you've created one breadwinner, but educate a female and you've improved an entire family).

Does the environment tend to suffer? Absolutely. Early development typically focuses on extractive industries, like mining, or simple commodity exports, like agriculture, so in that initial desperation for a better life, underdeveloped societies tend to exhaust their environment and their labor with little regard. Simply put, they make hay while the sun shines, and it's hard to expect the deeply impoverished to do otherwise. But the important thing is that the process of development is jump-started. You can't ask people to value the environment over their basic well-being, and the quickest way to get them to care about their environment is to meet their basic needs through economic development, followed by diversification away from dependency on commodity exports.

Once a country achieves broad economic development, limiting its poverty to pockets here and there, then there is the natural tendency to want to slow things down somewhat. At that point, connectivity stops being an imperative and starts being a choice, especially if certain forms of connectivity, such as the freest possible trade relations, sometimes generate unacceptably high or rapidly generated pools of losers. When that happens, it only makes sense that a state seeks to modulate and moderate connectivity so that the widest array of winners are created, while losers are given sufficient time and support mechanisms (e.g., lost wage benefits, education and retraining) to resurface in winning industries and/or job categories.

On one level, the disagreement between Old Core pillars America and Europe concerns the acceptable level of churn, meaning that portion of your society that's being forced at any one time by globalization to undergo such reinvention. Europe prefers to offer substantial safety nets to losers, while the United States prefers to focus on the creation of new jobs and thus expanding the pool of winners. As such, Europe is willing to slow down connectivity to keep the pool of losers from getting too big at any one time, while the United States tends to favor steady or constantly expanding connectivity as the best route to trading up within the global economy, meaning we're always searching for the "next big thing" that generates plenty of whatever the next great job will be. So Europe is basically willing to live with less overall growth and a slightly lower standard of living to keep the pool of losers acceptably low, while the United States typically pushes ahead aggressively in the hope of always generating higher numbers of new winners than new losers. Which approach is better? Well, that depends on whether you think a two-week vacation is excessively long or unbearably short. Me, I tend to get a little antsy about ten days in.

If it were just a clash of competing lifestyles (European versus American), that would be one thing, but our differences are much deeper than that. We also have very different views of globalization as a historical process (i.e., how fast it should unfold) and whether or not it needs a bodyguard (i.e., is the spread of globalization worth fighting for?). Inside the Core the speed question is really a postdevelopment choice, which is really a *why* sort of question, as in, "Why should I keep working so hard once I've *made* it?" Inside the Gap, this choice really doesn't exist for most people, because development is dependent on a number of factors, some of which are beyond a society's control (geography, soil quality, climate) and some of which are simply quite hard to master (good government being the toughest).

When Core countries talk about the speed question with regard to the Gap, it is really a series of *how* questions, as in, "How can we encourage the spread of the global economy into these more challenged environments?" In general the Europeans favor developmental aid as a way to bring underdeveloped countries up to speed in a slower, more controlled fashion, whereas the United States favors the faster method of lowering trade barriers (i.e., pushing poorer countries to "play up" to our level as quickly as possible). Given the right sort of government and a little bit of geographic luck, the free-trade route does work better. Check out the countries with the highest inflows of foreign direct investment or the highest trade volume as a percentage of GDP and you will find countries that are growing. Conversely, look at countries that are the highest recipients of foreign aid as a percentage of GDP and you'll find countries experiencing negative growth. That's not to say aid is a complete waste of time, just that it never seems to change anything all by itself.

Why is that? Most aid tends to go to the worst-off countries inside the Gap, and the worst-off countries tend to come in two forms: dictatorships (too much government) and failed states (too little government). That gets us to the question of globalization's bodyguard, because—not surprisingly—dictators tend to be associated with transnational terrorism (it is a way to make mischief beyond your borders, something all dictators love to do), and failed states tend to attract transnational terrorists (they're great places to hide out and conduct business because of the loose or nonexistent rule sets). Now, that's not to say that every country that gets aid in the Gap is either a dictatorship or a failed state, because they're not, but by definition, every state in the Gap suffers by geographic association with such states, because they create generalized conditions of regional insecurity either through the violence they perpetrate (dictatorships) or the violence they allow to occur (failed states). So, as I argue, if the Core isn't willing to do something about those bad states, it won't matter whether or not the Core gets the right mix of aid and trade with the good states, because investment flows seek secure locations, and the very existence of bad states inside the Gap depresses those flows.

For purposes of discussion here, let's stipulate that the Core needs to make a certain security effort inside the Gap to enable both trade and aid to work their magic there. Once that effort is made, the question still remains, How fast should Gap countries seek to globalize their economies and societies? In other words, understanding that speed is a choice for the most developed Core countries ("Where do we want to go from here?") and not much of one for the Gap's worst states, because both dictatorships and failed states scare off investors, what about those states in the bell of the bell curve? How do we synthesize America's Go Fast ideology with Europe's Go Slow vision for all those countries inside the Gap that aren't bad states and desire connectivity? Pure speed certainly isn't the answer, as the Shah of Iran proved in the 1970s, because going too fast with a traditional society is going to get you a god-awful backlash (no pun intended). But likewise, as most of Africa has shown in recent decades, going slow is no way to overcome the amazingly large deficits that many Gap states face, because a little trade and a little aid simply don't pull any of those nations out of the huge hole they're in. So where do we find the happy medium between shock therapy and hospice care?

I think the answer is found in the recent experiences of the New Core pillars, particularly Brazil, Russia, India, and China. I think these emerging (or, in the case of Russia, recovering) economies give us a sense of what economist Jagdish Bhagwati calls "optimal speed."

Here's how I like to describe it: The Train's Engine Can Travel No Faster Than Its Caboose theory. That phrase popped out of my mouth during one of those fabulously long banquets that my wife and I enjoyed in Beijing with our Chinese hosts. It occurred, quite naturally, during an extended discussion of President Hu Jintao's Theory of Peacefully Rising China, which most Western analysts tend to interpret primarily as a foreign policy vision, when in reality it is primarily a domestic policy imperative.

Because China's national leaders are facing numerous social and political challenges regarding the differing rates of economic development between the country's booming coastal provinces and its lagging interior ones, the so-called Fourth-Generation of Leadership fronted by Hu Jintao has come to the conclusion—quite logically, in my view—that the regime's future legitimacy will depend in large part on its ability not only to keep the juggernaut of the coastal provinces moving at top speed but also to do so in such a way as to spread that wealth throughout the rest of the country. To fail in this process is to risk great social and political instability in China, even to the point of significant civil strife. The only way Hu can keep that economic juggernaut moving is to convince the West that China's overall economic growth is not a military threat, because if it is perceived as such and, say, the United States tries to contain China's rise by denying it access to trade or investments, then the government's great gamble of opening itself to the outside world may backfire internally.

In my mind, then, Hu needs to sell the world on his Theory of Peacefully Rising China for all the same reasons that President Bush needs to tie his global war on terrorism to globalization's progressive expansion: Both visions ultimately spring from the recognition that disconnectedness defines danger, and that serious pockets of disconnectedness arise whenever large portions of any community are left behind while others move rapidly ahead. This is true for the Gap vis-à-vis the Core just as much as it for interior China vis-à-vis coastal China. The Core is clearly the engine to the train called globalization, but the Gap is its caboose. The military-market nexus is embodied in the inescapable reality that the Core will never be truly secure so long as the Gap falls farther behind. Simply put, globalization is not a foreign aid issue but a domestic security issue. That's what America realized thanks to 9/11, thus our renewed sense of urgency to speed up globalization's advance. But Hu's Theory of Peacefully Rising China reminds us of the inescapable reality on the far side of this equation: the Core can't expect any Gap state to move any faster in globalizing its economy than the weakest parts of its society can handle, otherwise we're not buying connectedness and safety but probably explosive internal instability that inevitably disconnects the country further.

New Core states have demonstrated this potential political blowback numerous times in recent years, most notably in elections. Inside the Old Core, elections tend to be boring, and inside the Gap they tend to be matters of life and death, as recent elections in Iraq and

Afghanistan have proven. But inside the New Core, elections are all about speed, as in, "How fast can we go without coming apart politically?" It's that domestic political fear that represents the greatest brake on globalization around the world today, but mostly in a good way, so long as leaders listen and heed these expressions of anxiety. Brazil's own Gap spoke in the election of Luiz Inácio Lula da Silva in 2002, slowing down that government from its previously more rapid globalizing pace. India's own Gap triggered the return of the Congress Party in 2004, with its leadership immediately pledging more attention to the rural poor, who increasingly feel that they don't belong in "Shining India." Ukraine's contested election of 2004 spoke to all the same dynamics, as the less connected eastern half of the country expressed its fear of being left behind while the more connected western half turned toward Europe.

In Russia, Vladimir Putin's recent turn toward authoritarian tactics likewise betrayed his government's growing fear that this former superpower was being left behind while emerging powers like India and China seemed to be getting all the West's attention, not to mention their growing respect (e.g., the G-8 inviting China to a summit meeting). Putin's crudely staged renationalization of the oil giant Yukos exemplified his nervous signaling to the rest of the Core that Russia-the-state would still matter in coming years because it has the capacity to deliver energy that isn't subject to the political instabilities of the Persian Gulf, despite its rear-guard conflict in Chechnya. Internally, Putin has likewise displayed a greater reticence to alienate the country's aging Soviet pensioner generation.

All these "reversals," as many of them are described, speak less to the limits of globalization's appeal than to the logical speed limits placed on not just its advance into the Gap but likewise its deep and permanent penetration inside the New Core. Anything that moves with the swift, reconfiguring power (meaning, destructive to old patterns) of globalization naturally engenders social resistance, no matter how mature the economy. So, in many ways, the appearance of what I might call "caboose braking" inside the New Core is just another variant of what we call "antiglobalization" inside the Old Core or West, although there the braking phenomenon tends to have less to do with economic fears than with social ones associated with the perceived loss of the "American way of life," Europe's Christian identity, Japan's racial homogeneity, and so on. George Bush won his "red state" victory in 2004 *despite* his support for globalization and primarily out of the sense that he would continue to vigorously represent America's core social values—especially in the ongoing global war on terrorism.

The New Core's "caboose braking" will continue to define those nations' pathway toward deeper integration into the global economy, and in that definition the world as a whole will find a sense of balance to apply to globalization's myriad disorienting effects. America's Go Fast approach will work for America and largely America alone, but in that bow waving of the future—that breaking new ground—we do more than run ourselves ragged, we set a course for others to follow. That the speed of others never quite matches our own should never be a problem, because our long familiarity with this experiment in multinational union called the United States means we can afford to dream not just for ourselves but for the world.

But America's pathfinding role imposes as many responsibilities as it offers privileges. We can never get too far out ahead in our creation of new rules, for if the rest of Core, and especially the New Core, no longer imagine themselves capable of tracing our journey, then we have let our sense of exceptionalism blind us to our real historic role of *always getting there first*—not uniquely, not providentially, just *first*. As we work to move globalization ahead and extend its benefits and connectivity to the rest of the planet, our blueprint for action must always factor in a realistic sense of speed. We may go fast, others slower, but we can never let our definition of progress disconnect us from those who simply fear being left behind.

The train's engine can travel no faster than its caboose. Globalization must proceed as fast as possible, but no faster. The Old Core must lead, and the Gap follow, but the New Core must set the pace and—by doing so—keep the entire train intact.

That's what I mean when I say, *The New Core sets the new rules.*

Chapter Four

SHRINKING THE GAP
BY ENDING
DISCONNECTEDNESS

WHEN C-SPAN BROADCAST MY PowerPoint briefing a slew of times in the fall of 2004, I found myself inundated with a steady flood of e-mails, at one point being forced to answer them virtually nonstop for about a week, which really begins to hurt after a while! The volume stunned me, because—frankly—I've never written a letter over anything I've seen on TV. But the contents of the e-mails were instructive in this regard: they overwhelmingly expressed a sense of gratitude for hope restored. That theme was conveyed over and over again, from the young and the old, from the Left and the Right, from states blue and red. The only thing I can compare it to is when you're fortunate enough to return a missing item to someone who's been desperately upset that it was gone for so long—as in, "I just don't know what I would have done if I had lost that forever!" It was that powerful feeling of balance restored: these individuals now had a sense of where they stand, what lies ahead, and why it matters. A lot of the people actually said they got their first good night of sleep since 9/11.

At first, you're kind of embarrassed with gratitude expressed on that level. I mean, you feel as though you found someone's wallet and nothing more. But over time, as I got more familiar with the emotions being expressed, I began to realize why it was so crucial to move beyond the first book's broad diagnostic approach to this volume's far greater focus on prescriptions—a plan of action. Eventually, that buzz wears off. It's as if you were full of all these fears about your declining health and then finally go to the doctor and get the diagnosis that dispels all your uncertainty, and even though it's not an easy diagnosis to swallow, you're just so damn happy to finally know what the hell's been going on all this time that even the challenging bit of "bad news" seems like a gift from heaven. They must have a cure for this, right?

Well, you can't just leave people hanging like that. You can't just get them all jacked up with no place to go. When people say they're a "convert" or "sold," you'd better have a better comeback than just "That's nice to hear." Moreover, your vision of the future can't just be some splendid description of a world they've got little hope of actually visiting. No, it needs to seem familiar enough that they can imagine themselves not just living there but also actually making the journey. The tale should be heroic all right, because that imparts meaning to sacrifice, but it can't be fantastic, meaning no "flying cars" or any other imagined technologies that save the day all on their own. People don't want their future handed to them on a silver platter; they want to build it on their own. What they need from you, the futurist, is just enough information—just enough vision—to give them the confidence to start hammering some stakes into the ground. They want to get rolling, because in the end, they're not interested in following you. They just want you to point the direction and then get out of the way.

That's what is so exciting about crafting a strategic vision: if you do it right, it unleashes so much pent-up energy—especially among the young. It's easy sometimes to think all that passion is about you, but whenever I'm tempted to go down that path, I just visit a few chat rooms where college kids are vigorously debating the book or my

SHRINKING THE GAP BY ENDING DISCONNECTEDNESS   205

articles and I soon realize I'm rather superfluous to the process. Again, if it's accurate and simple and direct, people are going to be able to digest it and make it their own rather effortlessly, my blessing being neither required nor—in most cases—desired. So yeah, you can make people believe again, you just don't deserve anything more than the simple "thank you" for your efforts. In the end, they're going to do all the hard work anyway.

And yet it's amazing how simply having a vision that people can sign up to seems to most of them as completing the hardest part of the process. In other words, what holds up most solutions to chronic problems is simply getting the consensus on (1) defining the essential nature of the problem; and (2) deciding that a process is needed to reach that desired solution. Once people agree on the destination and the essential need to make that journey, everything else begins to fall into place. That sense of wandering around aimlessly disappears, replaced by a sense of both definable purpose and demonstrable progress. So when people see a wave of democratic yearnings begin to sweep the Arab world following the successful Iraqi elections of January 2005, they not only sense a reason to hope, they get this feeling that "Hey, we're making good time!"

Having that hope in the future is our most important weapon in this global war on terrorism. Knowing you're right is nice, but knowing you're going to win is a whole lot better. War isn't a force that gives our lives meaning, only pain. But within that pain there are sacrifices to be recognized, connections to be forged, and paths to be chosen. The near term is always about hard choices and difficult tasks, and pragmatism isn't just warranted, it should be ruthlessly applied wherever circumstances demand. What keeps you grounded in all those short-term choices, though, is your sense that no matter how hard today is, it's going to get you closer to the future you know is out there, just waiting to be created.

So you can't be just about peace in this quest, because that's like pretending you can fashion a world with neither crime nor police. It just doesn't work that way, and it never will. So keeping it real means it's not simply a matter of constructing a military able to move beyond just waging war to truly waging peace. No, you have to be able to draw convincingly the connection from peace *back* to war. It's a two-way street. We have to be able to understand not just the journey from war to peace but also which developments achieved along the way render that peace both just and lasting. This is important to remember, because most of our victories in this grand struggle won't involve the military. In the end, it'll be mostly the work of private individuals that'll secure the victory, capitalizing on what the military effort made possible but could never come close to completing. So this trip isn't going to be one of those "wake me up when we get there" things.

This journey involves a number of key building blocks, and I want to touch upon the three most important ones in this chapter: namely, the importance of good governance in the political development of any Gap state, the crucial role played by women in the social development of any Gap nation, and how the individual's access to financial capital determines the market development of any Gap economy. But before I do that, I want to give you a clear sense of how I imagine the Gap can be successfully shrunk on a region-by-region level and how that journey will look and feel for individual states as they migrate toward the status of Seam States (i.e., those countries lying on the frontier of globalization's advance) and eventually join the New Core. By doing so, I hope to impart a sense of that journey from war to peace, from sheer disconnectedness to deep connectivity, and from Gap to Core. More than that, though, I want you to recognize the *everything else* that goes into this grand strategy, seeing this process as fundamentally one of building a better world from the ground up: to shrink the Gap, you need integrated regions; to integrate regions, you need states able to open up to the outside world; to get globalizing states, you need more competent and confident governments; and to get governments of that caliber, you need women empowered by education and entrepreneurs empowered by capital.

THE COMING CHOICES

There is a place—a sweet spot, if you will—for a well-crafted grand strategic vision. It lies just on the edge of plausibility. If you hit that sweet spot, the first response you're going to get from most people is this: "It's never gonna happen . . . but, you know, it does make a lot of sense when you think about it. But it'll never happen." That's exactly the discomfort zone where grand strategy should hit: just beyond the average person's sense of what's possible, but still just logical enough and optimistic enough so that it's hard to dismiss and still harder not to like. You want people to smile unconsciously even as they're shaking their heads no. That's exactly where you want them, because if you're not pushing people to think beyond today's obvious possibilities, which are always greatly restricted by the crushing combination of past legacies and current responsibilities ("Oh, I could never do that! Or could I?"), then you're not offering them any wiggle room, and everyone—especially political leadership—wants wiggle room.

Wiggle room is always about the future, because that's where you start creating legacies and downstream outcomes that will serve to constrain the choices of future leaders, just as past leaders did unto us. Dealing with those constraints is something our military does fairly well, but expanding that wiggle room for political leaders is something it has a hard time accomplishing. The Defense Department, for example, spends a lot of time modeling the ramping-up of crises in the direction of war, while the State Department and the U.S. Agency for International Development spend a lot of time examining the far side of conflict—namely, the reconstruction of damaged societies and their reintegration into the global community of states. But what the U.S. Government doesn't spend a lot of intellectual capital on is thinking about that transition from war to peace, and you know what? That's where all the wiggle room tends to be found. It's like that crucial point in any home remodeling project where the contractor's ripped out the old but hasn't yet started putting in the new. That's a serious wiggle zone where you can really recalibrate your approach, because at that point the old reality's been laid bare and you haven't yet committed yourself down any particular path, other than completing this project one way or the other.

We need to get a whole lot smarter about that transition space between war and peace. At this point in history the United States possesses an unparalleled capacity to wage war. We can certainly do a lot of good with it, but only if both we and the rest of the Core can learn not just to spot those moments of potentially transformative change in any troubled Gap state but get sufficiently organized to take advantage of them—to bring them to fruition. For now, we're like the doctor who knows how to conduct surgery but hasn't a clue about the patient's anatomy beyond simply realizing which parts you cannot remove without killing him. That's where the generation of new rule sets is so important: not in the war and not in the peace, both of which we understand fairly well, but rather in the space between them. Show me a mature A-to-Z rule set on how to process politically bankrupt states and I will show you more than enough wiggle room for the Core's political leadership to pursue a strategy of rapidly shrinking the Gap over the next twenty years. Practice will never make us perfect, but it'll make us smart enough so that there's no excuse for not trying.

But to get to that happy ending, we need more than contingency planning: we need a truly positive and ambitious strategic vision. Contingency planning is all about mitigating future failures, but strategic vision is all about exploiting future successes. Strategic vision isn't just about getting what we want, and it certainly isn't just about trying to get what we want all on our own. Strategic vision has to be about defining a future worth creating for the planet as a whole, because anything more narrowly defined is—by definition—unsustainable in a world where disconnectedness defines danger. So we cannot be safe until everyone has been invited into global economy in a deeply integrating manner that reflects not just order but likewise justice.

A strategic vision thus needs to be positive enough to justify the hard work between now and its ultimate realization, not simply to keep the American people on board but to attract the support of the rest of the Core's major powers. To get the latter, our strategic vision can't just be about increasing America's security; it also has to be about expanding the Core and the stable security rule set that defines its lasting peace and stability. This is crucial because to attack the problems of transnational terrorism and other forms of mass violence or military threat inside the Gap is naturally to increase their overall frequency in the short run. Sound counterintuitive? Not really. If you want to disarm the bad guys, you're asking them to give up that which makes them powerful, or what they believe gets them *their* future worth preserving.

So no surprise that when the United States takes up the challenge of a global war on terrorism, terrorism goes up in frequency. To expect anything else is simply not logical. To me, it's like walking into the office of Franklin D. Roosevelt in 1944 and saying, "We've been fighting the Japanese and Germans for three years now, and as far as we can see, not only are we fighting more intensely but there seem to be more people fighting on their side!" In effect, we employ the language of war and then judge it in terms of police statistics—as in, "Crime is going up!" That's not to say that the police metaphor is misplaced, because it's not, so long as we're talking about results inside the Core, but inside the Gap such a metaphor is simply premature. Through long-term integration of these disconnected regions into the mature global economy, we can talk about shifting our sense of measurements from war to peace, or from military to police. But until a certain threshold is reached, it remains a war inside the Gap, one whose success will be measured on our side, not by the diminishment of terrorism (or terrorists, for that matter) but by its progressive geographic retreat deeper into the Gap as globalization's deep connectivity extends itself and less-developed regions are progressively absorbed into the Core.

In many ways, then, our efforts to shrink the Gap involve us in a number of implied races with the terrorist networks that plague so many societies there. We seek to create a bandwagon effect across the global economy, enlisting the support of our logical allies in this struggle. Conversely, our enemies seek to create bystanders by targeting our weakest links, or those Core states most vulnerable to their

terrorist acts. We target rogue regimes that support transnational terrorism, while they target preglobalized states (typically failed regimes)
for sanctuary, thus triggering our interventions and subsequent nation-
building efforts. We push toward a victory defined as eliminating all
their secure havens, while the terrorists fight essentially a defensive
war designed to motivate our retreat from their world and the establishment of civilizational apartheid. Our sense of progress comes in
isolating and disabling their network nodes, and theirs come in expanding the reach of their operations and the robustness of their networks. Despite both sides feeling as though they're trapped in a series
of never-ending races, each assumes time is ultimately on its side:
we're rich and getting richer (i.e., a preponderance of resources), but
they wage a calculated war of attrition designed to wear us down and
sap our sense of purpose and moral cause.

Let's be clear on that last point, because our enemy's success need
not require their discrediting of globalization as a historical process,
just the United States. Because once the world's sole military superpower is convinced to abandon its military efforts to defeat the forces
of disconnectedness inside the Gap, then the rest of the world's major
powers will simply conclude their separate peace arrangements as
required with the various dictators who will continue to flourish there.
They will do this because, without the long reach of the U.S. military's
power, Core pillars such as the EU, China, India, and Japan will have
no choice but to bargain for their continued access to the Gap's key
resources—especially energy. Over time, more of the Gap would suc-
cumb to instability and mass violence absent America's Leviathan-like
military presence, forcing great powers to increase their own military
spending to secure—in a zero-sum fashion—their desired level of connectivity to key sources of raw materials. Eventually, we'd see the return of the same colonial-style relationships that defined the global
economy in the first great period of globalization, stretching roughly
from 1870 to 1914.

Thus, if the United States fails in its current attempts to enlist the
support of other great powers in a shrink-the-Gap grand strategy,
we'll probably see those states try to carve out their own "spheres of

influence" there in much the same way the United States and the Soviet Union competed for allies in the Third World during the Cold War. But make no mistake, America's failure wouldn't eliminate the need for Leviathan and SysAdmin activities inside the Gap's troubled regions; it would just turn a potentially cooperative venture of great powers into a competitive one. So if you are offended by the notion of the Core's collective paternalism toward the Gap's less-advanced states, look at it this way: the alternative involves the world's great powers each doing similar things on its own, frequently at odds with one another. We can either share this burden collectively, utilizing the comparative advantage each of the Core's pillars brings to the table, or we can all replicate one another's efforts absurdly, spending a large part of our time engaged in useless competitions with one another inside the Gap.

So ask yourself, which is better? "Trapping" U.S. military power inside a Core-wide rule set that determines when and under what conditions it can be effectively employed (don't forget, we can always pursue pointless interventions on our own)? Or triggering a Core-wide arms race to see which great power can field the most frightening colonial corps? In the former, America gets the privilege of owning the world's largest gun, so to speak, but in the latter, we're looking at a number of rivals (perhaps the EU and Japan, and certainly China and India) who are similarly armed.

Wouldn't it just be better for the United States to accept such rivalry, especially if it's "inevitable" with China? That way we'd retain our freedom of action, even as we'd probably end up paying a steep price for staying ahead of our rival in military capabilities.

In the end, however, this route would probably damage our interests most of all. First, we wouldn't be able to afford that force, especially if the rest of the Core's major economies (Japan, China, South Korea) stopped treating the dollar as their preferred reserve currency, a frightening plot turn I would logically associate with this more conflicted scenario. Second, in a competitive race to recolonize the Gap, the United States would naturally find itself progressively shut out of certain regions. No longer the "indispensable nation," since we would have forced other great powers to replicate our military means (thus beggaring us all), we could expect our competitors to pursue regional integration schemes that raised barriers to our entry into their common markets and collective security alliances, meaning it would no longer be a given that we deserved a free seat at every important table.

As in most of my arguments, I'm not trying to convince you that my "naïve optimism" will win out in the end because it's virtuous and logical. Rather, this vision will ultimately unfold simply because alternative routes will prove far too costly and much too painful to endure over the long haul. America's growing debt crisis cannot continue indefinitely, and its pending resolution will force upon us a series of difficult choices and adjustments, in both our domestic and foreign policies. We might pretend we can bring "liberty and freedom" to the entire Gap all on our own, but the farther we move down this track, the more apparent it will become that (1) only the Core as a whole can effectively shrink the Gap; and (2) the most efficient division of labor would be to have the United States continue to provide the bulk of the high-end military capabilities (i.e., Leviathan) for that effort, with New Core powers like China and India providing the majority of the manpower-intensive resources (SysAdmin).

America possesses a Leviathan-like military *only* because the world's other great powers have chosen not to replicate those capabilities on their own. Eventually, our ability to retain, much less use, that Leviathan must be predicated upon our government's growing adherence to a Core-wide security rule set. That's not utopianism and it's sure as hell not one-world government. It's just being practical. In sum, we can certainly self-finance the military force needed to keep America safe from the Gap's instabilities, so long as we don't care about what happens to the global economy in the process. What we can't afford on our own is the military force that's sufficient to shrink that Gap over time—unless the Core's other great pillars support that strategy from A to Z. There's only one win-win route here, take it or leave it. We can rule the world militarily all right. We just can't do it by ourselves.

As I said earlier, I'm not talking about any "global test," but simply buy-in from the rest of the Core's biggest powers, to include China,

India, Russia, Brazil, Japan, and Europe. Frankly, as we look ahead it gets hard to imagine anything worth doing militarily inside the Gap that won't be met with the approval of these Core pillars.

But you counter, "Aha! What happens when the United States seeks to topple some rogue regime and that government's already deeply in cahoots with some other Core pillar—say, like China's growing ties to Iran?" In that case, I think we simply have to be realistic about what can be done. If China is pulled into an embrace with Iran over energy to the extent that Beijing simply won't tolerate the United States' imposing its will militarily on Iran, then we're simply looking at the converse of our relationship with Saudi Arabia. In such a case we need to apply the same logic to the Chinese-Iranian bond that we apply to our own with the House of Saud: the goodness of the many (the global economy) outweighs the badness of the few (the corrupt/authoritarian leadership in question). When a country like Iran has achieved that sort of leverage with China, we need to view that connectivity as the opportunity for influence that it represents, and not merely some obstructionist response on Beijing's part.

If we simply ignore that connectivity and go ahead with our military intervention despite China's overlapping interests, we'd better understand that the ultimate cost to Core unity—and thus to globalization's future—is likely to overwhelm any particular security interest that may accrue to us. Is the United States capable of such self-inflicted strategic wounds? Sure. In fact, I think we're far more likely to move in the direction of enmeshing our military power within some larger Core-wide security rule set *as a result of such abject failures* rather than any successes we might enjoy unilaterally in this global war on terrorism. Again, I believe this vision is inevitable *primarily* because our accumulation of failures will force America down this path—optimism tempered by realism.

Those failures will come in the following manner: our failure in controlling our debt will engender a balancing response from the Core's other major economies (Asia and Europe will stop buying our debt at the same rate); that debt "failure" will impose a budgetary crunch on the U.S. military that is profound; those lost capabilities will mean either that America is less likely to intervene in the Gap militarily or, if it does, that it's more likely such interventions will end very badly; that poor administration of security in the Gap will result in more violence emanating from those regions and affecting the global economy as a whole; and as the Core's collective pain level rises, the United States will be forced into acting in conjunction with other great powers to reduce that discomfort to some level acceptable to the American public.

Or . . . we can accept the inevitability of this scenario and move strategically today to avoid this outcome.

And no, I'm not the only strategist to have figured this out. Frankly, the rest of the Core's great powers are already preparing to make this scenario come about if we don't come to our senses.

Having said all that, I'm betting on the more painful route in our relations with the rest of the Core. Why? Until we create a significant bureaucratic center of gravity capable of executing a coherent, government-wide strategy to shrink the Gap (and no, that new puny postconflict stabilization office in the State Department won't do it), our efforts to defeat global terrorism will probably remain far more punitive than preventive, relying excessively on the use of military force. Over time and through subsequent administrations, either we'll just learn to live with the continuing frustrations associated with that one-dimensional approach or we'll back off from trying further.

Why? America won't get consistent support for its scattershot efforts from the rest of the Core's great powers. Instead, we'll be forced into relying on "coalitions of the willing" as a rule, and that sort of ad hoc burden sharing doesn't really work over the long haul. You can make it work here and there under the best of circumstances, but never consistently, because the temptation for free ridership (letting the "next guy" do it) simply overwhelms the logic of doing your fair share *absent* an explicit rule set that compels such behavior. Imagine the United States trying to rally Western Europe for each and every military standoff with the Soviet bloc across the Cold War *absent* the NATO structure.

If that seems fantastic to you, then how can you expect a better outcome in America's ongoing efforts to get the rest of the Core to help it eliminate the far less coherent threats arising from the Gap's disconnectedness? Without an accepted rule set that unites the Core in its approach over the years, we're likely to see various great powers strike out on their own in a series of disconnected preemptive wars that yield no lasting stability inside the Gap but simply preview return engagements, much as *Desert Storm* telegraphed its "sequel," *Operation Iraqi Freedom*. In short, America's efforts to maintain its "freedom of action" will inevitably create copycat strategies among what should be our main allies in this effort—a sort of use-it-*and*-lose-it grand strategy.

If we stipulate that the only way one can describe various sequences of Gap shrinkage over time is to accept the logic of a Core-wide effort, what are the most likely pathways?

Here I would offer three simple rules: First, shrinking the Gap is likely to occur in waves, meaning that regional collections of states will be integrated into the Core at roughly the same time, much the way NATO and the EU have simultaneously integrated the bulk of East Central Europe over the last decade. These package deals will reflect the simple reality that a critical mass of stability and connectivity is required for any region or subregion to be considered truly part of the Core. So yes, Singapore may be a magnet for global financial connectivity in the predominantly Gap-like Southeast Asia, but until the region as a whole finds itself safely integrated within a larger definition of Asia that includes at least China and probably must include both a united Korea and Japan, Singapore itself can't really be considered part of the Core. When enough such connectivity emerges, though, Singapore won't be the only member of the Association of Southeast Asian Nations (ASEAN) to enjoy that sense of membership, as ASEAN will graduate—so to speak—as a class.

Second, the scenarios by which Gap shrinkage are sequenced will always feature a certain contiguity, meaning the geographic extension of the Core will unfold in a domino-like fashion. In other words, we'll squeeze the Gap from the outside in, rather than integrate individual states in a scattershot fashion. This rule really only affects the deepest interior regions of the Gap, or those of sub-Saharan Africa, which are highly unlikely to be integrated in a fashion that leapfrogs either Northern Africa or the Middle East—that is, we'll have to get there from somewhere in between. This makes sense in two ways: first, there is the simple logic of physical networks and their extension in an outwardly growing, crystal-like pattern; and second, it will always make sense to keep today's fights contiguous with the newest of the Core states or those most willing to support the struggle over the long haul given the geographic immediacy of their interests.

Third, the process of shrinking the Gap will inevitably reshape the Pentagon's global command structure, known as the Unified Command Plan. Right now a total of four regional commands encompass the Gap: Southern Command, which covers Central and South America; European Command, which covers all of Africa except Egypt through the Horn; Central Command, which covers the rest of Africa, the Persian Gulf area over through Pakistan, and the Central Asian republics; and Pacific Command, which covers the rest of South Asia and Southeast Asia. Eventually, the U.S. military will have only three regional combatant commands: the current Northern Command for North America (eventually subsuming Southern Command's purview over Latin America); a command that facilitates military cooperation with the rest of the Core (probably centered on a combination of Joint Forces Command, Strategic Command, and Transportation Command); and one dedicated specifically to the Gap as a whole (a merging of the current Central Command with Special Operations Command). We already see this dynamic unfolding with the global war on terrorism, where Special Operations Command was given operational control over the entirety of U.S. direct actions against transnational terrorist networks throughout the Gap. The current Unified Command Plan divides the world in bands running north to south, whereas the enemies we fight in this global war on terrorism tend to network more in an east-west fashion, thus confounding our efforts by creating a host of unwanted seams in which coordination tends to break down among the current regional commanders.

Working off that basic rule set, I'll now break the Gap down into four constituent regions:

1. The Islamic world that encompasses Northern Africa, the Middle East, and Central and Southwest Asia
2. The Asia-Pacific Rim portion
3. The Latin American regions of the Caribbean, Central America, and Andean South America
4. Sub-Saharan Africa

Because the United States provides both the vast bulk of the Leviathan force and the "hub" of the Core's SysAdmin force, it's logical that America's sense of strategic priorities will guide the sequencing of Gap shrinkage over the years. As such, it makes sense to assume that all possible sequences begin with our current effort to transform the Middle East. Taking that as a starting point for any scenario, the question then becomes "Who will experience subsequent bursts of extended effort by the Core in a similarly 'transformational' manner?" Since the perception of threat drives this decision-making process over time, it truly does come down to a question of "What do we fear the most at this time?"

If we stipulate that all scenarios begin with the Bush Administration's Big Bang strategy in the Middle East, a total of six subsequent paths are possible. I'll explore each sequence in turn now, according to the threat definition I can imagine being attached to each strategy.

The Rogue-State Scenario

The most likely sequence would correspond to the Bush Administration's focus on the so-called axis of evil, which originally included Iraq, Iran, and North Korea but could easily be expanded to include others, such as Bashar al-Assad's Syria, Hugo Chavez's Venezuela, or Robert Mugabe's Zimbabwe. Accepting the notion that any attempt to deal with both Iraq and Iran in the Middle East would keep the United States there for a fairly long stretch of time, then the question would become "At what point does the situation in the Persian Gulf settle down enough to allow a new focus on regime change in North Korea and a ramping-up of efforts across Southeast Asia to deal with the threats of transnational terrorism and ideologically inspired insurgencies there?" Absent some settling in the Gulf, the question could also be rendered as "What kind of radical instability in East Asia would be required to pull the strategic attention of the United States out of the Middle East and shift it to Asia?"

As I indicated earlier, I see more danger in North Korea and more promise in Iran, so I would advocate co-opting Iran regarding its quest for nuclear weapons by accepting that status and using this newly granted "prestige" to facilitate a grand bargain between Washington and Tehran regarding a host of security issues in the Middle East, to include the long-term stabilization of a Shiite-dominated Iraq and the codification of the two-state solution for Israel and Palestine. At that point, I would advocate the United States targeting North Korea for regime change with an eye to erecting an Asian NATO in that effort's wake.

Beyond those two regions, a rogue-state focus would likely push the United States in the direction of Latin America next, with the settlement of Colombia's long-running civil war being the likely draw, although Hugo Chavez's growing penchant for meddling in the affairs of neighboring states (e.g., Colombia, Bolivia) might place him a close second.

As such, Africa would rank last in this scenario, as it has yet to produce a rogue state of sufficiently menacing threat to demand U.S. attention. Given Africa's limited economic connectivity to the Core, it would take a lot from a rogue regime to pull the United States in this direction ahead of the other three regions.

The Islamic Arc Scenario
The second most likely sequence would focus on integrating the Islamic world as a whole with the Core and, after the initial focus on the greater Middle East, would follow the same secondary path as the Rogue-State Scenario by moving next to the major Islamic popula-

tions of South and Southeast Asia. The main difference in this scenario would be the lack of any attempt to dislodge Kim Jong Il's regime in North Korea. Hence the focus would remain on the southern Asian littoral states, and this would only strengthen the evolution of the U.S. military away from traditional combat operations to counterinsurgency operations. The role of the U.S. Navy would nonetheless be highlighted in this path because of its capacity to engage local militaries in cooperative security ventures, such as multinational efforts to increase security in the various straits and key shipping lines that crisscross the Indian Ocean region. Also in this scenario you would see the United States and China continue to split the difference in their relative spheres of influence, with the United States sticking to the littoral nations and China increasingly dominating the Asian heartland's security scene. Additionally, this scenario would place a premium on U.S.-Indian naval cooperation to guarantee the secure flow of energy from the Gulf to Developing Asia.

Following that secondary focus, this scenario would concentrate next on sub-Saharan Africa, to which the global Salafi jihadist movement would be likely to migrate in its continuing resistance to the spread of globalization as part of Islam's slow but steady penetration of the continent. The Caribbean, with an overwhelmingly Christian population, would receive the least priority in this scenario.

The Failed-State Scenario

The third most likely sequence would involve a consistent focus on failed states as part of a larger strategy of defeating poverty inside the Gap. Following the initial focus on the Middle East, which could be lengthened in this scenario to include a significant effort at economic development in the Central Asian region, the focus would shift immediately to Africa—ground zero for failed and weak states in general. This scenario would see the Core's effort move in the direction of dramatically increasing the flow of official developmental aid to the continent along the lines called for in the recent Millennium Development Challenge project of the United Nations. As such, the U.S. military's evolution toward the SysAdmin function would be greatly accelerated in this path, as would Sino-American military cooperation on the continent, given China's rapidly rising economic interests there. In effect, America would set the table and China would eat the meal, treating its SysAdmin role as a market-conquering mechanism. How would America tolerate this development? Easy. China's got the people to throw at the problem of ground-floor economic development in Africa. Remember, in coming decades the Old Core will make its money in the New Core, and the New Core will need to draw an increasing percentage of its raw material imports from the Gap, so the division of labor makes sense.

Beyond Africa, a good argument exists for a subsequent focus on Asia rather than Latin America, primarily because state failure in the former has greater potential for damaging the global economy, as demonstrated in the Asian flu of 1997–98.

The main advantage of this approach is that it's most likely to garner European support for its focus on developmental aid, thereby achieving the greatest good most quickly. The major disadvantage is that the Core tackles the toughest nuts to crack first, raising the question of staying power in a strategy that does not focus on the most immediate sources of security threats to the Core (i.e., transnational terrorists).

The Homeland Security Scenario

The next most likely sequence would probably come about as a result of America's sense of exhaustion following the extensive effort to generate and guide positive political change in the Middle East. Once that process was pushed to the point of perceived success, a strong sense could emerge among the American public for shifting to matters closer to home. A focus on homeland security would get the United States to the Caribbean and the Andean portion of South America most quickly, out of a direct sense of the dangers presented by instabilities closest to our borders—namely, the illegal flow of drugs and immigrants into the United States from Latin America.

This scenario's subsequent focus would be more likely to fall on Asia than Africa, simply because Africa offers less in transnational terrorist threats and immigration flows.

The Energy-Independence Scenario

This sequence would see the United States show the least amount of interest in Asia, as, following our initial focus on the Persian Gulf and Central Asia, the next most compelling case would be Africa, followed by Andean South America. The likelihood of this path is enhanced to the extent that Asia's rising dependence on the Middle East pushes powers like China, India, and Japan to secure their own long-term access to the region through military means, leading the United States to focus more on Western Africa and the Western Hemisphere as its main foreign sources for energy. This strategy would therefore dovetail with domestic U.S. desire to "get off our dependency on Middle Eastern oil."

The main advantage to this approach is that it would probably be the least expensive in terms of military spending and developmental aid. The main disadvantages would be the assumptions that (1) if America got what it needed from the world in terms of energy, the rest of the Core would do just enough to make sure their neighboring Gap regions didn't get out of hand in terms of instability; and that (2) Core unity could be maintained despite the lack of much coordinated effort inside the Gap. As such, this scenario would come closest to the return of nineteenth-century colonialism, with the ultimate downside being that this would clearly be the slowest route to shrinking the Gap over time.

The Humanitarian-Aid Scenario

I consider this sequence the least attractive and therefore the least likely, because it does little to speed the global war on terrorism to its quickest conclusion. It is the scenario most likely to unfold following America's failure to transform the Middle East and would represent an inward turn toward revitalizing America's domestic economy and society while applying the Band-Aid approach to stemming bad things coming out of the Gap and entering the Core. The focus here would be on the most bare-bones System Administration function: treating the worst humanitarian disasters inside the Gap and waiting on the expansion of the global economy into Gap regions to do the rest, no matter how long that took. This approach would come closest to the Core fire-walling itself off from the Gap and simply sending in "ambulances" with armed guards to deal with any situations that frightened us to the point of reaction. Other than that minimal approach, we'd do little to secure the Gap's regions and encourage foreign direct investment. Thus, left to its own devices, the Gap would worsen over time, becoming ever more disconnected from the global economy.

In terms of regional foci, the U.S. effort would likely center first on Latin America simply because of its proximity and thus ability to generate economic refugees and traveling epidemics. This strategy would dovetail with a renewed focus on the war on drugs, probably coupled with intensified efforts to stem the tide of illegal immigrants from the South. Africa would receive the next greatest amount of attention, simply because the levels of pain and suffering there would be likely to outdistance those of Asia, where one could expect rising China, rising India, and perennial top aid donor Japan to pull their own weight sufficiently. To the extent that anyone felt responsible for any continuing lack of economic development in the Middle East, it would probably be the EU that made the largest humanitarian effort, as Asian powers, following America's abandonment of its security role in the region, would tend to be satisfied to cut the most cynical deals on energy with the surviving authoritarian regimes there.

Wild Cards That Prioritize One Gap Region over Others in Sequencing

The biggest potential wild card is easily an incident involving a weapon of mass destruction inside the United States. Although such an event could trigger a turn toward significant isolationism, the far greater likelihood is that we'd go on a headhunting tear that would make our efforts to date in the Middle East seem quite tame in comparison. The key factor here would be our perception of the Gap country most directly responsible for allowing whatever transnational terrorist group succeeded in employing WMD to operate from their territory in some manner. At the current time, the country that would most probably fit that bill, if the global Salafi jihadist movement were responsible for such a strike, would be Pakistan, and given the size of that country (over 150 million citizens), the profound nature of our military response would no doubt keep us focused on that part of the world to the exclusion of all else for quite some time.

Following that very negative scenario, the most powerful vignettes would naturally involve China. In my mind, the most frightening specter for the Core as a whole would be a crisis involving China that would trigger its resumption of a hostile and xenophobic approach to the outside world. The most likely path here is a domestic economic crisis leading the Communist Party leadership to resort to manufacturing some external crisis to buttress its otherwise collapsing legitimacy, with Taiwan being the obvious first target.

The most frightening external shock to China's standing would be likely to come in the form of some disastrous downturn in Persian Gulf stability that would trigger a panicked response from Beijing regarding its energy security, possibly pushing it to focus far more intensely on securing direct access to energy supplies in countries contiguous to its borders, such as Russia's Far East regions, Kazakhstan, and the significant undersea hydrocarbon reserves surrounding the Spratly Islands in the South China Sea. The crux of the danger here would be China's aggressive moves to create military dominance over such territories, triggering military resistance from the region's other major powers and probably from the United States.

The most frightening internal shock for China is an easy one to guess: a banking or financial panic leading to significant internal protest. If I were a betting man, I would lay my money on this one as being most likely out of all the wild cards. In some ways it's almost guaranteed, given the heat of China's economic growth. At some point there's going to be a financial meltdown of sorts, and people will become more than just angry. The real uncertainty here is twofold: how China's political leadership reacts and how the rest of the Core reacts. The best hope is that cool heads prevail on all sides, but I'll be happy with two out of three, or even just one out of three, so long as that one ends up being the rest of the Core.

Beyond the key pillars of the United States and China, the next most damaging scenarios would involve a nuclear exchange between Pakistan and India that would knock the latter out of the global economy because of the great economic and social devastation involved, and anything involving Russia that triggered its own version of preemptive wars in its "near abroad." Both would likely have the same effect of ratcheting up the U.S. level of effort in Southwest Asia to the point of precluding serious efforts elsewhere in the Gap for upwards of a decade or more.

The wild card most likely to generate a Core-wide response that's heavier on foreign aid and thus lighter on military interventions would be some massively destructive pandemic coming out of the Gap and killing millions across the Core. Statistically speaking, the most likely sequence here would be an influenza pandemic emanating from Southeast Asia, which, because of that region's growing connectivity with the rest of the global economy, would provide the greatest likelihood of a truly debilitating death count that reordered the Core's sense of security priorities. The second most likely geographic source would be Africa, but as evidenced from the Core's still slow response to the unfolding AIDS epidemic there (to include the huge medical bill that's building inside such New Core pillars as India, China, and Russia), the end result of such a scenario could well be to isolate Africa even further.

The wild card that would most quickly sap the Core's collective willingness to shrink the Gap would be some unprecedented series of ecological disasters stemming from global climate change, because such events would be likely to turn the Core's attention inward toward dramatic attempts to reshape their energy profiles as quickly as possible, effectively leaving the Gap to fend for itself.

Finally, there are a variety of wild card scenarios regarding war in the Middle East that would have the effect of trapping the United States militarily in the region for the long haul, with probably the most important one being Israel waging preemptive war against Iran as the latter gets close to weaponizing its nuclear capabilities. By and large, the main impact of all such scenarios would be to delay significantly all the sequencing possibilities outlined above, as the general upshot would be that the rest of the Gap could regress significantly (in large part because of the damage resulting to the global economy from such wars) while the Core's attention would remain inordinately fixated on the Middle East.

It's only natural to recoil at the specter of the long-haul effort involved in shrinking the Gap. The point of exploring these sequencing scenarios is to force a discussion of the competing logic attached to each strategic focus. Until we can wrap our minds around such arguments, the goal of shrinking the Gap will continue to elicit that sort of "It'll never happen!" response that will only grow more pervasive the farther we move away from the wake-up call that was 9/11.

While consideration of cost versus benefit will always be called for, especially when our sacrifice includes loved ones dying distant from our shores, a sense of perspective is in order. We lose far more "System Administrator" forces at home each year (e.g., cops, firemen, other emergency responders) than we do abroad. While that realization is not meant to diminish the sacrifice of our military personnel, it does serve to remind us that all societies—from the national to the global—come with a human price tag in the maintenance of security and peace. Given the extent of our society's never-ending sacrifice to maintain the peace at home, we need to ask ourselves as a nation what level of effort would ultimately be warranted to achieve the same in a world without war. For if we are not prepared to provide our fair share to such a global effort (defined in terms of our wealth, not our population), then there really is no lasting purpose in waging a global war on terrorism.

There's no sense in starting a journey to a world we don't care to inhabit. We cannot imagine what we cannot describe. The future worth creating is worth creating now, otherwise it remains an abstraction that forever falls short of constituting a genuine blueprint for action.

TIPPING POINTS IN THE JOURNEY
FROM THE GAP TO THE CORE

Since the terrorist attacks of 9/11, the U.S. Government's bureaucratic responses give off that usual American sense of "We have identified the problem and we can fix it." The problem is, we tend to identify ourselves as the problem, when nothing could be further from the truth. America continues to serve as globalization's bow wave, meaning we're constantly charting new waters as we struggle to figure out what all this growing connectivity imparts in both promise and peril. The 1990s featured a huge expansion of the global economy, surprising both experts and average citizens alike, so it's little wonder that we felt plenty behind the curve when 9/11 came along and smacked us upside the head.

But instead of realizing what an amazing process we've set in motion through our longtime role as globalization's bodyguard (i.e., first to the West in the Cold War and now to the Core as a whole), we've wasted a lot of time and effort since 9/11 blaming ourselves and acting as if the weight of the entire world sits atop our shoulders when the good news is, we're just reaching the point in history when America no longer defines globalization's advance. In other words, help has arrived in the form of Old Core allies (Europe, Japan) who now—in general—want to do more and potential New Core allies (Brazil, China, India, Russia) who should be similarly tapped for what they can bring to the table.

But instead of realizing that we stand atop a tipping point of expanded partnership with all these powers, America has gone in the opposite direction of acting as though securing our country is the same as securing globalization's future, when that is no longer the case. Globalization's Functioning Core has simply gotten a whole lot bigger than just America in the last decade and a half, and that's been all for the better. Rather than reaching out, though, we spent most of our efforts since 9/11 getting ourselves in order (e.g., Department of Homeland Security, intelligence community reforms) and striking out (Afghanistan, Iraq) with little regard for how the rest of the Core comes to view these acts. The problem is, of course, that the sum total of our responses comes off as both selfish and myopic, not to mention awfully egotistical ("It's all about me—America!").

The tendency to confuse globalization with Americanization is widespread, when in reality globalization has already moved well beyond that narrow cultural definition—beyond that of Westernization itself. In ten years' time, no one with a decent understanding of how the world works will be able to pretend that globalization is an American plot to rule the world. That's because we won't be the only superpower on the block. Just like the many facets of human intelligence (e.g., linguistic, logical, spatial, musical, interpersonal), globalization's power structure will be defined in numerous ways.

The European Union is becoming a superpower on two crucial levels. First, the rise of the euro creates an alternate global reserve currency that will increasingly balance that 800-pound gorilla called the U.S. dollar. That's crucial, because without such an alternative, there's nothing and nobody in the Core that can push the United States toward better long-term fiscal responsibility regarding such issues as its aging population and its skyrocketing medical costs. The euro also offers other Core powers an alternative to linking their economies so extensively to the dollar, which gives them more flexibility in managing their own economic-growth trajectories. Plus, having the European Central Bank join the U.S. Federal Reserve in the role of managing the global economy's money supply is just one of those two-heads-are-better-than-one things that intrinsically make sense.

But Europe also emerges as the great alternative to America's advocacy of minimal rule sets for globalization's advance, especially in economics but likewise in military interventions to shrink the Gap. Unlike America, which really pulled its fifty member states together first before opening up a lot more to the outside world, Europe is already quite integrated with the global economy as it seeks to deepen its own internal integration process while admitting new members from the former socialist bloc. As such, the EU is forced to deal with a lot of difficult questions on the table right now regarding the Union's collective standards for products, labor, technology, and so forth, and in defining those standards the EU is—in many ways—establishing global standards. So if the United States tends to define globalization's rule-set "floor," the EU tends to define its "ceiling."

The same thing will ultimately happen in terms of military interventions: America defines the floor, or the minimal effort required to take down the "bad," while Europe, through its strong advocacy for multilateralism and UN involvement, will increasingly push for definitions of the maximal effort required to set up the "good," meaning they'll push us to define the upper limits of our responsibility for postconflict stabilization and reconstruction—aka, nation building. This is where our desire to "rid the world of evil" will naturally marry up with Europe's more humanitarian focus on relieving suffering inside the Gap. All Europe really has to do is simply move beyond criticizing us for waging war "unilaterally" and start pinning us down with new rules for waging peace multilaterally, making clear the bond of responsibility that links the two halves—that is, don't plan to win the war unless you plan to win the peace. In short, neither the United States nor Europe can get what it wants in places like Iraq (the United States wanted war, Europe passed on the peace) and Sudan (Europe wanted peace, the United States passed on the war) unless we work together. This is globalization at its best: forcing nonzero outcomes where we either win together or lose together but never really win separately.

Beyond Europe, the rest of the Core will offer several similarly important sources of globalization's future rule sets, and in each instance America should not view these "emerging powers" as threats or even competitors so much as additional hands to guide globalization's advance.

Japan's status as a design superpower and major cultural content exporter will also reshape the face of globalization, giving it a decidedly stronger Asian look and feel. If it's suddenly a lot more hip to be Asian around the world (especially among youth), Japan is the big reason why. In my household of four kids, I can tell you that while Disney movies ruled in the 1990s, it's Japanese anime that rocks our boat today. Whether it's my five-year-old's love of Pokémon, my ten-year-old's devotion to his Sony PSP, or my thirteen-year-old's extensive online postings of her manga-inspired drawings, all of my non-Asian kids seem to be turning Japanese before my eyes. My eldest, Emily, is already threatening to learn Japanese and emigrate to the Land of the Rising Sun to spend her life drawing anime vampires.

The reason all my kids look eastward for their creative sources is that Japan has learned to mass-market mass culture in ways that supposedly only that cultural Cuisinart known as America could manage. I used to think the Japanese suffered some strange self-loathing because so many anime shows feature Western-looking characters, until I realized this was just standard practice for these savvy marketers, who now set global standards for cool in such diverse fields as pop music, consumer electronics, architecture, fashion, animation, and cuisine. It's not just anime and sushi, but the larger sense of postindustrialism that ultimately defines the Core's growing cultural unity, and Japan, the most postmodern society of them all, is defining that fusion of national cultures more and more. Is Japan viewed around the world as a "cultural imperialist"? No, but rather as a cultural synthesizer with a softer touch than America, and by setting this sophisticated example of cultural inclusion, despite its well-deserved reputation for xenophobia regarding immigrants, Japan changes the face of globalization from being merely American or Western to something far broader.

China's emergence as a manufacturing superpower is already resetting rules throughout the global economy in commodity markets, and its vastly expanding transportation needs, both on the ground (cars) and in the air (airline industry), have the potential to push the Core as a whole in much needed directions of technological innovation. You want to get to the hydrogen age? China's your best bet, not America. China's huge growth in automobile traffic over the coming years will push it ever faster toward a tipping point on air pollution, in addition to ratcheting up its dependency on foreign sources of oil to a frightening degree. Neither condition will come about in the United States to anywhere near the same degree. Most important, because China's in the process of *creating* a car culture and not recasting one, it'll be far easier for China to choose the alternative pathway of introducing hybrids and ultimately hydrogen fuel-cell cars far earlier in its growth trajectory. The fact that China will soon represent the world's largest car market can trigger changes in car cultures the world over, including the United States, making the Core's transition to the hydrogen age all the faster.

Other New Core pillars of note:

+ India has not only remade the face of both the American information technology sector and its medical field, it is doing the same on a global scale, setting the example for any Gap nation that wants to excel at insourcing service-sector jobs and pioneering the phenomenon of "medical tourism" (traveling to India for the same major surgery that might cost several times more in the Old Core). Then there's Bollywood's rising profile in global cinema. Read *Variety* (Hollywood's bible) sometime. You'll be amazed at how much of that magazine is now devoted to covering India's film industry.

+ Russia's emergence in global oil exports has done a lot to reshape current market flows, but over the longer haul it will have a far greater influence in reshaping the natural gas industry as the world's largest reserve. Between Russia and the Caspian Basin states, including #2 reserve power Iran, Russia could easily form the centerpiece to a natural gas equivalent of OPEC, playing the same role there that Saudi Arabia does in oil.

+ South Africa, as long predicted, is emerging as the economic pillar of sub-Saharan Africa, the flow-through point for global foreign direct investments on the continent and the "lead goose" on technology adoption and network construction. When many African states eventually join the Core, they will probably do so much in the same manner as South Africa, leveraging their abundant mineral resources into infrastructure development.

+ South American New Core powers Argentina, Brazil, and Chile are collectively emerging as the world's agricultural superpower, with Brazil already the world's largest beef exporter. Along with India, Brazil has also become a key pharmaceutical exporter to the Gap, putting that nation at the forefront of treating the global AIDS crisis and transforming it into a leading champion of Gap trade rights with the Core in the Doha Development Round of the WTO. Brazilians also represent a rapidly growing and ever more influential population on the Internet, thanks in no small part to Brazil's decision to make itself a center of the world's open-source software movement.

In his classic description of globalization, *The Lexus and the Olive Tree*, Thomas L. Friedman quoted an Egyptian professor asking, "Does globalization mean we all have to become Americans?" That sort of logic may have made a lot of sense in the 1990s, but in ten years you will be hard-pressed to find informed people anywhere in the world who still see globalization as being solely in America's image.

That's not just a good thing, it's a great thing, because if America isn't *all* of the problem, then it certainly shouldn't be *all* of the solution. Winning this global war on terrorism isn't about replicating our country the world over to assure we'll be safe because we're both universally emulated and thus universally loved. It is about shrinking the Gap, which means turning Gap states into New Core states, and that means the most important exemplars of the way ahead will be countries like Brazil, China, India, Russia, and South Africa—not the United States.

And this is where many of our responses since 9/11 seem to be misguided. First, in making it harder to visit and study and do business in the United States, we may scare off a few Gap terrorists, but we'll also decrease a lot of useful social, economic, and political connectivity with New Core pillars right when we should be drawing them closer.

Second, we should abandon efforts to create a U.S. Government–wide "strategic communications policy" designed to win the "hearts and minds" of young males inside the Gap who are perceived to be at risk for becoming terrorists. Such an approach only reinforces the notion that somehow globalization is really all about Americanization, when it isn't. We have no more need to explain ourselves culturally or politically to the Gap than do the citizens of Brazil, China, or India, three countries whose competitive rise in the global economy increasingly presents more challenges to Gap states than do the policies of an established Core power like America.

Finally, no amount of centralized control in the intelligence community (e.g., the creation of the Director for National Intelligence, tighter budgetary control over the community's fifteen separate agencies) is going to buy us the long-term safety we need. In our increasingly networked world, "czars" will never be the answer. Nor should we swap out—in wholesale fashion—our old pool of intelligence analysts, who tended to focus on New Core military threats like Russia and China, for an entirely new cast of analysts focusing exclusively on the Middle East. Switching from one stovepipe to another isn't the way to go. Rather, we need more expertise, both in our intelligence and our developmental aid communities, on translating the development experience of New Core globalizers for the Gap environment. We need experts on making Indonesia more like China, Iran more like India, Angola more like South Africa, Algeria more like Spain, and Bolivia more like Brazil. These New Core states represent the near-term pathways of success, because while the Old Core's tide lifts New Core boats, it will largely be the New Core's tide that lifts Gap boats. This is yet again why it is so crucial for the United States to view New Core pillars like Brazil, China, India, and Russia as neither threats nor competitors but as key allies in winning this global war on terrorism. They define the path of our eventual victory, their experiences forming much of our own blueprint for action.

So ask yourself: What made these former outsider states part of the new inside? How did these New Core states join the global economy?

Clearly, a lot depends on how these countries are perceived by advanced economies and their investors. What's the difference between an LDC, or less-developed country, and an LCC, a low-cost country? Not as much as you might think. First off, there has to be some baseline of security, because no one wants to plunk a multimillion-dollar factory in some backwater that's about to be overrun by rebels. Once that's established, what is needed next are the basics of infrastructure and sufficiently strong legal rule sets to protect investments once made. Neither has to be perfect beforehand, as private-sector foreign investors are willing to help build both if the period necessary for earning back those initial investments seems reasonable given the potential gains. Yes, the more money flows in, the more foreign investors demand transparency in both political and economic decision making, even to the point of the currency being convertible and thus transparent in its reaction to external monetary pressures.

All these transactions trade sovereignty for connectivity, as domestic power shifts from the public to the private sectors and the domestic economy comes under the increased influence of foreign players. But to Gap states, insourcing jobs equates to "in-coring" their economies, hard-wiring their labor into the Core's service and supply chains. We buy an item in Wal-Mart this afternoon, and its stock replacement gets assembled in Malaysia within hours. Today's Gap company may just be an OEM, or original equipment manufacturer, of other nations' products using other nations' technologies, but over time it moves up the production chain, just as so many firms in the Asian "tigers" (e.g., Singapore, South Korea) did in the 1980s and China and India did in the 1990s. Eventually, that unknown firm becomes an ODM, or original design manufacturer, creating its own products and using its own proprietary technologies.

Sound inconceivable? I'm just old enough to remember when "Made in Japan" was a bad joke, indicating a product of the lowest quality. Now, of course, it represents the highest of high tech. So we know this journey can be made, and none is traversing this territory faster than China is today.

And such journeys from the Gap to the Core will be dotted with inconceivables, or events and developments you were sure you would never read about, such as a natural gas pipeline that runs the width of Pakistan and connects its archenemy India to natural-gas giant Iran. Not possible given all the military tension, you say, but conceivable once India's thirst for energy makes it so, and thus former foes become financial partners. India is itself a wonderful source of such "inconceivable" stories, such as the U.S. Catholic Church outsourcing "special-intention masses" to Indian priests, thanks to the shortage of clergy in America, or the "Black Hole of Calcutta," now called Kolkata, becoming IBM's second largest investment target in the country after high-tech Bangalore. If you can outsource prayers to India, I guess you can build production facilities in Mother Teresa's old neighborhood.

So if you're currently living in the Gap, what will this journey toward the Core look and feel like from your perspective?

As all these "inconceivables" begin to pile up and investors start labeling you an "emerging market," the tipping points will begin coming at you in waves. One of the first will be a dramatic ramping up of your pollution, especially air pollution. Cities will be transformed from what they've been for centuries, as the past is wiped out in favor of huge blocks of new high-rise developments. Many lower-class people will get priced out of their longtime homes, and real estate bubbles will expand and burst with painful regularity. Disorientation will be the order of the day, but if you're lucky, enough of your population will be enthralled by opportunities for lifestyles that would have seemed—there's that word again—*inconceivable* to their parents.

With all that change and opening up to the outside world, your youth will represent everything that's new and aggressive, and your older generations everything that's dated and out of style. Young people will simultaneously display an insatiable taste for all things foreign *and* a new heightened tendency toward rabid nationalism. What'll hold these two opposing concepts together will be a profound sense of idealism: these kids will *expect* a much better future and they'll *expect* their leaders to provide it or get out of their way. But a youth-tilted culture will also just want to have fun, so you'll know you've made it (or are making it) into the Core when there is a specific MTV network dedicated to your nation (Brazil, China, Germany, India, Ireland, Italy, Japan, Korea, Taiwan/Hong Kong, United Kingdom) or region (Europe, Latin America, Southeast Asia).

As your country becomes a place with a future, all those young brains that have been draining overseas will begin to come home. They'll come back not only because it's a place where they can imagine forging a lifetime's worth of a fulfilling career but also because they no longer see it as a challenging place to raise a family compared

with the West. You'll know you've really made it when young Westerners themselves actually start "outsourcing" themselves to your nation
because they feel the same. Moreover, expect more than a few Western
retirees to appear on your shores to start one last career adventure.
You'll need as many of those as you can get, for their unique skills and
long managerial experience.

The closer your nation moves to the Core, the more you take on the
trappings of a "made" state. You become a place where Olympics can
be held, like Seoul in 1988 or Beijing in 2008, and you're granted your
own Magic Kingdom from Walt Disney, like the new one going up in
Hong Kong (its exact location determined by feng shui considerations, of course). Your country thus becomes a new hot spot for global
tourism, and your history is "rediscovered" as though it had been accidentally lost for many centuries. Your public starts becoming a major
market for Hollywood, and the world's biggest music acts start touring in your major cities. Eventually, you become a media content
exporter, as your music, your movies, and your stars start becoming
bigger than the country itself. Plus, it starts becoming a big deal for
Westerners to become famous in your market, because there's real
money to be made in that achievement.

Such connectivity tends to go both ways, so your citizens begin to
travel abroad in record numbers, as in the expected tenfold increase in
Chinese tourists over the next two decades. By 2020, China will provide the global travel industry over 100 million customers annually.
What does that mean for Pacific Rim nations? It means a lot of people
will need to know how to speak Mandarin in coming years, increasing
China's global connectivity all the more. That rising external mobility
will be matched by growing internal mobility. China, for example, is
opening 150 major airports in the next twenty years, while becoming
the world's most dynamic market for passenger jets. Soon, Boeing will
depend more on China than on the Pentagon for its profits. Meanwhile, India just got its first budget-fare airline, called Air Deccan,
which is poised to become the Southwest Airlines of India as the country grows from 15 million air travelers per year today to as many as
70 million by 2010.

As your economy becomes more and more integrated with the outside world, your political system struggles to keep pace in both domestic rules and diplomatic relationships with countries that increasingly share your economic fate. Your country's leadership finds itself having to explain things it never had to explain before, like your companies' tendency to ignore other countries' intellectual property rights. This wasn't a big deal in the past, but as your economy grows in size, it stops being just a nuisance to your global competitors and they start defining it as both a threat and an unfair trade practice. And so you slowly but surely accede to these demands for better rules, because you value the economic connectivity more than the additional profits you keep, and because you can imagine a future when your companies will want the same protection abroad—today's counterfeiters are tomorrow's patent protectionists.

All this growing economic activity fuels a lot of social change, and your population naturally demands more accountability and responsiveness from your government institutions. But while pluralism is always on the rise, most states will remain single-party-run governments for the vast majority of the journey from Gap to Core, because they will favor order over freedom, plus they know a more authoritarian state can mandate changes needed for globalizing the economy more quickly and with less fear of a popular political backlash—so long as the rural poor aren't left too far behind. Naturally, many Core societies will be troubled by your government's authoritarianism, believing that it gives you an unfair economic advantage in certain respects and that it's morally wrong on many levels. But you notice that many nations on your same path are single-party states like your own. In fact, most of your best friends are single-party states.

Your leadership knows that the nation's development needs to cover the physical basics of food, housing, and infrastructure before moving on to the broader social needs for economic and political freedom. Rome wasn't built in a day, and it wasn't built as a democracy. But there's a natural economic progression from collective order to individual freedom over time: for example, state monopolies are great for building networks, but over time free markets are much better at running them. The same is true for the political life of nations: autocrats are great for building nations, but over time democrats are much better at running them.

This philosophy tends to hold true in your foreign policy as well, as your leaders, while often defending themselves from the Old Core's charges of being undemocratic, nonetheless routinely champion the rights of Gap nations vis-à-vis these same states, arguing that it's unrealistic for poorer states to be democratic so long as they're locked into unequal economic relations with richer, more democratic ones.

As your nation moves into membership in the Core, your leaders will swallow their pride on many occasions in order to gain admittance into the halls of power and decision making, but their long-term goals are clear: "Today we take *their* rules, tomorrow they start taking *our* rules." As you therefore move into New Core status, you find your neighbors start making diplomatic and economic efforts to hedge against your rise, and this complicates your relations with the Core incredibly, because your emergence is viewed there with a complex mixture of delight and dread. But the more you integrate economically with the Core's major players, they slowly but surely move from fearing you to needing you, and your diplomats' trick is to make sure that transition is a smooth one. This, of course, seems odd after all those years of your fearing the West and its tendency for colonial aggression, but your leadership learns to take this change in stride because it's a product of your economic success.

Another product of your economic success is less welcome, and that's how your country now can be far more easily swept up in the "network failures" and system perturbations of the Core. When you were a truly Gap economy, you never had to worry about such things, for the Core's economic crises tended to be as distant to you as the Gap's security crises are to the Core. But as your nation integrates itself with the global economy far more deeply, your definitions of military and economic crises overlap more and more with those of other Core nations, meaning you likewise begin to see fellow Core states as sources of stability and the Gap as the wellspring of danger and violence that threatens system stability.

As you become more interdependent with the Core on security matters, it is tempting to use your youth's rising nationalism as a barrier or
shield, but this gets both harder and riskier over time, because the youth
are the segment of the population most networked with the outside
world, so they're the hardest to hide the truth from, plus their passionate
nationalism is a double-edged sword that can end up harming your
regime's legitimacy far more than it protects you from outside influences.

As your nation joins the New Core, you are struck by the great similarities between your own society and that of America. Historically
speaking, you may seem vastly different, but in terms of vibrancy, constant change, and unleashed popular ambition, our two nations are
now much more similar than they were in the past. The strange thing
is, because you're a rising power and America is the military superpower, you may be quite surprised to find your nation's motivations
and actions under greater scrutiny from the United States *after* you
join the Core, despite that journey being of obvious good to America
and fitting with its long-expressed wishes. Over time, you come to
realize not only that America is somewhat paranoid about its grip on
military supremacy but also that the same hypercompetitive spirit that
made America what it is today is the fever that has gripped your rising
nation and that—in this regard—similarities tend to repel.

This can be a dangerous situation for both the New Core power
and the United States whenever a crisis afflicts the system, because, in
many ways, their levels of connectivity with each other are seriously
out of balance. In general, Old and New Core states tend to have far
stronger economic connectivity with each other than political connectivity, and far stronger technological connectivity than security connectivity. Their fates may well be linked, but they tend to look at the
world and at each other through very different eyes. The danger is, of
course, that the stronger forms of connectivity (economic, technological) will trigger disagreements and crises that overwhelm the two
sides' ability to handle them, given their limited political understand-
ings and security bonds. Here, mistakes *can be made,* because perceptions differ greatly, no matter how compelling the underlying
economic rationales.

Often, these political-military crises tend to revolve around the actions or fates of the Seam States that lie on globalization's frontier, being part Core and part Gap in their orientation. Most Seam States are reasonably well connected to the global economy but remain essentially outsiders to its insider decision-making venues, in large part because they're considered the Core's security bulwarks against the vagaries of the Gap's chronic instabilities, to which they themselves are periodically subject. Turkey and Pakistan are probably the two most emblematic Seam States right now, because the Core needs both countries to do well if we're going to effect long-term change in the Persian Gulf and Central Asia. In both cases, though, the Core has asked for plenty of cooperation on security affairs without—in effect—compensating the country economically. Turkey, for example, has been important enough to the West to enjoy NATO membership for several decades now, but it still sits outside the EU for being too culturally "different." Meanwhile, Pakistan has been, for all practical purposes, a major non-NATO ally of the United States for decades, and what does it have to show economically for all that effort? Just a free-trade agreement, recently concluded, that will have minimal effect on bilateral trade.

If the Core is going to be successful in shrinking the Gap over time, we can't settle into permanent "frontier outpost" mentalities with Seam States such as these, or others like Egypt and Thailand. If a country is important enough for the United States to lavish on it a certain amount of military cooperation or even substantial amounts of aid, like Egypt, then we need to go out of our way to reward such countries with far greater amounts of economic connectivity over time, in effect signaling not just the utility of such cooperation but the progressive advance of globalization itself. The European Union seems to be able to make this sort of dual-package approach work with the former socialist states of Eastern Europe, but anywhere we're talking about essentially non-European cultures, the Old Core doesn't seem to be following up whatsoever in matching economic connectivity with military connectivity, except for the U.S. decision to bring drug-war ally Mexico into the North American Free Trade Area (NAFTA) in the 1990s.

In effect we need to put our money where our mouths are in this global war on terrorism as we did during the Cold War, where we not only defended Japan, South Korea, and Western Europe but also went out of our way to establish broadband economic connectivity between these states and ourselves. In the current situation, we need to do more than just hold the line; we need to keep growing globalization by extending the military-market nexus through Seam States and into the Gap. Otherwise, what are we really selling to Seam States in this global war on terrorism? "You keep holding the line militarily so we here in the Core can keep on integrating our markets and living the good life?"

Of course, when Seam States, who seem permanently trapped in this unenviable situation, go overboard now and then in their military prosecution of whatever war we ask them to wage (e.g., drugs, rebels, terrorists), the United States tends to point fingers rather quickly, even when it can seem awfully hypocritical for us to do so. So as far as we're concerned, Mexico never seems to do enough in the drug war, and Pakistan should be able to root out the terrorists in its northwest territories after years of supporting such activities against the Soviets in Afghanistan at our request, and Thailand should be careful not to crack down too indiscriminately on Islamic terrorists within its borders even as we wage fierce battles on a city-by-city basis in Iraq or suffer the embarrassment of the Abu Ghraib or Guantánamo prisoner-abuse scandals. But where is the much-improved economic connectivity that should accompany these great security efforts, and if they're not coming fast enough—or deep enough, as in the case of Mexico—then should the United States be surprised that our security aid to and cooperation with these regimes often lead to unsatisfactory outcomes? If you're Turkey and you're still looking in at the EU after all these years of asking, why should you feel a special obligation to help the United States transform the Middle East?

The reward for serving on the front line of the global economy's advance into the Gap has to be getting off that front line over time, otherwise what's the point? For example, Mexico joined NAFTA over a decade ago and the war on drugs is still being fought primarily at the

U.S.-Mexican border, not farther south. We need to be generating the reverse of the domino effect we once feared in Southeast Asia with the Communists: to make the effort to shrink the Gap at America's side means you're not only invited into the Core, but the Core makes a special effort to trigger similar integration for the countries around you.

Look at China's current impact on Southeast Asia: The more China globalizes and marketizes its economy, the more it forces other smaller states on its rim to do the same, partly as a defensive reaction but likewise to keep pace with China's development. That's what gets you a Vietnam working hard to join the World Trade Organization, or an ASEAN stepping up its own program of internal economic integration. If China can have that kind of positive impact on the region without making any special security demands from these states, then how much more should the United States be willing to do if it asks certain Seam States to stick their necks out militarily in the global war on terrorism?

And when such economic quid pro quos aren't forthcoming, should we be surprised that Seam States appear to lose interest in our security partnerships? Ask yourself, for example, what Russia has won from the United States as a result of its early support in the global war on terrorism. When Russia agreed to ratify the Kyoto Protocol on global warming, the Europeans stepped up immediately to support Moscow's bid to join the WTO. But what has Washington done in exchange for the Russians' accepting our new military bases in the former Soviet republics of Central Asia? The EU wants to lift its self-imposed ban on military sales to China, and the United States says no, so why should China come to America's rescue or support anywhere in our global war on terrorism?

If the Core hasn't moved beyond great-power war, then why are global nuclear stockpiles inside the Core now less than one-third of their Cold War highs? Have we evolved past such competitions and suspicion inside the Core? And if we haven't, then how can we pretend to be waging anything but another pointless war of attrition on transnational terrorists, just as we've long waged on global drug traffickers and other chronic scourges inside the Gap, like AIDS? If transnational terrorism is just another of the Gap's chronic illnesses, then the United States cannot be surprised to find itself waging the same sort of lonely war that we now wage on drugs in Latin America—just another one of those crazy American obsessions that generates a lot of suffering and death distant from our shores, while back home we continue to enjoy cheap gas and potent cocaine.

I'm not arguing for the heavily cynical route of waging perpetual war inside the Gap just to keep the pot stirring over there and prevent too much of that nastiness from seeping into our safe lives, because that's not a grand strategy for anything but wasting a lot of young lives on both sides. Either we marry up this global war on terrorism to the goal of progressively moving all the Gap's regions toward the tipping point of both security and economic integration with the Core, or we accept Osama bin Laden's offer of civilizational apartheid and let Islam fight out this civil war on its own terms.

But I honestly believe that shrinking the Gap would have been America's natural choice for a grand strategy with or without either 9/11 or the subsequent global war on terrorism. We spent the 1990s going inside the Gap militarily like never before. Putting aside all our efforts on global terrorism since 9/11, God knows we could still fill our plate with what's going on elsewhere in the Gap—in Sudan, in Bolivia, in Zimbabwe, in the Democratic Republic of Congo. If the global war on terrorism doesn't warrant a long-term strategy to shrink the Gap, then we should abandon it and live with the security consequences, because with all the suffering that's currently going on inside the Gap, waging such an effort for anything less is simply not defensible on a moral basis. It is not defensible because it merely substitutes the global Salafi jihadist movement led by al Qaeda for the old Soviet threat, saying to the disconnected parts of the world, essentially, "We'd love to help, but frankly, we are too focused on containing this long-term threat to make any effort on your particular pile," no matter how much that suffering or disconnectedness is fueling that same threat.

Moreover, if we're not committed to following through on the larger logic of shrinking the Gap and making globalization truly global, then this war on terrorism really is just a knee-jerk reaction to 9/11 that may or may not have been cynically manipulated by the Bush Administration to get Saddam and little else. And if that's true, then all China needs to do is make the right sort of military crisis happen over Taiwan and we can get right back to the business of focusing on great-power war.

But I honestly don't believe that any of those things are true. I think America and Americans know better than that. I think we took away more from 9/11 than a need for retaliation or a self-righteous need for American justice. I think we understood that there is a world of pain beyond the expanding global economy. I think we see one-third of humanity with noses pressed to the glass, wondering what it will take for them to come inside and enjoy the same sense of security and economic opportunity.

And I think we as a nation are committed to doing something about all that—something that tries to make it come out all right in the end. If that's a future worth creating, then we need to commit ourselves to understanding both the journey we expect Gap states to make and the aid we'll need to offer them in this process.

Here is my sense of how we can describe the goals we seek:

In terms of economic development, we need to understand that inside the Gap, geology is destiny. The poor soil quality that afflicts much of the Gap means that too many nations there simply can't feed themselves. The recent effort by the world's best scientists to define the most advantageous routes to tackling some of the Gap's most persistent problems, called the Copenhagen Consensus, recently came to the conclusion that providing Gap nations with better agricultural technology, including the advances provided by bioengineering, offers the fastest pathway to routing hunger there and moving poor Gap nations beyond sustenance farming. You can't join the New Core until you can feed your people with relative ease. Most of today's New Core states accomplished this through the so-called Green Revolution effort of the West in the 1960s and 1970s.

If we want to start building the next contingent of New Core regions, we need to make a similar big push today, much as economist

Jeffrey Sachs argues for sub-Saharan Africa. So the desired progression here is from "can't feed themselves" (Gap) to "can feed themselves" (New Core) to "don't even have to try anymore" (most of the Old Core). To take this to its logical conclusion, the Old Core needs to find real partnership with the Gap in letting those regions pick up a larger share of feeding the world as a whole, which means ending our unfair subsidies to domestic agricultural industries. Otherwise the Old Core is guilty of trying to maintain its status on the upper reaches of the global production-value chain while denying the Gap's successful entry at its lowest levels.

The Core likewise needs to rethink its foreign aid in the manner suggested by the Bush Administration's Millennium Challenge Account, which, in theory if not yet in practice, holds much promise. What's important about this reform effort is that it tries to link aid with positive reform on the part of the recipient, thus pushing both donor and recipient toward the ultimate goal of ending this charitable relationship according to the latter's rate of success. For far too long now, foreign aid has generated long-term dependency relationships between the Old Core and the Gap, when we know full well that moving into the New Core means a nation moves off of official developmental aid from rich countries and instead attracts large flows of those economies' foreign direct investments, as China has successfully managed in the last twenty-five years. By 2025, China should be one of the Core's biggest aid donors to those still left behind in the Gap.

In terms of extending our developmental expertise to the Gap, we need to push the following progression: from foreign development experts (Gap) to insourcing jobs themselves (New Core) to outsourcing jobs (Old Core). Most of what the Gap suffers is not the lack of local entrepreneurial expertise but access to foreign capital. Our efforts at telling Gap states how to develop should only proceed as far as doing what it takes to attract foreign direct investment that propels the insourcing of jobs from the Core. When a country develops to the point of shedding its lowest level of insourced jobs, as China has already begun to do in certain industries, then it naturally proceeds to outsourcing those jobs to lesser economies (or, in China's particular case, perhaps just to its inner impoverished provinces) and continuing its climb up the production-value chain.

As to how countries treat their private sectors, the push needs to be toward moving countries from heavy state-sector involvement (Gap) to privatizing those entities (New Core) to limiting activities to bailouts of key industries when globalization's rough-and-tumble action cycle may warrant such government interventions, as well as government-funded programs designed to retrain workers whose industries either can't or shouldn't be protected by such interventions (Old Core).

On the migration of labor, here's the progression suggested to me by Robert Hormats of Goldman Sachs: we need to move the Gap from the conditions of "have gun, will travel" (transnational terrorists) and "need job, will travel" (guest workers), to the New Core's "have job, don't need to travel" (insourcing) to the Old Core's "have skills, don't need to travel" (the ability to move up in jobs). In more personal terms, we need to move states from the Gap's requirement that the son leave home for work, to the New Core's ability to attract that son back home, and finally to the Old Core's ability to keep that son from ever having to leave in the first place.

On the development of infrastructure, we need to move Gap states beyond their frightening tendency to treat communal networks as the first thing to be cannibalized whenever the economy sours. A good example of this is when Africans tear down their own communications and energy infrastructure for these items' value as scrap metal—the developmental equivalent of eating your own seed corn. As foreign direct investment begins to flow in, it's more than okay for state-directed monopolies to be in charge of developing network infrastructure (a common feature of New Core economies), but once they're sufficiently in place, global investors are right to press for these public companies' privatization. Again, monopolies are great for building networks, but markets are better for running them once they've matured. Otherwise, you typically end up with control-freak state enterprises that limit network capacity, something we see time and time again in the telephone industry.

On sovereign debt, too many Gap states are stuck in the "have crushing debt, can't pay back" mode, so debt forgiveness, when combined with banking sector reforms, will be warranted in the most impoverished situations, such as numerous countries in sub-Saharan Africa. Once states move into New Core status, their ability to float and pay off sovereign debt is typically not an issue, and frankly, once you achieve the credit status of an Old Core state, maintaining a permanent national debt really stops being an issue altogether, so long as the system as a whole can exert pressure on any state's ill-considered financial strategy through monetary interventions designed to weaken the currency at a reasonable pace.

When it comes to Gap states that are "cursed" by their ongoing dependency on raw materials (especially energy) for the bulk of their export earnings, we need to encourage these governments to stop treating their natural resources like a national trust fund to be "preserved." While some Gap states have gotten cash-rich in this manner, none has achieved broad economic development, in large part because the government's fears of losing control over this "national treasure" push it to restrict the ability of foreign capital to access those industries specifically and the overall economy in general. Plus, the whole trust-fund mindset tends to diminish public efforts at education, leaving the bulk of the population without the necessary skills to compete in the global economy. In combination, this is a disastrous double whammy that yields too little human and financial capital for long-term economic growth. Meanwhile, as history has amply demonstrated, global prices for such commodities decrease in real terms over time, trapping the population in a downward spiral of declining national wealth. In sum, being rich in natural resources alone has never proven to be a fast track to economic development. Instead, it tends to be a dead end.

All these economic shifts are difficult, because they push societies from their communal past to a far more individualized future where it no longer feels like "we're in this together." The group-think of more communal societies places a premium on age for leadership, which is fine, but it tends to result in younger generations' not being sufficiently educated to think for themselves, hence the tendency to substitute religion for free thought. Moving off that dime isn't easy, because the elders in any communal society don't care to give up their authority. And the youth aren't particularly ready to think for themselves, plus when they are given the chance too rapidly, you can end up with a rather revolutionary cohort of young people who don't just want to think for themselves, they want to smash the old system and replace it with something better. Given their limited sense of the outside world and its possibilities, such revolutionary youth in a more traditional society will often, as the Salafi jihadists do, reach for some "pure" vision of the past, before all the "corruption" of the present accumulated.

To say education is the key may seem trite, but it is. Not in the sense that we seek to free their minds from the past so much as simply zero in on usable skills that give them the confidence to approach fulfilling careers in a connected world. So by and large, I advocate skipping the "war of ideas" with youth in the Gap, focusing on sellable job-skill training, and letting them come to their own intellectual growth and conclusions through successful experience in the job world rather than trying to "rehab" or "brainwash" them up front out of fear that they'll turn into terrorists. America has long had the capacity, as Michael Barone has pointed out, to produce some of the world's least impressive eighteen-year-olds who somehow, over the next twelve years, end up becoming some of the world's most impressive thirty-year-olds. We don't do that by "saving" them from anything (like religion), but by connecting them to various experiences and opportunities for self-definition that apparently migrate them quite successfully from adolescence to adulthood. We need to tailor our educational aid to the Gap accordingly.

The journey from the Gap to the Core is essentially an aging process, then, from the Gap's youth to the New Core's middle ages to the Old Core's maturity and high proportion of elders. So the process is one of moving from a focus on educating the young to providing them fulfilling careers to erecting the social safety nets and financial networks that allow for postretirement lifestyles that aren't just free from want but are fulfilling. This journey is a daunting task, as we in the Old Core are finding out as our populations age rapidly, but it is one all countries must make if we are to shrink the Gap.

There is a key maturation point along the way in this process, and it is an important one to manage. Morris Massey is a psychologist who has spent his career studying key transition points in life that we all experience. He makes the argument that "what you are is where you were when . . . ," meaning every individual reaches a point in his life when he discovers a world larger than himself, and that coming-of-age moment tends to define people in a lasting way, centering them in time. For most people, that time tends to happen in their teenage years, which explains most people's tendency to stick with the popular music of those years throughout the rest of their lives.

Massey's useful observation about individuals can likewise be applied to states, as every society tends to reach a point where it emerges from its shell of self-absorption and realizes its place in the larger scheme of things. For the United States, that moment occurred in the early years of the twentieth century, or roughly around the time of Teddy Roosevelt's presidency. Before that moment, America was mostly focused on itself, but since that moment, America has also been quite active in shaping the world at large. The process of moving from Gap to Core will inevitably feature this sort of emergence-defining moment, and so it behooves the Core not only to be aware of this process but also to seek to manage it as positively as possible so that emerging states come through it with both a sense of confidence of where they fit into the Core and what assets and skills they bring to the larger world.

I see the progression of this self-discovery process as follows: While you're in the Gap, it's all about "what the world owes us." Moving into the New Core triggers that moment of discovering the larger world, and it is fraught with the dangers of explosive nationalism as a result, which is a normal fear-threat reaction upon realizing there's a bigger world out there. The trick for managing this process is moving New Core countries off that discovery process into some positive definition of "what we owe the world." The problem is that many states in history, having achieved this breakthrough moment of development, have subsequently gone overboard in that "what we owe the world" definition, deciding that what they owe the world is their empire or revolutionary movement. What we need to promote in this process is exactly what China is trying to sell right now with its Theory of Peacefully Rising China—namely, a sense that this emergence process is both nonthreatening and mutually beneficial.

This guiding process should never be characterized by a heavy-handed or patronizing approach, but rather a skillful opportunism that turns sows' ears into silk purses. Here's a good example: The Asian tsunamis of 2004 were a great opportunity for countries like India, Indonesia, and China to show their rising competence at dealing with a system perturbation of this stunning magnitude, to demonstrate their capacity for regional leadership. None was going to be able to shower locals with the large sums of disaster-relief funds as the United States and Japan had, but all had the chance to prove themselves as pillars of stability under dire circumstances. India passed this test, displaying a private-sector response that was impressive and a military response that was highly professional. Indonesia faltered at moments politically and yet saw its military-to-military relations with the United States significantly repaired by the joint cooperation that emerged—even in the politically volatile Aceh region.

China, however, was really missing in action. Yes, its private-sector giving was unprecedented, and yes, the government delivered a modest amount of aid, but here was a huge opportunity for China's growing military to play the kind of role that America's Navy mounts effortlessly around the world on a regular basis, achieving great goodwill in the process. A lot of strategic analysts in the West noted this lapse with some satisfaction, citing it as proof that America remains the region's only military superpower, but that observation, while true, misses the larger strategic opportunity. Just as important as spreading America's goodwill in the region was the chance to forge a new venue of U.S.-Chinese military cooperation in a disaster situation that offered win-win outcomes for both sides.

Here's my essential point: Rising powers don't act responsibly until established powers grant them responsibility. If we want to shrink the Gap, we'll need to grow the New Core, and that process must include openly acknowledging these rising powers' natural pride in the journey made, the skills they add to the Core's growing resource base, and their capacity to help us put into action a collective blueprint for a better world.

ESSENTIAL BUILDING BLOCKS FOR SHRINKING THE GAP FROM WITHIN

The great limitation of *The Pentagon's New Map* was that it argued for a national grand strategy to change the world but did so from the initial perspective of the U.S. military. It was an inside-out argument that began within the Pentagon but only seemed plausible once you extended its logic beyond war and into the *everything else*. The great misinterpretation of the book, much like that of George Kennan's original enunciation of the containment strategy for dealing with the Soviet threat after World War II, was that it proposed a military-*only* solution to the security problems engendered by globalization's progressive advance around the planet. So the taglines for the most reflexive reviews were "perpetual war for perpetual peace" and "war only leads to more war." The bottom line was, no matter how much I said the military was only a small part of the solution set, once I added the military to the equation, that's all many readers ever saw.

So why argue from the military outward for a grand strategy to enable globalization's advance? The great gift of 9/11 was that it reminded us that globalization needed a bodyguard, that this historic process wouldn't simply move ahead on its own, because history had demonstrated—yet again—that there would be forces in its path that would violently oppose it. The global Salafi jihadist movement fears the liberty globalization will unleash, because this individual freedom precludes its ability to create an Islamic superstate in opposition to all the "negative" cultural influences globalization brings from the West. So pushing globalization hits transnational terrorism where it lives.

Does this approach constitute a global war on terrorism? No. Killing terrorists and disrupting their networks constitute a global war on terrorism. Using the military to enable the spread of globalization is about unlocking the Gap's potential for self-development, and that economic development, in conjunction with the connectivity it creates between societies there and the world outside, is what ultimately *wins* a global war on terrorism. This war on terrorism must be viewed as just one small aspect of that larger grand strategy, the most important elements of which should involve the Core helping Gap states to unlock their own, *internal* potential for economic development. Along these lines I see three essential building blocks: good governments, educated women, and ready access to capital. Let me deal briefly with each.

Good Markets Need Good Governments

The marginalization of the one-third of humanity living inside the Gap creates long-term security problems for the Core, one of which is transnational terrorism. But frankly, terrorism is nowhere near the biggest killer of people and connectivity inside the Gap.

What really accounts for the lack of security and connectivity inside the Gap is the paucity of good governments. What's a good government? My definition is a simple one: a good government enables broadband economic and network connectivity to arise between its public and the outside world. Notice I didn't say *democracy,* or *pluralism,* or *secular.* I just said *connectivity.* How any government handles the content flows that result from that connectivity has to be its own business, because a rate of modernization that destabilizes the society will inevitably destabilize the government, often through the creation of rebel groups or terrorists who seek political change through violent means. So not only is *speed* not of the essence, neither is any particular political format. *Connectivity is of the essence,* because connectivity unlocks the society's potential for growth and development, and it is that growth and development that eventually dictate political reform in the direction of pluralism.

Democracy is not a means but an end. There is no such thing as waging wars for democracy. We're talking about a process that is historical in scope, because the change it demands from individual cultures is profound.

But what globalization promises on the far side of that difficult change is likewise profound—and quite positive. As the global economy has spread dramatically from the West to the East and the South over the last quarter-century, the world has experienced the greatest reduction in absolute poverty in human history. In 1980, there were approximately 1.5 billion people in the world living on less than a dollar a day. By 2001, that number had been reduced to 1.1 billion, meaning 400 million had escaped the crushing limitations of poverty thanks to globalization, with most of those people living in Asia. As a percentage of our growing global population, that means 40 percent of the world lived in stark poverty twenty-five years ago, whereas only 20 percent do so today.

This development is due fundamentally to the rising connectivity between national economies. This connectivity wasn't mandated by international organizations like the World Trade Organization or the International Monetary Fund. Whatever perceived strength those organizations have in pushing new rules is simply a reflection of that growing connectivity, not the cause of it. The United States doesn't enjoy a magnificently connected national economy of fifty states because it has a strong federal government, it has a strong federal government in response to all that connectivity arising over the years. Take away that connectivity and there would be no strong central government, leaving the individual states impoverished as a result, because the free movement of goods, services, people, and ideas would by definition be greatly diminished.

What separates the United States from the Gap is the amazing amount of connectivity that has developed among our fifty members over the course of our history. A good portion of that connectivity was enabled by the wisdom of our Founding Fathers and their amazingly prescient design of our political system. But that political system simply started the process of connectivity, whereas over time, because of the profound social and economic changes that connectivity triggered, these ever-expanding economic networks in turn generated a far better and far stronger political system whose rule sets are far more just in their definition, far more universal in their coverage, and far more effective in unleashing personal ambition and thus the pursuit of individual happiness. Good markets don't just require good governments, they likewise improve and sustain good governments.

You might think the last place you'd find antiglobalization sentiment would be in the Core, and yet that's where you find most of it. In general, the Gap welcomes globalization, overwhelmingly desiring the connectivity it offers. Yes, there are dictators and business elites inside the Gap who fear such connectivity because it threatens their ability to rule over the masses politically and economically. And yes, the Core has plenty of bad actors who support Gap dictators and elites out of greed for the profits that accrue to them in this villainy. Likewise, there are the fundamentalists willing to kill and die to prevent such "Westoxification." But in sum, none of this resistance poses a serious long-term threat to globalization's advance. Far more widespread and damaging are the sentiments of many inside the advanced economies of the Core that globalization is a bad thing, something that increases oppression and decreases wealth worldwide.

But of course this isn't true, otherwise it would be the Core that's plagued by endemic conflicts and not the Gap. What plagues the Gap is not globalization but the lack of globalization. Tell me which is worse: the alteration of "pristine" cultures inside the Gap or their continued isolation and primitive forms of impoverishment? It always amazes me how activists living in the Core agitate for the preservation of such "diversity" and yet would never advocate such conditions of disconnectedness for themselves or their own societies. More ironic, of course, is that such activists would never even know of these isolated cultures without the connectivity afforded by globalization.

Globalization provides overwhelmingly positive impact upon national economies, because trade is a win-win proposition that speaks to any society's comparative advantages so long as the rules of that trade are reasonable and fair. How do we know this to be true? Where does the bulk of foreign direct investment go in the global economy? It goes to the countries with the highest degree of labor regulations and social safety nets. The Gap is not yet flooded with such investments— far from it.

Would multinational corporations naturally seek to invest in Gap countries if certain conditions held true? Of course. By seeking out the cheapest labor on the planet, these investment flows access labor pools that have previously lacked such connectivity—hence their cheapness.

Once these corporations "invade" such cheap labor pools, are individuals there enriched or impoverished? The data here is overwhelming: when a Gap laborer works in a multinational corporation's factory, he or she typically enjoys a salary that's roughly 40 to 50 percent higher than other workers can achieve in that country. Guess what that does to families? Over time they tend to have fewer kids, and those kids will, on average, spend more time in school and less time engaged in labor. So globalization doesn't increase child labor, it increases childhood education, because it connects parents to higher wages and creates higher expectations for their kids.

As international economists love to point out, markets naturally want to globalize by crossing national boundaries, but states by and large do not, because the very definition of a nation stems from a definition of place. But if nationalism is a key ingredient for building a state, then globalism is a key ingredient for building a similarly binding rule set for the planet as a whole. If good markets need good government, then a good global economy likewise needs good states, whose ultimate definition of goodness is their adherence to the notion that increased connectivity is positive, while disconnectedness defines danger—especially when it's enforced involuntarily from above.

That sense of globalism, or a belief in the inherent goodness of connectivity, is what drives globalization's advance far more than either technology or the rare instances where military power is exerted. Throughout human history, we've consistently gotten better at transportation and communication, and those capabilities have essentially defined the reach of our ability to integrate with one another, first in small communities largely isolated from one another and now in a very globalized manner. As such, globalization is figuratively as old as human civilization, which is basically defined by such efforts at widening our shared networks so as to increase the social benefits that accrue to those who belong to their resulting communities.

So if globalization has always been driven by technology, what's made this era's version so profoundly different? The difference today is that the ideology of openness and connectedness is far more pervasive than it has ever been in history. Globalization is first and foremost a process of integration of national economies. That process is driven not by technology so much as the falling of trade and investment barriers among states. What has driven that is the spread of free-market ideas: open beats closed, connected trumps disconnected. If there's a race, it's not to the bottom but to the top, as the countries with the highest ratings for transparency and good governance attract the highest flows of foreign direct investment and trade.

If the ideology of connectedness has won out, then what are the great risks to globalization today? It's not great-power war, because the Leviathan status of the U.S. military, combined with the fact that most great powers possess nuclear weapons, essentially kills that form of warfare. Nor is a global economic collapse such as we experienced in the Great Depression of the 1930s particularly likely, the biggest reason being that the world's great currencies now effectively balance against one another in a system of floating exchange rates. The one danger that all advocates of globalization recognize as threatening its existence is merely the divergence between winners and losers, both within states and among them.

What can prevent these splits from overwhelming globalization's progress? Rules. The most important are rules within states that mandate—in my phrase—that the train's engine (globalization's winners) can't travel any faster than the caboose (globalization's losers). Next most important are those rules among states that define how the Core not only protects itself from the dangers and instabilities posed by the Gap but likewise seeks to shrink it overwhelmingly through peaceful, private-sector means at a manageable pace.

You Can Tell Everything You Need to Know
About a State by How It Treats Its Women

There is an old African saying that goes "The world moves on a woman's hips." What this is really saying, of course, is that women are central to the social order in their role as mothers, and that the strength of any society can be traced back to how women both provide, and are provided for, in that most essential of all futures worth creating—namely, the next generation of humanity.

There is likewise a modern saying: "You can tell everything you need to know about a man by how he treats his woman." I maintain that the same is basically true for states, as well as religions and civilizations: If a state treats its women primarily as birthing machines, it will neither develop economically nor succeed at globalization.

Much of this treatment is, of course, tied up in the tradition of agrarian life that dominated most of human history. So long as your society was mostly about growing food, women were for having children, and children were for working in the fields. It is only when a society moves beyond sustenance farming or a reliance on similar commodities for export that this tradition begins to break down. In short, solve the food issue and free the women. Once women are freed from the obligations of maximizing family size and related manual labor, they enter the larger, noncommodity workforce, as do their children. When a society has achieved enough success in industrialization, its children are subsequently held out of the workforce to be educated, and eventually the educational achievement rates of women approach those of men. At that point it is likely that you're living in a pluralist society, if not a democracy. It is also highly likely that your economy is globalized.

But if by some additional cultural rule set your women are kept isolated from your workforce and treated as de facto minors in your legal and political rule sets, then the odds are overwhelming that you are living in an authoritarian state that is not globalized.

In many parts of the Gap, the notion of empowering women is considered a subversive proposition. Indeed, few things scare the world's violent fundamentalists more than universal education. Why? Nothing empowers women more quickly than education equal to men's. Moreover, nothing is more effective for triggering economic progress than educating girls. The benefit from educating girls is very direct: delaying the first pregnancy/sexual experiences has a hugely positive impact on the rates of fertility and sexually transmitted diseases (reducing both). Plus, babies born to older females will tend to be healthier and better cared for, in large part because of the improved economic status that comes with both age and further education. Beyond that, a more educated female population tends to improve the existing labor force significantly, which in turn boosts female participation in the political process.

Show me a democracy and I'll show you a state that does not marginalize its females. You want to defeat global terrorism? Educate girls. Spread liberty and freedom around the world? Educate girls. Shrink the Gap? Educate girls. And I mean "girls" when I say this, because the surest route to women's rights is . . . you guessed it: educate girls. You can't wait until they grow up. The commitment needs to be there from the start, otherwise too many opportunities are precluded along the way. None of this is a secret. It has long been known in the development community that nothing fuels economic advancement faster than educating girls. Nothing. This is a tipping point in economic development that has no equal. Everything changes when you educate a girl.

Women's rights should be the Core's leading agenda item for any strategy to shrink the Gap because the payoff is so high and so permanent. Feminize an authoritarian political system and you will kill it— plain and simple. There is no mystery concerning the fact that our enemies in this global war on terrorism are almost exclusively men whose political and social agenda begins and ends with the subjugation of women (and yes, I know they consider that a "higher form of respect"). There is also little doubt that the population that suffers most inside the Gap is female. Women suffer the worst health care and health status. Women are the majority of victims in war and civil strife, constituting the bulk of economic and political refugees. No matter what the victimhood you might name inside the Gap, women bear the burden disproportionately, as they must in all patriarchal societies.

Why is pushing women's rights inside the Gap so difficult? Two reasons: First, inside some portions of the Core (read, the United States) the issue of birth control (read, abortion) has overwhelmed the subject to the extent that we have simply not emphasized it enough in our diplomatic and development dialogues with these regions. Second, conservative societies tend to consider gender issues in the same way many Americans fear the legalization of marijuana use—it's seen as a gateway to even worse things. So, too, many traditional Gap societies hold the line on women's rights, fearing a slippery slope to even more controversial debates on religious freedom and human rights in general.

In most patriarchal portions of the Gap, there is only one activity more dangerous for a woman than voting, and that is daring to run for political office. And yet nothing signifies victories in the global war on terrorism better than when women in these countries register to vote, cast ballots, and sometimes actually assume office. As one elderly Iraqi woman declared on her way to voting in January 2005: "I would go and listen to [the local cleric] and see if his words would be of interest to me. But when I go to the booth, I will do as I wish." While men tend to vote according to religion and ethnicity in such situations, women tend to vote more for those candidates who represent law and order. In other words, they vote for clear and universal rule sets.

In traditional societies, women also tend to favor globalization more than men. Since connectivity is gender-neutral, women benefit disproportionately from freer movements of goods, services, and capital. Women tend to dominate in microfinance or microloan programs inside the Gap, because they have always been starved for such access to capital. And women should welcome globalization's embrace of their societies, because the factories that follow globalization represent their best chance to escape the crushing burden of rural poverty, and by virtue of even these meager wages (by our standards), young women see their prospects for economic and social advancement transformed.

You should not be surprised to hear that the most prized category of labor in any emerging market is young women just off the farm. Once that migration begins, industrialization becomes possible on a serious scale. And if they arrive educated, almost anything is possible.

No Capital, No Capitalism

Most Gap regions suffer a dearth of readily accessible capital markets. Stock and bond markets tend to be undercapitalized, venture capital nonexistent, and foreign direct investment flows amazingly meager for the vast majority of Gap states. The great bulk of investments heading from the Old Core to "emerging markets" these past two decades has really gone to New Core economies with very little left over for the Gap. Why? Global investors are essentially cowards; when they see violence or instability or the "dead hand" of the authoritarian state, they naturally shy away. Bad governments breed violence and social unrest. They are likely to form disastrously inefficient monopolies that are rife with corruption. Especially in countries that rely primarily on commodities for export, such governments effectively kill all chance that their economies can grow, because monopolies, of course, like to keep things simple and undiversified.

By scaring off most foreign investors, bad governments force their citizens to rely on their own, typically meager savings to self-finance entrepreneurship, which is just about the slowest way to grow your own economy. Since many of these same economies receive significant amounts of foreign developmental aid (significant, that is, as a percentage of their GDP), there is the additional destructive effect often associated with such charity: it tends to infantilize the local social, political, and economic institutions necessary for broadband development. In short, aid has a nasty tendency to turn charity cases into basket cases. As Francis Fukuyama argues, what should be capacity building is, in far too many cases, often capacity destruction, "despite the best intentions of the donors."

A good example of this phenomenon comes in aid designed to develop infrastructure inside the Gap. The problem is that the development community tends to budget for construction but not for maintenance. This is the aid equivalent of the Pentagon's tendency to budget only for acquisitions and never for operations: unless you're prepared to pay for the latter, no amount of funds for the former will suffice. So, for example, the Gap often ends up with roads they soon can't use any better than whatever they had before.

As I noted before, I do agree with those, like Jeffrey Sachs and his Millennium Development Goals for the UN, who argue for massive infusions of new aid to the worst-off Gap states in the areas of health and education. But by and large I don't like to see development dollars go into infrastructure programs—I think history has shown that most of these programs tend to go awry in Gap states primarily because of the weakness and corruption of government institutions there.

However, it is wrong to think that foreign direct investment arrives only when the rule of law is perfectly in place in any developing economy. In truth, investors are willing to send their money in fairly early in the process and—by doing so—help set in motion the business community's growing requirements for government services and more secure economic rights, so long as the prospects for success are relatively bright, meaning the environment is secure from strife, the government is not overly corrupt, and enough of a legal system exists to grow in response to this rising demand over time. This is why connectivity is so crucial. Connectivity with the outside world generates higher transaction rates between the local economy and the global one. Those higher transaction rates demand a more efficient response from the government's legal system over time, forcing reform and maturation of the economic rule set, with the most important ones being property rights and contract law.

But as the noted Peruvian economist Hernando de Soto argues, some states inside the Gap are so mercantilist in their perspective, meaning zero-sum in their assumptions about the ability to create wealth through economic activity, that their governments would rather have a smaller economic pie that the elites could control than a larger one that would benefit broader segments of the population. If you believe that wealth is a fixed sum, meaning it cannot be created, only acquired, then this perspective makes sense. Not surprisingly, many such mercantilist governments exist in countries whose economic wealth is primarily derived from natural resources and agricultural commodities, both of which are attached to that eternal symbol of fixed wealth—the land.

In such governments (of which there are many in Latin America), there is the tendency to erect massive barriers to entrepreneurship through what de Soto calls the "legal tangle." For example, when I recently incorporated my sole proprietorship business, called Barnett Consulting, as an "S Corporation" (meaning small corporation), all I had to do in the state of Indiana was register at my county courthouse by providing proof of identification and a minimum of information regarding one or more directors (myself and my spouse) of the proposed corporation. That allowed me, under the USA Patriot Act, to set up a business account at my local bank. At that point, Barnett Consulting became a legal entity recognized by the state of Indiana, meaning I could sign contracts, accept payments, pay taxes, et cetera, under the corporate name "Barnett Consulting Inc." That was all I needed to do to start my own business in the United States: two easy steps that took less than half a day to accomplish.

As de Soto's pioneering research on Peru's economy showed, the "legal tangle" involved with starting a business in many Gap states is brutally complex and lengthy, requiring dozens of steps stretching out over many months. The purpose of this entire tangle is clear: to dissuade potential entrepreneurs from entering the market in the first place, thus securing the elite's ability to control the vast majority of economic activity in the country.

What is the response of the shutout would-be entrepreneur? It's what some call the "black market" but what de Soto likes to call the "informal market," meaning economic transactions, entities, and assets that are unrecognized by the state as having any legal standing. It's the sale that's not binding, the business that's not registered, and the house whose ownership cannot be proven—much less defended—in a court. It's the economic equivalent of America's Wild West, the difference being, as de Soto argues, that America's political system figured out ways to admit these informal economies through such legal mechanisms as "squatter's rights":

The crucial change had to do with adapting the law to the social and economic needs of the majority of the population. Gradually, Western nations became able to acknowledge that social contracts born outside the official law were a legitimate source of law and to find ways of absorbing these contracts. Law was thus made to serve popular capital formation and economic growth. This is what gives the present property institutions of the West their vitality. Moreover, this property revolution was always a *political* victory. In every country, it was a result of a few enlightened men deciding that official law makes no sense if a sizeable part of the population lived outside it.

All things being equal, no one chooses the informal economy over the formal economy. Because the efficiency and security of the latter are undeniably a better deal. The informal economy is an act of economic desperation. Nothing can truly be passed on to your kids; they simply have to get theirs, just like you got yours. As such, nothing accumulates in society; things just change hands with as much improvement as anyone dares to make when there's so little guarantee of a downstream payoff.

That brings us back to square one: Good markets need good governments. In their absence, only informal and hugely inefficient markets can arise. In the end, the Gap is plagued not so much by bad governments as by simply the lack of good ones. Our goal in shrinking the Gap must entail, therefore, increasing the number of good governments there, governments that extend the rule of law, develop the human capital of all citizens (and especially that of young females), and—most specifically—foster entrepreneurial opportunities by recognizing property rights and expanding contract case law.

Over the course of development, government will tend to get bigger, but so long as the scope remains modest, this growth in strength is not the issue. It's just that as an economy matures, states typically need to deal with aging populations, more environmental issues, and a greater need for education, infrastructure development, and maintenance and health care management (especially for elders). All these rising demands from the populace tend to grow the size of the state, which is why the states with the highest tax rates are overwhelmingly in the Old Core. Not surprisingly, as these governmental responsibilities accumulate over time, it tends to get harder and harder for such states to fund their militaries to any substantial degree, which tends to make for a more peaceful environment in which states pool their military assets in multinational security alliances like NATO.

In many ways, shrinking the Gap from within really has to do with managing the flow of people from the country to the city, for in that process women are liberated, capital is accumulated, and legal rule sets are generated by the expanded transaction rates that result. Globalization both engenders this process (when done right) and feeds off this process. If Gap countries are given the right sort of developmental aid to improve agricultural technology in climates featuring poor soil quality and if Gap economies are given free access to Core markets to sell those agricultural wares, then the migration from the country to the city is facilitated.

As that process unfolds, this mass movement of people enters the city under a variety of conditions. If the cities provide an environment of clear and universal rule sets, especially those involving contracts and property, then these new city dwellers should find real opportunity in the formal economy, so long as the country is globalizing and not remaining disconnected from the larger economic possibilities that lie beyond its border. But if such newcomers find themselves locked out of the formal economy by either de Soto's "legal tangle" or the lack of a sufficiently robust legal system, then these citizens have little choice: they can seek their way in the informal economy, become criminals, or become worse than criminals.

Thus, when the Core facilitates the effective movement of Gap residents from rural areas to cities, helping through institutional capacity-building aid or advice, as well as fair and just responses to the Gap's demands for fair entry into, and trade with, the global economy, we're not just improving the lives of people there, we're improving our security from the ground floor up. We're getting better citizens, better governments, and better states, all of which circumscribe the ability of bad actors inside the Gap to engage in nefarious activities.

If you want a global community where countries live in peace and individuals enjoy ready access to economic opportunity that yields a decent life for themselves and their families, the pathways to success are not that difficult to locate. As with the cases of violence inside the Gap, where all we need do is look into ourselves and our past to see similar challenges that we overcame in building these United States, this West, and this Functioning Core of globalization. All we need do to figure out how to truly shrink the Gap from within is likewise to remember the same rule-set resets that we were forced to engage in on a regular basis throughout our collective history of integration. There is no mystery to any of this, but rather a blueprint for action and a series of rule sets to guide our efforts.

The challenge is clear, the potential payoff quite large. Not all futures worth creating involve us directly, even as they benefit us magnificently. The only big push here involves our imagination for something better, to make others better.

Chapter Five

WE HAVE MET
THE ENEMY . . .

I HAVE BEEN STUNNED BY the amount of positive interest *The Pentagon's New Map* has received from religious communities across the entire faith spectrum. I've dialogued with more clergy in the last year than I ever would have suspected might be interested in a book about "war and peace in the twenty-first century," including my own parish priest of many years, Kevin Brassil, of Portsmouth, Rhode Island.

Now, you have to understand that Father Kevin, who recently retired, is about as liberal-minded a peacenik as you can find in a Catholic priest, so when he first approached me about my work, I was somewhat flabbergasted by his interest. Father Kevin's sermons tended toward the severely anti-Bush, antiwar, and pretty much anti-using-the-military-for-anything, but I have to say that our dialogue never suffered one whit from his strong bias, primarily because he and I share the same sense of moral outrage regarding the chronic violence afflicting the Gap and thus we both lack any sort of patience for go-slow approaches in trying to shrink it. Father Kevin's idealism, then, doesn't blind him to arguments—however compromising they might seem at first blush—that move the debate off the question of *if we do something* to *when we do something*.

Of course, I've never been shy about arguing that warfare has its purposes. I've just always tried to contextualize those arguments within the larger framework of the social, economic, and political realities of this grand historical process we call globalization—what I call thinking about war within the context of everything else. It's that connection to the "everything else" that has generated so many interactions with clergy like my parish priest: they're simply trying to contextualize their own faith communities' ongoing efforts to shrink the Gap within a U.S. foreign policy today that seems overwhelmingly defined by this global war on terrorism. If you want to be all about peace, you have to understand war. Because if you don't make that effort, all you can do is stand on the sidelines waiting for that deadly game to end, clucking your disapproval at the behavior of "lesser" individuals.

Seeing war within the context of everything else means you don't recognize anything or anyone as being on the sidelines—we're all connected or involved in some way. Sure, you can pretend to satisfy yourself spiritually by declaring your love for the sinner (military) despite the sin (war). But if you're not an active part of the peace solution, and I don't just mean complaining about the actions of others while doing nothing yourself, then you are—by default and extension—no less the sinner. If two individuals fight over some asset (e.g., food, medicine, security) and one dies in the process while you stand safely to the side possessing a supply that could easily encompass all three of you, then your moral outrage over this murder hardly answers the spiritual mail here. In a connected world, there's always plenty of guilt to go around, with every action triggering a reaction no more and no less than every nonaction.

The Core's faith-based aid and relief organizations understand the Gap is plagued with persistent pockets of mass violence and terrorism, and they are especially cognizant that when the U.S. Government makes a point of begging off any military response in these dangerous locales (such as Sudan in recent years or Central Africa over the past decade), their own potential for improving these dire living conditions is greatly reduced. Like it or not, the fate of this "everything else" crowd is just as tied to the strategic employment of U.S. military power inside the Gap as it is tied to them: we're working essentially the same set of problems. That doesn't mean the U.S. military is required for every scenario there—far from it. It just means that sometimes the military is a necessary but not sufficient ingredient for peace to unfold inside the Gap. What brings the faith-based community to the vision is simply these leaders' acknowledgment that they make up a big chunk of the "everything else" solution—or that which moves situations beyond the necessity of war to the self-sufficiency of peace.

In this chapter, I want to deal with the criticisms that are naturally launched against any vision that argues for a shrink-the-Gap outcome as constituting the true finishing line in the global war on terrorism. As I have encountered them, three big ones stand out most: (1) it'll take too long for a culture that expects easy answers and quick outcomes, so in our impatience we're likely to do more harm than good; (2) who are we—in our hubris—to impose our culture and its morals upon civilizations so different from our own?; and (3) even if we're successful we'll do more harm than good, because to make globalization truly global would destroy the planet's ecosystem. In my mind, all these arguments come far closer to selfish excuses for inaction than accurate critiques of my proposed strategy, speaking to the fear that we'll destroy the Core while trying to grow it. Simply put, I know we're smarter than that.

In *The Pentagon's New Map* I argued—using the "four flows" of people, energy, money, and security—that the Core's continued ability to generate a good life for its population *required* it shrink the Gap over time. In my "global transaction strategy," I described the necessity of both Core and Gap allowing that quartet of resources to flow from regions of surplus to regions of deficit (e.g., people from Gap to Core, energy from Gap to Core, money from Old Core to New Core and Gap, and security from Core to Gap), declaring those transactions were not only mutually beneficial to all but morally defensible as well, when viewed as a holistic model of globalization's successful expansion in the current era. What I want to do in this chapter is prove to you that while there is plenty of social, economic, and political friction generated by globalization's advance, the Core has it within its power to not only overcome those frictions with relative ease (meaning it beats the alternatives of inaction and/or selfish self-preservation), but do so while actually improving ourselves and our collective existence in the process.

Optimistic? Only if you believe the ingenuity and driving spirit that got humanity to this point in history is suddenly in great deficit today. I don't believe that. In fact I believe just the opposite: we've never been so blessed with talent in all of our existence.

THE RESUMPTION OF HISTORY AND THE LATEST ENEMY

The first great criticism of my vision for shrinking the Gap is that it demands decades of persistence from an America that is genetically predisposed toward attention-deficit disorder. My counter to this argument is that retreat from this long-term challenge is simply not an option, and that meeting it requires nothing more than efforts we've mounted similarly in the past. Violent resistance to the American-led globalization process did not die with the Soviet bloc, and if the 1990s lulled us into believing such resistance would never be made dangerously coherent again, then we were foolish to think that globalization's revolutionary effects had lost either their potency for social transformation or their capacity to motivate young men to more than just hoisting protest placards and vandalizing symbols of multinational corporations.

In many ways, the Cold War period was the easiest one we're likely to experience in this long process of making globalization global, because during that half century the global economy was effectively hemmed in by the Iron Curtain, unable to advance, and so its potential for luring us into combat with every local source of resistance was limited by the superpower rivalry. But when East joined West and the

Core was expanded, our Cold War victory set in motion globalization's rapid penetration of a host of tradition-bound, largely disconnected societies for whom this process would serve as a severely
radicalizing phenomenon. For decades on end, the so-called Third
World could bide its time, wondering which side, the East or the West,
would eventually prevail and force upon it a future for which it was
sorely unprepared. With the East's sudden ideological collapse and
subsequent transformation into the West's newly competitive capitalist "threat," globalization's Gap suddenly became the focus of the
great historical struggle between global capitalism and all comers that
has dominated world history for a century and a half now.

While balance-of-power academics spent the 1990s scanning the
strategic horizon for that Core power that must necessarily arise to
counter America's military supremacy (and we're still waiting . . .),
the Pentagon paid scant attention to the only logical source for the
next great opponent to the American-led globalization process—
those still on the outside who violently prefer to remain there.

And why can't they remain there, if it be their choosing?

Ah, but who is doing the choosing? Does Osama bin Laden speak
for the entire Muslim world when he says America's policies in the
Middle East are hypocritical and corrupt? Perhaps. But does he speak
to the future dreams of most Muslims living inside the Gap when he
speaks of permanent civilizational apartheid with the West, conse-
quently condemning hundreds of millions of young people to lives of
disconnectedness and deprivation? For if he does, then why did the
Muslim world remain silent while the U.S. military toppled the severely
fundamentalist Taliban regime in Afghanistan only to throw its arms
up in anger over the subsequent decision to dismantle Saddam Hussein's amazingly vicious but *secular* regime in Iraq? Why, then, did so
many ordinary Muslim citizens participate in later elections in both
Afghanistan and Iraq, despite the death threats and car bombs and
promises of certain retribution from al Qaeda–inspired terrorists?
Why did hundreds of citizen candidates run for only a handful of
seats in the capital city of Riyadh in 2005 when Saudi Arabia held its
first local elections in more than seven decades? Why has there been

such a profound surge from below for political reforms throughout the Middle East since the United States–led coalition invaded Iraq in the spring of 2003? Is this a civilization that just wants to be left alone or fears being left behind?

I believe it is the latter, and that, as many experts on the region point out, the revival of religiosity throughout the Gulf area reflects a population's desire not simply to resist our cultural "pollution" but to find some way to deal with undesired influences while adapting to much-needed and greatly desired economic connectivity that virtually all citizens there hope will lead to political pluralism over time.

Globalization will rule this planet or it will be ruled in pieces by forces far less beneficent than free markets and collective security schemes. We cannot turn off this hugely powerful process of global integration without triggering its opposite force—disintegration. Such a decision to withdraw from the world would send it into a fracturing spiral of unprecedented magnitude, precisely because the Leviathan's departure from the global security system would create a power vacuum that other Core pillars would feel compelled to fill with their own competing military activities. Globalization could easily split into a plethora of antagonistic blocs, replicating the sort of dynamics of the first half of the twentieth century. Make no mistake, the burden of picking up those pieces—yet again—would not somehow be magically outsourced to the rest of the world, or to "history," but to our children and grandchildren. Our parents once witnessed the demise of a global economy and sacrificed greatly across the two world wars that process spawned. What are successor generations prepared to endure?

Americans need to see the world for the ties that bind nations and their economies together, and not simply fixate on the vertical borders that give the illusion that the pain and suffering of the Gap can forever be kept distant from our shores. Helping fellow citizens understand that connectivity is my main goal, because an informed citizenry will not only demand better and more strategic global leadership from Washington, it'll better understand the long-term scope of this effort to shrink the Gap.

When you think horizontally on a regular basis, meaning you stretch your mind across numerous subjects rather than specialize over-whelmingly in any one, pretty much every experience in your life is an education. A visit to an amusement park becomes an exercise in not just physics, for example, but demographics, youth fads, and queuing strategies as well. Inspirations are everywhere, and everything is worth comparing with something else. I've rarely accomplished any serious thinking sitting alone in my office, unless I leave it vicariously by phone, e-mail, or surfing the Web. I have to be connected to some-thing or somebody else before I can draw a line from Point A to what-ever Point B presents itself. Typically, I locate Point B in the most surprising of places.

Last year I took my kids up to Boston, and during that trip we vis-ited the Museum of Science. It's a kid-oriented place, and my job was mostly to make sure my youngest son, Jerome, didn't run off into some crowd. Near the end of the day, after the lightning show and the planetarium, we stopped by an exhibition on archaeology, where the kids got to mess around with various assembled skeletons. So while they were stacking bones in one corner, I found myself scanning the room for something to look at. I was drawn to a world map hung on a nearby wall. On it was displayed the migration of humans from our earliest origins in sub-Saharan Africa, roughly 100,000 years ago.

Now, the first thought that hit me is one that I've heard many times in the past: the spread of humanity around the planet was the first form of globalization. But as I stared at the timeline legend, another thought occurred to me: the spread of the current model of economic globalization is really the reverse track of that original spread of humanity. Humanity first spread from Africa to the Middle East; then to Eurasia; then to Europe, Japan, and Australia; and finally into the New World of the Western Hemisphere about 10,000 years ago. So if you were going to date civilizations, the age ranking would roughly correspond to the spread of humanity, with Africa and the Middle East being the oldest and the Western Hemisphere being the youngest.

But today's version of globalization really began in the Western Hemisphere (the United States), then spread outward to include the

West (Japan, Australia, Europe), finally conquering the Eurasian socialist bloc in the last generation, and now finding itself fundamentally
stuck (no pun intended) on the oldest and least globalized parts of
the world—namely, the Muslim world and Africa. In effect, modern
globalization can be described as roughly a 150-year trek from the
"youngest" parts of the world to the "oldest," which is why it's gotten
harder and not easier with time, because it's had more and more tradition and custom and history to overcome at each stage of its spread.

Admittedly, this thought didn't come to me in a flash right then and
there, because, as always, I was pretty tired from chasing my kids
around that huge museum all day. What happened right there was that
a different thought that had been crystallizing in my head for several
days finally made sense when I saw the map. For that one, I have to
take you to my nightly exercise on the treadmill, where I like to watch
documentaries on my laptop.

Turns out a few days earlier I was watching Ken Burns's masterful
The Civil War, and listening to the descriptions of the conflict and
what was at stake for both sides, I couldn't help but think that the
American Civil War was really the first Core-Gap war of the modern
era. The North was the land of great cities, railroads, and factories,
bristling with connectivity to the outside world in all forms, but especially in terms of immigrants streaming in from Europe. In contrast,
the South was the bucolic, agrarian, and far more homogeneous landscape, largely disconnected from the outside world except for the
narrow but voluminous trade in cotton, and distinguishable fundamentally for its heavy reliance on slave labor, which further isolated it
from the rest of the world.

I know what you're thinking: substitute oil for cotton and Asian
guest workers for slaves and you've got some interesting parallels with
a United States–led Core coalition of states seeking to transform the
Middle East in another bloody war of conquest and occupation. The
Union didn't exactly invade the Confederacy to "secure" the cotton,
now, did it? And the reality today is that we don't need to invade the
Persian Gulf to "secure" its oil, either. Hell, given the region's great

dependency on oil revenue, the regimes there have far fewer choices about selling their oil than the rest of the world has about buying it.

Well, it was following America's Civil War that you really saw the second industrial revolution begin to flower in the United States, helping to speed up the westward expansion of the Union. Once the country became effectively networked with railroads, most of the movement of raw materials in our land fed the giant industrial beast rising in the northeastern quadrant of the continent. It was roughly in the last quarter of the nineteenth century, then, that the United States finally began to resemble the multinational economic and political union that it is today, with its amazingly free and efficient movement of goods, services, people, and information across dozens of states all bound together under a federal government made significantly more powerful through civil war.

Meanwhile, of course, while America was rising "peacefully" in the Western Hemisphere, Europe spent the nineteenth century expanding its vast network of colonial possessions around the world in a great race among imperial powers, giving rise to the first great modern phase of globalization (Globalization I), running roughly from 1870 through 1914. This globalization, though, was largely based on the uncompetitive movement of raw materials from the periphery (colonies) to the home world (Europe), and it was enforced primarily by the occupation of foreign lands by European nationals augmented by extensive military networks (primarily defined by navies). When that system of global economy self-destructed in two great world wars (1914–18 and 1939–45), Europe was divided between the two victorious external powers: the United States and the Soviet Union.

At that point, Western Europe was connected, along with Japan and Australia, to America's new version of globalization (Globalization II, from 1945–80), one not based on colonialism but on free markets, free trade, transparency, democracy, and collective security. On the other side of the Yalta line, Eastern Europe was disconnected from the rest of the world and fell under the isolating control of the Soviet Union for almost half a century. When China subsequently fell to the

Communists and South Asia broke free from Europe's colonial grip, basically the rest of the Eurasian landmass was lost to the socialist mind-set, remaining largely disconnected from the West's embryonic global economy for roughly a couple of generations.

After that period of blocked expansion, the Western-defined globalization process renewed its march eastward with the collapse of the Communist bloc in 1989, with China actually predating that conversion by several years, thanks to Deng Xiaoping's "four modernizations" push in the early 1980s, which marked the beginning of the third great age of modern globalization (Globalization III, from 1980 to 2001). At the end of the Cold War, only the former colonial regions of the Gap, which had overwhelmingly fallen victim to homegrown authoritarian regimes after the collapse of the European empires following the Second World War, remained fundamentally outside the global economy, with the two most disconnected regions being the Middle East and sub-Saharan Africa. Not surprisingly, the Middle East now defines the battlefront in the grand historical struggle between the Core's forces of connectedness and the Gap's most bloodthirsty foes of that integration process (Globalization IV, from 2001), and once it likewise falls to globalization's embrace, only deepest Africa will remain—that first cradle of humanity.

Realizing that modern globalization's advance essentially traces backward the earlier spread of humanity is important on another level: Modern globalization's advance has met with consistently violent resistance throughout most of its history from rejectionists armed with exclusionary ideologies. These rejectionists, starting with the slaveholding South and extending right on through to our current enemies, have always pleaded that mankind must be saved from the machine-driven logic and exploitation of the industrial world. Typically, these rejectionists not only have sought to resist integration into this industrialized world but also have proposed competing systems of government and economics that would both avoid this outcome and do it one better by leapfrogging humanity into some idealized alternative universe of near-utopian self-fulfillment.

The odd thing is that as globalization has progressively advanced in its technology and modernization, the rejectionist ideologies have been forced to retreat farther back in time to attempt to build their alternate universes. When Marxism began in the mid-nineteenth century, the assumption was that socialism would naturally be achieved at capitalism's pinnacle of development, or at the point of the super-abundance of goods. This ideology actually sought to extend the capitalist model of development beyond what were perceived as its logical limits. But since that ideology proved wrong in its diagnosis of capitalism's weaknesses, it fell to Vladimir Lenin to turn Marx on his head at the start of the twentieth century and argue that socialist revolution was far more likely to succeed in a largely precapitalist society, meaning not industrial Germany but Russia just as it was approaching what would have been its industrial phase of development.

Later in the same century, Lenin's great ideological successor, Mao Zedong, took his theory farther back in time, arguing that socialist revolutions made even more sense in largely agrarian societies like China, meaning a revolution led by rural peasants and not by an urban proletariat. Cambodia's subsequent Khmer Rouge Communist movement later took Mao's ideology to its logical extreme, not just engaging in "cultural revolution" against largely city-based "enemies of the state" but literally emptying the cities and forcing millions to endure "reeducation" (marking the revolutionary Year Zero that would reboot the system completely) and eventual genocide in the most backward rural areas of the country.

Meanwhile, with the fall of the Portuguese empire in sub-Saharan Africa in the mid-1970s, the Soviet Union's leadership, despite the complete lack of revolutionary spirit back home, nonetheless deluded itself into thinking that successful socialist states could be constructed in some of Africa's most backward economies, generating Moscow's brief but ultimately failed ideological fling with the so-called Countries of Socialist Orientation (e.g., Angola, Mozambique, Ethiopia). When the bankruptcy of that approach was made apparent in the failure of the Soviet puppet regime in Afghanistan at the beginning of the 1980s, the great collapse of the socialist bloc began in earnest, fueled in Asia by China's rapid turn toward market economics under Deng.

It was at this point in history that many political theorists began speaking of the "end of history," a phrase made famous by philosopher Francis Fukuyama, who, not accidentally, began his career as an expert on the Soviet bloc and its relations with the Third World (the subject of my Ph.D. dissertation as well). What was meant by that was the notion that no feasible alternative to democracies and capitalism seemed to exist anymore, signaling the historical supremacy of each in combination. As a great wave of democratization swept the planet in the wake of the socialist bloc's retreat and collapse, the judgment appeared warranted.

And in many ways this historical judgment does remain valid, for what has arisen in the years since the Cold War cannot be described as a full-fledged alternative model of development, since the Salafi jihadist movement promises no economic development whatsoever, but rather a strange sort of retreat into the past, with the utopian promise of somehow not only getting it right this time (i.e., returning to the golden age of the first several centuries following Muhammad's life), but doing so in such a way as to become far superior to the current perceived alternative ("Westoxification" at the hands of a corrupt capitalist world system). Indeed, the world witnessed this back-to-the-future outcome in the Taliban's rule in Afghanistan across the late 1990s, right down to its pointless destruction of all symbols of foreign religions, the banning of television and music, and severe restrictions on the education of females (the quintessential disconnect). In all, the Taliban's definition of the "good life" was almost prehistorical in its quality, demonstrating the absurd lengths to which the violent resistance to globalization has traveled in the current age.

Yet, despite this retreat into the past, which corresponds to globalization's progressive encroachment into the world's most ancient civilizations, the Salafi jihadist movement of today is, in the words of economist Brink Lindsey, "strikingly similar to its defunct, secular cousins." For like all the Lenins and Maos before it, al Qaeda's antiglobalization movement, while feeding off its adherents' sense of alienation from, and resentment of, the Western-fueled globalization process, is still nothing more than a naked grab for power over others, or what Lindsey calls "the millennial fantasy of a totalitarian state that is the fundamental feature and common thread that unites all the radical movements of the Industrial Counterrevolution."

But, unlike previous versions of ideological resistance to this expanding model of global economic connectivity such as socialism or fascism, which offered a marriage of conservative social values with modern technology, the Salafi jihadists promise simply the rejection of modernity—which, as Lindsey points out, effectively kills any sort of global appeal beyond their most like-minded coreligionists. So how can bin Laden and al Qaeda still maintain their widespread popularity in the Islamic world? Easy. Their main competition is the rigid, unimaginative authoritarianism that grips so much of the Middle East. With history "ended," where else can young Muslims turn in their anger over the lack of both freedom and development in their countries?

Martin Wolf, longtime writer for the *Economist* and author of the best book yet on globalization *(Why Globalization Works)*, argues persuasively that the two Western ideologies of nationalism and socialism have effectively run their course inside the Gap, because "socialism did not work, while nationalism became an excuse for grubby tyranny." So all that's left to rally resistance to globalization is some sort of Occidentalism, or fear and hatred of the West, which has served as an emotional wellspring for anticapitalist ideologies and movements throughout history.

As Ian Buruma and Avishai Margalit point out in their excellent work on the subject, Occidentalism is simply the mirror image of Orientalism, or the tendency of the West throughout history to view the East as corrupt, degenerate, and greedy in comparison with its virtuous self. All that the current expression of Occidentalism offered by radical Islam adds to that classic mix is to up the ante considerably by depicting Western civilization as "a form of idolatrous barbarism," because "idolatry is the most heinous religious sin and must therefore be countered with all the force and sanctions at the true believers' disposal." In the end, then, the Salafi jihadists' holy war isn't about America's policies in the Middle East or the fact that we're so powerful: "This is not about policies, but about an idea, almost a vision, of a machinelike society without a human soul." This is the globalization process so innately feared by our enemies: an almost *Invasion of the Body Snatchers*–like horror film where people's souls are removed from their bodies, leaving them permanently trapped within a global network of nonstop economic exploitation and sexual perversity. There is no policy the United States can adopt, change, or cease that will stem that powerful fear-threat reaction.

Occidentalism, as the authors note, is neither a left- nor right-wing phenomenon. It goes beyond such divisions to represent a profound fear of the invasive forces of the outside world. It is clearly not linked to a particular culture, for Japan spent the first half of the twentieth century in the throes of such Occidentalism only to find itself the target of these same ideas by the century's end. But of course this transformation has occurred time and time again as globalization has engulfed culture after culture. German fascism believed itself a pillar of resistance to Western corruption, only later to join and help define the West. The same is now happening with once socialist Slavophile Russia, longtime xenophobe China, and the eternally insecure India, three major civilizations whose progressive integration into the global economy moves it beyond its perceived Western limitations and demonstrates its potential for complete global reach.

This fear of losing one's soulfulness and grounding in tradition lies at the very heart of this journey from disconnectedness to connectedness, from Gap to Core, and—most important—from countryside to metropolis. Modernity is represented by the city, tradition by the farm, and so to migrate from the latter to the former is to suffer not just a change of place but of lifestyle as well. Questions of identity and existence are naturally raised by this journey. What was once viewed as stultifying tradition back on the farm is now firmly held on to as a connection to the past, something that centers the individual in a dizzying new world full of temptations and sin.

Occidentalism actually began in the West, with the wholesale migration of people from the country to the city. In these earliest expressions, the countryside represented the divine, the soulful, the pure, and the natural, whereas the cities were cesspools of heresy, machines, decadence, and the man-made. Naturally, the history of revolution against this pathway of development begins in the city, not in the country, because it's in the city where the sense of anger, alienation, and resentment grows, not in the disconnected countryside. To learn to hate the city/industrialization/capitalism/globalization, one needs to experience them firsthand, in the belly of the beast. Thus terrorists historically have arisen from well-educated, middle-class urban segments of society, not from the backward, disconnected rural segments, even as they are often enlisted as the foot soldiers of these revolutionary movements.

So it is managing that individual journey from the country to the city that lies at the heart of the Core's historic task of shrinking the Gap. If the Gap's populations cannot successfully make that trip, finding genuine economic and social connectivity, then there is little hope of making globalization truly global, for all that will happen with this migration is the concentration of disgruntled masses—the perfect source material for unrest, as noted by revolutionaries throughout history.

Such wars against "sin city," the West, and the "corrupt global economic order" have been declared time and time again in the past century and a half, as Buruma and Margalit point out, "in the name of the Russian soul, the German race, State Shinto, communism and Islam." All promised a better, universal alternative. This search for the great alternative will not end anytime soon, and so many more such "wars" will be declared in the future, by increasingly less-powerful foes, for this resistance represents not the historical momentum of global integration but the friction such a process naturally elicits from tradition-bound cultures forced to adapt themselves to new and seemingly alien rule sets of behavior.

In his book *The End of History and the Last Man*, Francis Fukuyama explored whether or not the twenty-first century would provide further impetus to history's exploration of the question, What is the best political order for societies? If it did not, then history would have truly "ended" with the demise of socialism, the last great alternative to free-market democracies. In the end, Fukuyama argued that much history still remained to be played out on this debate, as the spread of the capitalist world economy would trigger a natural resistance among outsiders regarding their struggle for recognition, meaning their fight would be less one against the economic logic of integration than one against the perceived loss of identity that would result from such a process.

And here we get at the essential truth of the matter: The current form of violent resistance within the Gap to globalization's creeping embrace is a rejection neither of connectivity, per se, nor of the economic benefits that accompany that connectivity. It really all comes down to the fear of lost identity in the highly networked, urbanized, atomized, and individualized existence of an increasingly globalized economy and society. In a nutshell, it is anonymity that is most feared, because the anonymous person can quickly become lost, discarding tradition and a sense of morality in exchange for opportunism and self-gratification without consequence. It is a world where distinctions of right and wrong, if not successfully internalized, are routinely ignored by individuals as they rush through their daily lives, rationalizing everything in the name of efficiency, utility, and personal gain.

If such prospects motivate many within the Core (especially in the United States and New Core pillars such as Brazil, China, and India) toward stronger reliance on religious faith, should we be surprised that violent resistance to this perceived inevitability inside the Gap results in a plethora of religious-inspired revolutionary movements? Not at all. These "wars of the spirit," as Fukuyama calls them, are precisely about the only thing left worth fighting over in a world where connectivity promises the superabundance of wealth—namely, one's sense of unique self-worth. People simply don't want to feel as though who they are is nothing more than the sum total of their material possessions or career achievements. They want to be connected to something higher, something more profound, something that promises a lasting sense of identity and self-worth in a world that seems constantly swamped by change.

Look at it this way: If we in the Old Core find globalization a frighteningly chaotic mix of new rules constantly undergoing revision by forces beyond our control, imagine how much stronger that personal sensation must be in New Core states undergoing that process of deep integration with the outside world, where the past seems to be swept away on a daily basis by crushing waves of rapid development. Then imagine how hesitant most individuals inside the Gap must feel at the prospect of throwing themselves on the mercy of this seemingly cruel process of absorption into a frighteningly anonymous and machine-like whole.

As we seek to shrink what remains of the Gap over the next several decades, we will rarely find societies adequately prepared—either intellectually or emotionally—for the travails that lie ahead. Instead, the elements most prepared will be those most willing to wage bloody resistance against this process: educated, worldly young men who are familiar with the future we offer and have already decided that it is corrupting beyond all reason. These revolutionaries and terrorists will wage wars of extreme perversity against both us and their own peoples, convinced as they are of their moral superiority in rooting out hypocrisy and heresy.

We will see, time and time again, atrocities committed by these actors that recall the chillingly murderous logic of Stalin, Mao, and Pol Pot, as they too seek to remake their own corners of humanity overnight so as to keep them safe and thoroughly disconnected from the evil of the outside world. These perverse acts of violence will be designed to shock us as much as their own people, in the typical "bloody nose" strategy that outsiders have attempted against the "weak" and "amoral" Americans going decades back in our history— at times successfully (e.g., Pearl Harbor, Tet Offensive, 9/11). As such, their strategy of resistance will specifically target—in the manner of Fourth-Generation Warfare—our morale and perseverance rather than our material strength.

This "silver bomb" strategy is not unlike the "silver bullet" thinking that has long impaired much of America's own military logic. While we constantly search for the "killer application," or decisive technology that will bring us instant victory, our enemies search for the "killer strike," or the symbolic targets whose destruction brings us to our knees and convinces us of the futility of fighting on. In this way, our current main enemies, the Salafi jihadists, are, in the words of that hardened revolutionary strategist Vladimir Lenin, almost "childlike" in their assumption that the right bomb in the right place at the right time will bring about worldwide revolution.

But their destruction is preordained by history, in a form of natural selection by which those who cannot ground themselves in anything but totalitarian schemes of power and domination over others must inevitably be weeded out so that others far more talented and imaginative can truly reap the benefits of a world without walls, without disconnectedness, and without war.

So yes, I do account for nonrational actors in my worldview. And when they threaten violence against global order, I say: Kill them.

THE CONVERGENCE OF CIVILIZATIONS

The second great criticism of my vision for shrinking the Gap is that it simply assumes too much rationality from the world as a whole and that the religious and cultural differences that divide us are just too great to overcome. In other words, no matter how much it may seem that economic logic *should* bring the world together, the planet is full of irrational people who will fight this "mixing of the races," this "mongrelization of cultures," and the "surrender of ethnic identities." I understand the argument and I appreciate the fear, but I also believe that fighting this global integrating process is both immoral and pointless. Given all the challenges of transracial, transreligious, and transcultural relationships, no one chooses this pathway except out of sincere and intense love for the others involved, and fighting love, as countless generations of human evolution have proven, is far more futile than fighting hatred and racism.

Plus, quite frankly, as the father in a transracial family, I simply like the idea that humanity started out light brown, then spread out into a great diversity of shades, only to someday return to that middling color. The symmetry of that journey simply appeals to me, especially as I know my own religion's founder, Jesus Christ, certainly walked this earth with that skin tone. So when I look into the eyes of my brown-eyed girl, I don't see an alien race, but the future of the human face—and I find it quite beautiful.

The goal of globalization must ultimately be finding space for all comers, not forcing all comers to fit into the globalization space. Whatever clashes emerge from this process are to be embraced, not feared, for it is in harnessing these differences that the whole grows into so much more than the sum of its parts. In many ways, belonging to a transracial family is twice the work (the perceived need to achieve a higher standard in damn near everything to justify your unorthodox choice), but with twice the payoff (think of all those extra holidays!). Globalization is transracial and transcivilizational many times over, and the real reason why it's unstoppable, if not sabotaged from within, is that inclusion always outperforms exclusion—economically, politically, militarily, socially, spiritually.

Don't worry. Human identity has an unlimited capacity for expansion. We'll never run out of hyphens or slashes, much less faces we find beautiful.

It is quite ironic to me that the man best known for popularizing the phrase "the clash of civilizations," Samuel P. Huntington of Harvard University, was one of the least judgmental teachers I ever encountered across ten years of college and graduate studies. In fact, I can remember few other thinkers I've ever met in my life who measure people more completely on the basis of their ideas and the soundness of their arguments rather than who they are or where they come from. An elitist in terms of intellect, certainly, but easily the most encouraging professor I ever studied under, and the first who imparted to me the recognition that I had a natural talent for big, powerful concepts.

Huntington is probably the most influential political scientist of his age, and his talent for taxonomies, or classification schemes that divide up the world into various categories, is legendary (his notion of "clashing civilizations" being only his most famous). In his latest book on the changing character of the American nation-state (*Who*

Are We?), Dr. Huntington divides what he calls the great themes of transnationalism (if globalization were a political movement, transnationalism would be its ideology) into three basic categories: universalist, economic, and moralist.

Before I get all professorial on you, let me explain why I want to run you through this drill. Huntington's approach of parsing out the logic of transnationalism—in effect, breaking it down into its various angles or constituent parts—is designed to make each seem narrow in its logic regarding means while remaining wholly unrealistic in its desired ends, like trying to build a fabulous mansion using only hammers as tools. By forcing us to choose among these perspectives, he makes them all seem suboptimal. Frankly, I don't see the need to choose between these artificially compartmentalized labels. But understanding how each perspective is criticized by opponents is useful, because you can't realize that the sum of all these parts is greater than the whole until you're confronted with such *either-or* logic, as in, "Either you're one or the other, but it's no fair mixing and matching pieces into something far more logical and coherent than any one of these caricatures!"

This won't be easy, so excuse the academic tone.

Huntington defines each approach as follows: The universalist vision argues the most expansive variant of American exceptionalism, or the notion that America's political evolution represents the future of the entire world, and, as such, we Americans are both specially empowered to and uniquely burdened with the responsibility of seeing our brand of government replicate itself around the planet. Imagine Microsoft as a model of a nation-state and you'll get what he means here. Being a white Anglo-Saxon Protestant (or WASP) who tends to highlight America's admittedly strong Anglo-Saxon roots, Huntington treats that viewpoint with great skepticism, believing few countries around the world possess the natural wherewithal to replicate America's political journey. That may seem awfully snotty to someone without the same cultural heritage, and yet there's no denying that most of the world's oldest and strongest democracies are former British colonies. But before you start hypothesizing about a democracy "gene" (easy does it, Darwin!), let's move on.

WE HAVE MET THE ENEMY . . .   285

Huntington's second category is that of economic determinism, a perspective I am accused of embracing on a regular basis. It's the notion that economic logic tends to prevail over all other rationales for collective human behavior, driving the planet toward ever greater and more elaborate schemes of integration through trade, shared investments, and connecting networks that facilitate it all. As some-one who used to teach Marxism at the Kremlin-on-the-Charles (Har-vard), I readily plead guilty to this charge. I believe that people, if left alone by the state *just enough*, will trade things with one another like crazy, actually preferring that to war and conquest (but still finding a place in our hearts for professional football, for example). Yes, yes, I know, the Gap is still full of people who simply *love* to kill each other nonstop, but I'm just inflexible enough to think that if you give them a real chance, even *those people* would rather buy and sell stuff than wage war to make their lives work. Ditto for big collections of *those people* called states, assuming—yet again—that the governments in question give individuals *just enough* freedom to pursue such economic connectivity on their own.

The last category of the trio Huntington calls the moralist view-point, or one that argues against the perceived sanctity of state sover-eignty, a notion that took strong root in Europe following its dual world wars of the first half of the twentieth century, two horrific struggles that in their aggregate now look, with the passage of time and the emergence of the European Union, like Europe's version of the American Civil War (i.e., the initial trigger sending the continent from their collective past as *these* European states toward their future as *the* European state). Eager to avoid any further repeats of these state-based wars of aggression, Europe subsequently identified itself with the preservation of state sovereignty around the world, *even* as its now growing European Union continues to do its best to reduce that notion among its own pool of members. As the EU's periodic national "no" votes prove, this is still a highly contentious political process of surrendering state sovereignty to higher authority—the *union*.

Nowhere is the sanctity of state sovereignty held in higher regard than in the UN, a characteristic that does much to explain that international organization's growing irrelevancy in the post–Cold War era. Such respect for state sovereignty was a very good thing during the decades-long nuclear standoff between antagonistic superpowers America and the Soviet Union. But it has clearly become a hindrance to the Core's collective ability to deal with the rising volume of subnational violence inside the Gap, as well as transnational terrorism committed by nonstate actors who—by definition—have to be acting with impunity from somebody's country somewhere in the global community.

Now, the argument of the moralists is that advanced states needn't be shy about intervening in those states from which threats emanate toward the world at large, or where citizens living within suffer either repression at the hands of dictators or deprivation and mass violence as the result of failed governments. This argument isn't so much about deterring the threat as it is about simply dealing with the bad situation that gives rise to that threat—on moral grounds. So, say your next-door neighbor is one scary guy who you think might harm you someday, but there's no reason to do anything but avoid him in the meantime, because, hey, it's a free country! Then imagine this scary guy is discovered to be abusing his wife and children in some horrific way. Now, if you have a strong sense of morality, it's society's duty to do something about this creep, if for no other reason than to save his wife and kids further suffering. If you make your neighborhood better in the process of putting this guy behind bars, then so much the better. But the main point is, it stops being a "free country" for this particular jerk once he starts harming others. At that point, his rights, or "sovereignty," disappear, and those of society grow paramount.

Now, when I'm confronted with this sort of category scheme, I know it's all about trying to pigeonhole me into one box or another, denying me the ability to build a case for action. So, for example, when I argue that the Core should end Kim Jong Il's rule, I'll read you an entire riot act of complaints: he's killed at least two million of his own people (moralist), his criminal activity (drug trafficking, counterfeiting) is very bad for the business of Developing Asia (economic), and his decrepit totalitarian regime has simply lived beyond its historical expiration date, so why not finally liberate that population and let it join democratic South Korea (universalist)? When you attack each argument separately, it's a lot easier to declare Kim Jong Il "not our problem," but when you add them all together, the case for his removal from power is a whole lot stronger.

Again, Huntington's point in presenting this typology of transnationalist thinking is simply to attack each position in turn—a divide-and-conquer approach. Why? Unlike Francis Fukuyama, who believes that globalization's economic momentum will eventually overcome the social friction it causes among the world's many cultures (and the "wars of the spirit" that friction regularly ignites), Huntington seems in awe of that friction's capacity to fuel long-term power struggles among the world's great civilizations, to include the reformulation of an effective East-West standoff (his favorite bet being a strategic alliance of the "many Non-West" against the American-led West). As such, he tends to discount transnationalism as a chimera of today's era of globalization, one that will fade as civilizational divides make themselves more apparent and intransigent with time.

What I find so damaging about Huntington's analysis is his penchant for turning America's exceptionalism on its head: rather than signifying over the long course of its political evolution the successful pathway the world might follow in economic and political-military integration, he tends to focus too narrowly on America's early years to explain the uniqueness of our country's formation and thus later success. So where I see the replicability of the American pathway, Huntington argues against such reproducibility around the world primarily because, in my opinion, he misses the trees for the forest.

America is itself the first embodiment of transnationalism, and our subsequent success in developing a strong federal state should not obscure either our origins or our successful growth from thirteen to fifty states. That much of our early success was greatly facilitated by a common ethnic, racial, and cultural background simply explains why America was able to accomplish what it did so many decades *before* similar developments finally took hold in Europe, by far the most advanced civilization of modern history. And the fact that our initial cultural homogeneity has been lost in the decades since (i.e., we're not all WASPs anymore), while we've continued to evolve as the world's most dynamic and creative society, simply underlines how important our historical pathway has become as an example to the rest of the world, which is only now encountering—thanks to globalization— many of the same splintering social pressures that America has long successfully endured, such as long bouts of massive immigration.

My point is this: There is no need for, or utility in, dividing the concepts of transnationalism into these seemingly conflicting categories, because all three ideas come together nicely in the American experience.

America's exceptionalism is not based simply on its success as a nation-state, but as the world's first and most successful multinational political and economic union. Its example does not speak to the individual futures of nation-states, but to their collective futures as larger unions and ultimately to the future of globalization itself. The European Union does not provide historical lessons to the United States, it receives them.

My God! How can the Europeans brag so about finally achieving a unified currency when our uniting states managed that feat a couple of centuries ago? Or a "supranational" legislature (the European Parliament) that rides herd over the member states' own legislatures? Or a "supranational" European Court that sits *supreme* above all other states' own court systems? Or (can you believe it?) an executive function that would seek to speak to the world on behalf of all European states regarding foreign policy and security matters? Is anyone really operating under the delusion that all of these transnational or supranational concepts didn't start first in America in 1789 (the year we forged our Constitution) rather than in Europe in 1991 (the year the Maastricht Treaty set in motion the formation of today's European Union)?

That's why I'm amused by those libertarians who love to accuse me of betraying America's Founding Fathers with all my talk of Leviathan and System Administrators. What they say is that our military should only concern itself with defending our country from attack, not enforcing a global peace (Leviathan) or trying to rehab failed states (SysAdmin). In sum, these political fundamentalists want to

WE HAVE MET THE ENEMY . . .   289

keep America off by itself in the global security environment, pretending we can isolate our security from that of others. By my reasoning, the architects of our original union of thirteen (count 'em, thirteen!) colonies purposefully created a multinational political system designed to accommodate both the future expansion of its political ranks and the deepening economic integration among its member states, while allowing for each state to retain its own unique identity and cultural attributes. It has been that political capacity for peaceful convergence among those states (remembering that we suffered one incredibly nasty civil war along the way) that has allowed America to process successfully such an amazing influx of immigrants over the decades, as well as finally move beyond the disastrous legacy that was slavery in the South—a gap that was shrunk over the course of roughly one century (from the 1860s Civil War to the 1960s civil rights movement).

The universality of that American experience is marked not so much by our exceptionalism but by our great good fortune in being the first part of the world to achieve this transnationalism. America does not lead globalization because it's exceptional. America leads simply because it got there first. The fact that we've continued to get there first, decade after decade, is in no small part due to our long-term adherence to the precepts of free markets, starting with the freest of trade relations among our member states, complemented with mostly free trade with the outside world. There is no either-or regarding American exceptionalism and economic determinism: we are so successful as a society simply because we consistently commit ourselves to the purest forms of capitalism that our inexhaustible pool of entrepreneurs can dream up.

So it's no great surprise that the world tends to conflate globalization with Americanization. How could it not?

Should this process be feared by the world for its homogenization of culture? I guess that would depend on whether you think California is a carbon copy of Alabama or that Texas and Massachusetts are indistinguishable. Convergence does not result in homogeneity, but in a superficial blending of external similarities, much like that light brown face that will someday define the bulk of the American population.

Deep down, we all remain distinct, as do our neighborhoods, our communities, and our member states. I personally have lived in the Midwest, the Mid-Atlantic, and New England, and I found each of these experiences quite distinct, despite the existence of McDonald's everywhere I go.

Huntington is absolutely correct in noting that America has essentially lost the original ethnic, racial, and cultural components of its identity, now leaving only a political concept that unifies the United States, the only country in the world whose official name denotes no geographic component whatsoever. What defines the United States? Simply the political decision of these states *to be united*. That is our identity, one that owes no allegiance to race or culture, but rather an exceedingly simple political rule set. Americans have always lacked the primordial attachment to the land that defines nationalism the world over. America has been and always will be defined by the pursuit of frontiers, wherever they may lie and whatever form they may take.

Probably the most important reason America has been able to move itself in the political direction of accepting all races, cultures, and creeds as essentially equal is that we have remained, throughout our history, a profoundly religious country. Not a country dominated by religions, but one imbued with great religiosity or a deep sense of spirituality. As with our politics, we Americans tend toward the most direct relationships with our faith, so our religious connectivity mirrors our political connectivity: we expect to speak directly to the "man" in charge. Our tendency to individualize our faith makes us the most independent-minded Catholics, Jews, Protestants, Evangelicals, Hindus, Buddhists, and Muslims in the world. To become an American is to automatically enter into your own personal Reformation, no matter what your faith, because our profound sense of individual freedom virtually mandates such an iconoclastic approach.

Our tendency toward passionate spirituality moves America down a pathway quite apart from Europe's, where—as many experts note— religion remains important but religiosity does not. As such, America will increasingly find far more in common with New Core states experiencing a resurgence of both religiosity and religions than it will with Old Core Europe. The same will also hold for America's relationships with the tumultuous Gap. We'll continue to be more accepting of immigrants streaming from there than Europe will be. In contrast to the resilient and much experienced United States, the rather adolescent European Union naturally fears the stronger religious bent of these "guest workers," believing it threatens the secular nature of its still embryonic political system.

There are strong differences between the types of Muslims who immigrate to America compared with those flowing into Europe. European Muslims overwhelmingly pick up the "3D" jobs in the economy, as in "dirty, dangerous, and difficult." In the United States, the 3D jobs tend to go to Hispanic immigrants, not the far smaller pool of Muslim immigrants, who come to America more often with advanced degrees and professional skills. Because European Muslims often occupy the lowest steps of the economic ladder, they also tend to live clustered in urban ghettos, not unlike the inner-city concentrations of African-Americans in the United States. Finally, in America, Muslims possess no residual anger over past colonial relationships, although there is, of course, strong resentment over certain aspects of U.S. diplomatic and security policies in the Middle East.

As such, Muslims in Europe are likely to identify themselves more in an ethnic or cultural manner, while in America it's more of a religious or mosque-based orientation. In America, organized religions no longer form the basis for voting blocs, as each faith tends to be as evenly split between the major parties as the next one, with the key determinant for voting Republican versus Democrat being the degree of religious observance—namely, the more often you attend church, the more likely you are to vote for conservative candidates.

In Europe, however, the concentration of Muslims in both urban centers and low-paying jobs places them overwhelmingly on the left end of the political spectrum, suggesting that over time Islamist parties that arise to represent this constituency will occupy much the same oppositional, minority-party space as Marxist parties did in previous

decades. As Islamic expert Olivier Roy notes in his impressive book
Globalized Islam:

> Twenty years ago these men would have joined a radical leftist move-
> ment, but such movements have disappeared from the spaces of
> social exclusion or have become more "bourgeois." . . . There are
> now in the West only two movements of radical protest that claim to
> be "internationalist": the antiglobalization movement and radical
> Islam. For a rebel, to convert is to find a cause.

While some might find this a frightening prospect, it's really just the
opposite. By channeling their sense of economic and social disconnectedness into political action, Muslims in Europe achieve connectivity with governments there that allow for their integration into
political life on a peaceful basis while preserving a sense of cultural
identity. Moreover, with time these political movements will be able to
force greater openness toward Muslim immigration to Europe in the
same way that America's rising Hispanic quotient will keep the United
States open toward Latinos migrating north. In Europe's case, this
isn't just a political release valve for both sides but an economic one as
well: Europe needs workers to balance its rapidly aging population,
while the Middle East needs to be able to siphon off a portion of its
huge youth bulge for emigration.

On a related note, the globalization of American hip-hop culture
may well prove to be a boon to the Core's overall efforts at channeling
similar feelings of social and economic exclusion among Muslim
youth in Europe. How? Youth culture everywhere is about establishing
a sense of identity that claims distinctiveness ("I'm unique . . .") while
expressing a desire to belong to a larger whole (". . . that's why I dress
and act exactly the same as everyone else in my gang!"). By identifying
themselves with American hip-hop culture, Muslim youth in Europe
simultaneously stake out an outsider space ("We're the niggers of
Europe!") while reaching out to like-minded youth the world over
("Rappers of the world, unite!"). A bit over the top? As I remember

from my years as a New Wave skinhead (okay, I shaved only the sides of my head), that's the whole point!

As in the case of their elders in the political realm, these youth have found a political space that allows for "marginal protest culture" (manifested in music, clothing, slang) commensurate with their lesser ambitions to find themselves, have a good time, and simply express their youth in a way that pisses off their parents—the goal of adolescents everywhere. In the end, my bet is that American hip-hop culture (thank you, Russell Simmons and Sean Combs!) does more to prevent Islamic terrorism around the world than the combined efforts of the U.S. Government and military, because it gives Muslim youth the two things they need most at that age: an identity that allows them to express both their distance from mainstream society and their underlying acceptance of its social norms against political violence. Give me one Jay-Z over ten John Ashcrofts any day.

The hardest part for Old Core Europe will simply be giving Muslim immigrants enough time to work past their sense of social exclusion on their own. Watching France's rather idiotic efforts to ban head scarves among Muslim girls attending public schools there should only remind us that change like this comes over generations. The most important thing, of course, is that Muslim girls are attending public schools, not the compromises they may make with their parents to allow their freer movement in society. There are plenty of political leaders in the Core who understand all too well that the real struggle is not between Islam and the West but within Islam *regarding* its convergence with the West and the historical force of globalization. Nonetheless, plenty of these same politicians cannot exhibit the same patience at home that they might demand of American or European foreign policy in the Middle East. For example, all over North America there are examples of Muslim women pushing for greater gender equality within their mosques. These "progressive Muslims" represent exactly the sort of Reformation the multiculturalists are waiting for within Islam (i.e., the individualization of religious worship), but again, can we show the necessary patience to let Muslims living in the

West make these necessary changes on their own schedule, or must we force confrontations and showdowns?

The counterintuitive reality of people migrations is that both societies, the receiving and giving ends of this transaction, tend to experience what sociologists call a "revival of ethnicity." So when Muslims emigrate from the Middle East and immigrate into Europe, both regions respond to this transaction by becoming, respectively, *more* Islamic and *more* European in the near term, until such time passes that new rule sets emerge to define these profound forms of social (family ties), economic (remittances), and ultimately political connectivity. While the movement of Core citizens into the Gap occasionally forces Core powers to defend them through military means, or what the Pentagon typically calls "noncombatant evacuation operations" (i.e., rescuing Americans living or traveling abroad when they're caught in some political-military crisis), a far more potent form of political connectivity comes in expatriate populations living inside the Core and agitating for their adopted nations to intervene militarily or diplomatically in their countries of origin in response to instability or political repression there. A good example of this, of course, is the role of Iraqi expatriates in the U.S. decision to lead a multinational coalition into that country in 2003 to topple Saddam Hussein's regime.

Of course, America's effort to transform the Middle East naturally triggered an even stronger uptick in Islamic revivalism across the region, in large part because this answers the need for strengthened cultural identity in response to greater cultural contact with the outside world. In the short run, that heightened identity is married to an intense form of anti-Americanism, but, as authoritarian regimes across the region are quickly realizing, once the United States reduces its visible military presence in Iraq, all that social anger will inevitably be redirected at them. For once Iraq proves the lie that Arab Islam is incapable of self-rule, that widespread social anger will refocus on the lack of economic opportunity in countries experiencing unprecedented youth bulges.

At that point, the convergence of civilizations inside the Gap takes on an Asian flavor, just as it does inside the Core, where new pillars India and China lead the way in defining new developmental models. For it is in Asian Islamic countries that Arab Islamic societies will find their "lead geese," or those states whose blending of Islamic identity with Western-style economic development will show the way ahead for the Islamic world as a whole. Who are the lead geese? Malaysia and Singapore and, to a lesser extent, the more troubled Indonesia. Malaysia, in particular, offers itself up, in the words of a *New York Times* profile, as "a progressive model to an Islamic world divided between Muslims who believe they can co-exist with the Western world and fundamentalists who say they can't and shouldn't try." A key component of this model is offered by Malaysian Prime Minister Abdullah Ahmad Badawi, who—not coincidentally—is an Islamic scholar. His notion of Islamic Hadari, or Islamic civilization, "emphasizes economic and technological development, social justice and tolerance for other religions." This is how Badawi's ruling coalition continues to defeat Islamist parties in elections, despite the country's 60 percent Muslim population.

Is convergence the only choice for Arab Islam? That depends on whether or not you think a model of exclusion based on interdiction and censorship of "dangerous" foreign influences represents a viable long-term strategy. The Soviet bloc once sought to preserve its model of "Soviet Man" in a similar fashion, and my reading of history suggests that Arab authoritarian regimes will experience similar dismal failures if they persist in this approach over the coming years and decades. Islam the religion simply will not stand by and wait to be overrun by foreign influences. Facing the threat of globalization, this religion has already, through the Salafi jihadist movement, sought to fight fire with fire—in other words, going global to counter globalization. This instinctive fear-threat reaction will not be contained by tired authoritarian regimes in the region, and it will force some sort of ultimate accommodation of modernity in the Middle East that will politically doom authoritarianism there, just as it once did throughout the socialist bloc. This is not economic determinism so much as social Darwinism, with accommodation being the only feasible alternative to atrophy and death, a pathway to which Islamic culture has shown itself highly resistant as one of the world's fastest-growing religions.

Of course, Islam is not the only religion growing around the world.

Christianity is experiencing a serious boom, not in the Old Core but in the New Core and Gap, and the forms it is taking are clearly biased toward greater connectivity and not disconnectedness, again signaling the convergence and not merely the clash of civilizations. By connectivity here I mean a focus on expanding membership in a nonexclusive manner, as in, "Join our faith and connect yourself to a larger, global community," as opposed to, "Join our faith and detach yourself from the larger world." Fundamentalism is essentially a disconnecting force, because it demands separation (sometimes by force) from the "corrupt world," but evangelicalism is—in many ways—just the opposite, demanding a proselytizing embrace of the larger world, primarily out of the desire to convert others to the faith. Despite popular perceptions, radical fundamentalism is seen to be peaking and probably on the decline around the world, according to the latest estimates by religious experts, while evangelicalism is clearly on the long-term rise throughout the New Core and Gap. Because the two are often lumped together in Christianity, this crucial tipping point is largely missed by mass media as well as most of academia. For example, not all of Islam, which is growing rapidly as a global religion, is—by any stretch of the imagination—fundamentalist, any more than you can say all Christians are evangelicals (even if they do represent the fastest-growing portion of Christianity).

Evangelical Christian faiths, such as the Pentecostal wing, which is the fastest-growing religion in the world (especially in New Core pillars South Korea and Brazil), emphasize an intense form of personal connection to God that empowers individuals to engage the larger world with their good deeds and—most important—their profound attention toward the suffering of others. This is why the strongest internationalists in America right now hail from what is typically described as the "religious right," historically a source of isolationist sentiment. Look at the groups arguing for stronger U.S. Government stances on human rights around the world, especially in societies suffering religious persecution, and you will see evangelicals leading the way, with Senator Sam Brownback of Kansas a leading figure of the movement. Look who's pushing for stronger environmental stances in global negotiations, or new international laws against human trafficking, or more aggressive AIDS funding and debt relief in Africa, or conflict resolution throughout the Gap. What you will see in front of the TV cameras will be the familiar internationalist Left (remember Nobel Peace Prize–winning Jimmy Carter?), but the biggest movers behind the scenes will hail from the so-called religious right (did you forget that Democrat Carter was our first born-again president?). Bono, shake hands with Pat Robertson!

How can this be? Just take a look at the profound shift in the global demographics of Christianity. What was once an Old Core–defined religion is now predominantly a New Core and Gap religion. Consider these rather fantastic facts: More Chinese partake in Sunday Christian services than do Western Europeans. There are far more Anglicans in Africa than in England and America *combined*. There are more Presbyterians in Ghana alone than in Scotland. There are roughly a billion Catholics in the world, and the large majority live in the New Core and the Gap, not Old Core North America and Europe. At the beginning of the twentieth century, eight out of every ten Christians lived in Europe and North America. Today that percentage is below 40 percent.

When you combine that demographic reality with the robust social networks that define the evangelical movement in America, it's a powerful package. Moreover, if the Republicans are approaching a permanent majority status and born-again Christians account for roughly one out of every four registered American voters, then we face, as evangelical expert Allen Hertzke remarks, a truly "mind-bending prospect: *evangelicals as a foreign policy conscience of conservatism.*"

If you fear that radical Islam is growing inside the Gap, I say relax, because most Islamic experts agree that its rise actually reflects mainstream Islam's desperate attempt to forge accommodation with globalization and the modernity it imposes upon traditional societies. Focusing on just Islam inside the Gap likewise misses the similarly profound penetration by Christian faiths and the long-demonstrated historical tendency of those faiths to push host populations toward stronger demands for pluralism and even democracy. We've seen in America what Christian churches are capable of in terms of mobilizing

298 BLUEPRINT FOR ACTION

political sentiment and, beyond that, voters, so there should be no surprise that we'll see these same networking capabilities at work inside
the New Core and Gap. Moreover, the political connectivity back
to coreligionists inside the United States should never be underesti-
mated, because these bonds represent a whole lot more than just an
expatriate-like community whose collective guilt at leaving the homeland expresses itself in occasional political lobbying; this is a highly
energized and deeply passionate political mobilization network
lodged within the world's sole military superpower.

In so many ways, it's wrong to write off this community as simply
the "religious right," because that political label disguises the fact that
significant portions of the "religious left" are found here as well. Why?
Religious faith is—yet again—a significant gateway for individuals
wanting to locate a moral rationale for caring about human rights
outside of the comfortable existence of the Old Core. Remember how
nineteenth-century colonialism went hand in hand with missionary
zeal? Well, we shouldn't be surprised that an era that demands a grand
strategy of shrinking the Gap would go hand in hand with a renewed
focus on proselytizing global faiths. While the more secular Left can't
possibly support U.S. interventionism abroad because of its association with military means, and the secular Right can't stomach the
"betrayal" of our "founding principles" for similar reasons, the religious community—both left and right—similarly can't stomach the
notion that America, with all its wealth and power, stands by while the
faithful in numerous Gap countries (and a few key New Core ones like
China) suffer persecution for their beliefs. To believers, then, the
Heavenly Father's admonition to spread the faith trumps the Founding Fathers' inhibitions on mixing church and state.

So let it be written, so let it be done . . . at least until the lawsuits
begin.

Yesterday's Protestant work ethic defined capitalism's rise in the
Core, providing what political scientist Robert Putnam calls "bonding
social capital" that knits an existing community together, but today's
Protestant evangelicalism may well define capitalism's ultimate tri-
umph in the Gap, providing the "bridging social capital" that links

faith-based communities throughout the Core to similar ones inside the Gap. So not only will the twenty-first century's religiosity far outpace that of the twentieth century, to the amazement of social scientists the world over, the ultimate impact of more religion will not be sectarian violence designed to drive religious communities apart, but rather increased social and political connectivity between Core and Gap that will definitely speed up the convergence of civilizations and—by doing so—facilitate globalization's spread around the planet.

Take that, Karl Marx!

A WORLD MADE ONE . . . OR JUST NONZERO

The third great criticism of my vision for shrinking the Gap is that, if achieved, it will bankrupt the planet. The oft-cited estimate by environmentalists is that we'd need something on the order of three to five earths if everyone in the world achieved the same standard of living as that currently enjoyed by Americans. This is, of course, a rather nonsensical projection, because the simple journey of shrinking the Gap would create vast waves of new rule sets (economic, political, social, military) that would simultaneously force compromises among the world's nations while pushing their societies to new heights of ingenuity and enterprise. To assume we'd make that journey and learn nothing in the process is silly, but this is a consistent mistake of most futurists: the assumption that somehow humans can achieve some vastly different world in the future and not somehow be changed by that process of creation. And no, I'm not talking about growing another brain or anything like that, just changing our behavior along the way.

There's a famous quote from a New York City financier of the telephone industry back in the late 1880s that demonstrates this sort of linear logic: "The possibility of a private home telephone system throughout the country is out of the question. Almost the entire working population of the United States would be needed to switch cable."

In other words, eventually there would be so many phones and so many phone calls that virtually everyone in America would have to be employed as a telephone operator for it all to work! Sounds as if we would have needed twenty additional Americas to pull it off, right? Well, it turns out that prediction was absolutely true, and yet it wasn't a problem at all, because Americans simply learned to dial a series of numbers on their own, without requiring help from telephone operators. It wasn't as though we had to sprout a sixth finger on each hand or anything too amazing like that, but rather that the growth of telephones simply generated a new rule set to which we all adapted without much thought, and without bankrupting our labor pool.

Futurists, by and large, tend toward rather dark views of the future and man's capacity to adapt to it. In part, that's the nature of the modern media age: if you want to get noticed as a futurist, it's far easier to do so by predicting lots of scary things than by simply telling people it will probably all work out. If you want to be positive, then you really have to go overboard to get noticed, meaning you're constantly promising flying cars and life expectancy of two hundred years and all sorts of wondrous stuff like that as always being right around the corner. Because if you tell people that everything will get steadily better but never instantly or dramatically so, that sounds too much like life as we know it, and nobody wants to think the future will simply be today's reality improved at the margins with time—even if that tends to describe the long march of human experience.

So, accepting that hyperbole is pretty much the order of the day when predicting the future, then why must so much of it be so dark? In general, we place a great deal of faith in technology, assuming it will always get better and consistently provide us with more amazing capabilities, and yet we're always so willing to accept the notion that humans themselves will inevitably employ these technologies in self-destructive and even suicidal ways, creating future dystopias by the barrelful with our insatiable greed. Sure, Jared Diamond, in his book *Collapse: How Societies Choose to Fail or Succeed,* can find you a number of obscure, outlier human communities throughout history that managed to cut down all their trees to spite their forest, ending their existence in the process. But the larger reality is that today there are more humans on the planet than ever before, and we continue to create new sources of wealth and higher standards of living while adapting the world to our needs and our needs to the complex mix of natural and man-made environments that results from that continuous process of change and development. Mistakes are made along the way, to be certain, and experiments on the margins constantly fail, but the human story continues and tomorrow always comes.

The truth is that most futurists possess very dark imaginations because they tend to be vertical thinkers with enormous knowledge in science and technology but far less so in human behavior. They are likely to be pessimists by nature, and not the happiest people you'll meet. Moreover, their views of humanity tend to focus overwhelmingly on the worst aspects, while heavily discounting the good ones. Overwhelmingly male, they've mastered their field of study to the point where they can tell you how it will "change life as we know it," while having almost no sense of how "life as we know it" will change and adapt itself to the "unprecedented breakthrough" in question. And yeah, it's a very guy thing to cast all such change in uncompromising, zero-sum terms. Present any man or woman with an adapt-or-die scenario, and odds are they'll naturally gravitate to opposite assumptions regarding the outcome—and thank God for that!

Most futurists have a horrific track record precisely because they're always predicting the worst possible outcomes (doomsayers from Thomas Malthus onward), while those who predict that things will get better (the so-called technoprophets going back to science fiction giant Jules Verne) are often far less cited despite getting it right the vast majority of the time. But the good thing about predicting disaster is that you only have to be right once to have your reputation sealed (Richard Clarke as Chicken Little made good). Too many celebrated writers in history (e.g., H. G. Wells, Eugene Zamyatin, Aldous Huxley, Philip K. Dick) simply picked out the worst aspect of life around them and then projected it whole across some future landscape, like George Orwell fixating on the totalitarian regimes of his day (Nazi Germany, Stalinist Soviet Union) and simply assuming that the entire world would be made up of such political orders by the year 1984. Oops! Current

Orwell aspirants (e.g., journalist Robert Kaplan, military writer Ralph Peters, economist Jeremy Rifkin, technologist Bill Joy) make similarly frightening extrapolations that narrow the mind. Kaplan, the U.S. military's favorite dystopian, would have you believe the entire future of the planet can be summed up in some stinking Gap metropolis overrun by suicide bombers and gangs of doped-up teenage hit men. This is the inescapable future! we are told. Why? Because all new worlds must be *brave* new worlds, never *safe* or *secure* or *peaceful* ones.

And yet the course of human history disproves these predictions time and time again. Right now, there is a smaller percentage of people on this planet preparing for or engaging in violence, either organized or unorganized, than at any point in human history. Simply put, we've all found better ways to get what we want. As Robert Wright argues in his book *Nonzero*, humanity has just progressively discovered, through trial and error, that peace beats war, that cooperation beats competition, and that win-win outcomes beat all alternatives. Why is globalization so inevitable? Because it's the ultimate non-zero-sum game, where all sides win and the planet's entire population is ultimately able to participate in this historical accumulation of growth and fulfillment, or what Wright calls "non-zero-sumness":

> [Non-zero-sumness] explains why biological evolution, given enough time, was very likely to create highly intelligent life—life smart enough to generate technology and other forms of culture. It also explains why the ensuing evolution of technology, and of culture more broadly, was very likely to enrich and expand the social structure of that intelligent species, carrying social organization to planetary breadth. Globalization, it seems to me, has been in the cards not just since the invention of the telegraph or the steamship, or even the written word or the wheel, but since the invention of life. The current age, in which relations among nations grow more non-zero-sum year by year, is the natural outgrowth of several billion years of unfolding non-zero-sum logic.

But because humans tend to define themselves in terms of place, and very local places at that, the global win-win is routinely cast as the cruelest and most violent Leviathan of them all. To many, globalization isn't the expanding pie but the rapidly consumed one. If China's billion-plus and India's billion-plus experience development, then *surely* we must lose in that process, because didn't they lose absolutely as a result of our prior gain? Isn't all wealth and progress built on the exploitation of others?

History would seem to indicate otherwise. At the beginning of the nineteenth century, the global population was roughly 1 billion people. At the beginning of the twenty-first century, it stood at roughly 6 billion people. Somehow, despite that sixfold increase in population and a gargantuan accumulation of wealth and prosperity across the planet as a whole, the percentage of people living in extreme poverty, defined as living on less than a dollar a day (adjusting for inflation), actually fell quite dramatically over those two centuries: from roughly 80 percent to approximately 20 percent. That's what two centuries of industrial revolution have done to the planet: added 5 billion people to our ranks while keeping the absolute number of impoverished individuals relatively fixed (e.g., an estimated 900 million in the year 1820 and an estimated 1.1 billion in the year 2001).

Seem impossible? It all depends on how you want to count things up. If the only categories that make sense to you are nation-states, then the gap between the average incomes of citizens in rich countries and those in poor countries is definitely widening with globalization. Ditto for living standards. But all that says is that living in the Core has never been better, while living in the Gap has never been worse.

But when you shift from the level of nation-states and focus on individuals themselves, globalization starts to look a whole lot more non-zero-sum. Inequality among individuals has not increased as the New Core states have joined the global economy over the past quarter-century, and income inequality *within* individual states has likewise not increased, except in the case of China, which, thanks to the anti-growth policies of Mao, entered the 1980s as a country where poverty was both rampant and equally distributed. Instead, the last quarter-century of globalization has seen a dramatic decrease in both the percentage of global population living in extreme poverty (from two-fifths to one-fifth) *and* an absolute drop in that number of roughly 400 million people. When the UN says that more has been done to reduce global poverty in the last 50 years than in the previous 500, they're basically noting that roughly 3.5 billion people have escaped the fate of extreme poverty since 1950—thanks to the rise of the global economy.

But it's not just monetary measures that have improved with globalization. Life expectancy is up dramatically and infant mortality rates have decreased significantly. Fertility rates have plummeted, as have child labor rates. At the beginning of the twentieth century, roughly three out of every four people living in developing countries were illiterate. Today, that percentage is less than one-fifth, although rates for females are still approximately double those of males. All this while we basically tripled the world's population over the past half century. When you add it all up, it's awfully hard to make the case that America's effort to regrow the global economy after its self-destruction in the first half of the twentieth century has been anything but a spectacular success that benefited billions around the planet.

Have we been too successful? Are we going to regret turning on the New Core over the past quarter-century because now these labor-rich countries will flood our markets with cheap goods that ruin our industrial base? Only if we stand still and assume that America's future industries must remain its previous successes. Manufacturing's share of American GDP has held steady for decades now at a level somewhere between 20 and 25 percent of total GDP (rising in real terms), even as the percentage share of our workers in manufacturing has declined dramatically. The alternative is to avoid rising productivity in that sector, hardly a growth strategy. So globalization has not resulted in the deindustrialization of the Old Core at the hands of the New Core. Instead, both the Old and the New Core economies have simply moved up their respective ladders of production, gaining productivity for the world as a whole in the process.

As part of this progression, China will end up buying what seem to be America's crown jewels of production, such as the Chinese company Lenovo's purchase of IBM's computer manufacturing arm in 2005. But this is hardly China stealing our industrial base, unless you think IBM should be "pioneering" PC production ad infinitum. Me? I want IBM to move onto its next great success, whatever that might be. As for the notion that China's "inexhaustible" supply of cheap labor will inundate the world with cheap goods, economist Martin Wolf's admonition in *Why Globalization Works* is worth remembering: "The world we know cannot suffer from a surfeit of goods. It can only suffer from inadequate purchasing power." So long as America's economy succeeds in creating better jobs, thus increasing that purchasing power, we move forward. But holding on to old jobs is never the answer, as romantic as that notion may be.

But if the world is forever buying more and using more, won't we exhaust our planet's natural resources? Shouldn't we preserve them for future generations? Swedish environmentalist Bjorn Lomborg argues:

> The issue is not that we should secure all specific resources for all future generations—for this is indeed impossible—but that we should leave the future generations with knowledge and capital, such that they can obtain a quality of life at least as good as ours, *all in all*.

Ultimately, the most important resource we develop over time is humanity itself, just as it has always been. We see this most clearly in fertility rates: the smarter and more developed we make people, the fewer we need of them, and thus our population growth slows down. When demographers point out youth bulges in certain regions and *then* cite future scarcity issues, they have it completely backwards. Large numbers of people don't cause scarcity; scarcity causes large numbers of people. When you don't have enough food, you tend to "grow" more people to help you man the farm, but once that food requirement is taken care of and you can move to the city in search of *better* jobs, you naturally have fewer kids, spending more on each because they in turn will have to be smarter to get the better jobs that will emerge down the road. Population control is never the answer to overpopulation. Economic development diminishes fertility rates, because it makes people more confident that they can get by with fewer kids to support them.

Globalization is succeeding in this regard to a tremendous degree. There is more food today for more people around the planet than ever before in human history. Moreover, it grows ever more inexpensive over time. Caloric intake has increased globally by one-quarter over the past four decades, rising almost 40 percent in developing economies. Meanwhile, global food prices are roughly one-third of what they were four decades ago. As a result, the percentage of the world's population suffering from starvation has dropped dramatically. In 1970, more than a third of the world's population was starving, meaning they weren't getting enough food to perform light physical activity. By 2010, it is estimated, that percentage will have declined to just over 10 percent. More amazing, as Bjorn Lomborg points out in his classic book *The Skeptical Environmentalist,* is the fact that the absolute rates of starvation have decreased since 1970, despite the huge growth in population. In the 1970s, just over 900 million people were starving, but by the late 1990s that number was below 800 million, and it is expected to drop to fewer than 700 million by 2010. Is that still too many? Of course. But telling poor people to stop having babies isn't the answer, because humans instinctively seek safety in numbers.

Population growth is concentrated overwhelmingly inside the Gap, as is the lack of development—by definition—in the global economy. Shrink the Gap if you want to control population further, and trust that we'll do better by the planet as a whole by taking that path than by pretending we can ask Gap economies to do better by their environment by remaining underdeveloped.

But don't advanced, industrialized economies damage their environments more than less-developed economies? No, they don't. Check out any number of "environmental sustainability" measures or indices that rank nation-states and what you'll find is that the countries with the best environmental records are those with the highest rates of economic development, whereas Gap nations overwhelmingly rank among those who abuse and use up their natural environment in the worst ways. As for the socialist alternative, let's just say that no countries in human history have had the same horrific record of abusing their environments than did socialist-bloc nations over the second half of the twentieth century, with Russia itself being the poster child of this well-demonstrated tragedy.

This is why the world has actually gotten better at utilizing natural resources in recent decades as more countries have either escaped underdevelopment or discarded socialism. You want a global environmental movement? Then make globalization truly global. Otherwise, expect to see environmentalism remain a splintered special interest movement overwhelmingly limited to the Old Core, where too many of us remain fat, dumb, and happy on these issues. Inside the Gap, however, you'll find plenty of skinny people who know better, even as that knowledge makes far too many of them more angry than enlightened.

There is a boom right now in the field of international relations for books and analysis that suggest that the future will be full of "resource wars," as countries fight over raw materials such as oil or substances far more immediately necessary for life, like water. No surprise on this one, as basically every named "hot spot" in this regard can be found inside the Gap or along its Seam. Why aren't there any good prospects for "oil wars" and "water wars" inside the Old Core? Simply because we've got both the money to work around such scarcity issues and the necessary legal rule sets to prevent conflicting claims over jointly shared resources from escalating into violence.

Water is a good example of why the concept of "resource wars" is deeply misguided. Humanity has increased its use of water fourfold since World War II, and yes, in many key locations around the world we've seen local populations grow very close to maxing out their ability to draw upon fresh-water supplies. But to say the planet is running out of water is a gross overstatement. What's true is that we don't price water very effectively, and whenever humans treat a resource as both cost-free and inexhaustible, they waste it like crazy. Good studies show that virtually any country in the world could cut its water use by an average of 50 percent simply by utilizing and transporting water more carefully, basically eliminating all predicted future water shortages. But here's the larger point: It is poverty that creates water shortages, not development. If you're developed, then your economy will be more than able to price water as it should be priced, employing desalinization plants where required. Kuwait, for example, is one of the most water-distressed countries in the world by standard measures, and yet no water shortages exist there, simply because Kuwait has enough money to buy fresh water made from seawater.

All the countries currently predicted to experience stressing water shortages in coming years are found inside the Gap, with the exception of rapidly growing China. But guess what? China's rising wealth will take care of the water issue there because the economy as a whole will be able to price that resource more effectively over time, plus pay the expenses associated with improved use (e.g., most water waste is due simply to leaking pipes). The real question for the countries inside the Gap is, Will they develop fast enough to provide the wealth to deal with their growing water scarcity, or will that scarcity cause conflict? On the latter point, let me point out that exhaustive research on "water wars" throughout time demonstrates that, as far as we know, *there has never been a war fought primarily over water in human history.* Instead, what the record shows is that when water issues arise among states, the states' response is typically to sign treaties that settle the issue peacefully.

How about deforestation? Aren't we cutting down all the trees as part of globalization? Again, the record here, as Lomborg points out, is far better than popularly realized, with all the real problems existing inside the underdeveloped Gap. By our best estimates, we've lost roughly one-fifth of the world's forests in the modern era of economic development, leaving roughly one-third of the world's landmass still covered, a percentage that hasn't changed much at all since World War II. The global economy should easily be able to satisfy its paper requirements in the future through the effective use of a very small (less than 10 percent) portion of the current forest cover.

The real problem with deforestation lies inside the Gap, where losses of tropical forests are dramatic. But again, as anyone familiar with development issues inside the Gap will tell you, what drives that deforestation is not development there but the *lack* of development. Deforestation is often cited as a big trigger for larger environmental catastrophes inside the Gap, and those environmental disasters often exacerbate the impact of natural disasters, such as the hurricane that triggers massive mud slides because the trees are no longer there to secure the topsoil. This is basically what happened with Haiti as a result of Hurricane Mitch several years back. This problem is real, but again, ask yourself why Haitians, for example, felt the need to cut down virtually all their trees while citizens in the country occupying the other half of their island, the Dominican Republic, did not. The answer is simple: the Dominican Republic enjoys a much better level of economic development, so their trees are spared and the hurricane did far less damage there.

In general, though, the world is not suffering more deaths from natural disasters over time; they're just becoming more expensive, thanks to rising levels of development around the world. When a hurricane hits an undeveloped coastline, the cost is negligible. But fill that coastline with houses and ports and all manner of economic development, and the same hurricane is an economic disaster of huge proportions— at least in monetary terms. In terms of human deaths from disasters, though, the numbers have improved dramatically over the past half century, thanks to better medical care, better warning systems, and better emergency relief responses. In the 1940s, the world suffered death rates (measured as a percentage of population) that were roughly seven times those we experienced in the 1990s, reflecting a decline of over 90 percent. So Hollywood disaster movies aside, the future is not likely to be one of mass death around the planet from globalization-fueled catastrophes.

Turning to nonrenewable resources, certainly here we can cite a growing scarcity, yes?

As Lomborg argues so effectively, what drives companies to discover mineral and energy resources is high prices. When prices are lower, companies make less effort to find new reserves, but when prices are high, companies spend more money seeking out new reserves. As such, we really don't have as firm a sense of what our "known reserves" are as we might think, because whenever prices rise—for example, in the energy sector—our historical record is that we routinely find more reserves or figure out how to utilize a broader array of such reserves to achieve the same output (the oil industry turning increasingly toward oil sands and oil shale as reserve sources is a good example of this). Lomborg's best point is this: Getting all jacked up about "known reserves" is a little bit like measuring your personal food security by checking out your refrigerator and assuming that you'll run out of food after three days. The answer is, of course, you won't. Assuming you have money, you'll simply go to the supermarket and buy some more. In many ways, energy markets are like that: they tend to seek out new "known reserves" only when existing supplies get low enough to drive prices up.

So are we running out of oil? Some experts would have you believe the peaking of oil production is just around the corner. But while private oil companies are mostly in charge of refining and distributing oil, it is national oil companies that control the vast majority of the world's "known resources," and guess what? These national oil companies tend to keep their cards pretty close to their chests in this poker game, leading many experts to conclude that reserve levels are much lower than realized. Why do countries do this? Well, it's not a bad way to justify currently high prices. But guess what happens whenever a country with lots of "known oil reserves" lets in private companies to conduct more extensive prospecting efforts? Lo and behold! The oil companies tend to discover a whole lot more reserves. This has just happened with Russia, and it's going to happen with Libya now that it is back on the oil market in a big way following the ending of terrorism-related economic sanctions. Most of Libya's suspected oil fields, for example, have never been seriously explored.

So will we run out of oil anytime soon? My sense is that history will continue to demonstrate that as we need more oil, we will find more oil, paying incrementally higher prices over time to achieve more "known reserves." But this does not mean that we will stay in the oil age ad infinitum. We didn't leave the Stone Age because we ran out of stones, and we won't leave the oil age because we run out of oil. We will move on to hydrogen simply because it is a better technology and because it is easier on the environment.

WE HAVE MET THE ENEMY . . .   311

For similar reasons in the area of electricity generation (remembering that oil is primarily about transportation), expect to see a huge movement toward nuclear power in coming years. Nuclear power may be a scary prospect to most citizens in the United States, but frankly, we're largely alone in our fears. Elsewhere in the Old Core, nuclear power provides a far greater percentage of current electricity needs, and in the New Core, the push for expanding nuclear power is large and getting larger still with time. While the United States occasionally has had bad experiences (e.g., Three Mile Island) with its original generation of nuclear power plants, current technology in the field, such as that of pebble-bed modular reactors that are far more scalable in size and offer far greater safety margins, not only makes nuclear energy cost-competitive in a per-unit sense but also allows advanced economies like the United States the shortest route to reducing our emissions of carbon, the leading cause of undesired global climate change. For example, to reduce U.S. carbon emissions by 15 percent in coming years, we could increase our current solar energy capacity by 6,000-fold, grow our wind energy capacity 300 times over, or pursue five times as much nuclear energy production as we currently have.

But as we'll see time and time again in the future, it'll be the New Core that sets the new rules, because it will have the economies experiencing not just the highest rates of growth but the highest resulting pollution effects. So as the Chinese increase their car population severalfold in coming years while tripling their electricity requirements, we should expect their economy to take the lead in developing hydrogen-fueled cars and pebble-bed modular nuclear reactors. Simply put, America won't experience the same up-tick in pollution that China will in coming years, plus America is a far richer economy and so it won't feel the same need to avoid higher energy prices from more conventional sources.

This may sound like I'm expecting an awful lot of farsighted planning from New Core pillars like India and China, but I'm not really. I'm just expecting them to go through the same sort of pollution "peaking" that every Old Core economy went through in previous decades. So no surprises here, just an expectation of the same old same old.

History shows that local air pollution grows dramatically for an economy as it moves from undeveloped status toward development, meaning that pollution increases in the early stages of industrialization as measured by a rise in GDP per capita. What happens, typically around the time the country hits a certain level of development (i.e., surpassing the World Bank's current threshold of "medium income"), is that its local air pollution problem peaks and then experiences an improvement curve that tracks with further economic development, meaning the richer the country gets, the cleaner its air gets. How does this happen? First, production technologies improve with economic development. Second, pollution abatement technologies are employed to a greater degree, again reflecting higher development. Third, the public, growing wealthier over time, tends to become more concerned with increasing pollution and naturally demands improvement from the government (typically a grassroots process that encourages pluralism within more authoritarian governments), which in turn tends to regulate industry more stringently. Fourth, the economy's industry as a whole advances up the production ladder, thereby, as a rule, engaging in less polluting means of production.

But here's the hitch: Local air pollution—for example, sulfur dioxide (SO_2) and nitrogen dioxide (NO_2)—tends to improve with rising economic development levels. But global air pollution—for example, carbon dioxide (CO_2)—tends to worsen. But again, where does that knowledge lead us in considering the cost of shrinking the Gap? To me it says that we accept the reality that shrinking the Gap will increase local pollution in the short run but decrease it over the long haul as areas in the Gap develop and join the Core. But it also says that growing the Core will result in more global pollution, thus necessitating ever more environmental cooperation across the Core as a whole. In general, then, this is all a question of timing. The problem the Bush Administration had with the Kyoto Protocol on global warming was that it excluded India and China, which may have made sense ten years ago but certainly won't make sense a decade from now.

As always, it is connectivity that drives increased awareness of global environmental issues, just as it drives economic development. Right now Africa is largely an environmental disaster, as well as a security sinkhole, and the two problems are intimately linked. Africa relies far too much economically on the exporting of raw materials, which keeps countries there trapped in underdevelopment. That underdevelopment results in higher rates of environmental damage. Additionally, Africa is subject to more armed conflict in large part because that great dependency on raw materials encourages struggles over control of those resources. These outbreaks of war and mass violence also damage the environment and spread disease. The combined effect of all these problems is to keep many African states mired in underdevelopment, likewise keeping their populations largely disconnected from the global economy and the benefits it offers.

Is there any one solution to this complex mix of problems? No. But the costs associated with solving all these problems is not as high as you might expect, in large part because these investments trigger a virtuous cycle of development that benefits both Core and Gap.

The Core is going to need a lot of cheap labor inside the Gap in coming decades, both as a source of lower-end industrial production as the Core progressively moves up the ladder of production itself and as a pool of replacement labor through migration to the Core as those countries age demographically and need to maintain their worker-to-retiree ratios. Fortunately, the Gap is going to need to dispense with a lot of extra labor it cannot employ. When that labor makes its way to the Core, typically it will send back to its country of origin more in remittances than that Gap nation receives from the Core in Official Developmental Aid. Those remittances help fuel, along with foreign direct investment flows from the Core, economic development inside Gap economies.

Facilitating that flow of Gap populations (both from the Gap to the Core in terms of immigration and within Gap countries from rural areas to urban ones) should therefore become an economic imperative, meaning the Core will have to do what is necessary to solve the issues that prevent such flows from effectively happening, such as chronic illnesses within Gap countries, those countries' reliance on raw materials and commodities as their prime exports, and their inability to solve issues of food production. In every instance, what we pay to mitigate the downstream negative impact of these chronic issues dwarfs what we would need to pay up front to solve these problems. For example, the vaccine that prevents the disease obviously costs far less than the lifetime medical care burden that results from the disease. As we've seen with the spread of the worldwide disease burden that is AIDS, prevention is eminently cheaper than treatment.

The most telling example of misplaced funding priorities is seen in what the Core currently spends on agricultural subsidies to its own farmers versus what it would need to spend to eradicate hunger inside the Gap. Even if you put aside the enormous moral quandary associated with this gross hypocrisy on the part of Old Core countries, just ask yourself how much sense it makes for our government to pay our farmers to grow (or worse, *not* grow) food that we don't need while simultaneously paying to treat hunger and all the ancillary costs associated with that deprivation inside the Gap. Toss in, if you will, what we end up paying to interdict the flow of illegal narcotics from the Gap to the Core (plus to eradicate those supplies in the Gap in the first place) from farmers there who are otherwise denied effective access to our legitimate markets, and it adds up to be quite a stunning sum of money—easily severalfold more than what we'd spend to jump-start agricultural development in the Gap.

Because we don't facilitate agricultural exports from the Gap to the Core, we inadvertently lock many of those nations in to long-term dependency on commodities as their main exports, delaying their industrial development. The less connected these states are to the global economy, the more likely they are to fall into conflict and instability. There is no mystery to any of this, or to regarding both the safety of bioengineered crops and their great utility in promoting agricultural development inside the Gap. But antiglobalization forces, especially centered within the Old Core's environmental lobby, fight this flow of technology tooth and nail and, by doing so, inadvertently probably do more than any "evil" multinational corporation to both block economic development inside the Gap and—by extension— exacerbate a raft of environmental problems there.

But those most guilty of denying the Gap's positive movement toward integration with the Core are the antiwar protestors within Old Core nations who agitate against any and all military interventions by the United States to quell conflicts or topple dictatorships there. I judge them so because the deficit of security is the biggest single hindrance to economic development in the Gap, not to mention a huge source of death and destruction, as well as a spreader of both disease and distressed refugees.

While I hear plenty from readers and critics about how much my vision to shrink the Gap militarily will cost, what I never hear from them are the costs associated with doing nothing. Let's consider just some of the more obvious ones:

- Think of all the military spending inside the Core that is directed at defending powers there against one another. Given the integrating forces of the global economy and our shared interdependency, this is fundamentally money spent to no purpose. A Core united in its understanding of its collective security strengths and responsibilities would be able to redirect the vast majority of that money toward dealing with security problems inside the Gap.
- Then think of all the money Core governments currently spend on military aid to states inside the Gap.
- Then think of all the money Gap nations spend on purchases of military equipment and services from private corporations located almost exclusively in the Core and—within that— overwhelmingly inside Old Core Europe and the United States.
- Then think of all the money spent inside the Gap on these conflicts and wars.
- Then think of all the money spent by Core militaries in their responses to these conflicts and wars.

+   Then think of all the money spent by Core governments in their
     relief and development efforts to these states following all their
     conflicts and wars.
+   Then think of the economic losses by all the Gap economies in
     these conflicts and wars.
+   Then think of the economic opportunities lost by Core econo-
     mies because so many Gap states suffer these conflicts and wars.

Then tell me it's far too costly to consider massing the Core's collective military might to impose peace upon the Gap, where—at any one
time—roughly a dozen chronic conflicts are raging.

Because at that point I will tell you this: What it costs the Core to
send postconflict emergency aid to a Gap state following civil strife is,
on average, half as much as what it costs that nation in lost economic
development when, as a result of being unable to keep the peace on its
own, it slips back into conflict. Comparing just those two measures
alone, out of all the ones I've named above, gets you at least a two-for-
one return on your investment. Spend $10 billion on SysAdmin recon-
struction work inside the Gap (I'll get to the military costs in a minute),
and you'll save the global economy a good $20 billion or more.

Where does one come up with such estimates? The Copenhagen
Consensus project brought together a host of scientific experts from
around the world in the spring of 2003 to address the question of how
best to prioritize the world's problems. One of the top ten priorities
ended up being conflict prevention, and in the analysis offered in their
final report, entitled *Global Crises, Global Solutions,* the authors,
using various econometric models, calculated how much money could
actually be saved by applying military force in the manner that I just
described.

By the Copenhagen Consensus's best estimates, preventing the
average civil war inside the Gap saves the global economy in the range
of $65 billion over the lifetime of that conflict (on average, civil wars
last seven years). On average, there are seventeen civil wars going on
inside the Gap or along its Seam, with two new ones beginning each
year as others settle into postconflict periods. When external powers

step into any civil war to shorten it by just one year, the estimated savings per conflict in terms of lost economic development is roughly $10 billion.

Once a state exits a civil war situation, it must endure a roughly ten-year recovery period during which it builds its economy back to where it was prior to the civil war. During that ten-year period, the country has about a 4-in-10 chance of lapsing back into civil war during the first five years and a 3-in-10 chance over the second five-year period. At any one time, there are roughly twelve such states inside the Gap in this situation. What the Copenhagen Consensus data shows is that one of the biggest triggers for renewed civil war is the tendency of the surviving state to spend prodigiously on arms in the years immediately following the conflict, which in turn tends to provoke the suspicion and renewed aggression of rebel parties. What tends to dampen such spending most is the introduction of foreign military troops to keep the peace. If such troops can be offered for approximately five years on average, then the country in question typically hits a growth-recovery spurt in years 4 to 7 following the end of the conflict, and when the bulk of the country's postconflict economic recovery is achieved, the odds of slipping back into civil war decrease dramatically.

What this tells us is that the best payoff for the Core comes in stabilizing Gap nations with peacekeeping forces following conflicts. The Consensus's best estimate in this regard, using historical averages, was that "an outlay of less than half a billion dollars secures benefits in excess of $30 billion" and that was with "very pessimistic assumptions about risks after the withdrawal of external forces." The world's second-best option, as defined by the Consensus, was reducing the length of civil wars through international controls over commodity exports from afflicted countries—again, gaining on average $10 billion in savings for each civil war shortened by one year's time.

So two seemingly counterintuitive realities emerge in the current globalization era: (1) the biggest cause of civil wars is civil wars (namely, lapsing back into civil strife following extended civil war); and (2) peace costs less than war (i.e., the return on investment for peacekeeping is nothing less than staggering). And to that I will add this important corollary: When it comes to shrinking the Gap, action costs much less than inaction. Beyond that basic truth, my real point in tossing out this sort of data analysis is to note that we're just beginning to think through the full dimensions of what could possibly be gained over the long haul by committing our nation in particular and the Core as a whole to this worthy goal.

Right now the U.S. military is undergoing a massive shift in its budgetary, training, and operational priorities, all of which are being redirected from a previous focus on major wars against fellow Core powers to smaller and longer-drawn-out interventions against rogue regimes and failed states suffering civil strife inside the Gap, in addition to the specific tasks associated with fighting transnational terrorist networks operating across the Gap. The invasion and occupation of Iraq was a huge turning point for the ongoing transformation of the U.S. military from its industrial-era roots in the Cold War to its information-era strengths of the current age of globalization. This transformation will ultimately yield a Leviathan force capable of defeating all traditional military opponents, along with a core SysAdmin force, which, when coupled with sufficient resources and personnel from other advanced powers, will be more than capable of waging peace in any Gap environment. As these combined military capabilities emerge, we need to move our political thinking beyond the conventional wisdom that says the Gap is unshrinkable and—even if it wasn't—that it would cost the world too much to do so.

Absent the right tools to deal with the underlying security issues of the Gap, the conventional wisdom will continue to hold sway, if for no other reason than that the Core's political leaders will lack both the will and the resources to imagine any better outcome for the global war on terrorism other than simply continuing to kill the bad guys. Frankly, America doesn't need to transform its military simply to achieve that lesser goal, but by doing so we are setting in motion the development of the means to do so much more. We are setting in motion the capability to end war as we know it inside the Gap and—by doing so—to make globalization truly global.

We will not need five earths or even two earths to accommodate this desired outcome. All we really need is a Core whose main military powers move beyond the zero-sum, balance-of-power thinking of the past and embrace the notion that shrinking the Gap militarily will expand the Core's economic pie dramatically. I believe that getting the Core's military establishments to accept this vision will be much easier than getting the Core's public constituencies to believe in the vision's feasibility, such are popular fears about globalization and its growing impact on our daily lives. Thus, to set in motion this blueprint for action, educating the American public about what is truly possible is easily more important to our national security over the long haul than all the efforts we will undertake to secure our borders, our cities, or our homes from possible terrorist attacks. Like all education, this will be about tearing down walls instead of erecting them. Otherwise, the global future worth creating will remain undiscovered in those countries ignored by our generation, isolated by globalization, and ultimately abandoned by history itself.

CONCLUSION: HEROES YET DISCOVERED

I AM OFTEN APPROACHED BY experienced bureaucratic and political players in Washington who, after telling me how much they admire and support the notion of the System Administrator force, suggest that I come up with a different name for it. In their minds, SysAdmin isn't an important-enough-sounding phrase and it's too hard to explain to people. "Most people of our generation," they tell me, "tend to look down on these computer people as just the 'tech help.'" My reply is always the same: "I didn't come up with the phrase so that it would make sense to your generation, but to the one that's coming up next."

The Echo Boomers, or the huge 80-million-plus generation of Americans born between 1980 and 1995 (the largest generation this country has ever known), are the real target audience for this vision, because come the year 2025, they'll be the cohort (age thirty to forty-five) that's doing the most moving and shaking in our economy and political scene. In the same way that I spend the vast majority of my time now working the youngest officers of the U.S. military on the security implications of this grand strategy, over time I'm most interested in winning the hearts and minds of the Echo Boomers regarding the economic, political, and moral implications of this vision. Why? The Echo Boomers will constitute the generational follow-through. If they can't stay the course, then there will be no course. It'll be their system to administer, so they will need to be able to wrap their minds around it and claim this responsibility as their own, just as their contemporaries all across the Core will be required to do eventually.

And the Echo Boomers couldn't be a better fit, in many ways.

The children of the Boomers are probably the most overly programmed and overly protected generation that America has ever produced. As *60 Minutes* correspondent Steve Kroft put it in his profile of the cohort, "Echo boomers are the most watched-over generation in history. Most have never ridden a bike without a helmet, ridden in a car without a seat belt, or eaten in a cafeteria that serves peanut butter." As a result, they are naturally team-oriented overachievers who, unlike previous recent generations, trust the government, hold traditional values, and emulate their parents instinctively.

The Echo Boomers are also natural networkers. They build their own Web sites, burn their own CDs, and edit their own DVDs. They distrust slick packaging and mainstream media, preferring to share information among themselves to a degree never witnessed before. They are the ultimate word-of-mouth generation.

Natural multitaskers because they grew up in conditions of universal connectivity (the oldest came of age right as the Internet blossomed into a global phenomenon), the Echo Boomers are, in the words of one demographic study, "totally plugged-in citizens of a worldwide community." As such, they know multiculturalism not as something to be accepted, but as simply a fact of life, since over a third of this generation is nonwhite. Probably the least "churched" generation in U.S. history, they are nonetheless deeply interested in making the world a better place. As historian Neil Howe describes Echo Boomers, they are far closer in outlook to the "greatest generation" from World

War II than their egocentric Baby Boomer parents. In short, they're "more interested in building things up than tearing them down."

This generation is far enough removed from the sensibilities of their parents that "the bomb" is their slang for cool, and "gay" has mutated into an all-purpose put-down for nerds and geeks. But like Pearl Harbor served as a wake-up call for their grandparents' generation, 9/11 is their historical touchstone. And like their parents' fixation on the Vietnam War, their sense of the world is being dramatically shaped by the global war on terrorism.

Put this package all together and you basically have my ten-year-old son Kevin, who's completely at home playing Nintendo in the back of the car, listening to his favorite band over the stereo, and talking with a friend over a cell phone while Dad, the only coach he's ever known over five years of playing three sports, drives him to his weekly piano lesson. Kevin knows more about World War II–era weaponry and tactics than I know about current U.S. military operations, thanks to his having replayed virtually every major battle of that war in a variety of first-person-shooter video games of stunning complexity—at least to his dad, whose own "war" game as a kid consisted of picking up a stick and running around the yard shooting imaginary German soldiers. Kevin also likes to remind me that we should go to church more often, that smoking cigarettes is just this side of suicide, that we need to donate money to environmental groups the world over, and that someday he wants to grow up to be just like me so he too can earn a living writing stuff and sending it over the Internet.

Oh, and for Christmas Kevin wants a Mac Powerbook laptop so he can self-publish his book about a superhero named Ray Trinity who routinely saves the world from fanatical terrorists hell-bent on destroying it.

Kevin is keen on heroes, especially ones who fight the good fight, like Luke Skywalker, King Aragorn, and Spiderman. He's less concerned with success than with playing by the rules, and he's pretty sure he'll spend his adult life "doing things that'll help other people," even if he's unclear right now about what that might entail. He knows there are some things worth fighting for, but that—in the end—we all have to get along because it's a small planet and we all need to share, especially when somebody gets into trouble. So Kevin thinks nothing of saving up his money from chores only to turn it all in at school for some relief fund targeting disaster victims on the other side of the world. "Dad," he says when I ask if he'd rather not save his money for that laptop he keeps talking about, "those people over there are just like Vonne Mei, and if she got in trouble, you'd want me to help her out too, wouldn't you?"

Indeed I would Kevin, indeed I would.

Rather than end this book with a long list of things the next generation of leaders will need to do, let me offer up a host of heroes whom I believe we will encounter along the way to fulfilling this blueprint for action. I provide these quick character descriptions for several reasons: First, I want you to recognize these people when you see them, understanding what they represent. Second, I want you to be ready to support these leaders as they arise, realizing that implementers are far more important than visionaries if anything truly lasting is going to be achieved. Third, I want you to raise these adults from childhood, understanding that the future worth creating will largely come from their hands and their imagination. Whether they end up leading or following is unimportant, so long as they see themselves as being part of a larger team, with larger goals and responsibilities beyond just getting ahead or taking care of their own. Finally, if you're of the right age, I want to encourage you to become one of these heroes, not out of duty or guilt but because you can find yourself within these tasks.

Within the world of the military, some of the heroes yet discovered would include:

+ *The four-star military police general:* The U.S. military currently lacks someone of this rank, and it shows in the budgetary priorities regarding the SysAdmin force. When waging peace becomes as celebrated as waging war, this flag officer's fourth star will signify the ascendancy of the "second-half" force. It will also signal to the world America's long-term commitment to peacekeeping operations.

- *Japan's first combat casualty since World War II:* Where this can't happen is somewhere underwater along China's coast. Where this should happen is probably Africa, in a country of virtually no economic importance to Japan. If Japan is going to become a normal great power, its soldiers will have to die waging peace inside the Gap just like everybody else's.

- *America's first SysAdmin force civilian held captive by the enemy:* The ultimate backdoor draft is the one we have now, where civilian relief agency workers are forced by circumstances to work alongside U.S. troops in low-intensity conflict environments. Until such time as SysAdmin troops can secure a country, those relief workers on site should be uniformed and officially part of the civilian coalition force—in effect provided the same security guarantees as the military personnel in the event of being taken prisoner or hostage. Otherwise, our efforts will be met with asymmetrical responses targeting the coalition's weakest links.

- *The "father of postconflict stabilization and reconstruction ops":* The Pentagon needs to find the same sort of visionary leader for the SysAdmin force that it has found repeatedly for its Leviathan force over the decades, the most recent one being Vice Admiral Arthur K. Cebrowski, the "father of network-centric operations." We need someone of Cebrowski's stature to define these operations' doctrinal pillars.

- *The first SysAdmin soldier to win the Congressional Medal of Honor:* This soldier should be the archetypal equivalent of World War I's Sergeant Alvin York, but instead of being someone famous for killing great numbers of the enemy or saving the lives of many fellow soldiers, he or she should be famous for preventing the deaths of great numbers of noncombatants under conditions of great personal risk. By recognizing such an accomplishment, we honor all those who've paid the ultimate price in similar peace-waging situations.

- *The inventor of the Peacemaker, "the nonlethal weapon that settled the Gap":* Gunsmith Samuel Colt designed the Colt .45

handgun, later called "the gun that settled the West." The Sys-
Admin force will need numerous nonlethal technologies to prevent warring parties from firing on one another or targeting
noncombatants as part of their tactics. Nonlethal weapons have
been the "weapons of tomorrow" for quite some time now. That
needs to change. We need great inventors to step forward and
make these technological breakthroughs happen, and we need
the Pentagon to put up enough funding to get these systems into
the field as quickly as possible.

→ *The Secretary of Everything Else:* At some point in the future,
after yet another badly run military occupation of a Gap state,
the President of the United States will need to demonstrate
America's long-term commitment to providing lasting security
inside the Gap by creating a cabinet-level position to oversee such
efforts. This function will never be adequately served within
either the State Department or the interagency process overseen
by the National Security Adviser. Instead, the SysAdmin force
will be grown within the Defense Department and eventually
spun out across the river to a separate federal agency, primarily
because the Pentagon will want to get out of that complex business and return to being exclusively focused on warfighting.

Beyond the Pentagon and the national security establishment, we'll
need to find several important political voices who will serve to enunciate the real challenges America faces as we seek to shrink the Gap:

→ *The feminist neocon:* We need a strong voice from the Right for
women's rights inside the Gap. This person, male or female,
needs to highlight the U.S. foreign policy goal of pushing the
rights of women as a profound subversion of the status quo in
traditional-bound authoritarian regimes, as well as a direct repudiation of the long-term goals of the Salafi jihadist movement.
Such a voice would have to acknowledge the disutility of continuing to let America's support for women's rights in developing

countries remain hostage to the white-hot politics of abortion rights back home.

- *The reeducation president:* Everyone runs for the presidency promising to do more for education. What we really need is someone committed to promoting lifelong learning programs throughout the economy that allow workers displaced by globalization's negative effects to seek retraining opportunities that get them back into the workforce as quickly as possible. It used to be enough to say, "My child will do better," but now individual workers need to be able to upgrade their careers on a regular basis because of the speed of change forced upon the U.S. economy by globalization. Meeting this fundamental need keeps America's "caboose" from braking the entire train. Without it, we risk losing the public's long-term support for the strategy to shrink the Gap.

- *The last Secretary of the Department of Homeland Security:* I think the Department of Homeland Security was the one great strategic mistake we've committed so far in the global war on terrorism. Rather than watch it drift into budgetary irrelevance over time as its funding is hollowed out in deference to more pressing needs, we should disestablish this department in the direction of reestablishing it as the ultimate home for the SysAdmin force. Many of the skill sets and personnel best suited for the SysAdmin function are trapped within the Department of Homeland Security, their talents largely wasted. This "keeping our powder dry" strategy is both wasteful and selfish, because these great capabilities should be informing our nation-building and disaster-response efforts abroad.

- *The first Hispanic major-party nominee for president:* This one will happen sooner than people think, and it can't happen fast enough. America's relationship with Latin America is the strategic partnership most dangerously put at risk by the global war on terrorism, in part because it has forced us to tighten our borders excessively against economic immigrants from the South, diverting a significant portion of that flow to Europe. America's demographic future is threatened by this development, as is our economic viability over the long run. A Hispanic president will represent a major turning point in our relations with the rest of our hemisphere, forcing us to concentrate finally on shrinking the Gap in our own backyard.

✦ *The first governor of the fifty-first state of the union:* At some point America needs to stop being a closed club. If the European Union can add member-states, then so should we. The first new member will be the most important one, because it will signal that the United States is back in the business of adding new states and growing this political and economic experiment that serves as source code for the current age of globalization. Regulatory competition has fueled the spread of free trade around the world. Now the competition offered by formal political integration should be added to the mix of forces promoting the Core's expansion.

✦ *The first "Chinese daughter" to run for major political office:* American couples have been adopting Chinese female babies by the thousands for over a decade now, setting in motion an amazing social experiment, because these girls will someday move beyond their status as trophy kids without peer to become amazingly well-educated and highly driven adults whose transracial family status will make them akin to a small army of Tiger Woods–like talents unleashed upon America's economic landscape and—inevitably—its political scene. Eventually, China's political and economic leaders will find themselves staring across conference room tables at these "lost daughters," signifying yet again America's unprecedented capacity to integrate all cultures under all circumstances.

✦ *The Echo Boomers' "George Kennan":* George Kennan was the Greatest Generation's most famous grand strategist, or the diplomat who first enunciated the Cold War strategy of containment. Echo Boomers tend to look to one another for guidance, so eventually a George Kennan–like figure will need to arise from their ranks to enunciate their generation's major tasks in shrinking the Gap. Given the current pace of events in the global war on terrorism, their generation's main strategic focus will probably end up being Africa.

As we move outward from the United States, our focus switches to leaders who help break the mold of balance-of-power politics inside the Core:

- *The European Union's "Woodrow Wilson":* The EU is setting up a constitution that will create a Secretary-of-State-like position of Foreign Minister to speak on behalf of the entire continent on global diplomatic and security affairs. This official needs to occupy a special role in the Core's efforts to shrink the Gap, one that fundamentally focuses on the promotion of democratic rule there. As the United States will always be cast in the role of military lead, its diplomatic focus will naturally remain on the removal of bad regimes inside the Gap, as opposed to the creation of good ones. The EU's new foreign minister needs to play "good cop" on this one, constantly holding America's feet to the fire regarding our nonstop rhetoric of promoting freedom around the world. This official needs to be our moral conscience, not in an effort to obstruct the employment of the Leviathan but to make sure the Core as a whole follows through adequately with the SysAdmin.

- *The first Brazilian chair of the G-20 summit:* Eventually the G-7 needs to grow beyond just tolerating Russia's presence as the eighth member and expand itself to include fundamentally all the Core's major economic pillars. A key moment in this expansion will come with the first summit hosted by a New Core pillar such as India, China, Russia, or Brazil. Of that quartet, Brazil has recently gone out of its way to establish itself as the great champion for the Gap in its economic negotiations with the Old Core in the Doha Development Round of the World Trade Organization. When the G-20 eventually meets in South America, the

Core's largely northern flavor will be suitably recast by this greatest of all southern economic pillars.

- *Russia's "Bill Clinton":* Russia under Vladimir Putin has slipped back into Gap-like status in its most important economic sector: energy. This does not bode well for Russia's long-term economic integration with Old Core Europe, because it encourages the European Union to view it more as a non-Muslim OPEC than as a future potential pillar of its membership. Russia needs a Bill Clinton–like leader who uses the office of the presidency to promote economic connectivity between the nation and the global economy beyond Putin's narrow focus on energy. Moscow needs a salesman in that position, not just a former cop who makes the gas flow on time.

- *The "Martin Luther King" of Islamic Europe:* Europe's growing Muslim population needs a political voice that galvanizes that community's sense of exclusion and discrimination, someone who projects simultaneously an image of moral authority and nonviolent protest. This leader needs to define a positive agenda of both economic equality and political participation for the ghettoized Muslims pocketed across Europe, taking advantage of the European Union's political integration process to stake out a fair claim on political leadership for this marginalized population.

- *The "Serpico" who blows the lid off human rights abuses in the global war on terrorism:* It took one man with a conscience to shine a light on Abu Ghraib, but there will logically be many more such abuse situations emerging as the Core increasingly comes together to wage joint warfare against the Gap's many terrorist networks. Frank Serpico was a New York City police detective whose efforts to uncover police corruption eventually led to a major reform commission being launched by the mayor of the city. As we move ahead in the global war on terrorism, we're going to need a lot of Frank Serpicos—a lot of guys who do the right thing.

✦   *The first Russian Secretary-General of NATO:* Eventually, NATO must take Russia into more formal membership than it currently has via its "joint council" arrangement, but that won't happen so long as Moscow continues to act as though every turn westward by its former republics (e.g., Ukraine) represents a zero-sum loss for its perceived sphere of influence. Russia needs to move toward a European definition of its place and power within the Core, and when this happens, we'll see Europe reward Russia with far more trust and authority within NATO.

✦   *The first Old Core company to pay reparations to Gap victims:* Certain German companies that were allied with the Nazi regime in the 1930s and World War II were later made to pay reparations to Jews forced to work in their factories as slave labor. As we saw with Saddam Hussein's regime and the UN's Oil-for-Food Scandal, there are always Core companies that support criminal regimes inside the Gap for financial reasons, thereby extending and facilitating the suffering of people there. Eventually, such a relationship will be uncovered in subsequent international court proceedings so as to allow for similar financial penalties to be employed. This will have a wonderfully chilling effect on other Core companies engaged in similar ongoing transactions.

China's pathway toward firm pillar status within the Core will likewise require the emergence of a number of as-yet-undiscovered heroes:

✦   *China's "JFK":* China will reach a historic tipping point sometime in the next decade, when it will become apparent not just to the leadership but to the country as a whole that the nation is no longer one that asks the world what it can do for it but increasingly is asked—in an echo of John F. Kennedy's famous inaugural speech—what it can do for the world. On an individual level, China's governments have asked the people to do plenty over the centuries, but the world has not really asked the Chinese people to be anything other than concerned with themselves and their own needs. Eventually that sense of growing internal confidence will be met by a growing sense of global expectation, and a leader must emerge within China to rationalize the two with some expressed vision of China's positive *and* active role in world affairs.

✦ *China's "Erin Brockovich":* Erin Brockovich was a legal aide who was instrumental in the successful pursuit of a huge direct-action lawsuit against a major American corporation regarding its criminal negligence in allowing citizens to become poisoned by its operating facilities. China is experiencing a tremendous amount of environmental damage as its economy develops rapidly, generating huge numbers of long-term medical victims among its population. The Chinese Communist leadership is beginning to display a real willingness to let the public confront businesses in this regard through legal means, so long as such efforts do not threaten the party's legitimacy. Eventually, the Chinese government will need to allow the courts enough leeway to begin leveling large financial penalties to deter future negligence by private-sector and even state-run companies. In this process, many stories will unfold of courageous individuals standing up to corrupt companies in courtroom dramas.

✦ *The first Chinese General Secretary of the North Pacific Treaty Organization:* Eventually, the United States and China will need to establish some sort of NATO-like military alliance in Asia that binds these two military powers together in a strategic partnership. As that organization matures, the position of general secretary will probably rotate through the major Pacific Rim powers that are party to the agreement. While China is unlikely to be granted that post at the start, out of deference to America's long-term military allies in the region, eventually the post will rotate to Beijing, and when it does, it will represent China's emergence as America's diplomatic equal in the Pacific—a real turning point in the history of the world.

✦ *China's "Billy Graham":* Christianity is exploding inside China, although currently most Chinese Christians belong to unregistered and unapproved congregations that are routinely branded by the Chinese Communist Party as "illegal cults." Eventually, as this growth continues over time, popular religious leaders will emerge from the population to begin a process of negotiation with the Chinese leadership for greater acceptance of these churches in light of their positive role in community life. This is likely to be a tense process, within which various government crackdowns and arrests interrupt the inevitable progress toward official tolerance of religions with strong connectivity to the world at large. The establishment of official diplomatic relations between Beijing and the Vatican will constitute an important early milestone.

◆ *The first Chinese commander of a joint Sino-American Sys-Admin operation:* China's military will never match America's in terms of Leviathan power-projection capabilities, but over time its contributions to a Core-wide SysAdmin force capability will be substantial, eventually triggering a situation in which U.S. SysAdmin forces will fall under the command of Chinese officers in the same way our peacekeeping forces have fallen under the command of European officers in joint NATO efforts. When this happens, and it will probably happen first in Africa, China's military strategic partnership with the United States will have matured to the point of no possible return to hostile intentions.

India's rise as a Core pillar will likewise involve the emergence of several important heroic figures:

◆ *India's "Margaret Thatcher":* India sees itself as the major security pillar of South Asia, which sits between the energy-rich regions of Central Asia and the Middle East and the energy-dependent region of East Asia. India's Margaret Thatcher will be a prime minister who, confident of her country's economic status in the Core, will begin to seek out opportunities across the board to demonstrate to the world India's ability to take firm leadership of security-enhancing efforts throughout the Indian Ocean rim as the trusted junior ally of the United States, in contrast to the more hesitant Japan and the less confident China.

◆ *India's "Bill Gates":* In many ways, India already has several such individuals operating powerfully within its private-sector economy, but none yet that simultaneously wields the same sort of influence in the world of charitable giving and public policy formation both at home and abroad as Gates, who has emerged in the United States and globally thanks to the world's largest private foundation, which bears his name. As we saw with the Asian tsunamis of 2004, private charitable giving in India has reached a new age, and, as home to the world's largest number of millionaires, India's private-sector philanthropic reach should eventually extend beyond its own multitude of poor to become an important regional influence.

◆ *India's first Oscar-winning Best Picture producer:* India's Bollywood is one of the world's leading filmmaking production centers, cranking out significantly more movies each year than Hollywood and serving as a major cultural force throughout Asia and across much of the Gap. India's more G-rated fare will increasingly compete with Hollywood's more violent and sexually explicit material for global marketplace shares, forcing the latter to tone down its material to remain competitive. This will be a prime example of the New Core setting the new rules as globalization's "face" becomes increasingly less American.

In the Islamic Middle East, numerous heroes must be located as that region effectively joins the Core over time:

◆ Wired *magazine's "blogger of the year" award winner:* Middle East bloggers have already emerged as a potent connective tissue between Islam and the West. The blog "Iraq the Model," for example, has had an inordinate amount of influence in shaping American perceptions of the postwar occupation of Iraq by coalition forces. Although the region features some of the world's lowest Internet penetration rates, the simple fact that authoritarian regimes there control mainstream media only highlights the role of alternative media as a forum for grassroots political dialogue between Islamic populations and the Core, as well as within the Islamic world itself among reformist elements.

✦ *The first Arab political leader who leaves office when his legal term ends:* In general (meaning seemingly everywhere except Lebanon), political leaders in the Arab world have only one term limit: death. Because of the longevity of such rule, even the regimes that pretend to be "republics" invariable pass power from fathers to sons. When this event happens in a country whose government isn't overshadowed by a more powerful theocracy, such as Persian Iran, then a powerful example will have been created for the region as a whole.

✦ *The "Eminem" of Muslim rap:* Hip-hop is already a globalized cultural force of great potency among young people the world over, allowing for cultural expression on both sides of any divide you can name in the Middle East: Arab-Israeli, progressive-fundamentalist, Western-traditional. What Middle Eastern rap has yet to produce is an artist who explains Arab Islamic culture to the world outside. When that happens, an important social bridge will have been built, even as the material will be likely to prove highly controversial to most Western listeners.

✦ *The first Islamic religious leader to win the Nobel Peace Prize:* Of course, the temptation here is to suggest that Iraq's primary Shiite religious leader, Grand Ayatollah Ali Husaini Sistani, has within his grasp the current opportunity for such greatness in post-Saddam Iraq, exerting such control as he does over the political evolution of the country. But if not there, such a development must happen eventually somewhere as part of Islam's inevitable Reformation-like recasting of itself in the region, so as to allow countries there to build sufficient economic connectivity with the outside world to accommodate the growth in job creation necessary to process the huge youth bulges currently making their way through societies.

✦ *Iran's "John Marshall":* John Marshall was the first great Chief Justice of the United States, who, more than any other figure in U.S. judicial history, established the independent role of the Supreme Court within America's federal government. What Iran currently lacks is a judicial authority that is free and clear of the influence of the unelected supreme leader, or ayatollah. When the role migrates from the ranks of unelected leadership to the elected government, this will be the clearest sign that Iran's theocracy has come to an end.

+ *Last peacekeeper killed along the Israel-Palestine security fence:* Foreign peacekeepers will end up guarding the border barrier between Israel and Palestine for many years in what will be one of the most thankless jobs inside the Gap. But it will not be wrong to ask some soldier to be the last man to die for this necessary effort, for eventually the wall will wait out all the hatred and anger on both sides.

+ *The first female leader of an Arab state:* One of the great deficits in the Middle East is the broad exclusion of women from economic and political life. No nation has joined the global economy without first liberating its women, at least within the economic sphere. With such liberation eventually comes bottom-up pressure from the public for a greater political participatory role for women. The great wild card here would be the emergence of a female political leader of note among either the Palestinians (who already feature several notable local female politicians) or the Iraqis (where the United States mandated that a certain percentage of political candidates be female, along with a certain portion of government appointees).

Finally, Africa, as the deepest interior portion of the Gap, must produce a number of significant heroes along its pathway to connectivity with the Core:

+ *The first VJays of MTV Africa:* It may seem like a trivial thing at first blush, but consider where young people in the United States get their information about the world beyond our borders. MTV has extensive regional networks throughout most of the world, and until recently, only Africa lacked a channel specifically customized by local content. Africa joined the global network with the launching of MTV Base in Africa, operated out of MTV Europe, in February 2005. Only 1.3 million households will be reached at first across the continent, but even that sliver of connectivity is worth something in a region overwhelmingly skewed to youth demographics.

- *The first African Pope:* The Roman Catholic Church has become demographically skewed toward both Africa and Latin America over the past several decades, raising the inevitability of a non-European Pope. Following the passing of John Paul II, the Catholic College of Cardinals voted for a new leader of the global church, and for the first time in its history this body was not dominated by a European bloc of senior clergy. To the surprise and disappointment of many, the conclave nonetheless voted for an Old Core pontiff, a German. By the time the next pope is selected, the pressure for a pope from the Gap, probably Latin American, will be overwhelming. Eventually, for the same reasons the UN went with African Kofi Annan as its Secretary-General, expect the Roman Catholic Church to select an African cardinal to succeed that pope, creating yet another important political bond between the Core and Africa. There have been three African popes in the past, but none within the last fifteen centuries.

- *The great African-American political spokesman for African security issues:* The African-American community made one great effort in the last several decades to focus U.S. Government and public attention on a security issue in Africa, and that was apartheid in South Africa. Other than that one successful mobilization effort, the African-American community has been amazingly silent over the years concerning all the wars, civil strife, and pandemics that have afflicted Africa. Lacking any local citizen pressure and absent the rise of compelling national security issues, such as the extension of the global Salafi jihadist movement into the region or China's perceived rising influence there, the U.S. Government continues to remain reticent to get involved militarily in the region. The concerted efforts of national political leaders from the African-American community could change that stance, but only with considerable effort.

+ *The first African "Big Man" to surrender power on an ICC plea bargain:* African dictators have abandoned their regimes in the face of external military pressure, and recently Charles Taylor of Liberia left to seek exile in the Congo rather than face war-crime indictments from an international tribunal run by the UN in Sierra Leone. The next step up would be for the international community to be able to exploit the threat of prosecution of war crimes such as genocide by the International Criminal Court as a means to plea-bargain criminal leaders out of power without the use of military force. In many ways, such an outcome has been sought with regard to the Darfur crisis in western Sudan, in large part because of the unwillingness of Old Core Europe and the United States to get involved militarily and the inability of the African Union to mount an effective peacekeeping presence.

+ *The first U.S. military commander of African Command:* The United States will be forced by circumstances in the global war on terrorism to refocus more of its military attention on sub-Saharan Africa over time, eventually recasting its Unified Command Plan to create a specific African Command. This will represent a huge commitment on the part of the Pentagon, which historically has shied away from any major efforts on the continent. At first, African Command will be a lot like Southern Command, which covers Latin America: lots of geographic responsibility but little in the way of troops and resources. But as the Middle East settles down and NATO builds up its capacity for extraregional operations, Africa will become the main focus of the Core's SysAdmin force.

+ *The African Union's peacekeeping troops win a Nobel Peace Prize:* This scenario may seem far-fetched at this point, because it requires a significant Core effort on the part of the United States and NATO to provide training and logistical support across a sustained period of time in order to build up local capacity. Even if such capacity were to be established, it's likely that real-time support funding would be needed throughout any extended effort by the AU. But there's little doubt that if such a regional capacity could be developed and effectively employed, it would save large numbers of lives in any number of ongoing or future conflict scenarios.

These are all real needs that eventually will either be expressed by the suffering of real people or be met by the emergence of real heroes, but almost none will go away on its own, meaning without *somebody somewhere* standing up and trying to make a difference. What I've drawn in this book is a blueprint for action: a linking of readily apparent needs with readily developable tools and institutions. None of this is beyond either our grasp or our imagination, but almost all is beyond conventional wisdom and our current comfort zone of expected historical pathways. As such, these are unreasonable demands. George Bernard Shaw once said, "Reasonable people adapt themselves to the world. Unreasonable people attempt to adapt the world to themselves. All progress, therefore, depends on unreasonable people." It is my hope that this book has made you feel as unreasonable about the world as we find it today as I have become. It is my hope that in some small way, it has enabled you to see a future world worth creating.

AFTERWORD:
BLOGGING
THE FUTURE

IN MANY MOVIES, especially war films and crime capers, there is a scene somewhere in the middle where the rest of the plot is essentially revealed, meaning "the plan" is laid bare for the audience. The filmmaker George Lucas describes this as the "pointer scene," like the one he used in *Star Wars* to describe how the rebel alliance was going to destroy the Death Star. Scenes like this are essential in action movies, Lucas argues, because they forecast the story's most likely ending, in effect giving the viewer a series of handholds for the fast-paced action to follow. In other words, it is protection against losing the audience's understanding over the course of the film.

Within the ever-expanding sphere of global media, the function of bloggers is similar in many ways to that of pointer scenes in movies. Most blog posts are essentially "pointers," meaning they direct readers by hot links to pertinent news provided by other, typically more established sources, such as the online version of the *New York Times*.

What the blogger offers, in addition to the link, is usually some contextualizing analysis that says—in effect—"this is why this story is
important." The best blogs tend to be future-oriented, meaning they
help readers think ahead to trends and changes that will impact some
sphere of life about which they care deeply—like the future of war and
peace.

I've been blogging at a prolific rate (meaning, several thousand
words a day) on my Web site since about a month before *The Pentagon's New Map* came out, in the spring of 2004, providing readers of
the book my ongoing analysis of current events within the framework
of my vision for the future. In effect, my blog is a nonstop pointer
scene for the story line known as the global security environment.
Each news article that I cite and annotate is my attempt to tell the
reader, "Hey, this story really speaks to (or against) a future worth
creating!"

In this book, I blogged the future with a vengeance, laying out argument after argument for new institutions, new rule sets, and new
tasks. In doing so, I hope I provided one big "pointer scene" for American foreign policy over the next years and decades. I think that sort of
global plotline projection is incredibly useful. For example, it can
inform American citizens who need to think about which candidate to
chose in future elections and which policies to support. But I think it is
also essential for the world as a whole, because global understanding
about our nation's intent in any grand strategy to shrink the Gap will
fundamentally determine our government's ability to enlist allies in
this historic quest.

The following is a device I've used many times in various wargaming exercises that I've conducted with strategists, business leaders, and academics: You give them your preferred long-term scenario
and then ask participants to come up with newspaper headlines they'd
expect to read if that future were to indeed unfold as described. The
upshot is that your imagined plotline gets fleshed out in a way that
people find plausible, meaning they can imagine actually living in
that world.

I don't just want you to imagine living in this hypothetical world, I want you to be so convinced of its plausibility and desirability that you'll be willing to work for it—whenever and wherever possible—over the course of your life. Moreover, I want us all to raise future generations that not only expect such positive development but come to demand it.

Here, as a parting note, are headlines from the future—both good and bad—that I expect to blog someday. The year headings refer to the time by which I expect each event to unfold—give or take an independent variable or two! ;<)

2010

"'Nixon' Goes to Tehran: Grand Bargain in the Works Between United States and Iran"

I know, I know, "axis of evil" and all that. But common sense says that, absent 9/11, some "Nixon" should have made it to Tehran by now. Why? First, it was going to take us roughly two decades to get over the embassy hostage crisis, just as it took us roughly two decades to get past the fall of Saigon and finally recognize Vietnam. Second, the Shiite revolution is a spent force in Iran: the mullahs pretend to rule and the masses pretend to obey. To me, that's similar to the Soviet Union in its Brezhnev phase, and that means it's time for a détente designed to kill the regime from below with connectivity for the masses. Finally, paint me a future picture of a stable Middle East where Iran isn't a major security pillar—nukes or no nukes. You can't. That's why "Nixon" has to go to Tehran.

"Doha Round Agreement Hailed as Historic Breakthrough for Struggling Economies"

The so-called development round of trade negotiations within the World Trade Organization began in the shadow of 9/11, lending it a sense of real urgency, because it mostly involves a struggle between the

Old Core and the Gap, with New Core pillars like China, India, and Brazil in between. By and large, the New Core advocates for the Gap, especially on issues like the Old Core's long-standing agricultural protectionism and stinginess on pharmaceutical patents, but as we see with China regarding the new global rule set on textiles, New Core economies are often most likely to dominate when Core-Gap trade is opened up for fair competition, leaving many struggling Gap economies in the dust. But this deal is a must, and its basic outline is no mystery: the Gap opens up in accepting the Core's industrial products and financial services, while the Core opens its markets to the Gap's agricultural exports and low-end manufactures.

"Kim Steps Down After Joint United States–China Ultimatum; Korean Reunification Near"

This one is long overdue. Kim Jong Il's got the blood of roughly two million of his citizens on his hands, thanks to the entirely preventable famine that he let decimate North Korea's countryside in the late 1990s, all the while denying entrance to the world's relief agencies, which were desperate to step in and help. The key here is China, Pyongyang's longtime ideological and economic patron. Since neither tie makes sense anymore for increasingly capitalistic Beijing, determining that leadership's price for a unified front vis-à-vis Kim is the essential task at hand. The opening bids (America's blank check on Taiwan's defense comes off the table, and it promises troop reductions in both Japan and the ultimately reunified Korea) aren't easy, but it's something we need to do if we're ever going to shift military resources from East Asia toward the Gap. The easier give comes on missile defense, where it's not only the U.S. military's dream of a shield for Japan that has to be sacrificed but also ultimately the entire concept of ringing America with a defense perimeter. Sound hard? Only if you believe in the $100 billion-plus boondoggle called Star Wars Lite.

"Super Flu Overwhelmed Most Nations' Medical Systems; Half of Deaths Preventable"

The world's been tested by a pandemic flu roughly once every generation or so, going back to the Godzilla of influenzas, the Spanish flu of 1918–19, which killed at least twenty million worldwide. Flu viruses mutate on a yearly basis, which is why the medical community needs to come up with a new vaccine each winter. A pandemic flu is one whose "antigenic drift," or mutation, is so profound that an entirely new strain emerges, meaning one for which a suitably effective vaccine is not easily found. If it's especially infectious and features a high mortality rate, then twenty million dead around the planet could be a low-ball estimate, especially since the vast majority of vaccines are sold to Core states, leaving two billion in the Gap essentially unprotected. The scary thing is, of course, the Core's tendency to respond slowly to Gap-heavy pandemics, as we've seen consistently with HIV-AIDS. But in an increasingly connected world, eventually this nightmare scenario is going to jump up and bite us, triggering a massive rule-set reset in the process.

"Iran-Israel Agreement on Nukes Triggers Tehran's Recognition of Jewish State"

I understand that it seems crazy to trust an authoritarian regime with nuclear weapons, especially one propped up by a bankrupt revolutionary ideology and a long history of supporting terrorist groups beyond its borders. But remember back to the Cold War: that's exactly what we did with the Soviets, whose ideology was just as decrepit and whose terrorist support network dwarfed anything Iran's ever attempted. So if the United States could hold its nose then, it can do so again in the future. Anyway, Iran's getting the bomb whether we like it or not. The only question that remains is, What do we get in return? What we ought to get is the opportunity for a stable MAD (as in, mutually assured destruction) situation to emerge between Tehran and Tel Aviv. At that point, the Muslim Middle East would have its own nuclear power able to sit across the table from Israel, who's long had the bomb and made no secret of its willingness to use it in extremis. Think that doesn't matter to a Middle East peace? Think again.

"National Security Act Establishes Department of Overseas Contingency Response"

Admittedly, this one is both self-servingly central to my vision and seemingly hard to imagine, given that we just created the Department of Homeland Security, but you know it's going to happen eventually, not because it's a neat idea but because either our repeated failures or the growing magnitude of the task will demand it. The Iraq occupation failed on so many fronts because no one cabinet-level department owned it, and no amount of fiddling with the "interagency process" lorded over by the National Security Council is going to change that. Defense will still want to avoid nation building, and State will still want to avoid regime change. Meanwhile, the National Security Adviser will still want to make sure the President's not to blame for any of it. The shame of that tug-of-war is that most of what this System Administrator–type department would really do involves the everything else—not war. This is the department that should have led America's full-spectrum response to the Christmas tsunami disaster in Asia. When we win those sorts of victories in a global war on terrorism, we do so without firing a shot. Tell me that's not worth a new department.

"Iraqi President Lifts Emergency Decree, Immediately Relinquishes Military Post"

This one speaks to the reality that Iraq has to devolve from its authoritarian past before it can evolve toward its democratic future, and it ain't going to be pretty. Like many Gap states, Iraq is essentially a made-up country, stitched together from old imperial provinces established decades earlier by a now-departed colonial master. Saddam Hussein's rule did generate some real nationalism, but at the cost of a lot of lives in a part of the world where such crimes against tribes rarely go unavenged. So, like the conflict in the former Yugoslavia, the post-Saddam civil war in Iraq was preordained in animal spirit if not in deeds. America's Big Bang strategy of rapidly toppling Saddam's cruel regime, after a decade of no-fly zones both north and south, left behind a trio of peoples with very different desires, expectations, and grievances against one another—not to mention different capacities for self-rule (with the Kurds way out ahead). If we're lucky, Iraq will end up being a slightly better version of Pakistan, meaning America will have solid ties with the military, which in turn will have to step in now and then to make sure intertribal relations don't explode into full-scale civil war. So start looking for your General Musharraf now, and if we can't find one, we'd better train one.

"China-ASEAN Pact Accelerates Agenda for Asian Free-Trade Area; Japan, Korea Next"

The Association of Southeast Asian Nations (ASEAN) comprises all the little countries in the region that most people can't find on a map, their main attributes being that they're not Japan, Korea, China, Australia, or India—thus their need to bond together in their relative smallness. Of course, not all of ASEAN is so little. Indonesia, for example, is the world's largest Muslim state, but even here we're really talking about an archipelago of lots of smaller tribes all slightly disorganized under the notion of a nation-state, so breakaway republics and rebel movements are to be expected. ASEAN's main purpose today and into the future is figuring out how not to get squashed under the big economic footprints of the far larger emerging economies that surround it—especially rising behemoth China. So expect ASEAN to make China an offer it (meaning ASEAN) cannot refuse. Then expect a bandwagon effect where no other major economy wants to get left behind in all that economic integration driven by China's insatiable import needs.

"Synchronized Attacks Drive G-20 to Create World Counterterror Organization"

To me, the question that really remains after 9/11 is, What would happen if someone figured out how to fight 9/11-like in a sustained fashion? I tend to doubt a transnational terrorist movement is capable of this (at least on our shores), simply because of the logistics, resources, and coordination required. In short, terrorists can pull off a vertical scenario like 9/11, but it tends to take a state—or at least some serious state backing—to stretch a string of 9/11-like attacks along a sustained horizontal scenario. And yet some terrorist network, with or without significant state backing, will eventually crack that nut, and the shells are far more likely to be exploded in Europe than in the United States. Since Europe prefers the police model to America's military model of dealing with transnational terrorism, I expect the push to come from the other side of the Atlantic for some sort of members-only counterterrorism coalition. Not some sloppy Interpol, mind you, but a serious Star Chamber–like organization that makes bad guys disappear quietly. Messy at first, but that's how the Core-wide rule set will eventually come of age.

"China's Demand for Resources Provided Economic Liftoff for Southern Africa"

China's fantastically rising demand for raw materials is reshaping commodity markets the world over. That's the new global rule set that accompanies the rise of a manufacturing superpower: trade patterns change, once-moribund national industries are revived, and secondary and tertiary spillover effects abound. For example, when China wants a couple of hundred million tons of iron ore, that not only perks up that sector of the mining industry in South Africa (and all the attached equipment suppliers), it triggers significant expansion of infrastructure like railroads, which in turn increases the need for railroad cars, and so on. Africa's saving grace is its enormous mineral wealth, so when the emergence of the New Core states effectively doubles the global labor market, those are a lot of manufacturing hands to get busy, and that opportunity encompasses even fragile, far-too-corrupt Africa—if the right local rule sets can be put in place and security maintained. Point being, Africa has an invitation to connect better to the global economy, and that invitation's postmarked from Asia, not the West.

"Nuclear Detonation in Northwest Pakistan Described as Terrorist 'Mistake'"

What's scary about Pakistan is that it's one of the Muslim world's best examples of a functioning state (e.g., reasonable rule of law, largely secular state, decent on women's rights), yet it still doesn't control large swaths of its own territory! Yes, America facilitated the resiliency of this mess (i.e., the ungovernable northwest territory) by encouraging Pakistan's support for the Afghani mujahideen against the Soviets (enough said on that one), but frankly, it's been that way all along. I mean, there's a lot of good reasons why Osama bin Laden's probably hiding out in the open in some city up north, and those reasons will eventually bring the Core's major powers to that messy border area that links China, India, Pakistan, Afghanistan, and Tajikistan. Why posit a nuke? Check out Pakistan's record on selling bottles of that genie and tell me it doesn't scare you. But the simpler rationale is this: high-end bomb making is tricky, so we're just as likely to see one go off accidentally in the hands of a terrorist group somewhere in the Gap as we are to witness its effective employment inside the Core.

"China's 'Black Summer' Triggers Unprecedented Social Unrest; Tipping Point Seen"

I spent one long, hot August traveling through China last year, and I can personally vouch for the fact that it suffers the most amazingly high levels of air pollution I have ever endured. Guangzhou, described as China's "Los Angeles," suffers smog that effectively blots out both sky and sun, even on what are theoretically cloudless days! Between the constant headaches, sore throats, and stuffed heads, it is simply hard—physically—to live in Guangzhou. Not surprisingly, nineteen of the twenty-five most polluted cities in the world are located in Asia, with nine in China alone. A tipping point is coming on environmental stress in China, one we've seen before in industrializing countries as the masses simply begin to recognize a clear trade-off between that extra slice of GDP per capita and the instinctive desire to be able to

suck in a chestful of air without it burning. The grassroots environmental movement is growing in China, and eventually some horrific
example of mass suffering will trigger an explosion in political demands for something better.

"Putin's Handpicked Successor Bows to Massive Protest, Accepts Election Defeat"

So far, Vladimir Putin has gotten Russia moving economically across
his two terms, but at the cost of significant amounts of political freedom and the reinstitution of state control in the commanding heights
of the economy—namely, energy. More House of Saud than House of
Rothschild, Putin's betting that Russia's ticket to great-power status
will ultimately be its enormous reserves of natural gas (smart man), so
what's good for the Kremlin is good for Gazprom—and anyone it supplies. Naturally, such a tight intertwining of economic and political
interests means Putin & Co. won't stand for just anybody succeeding
him in 2008. Assuming no president-for-life scenario emerges (not a
small assumption), will the public go along in his choice? Ukraine has
historically been the viral route through which "dangerous foreign
ideas" have entered Russia's political bloodstream, so if the "orange
revolution" that reversed Viktor Yushchenko's initial election loss in
2004 serves as any sort of example, Russia's "Pinochet period" may
well be shorter than most pessimists expect.

"Asia, EU Propel Negotiations for South American Free Trade Zone, Not U.S."

In December 2004, South America's two standing economic group-
ings, Mercosur (Brazil, Argentina, Uruguay, Paraguay) and the Andean
Community (Bolivia, Colombia, Ecuador, Peru, Venezuela) announced
a merger that when truly put into effect would create an EU-like economic union (similar in population size with NAFTA but at only a
fraction of the GDP power). Most skeptics don't give the project much
chance of success, in large part because both constituent trade groups
haven't been particularly successful in reducing trade barriers among
their respective members, much less achieving any serious integration

of national economies, which tend to be competitive with one another in exports. But two external forces should help to move this bureaucratic pile up the hill. First, the EU prefers bloc-to-bloc agreements, in contrast to the United States, which leans toward bilateral accords. Second, China's growing pull on South America's commodities will encourage a more unified stance vis-à-vis the outside world simply to increase those states' collective bargaining power. South America likes to say that the United States only pays attention to it when it causes trouble, so in the meantime expect Old Core Europe and New Core China to remain far more interested.

"Turkey's Surprisingly Rapid Entry into EU Signals Europe's Tilt Toward Arab World"

I know there's a lot of skepticism about Turkey's *ever* getting into the European Union. After all, it took decades of Turkey's asking just to get formal negotiations started, and even those are projected to take another decade. But I expect it to go faster than that, primarily because Europe needs to signal to the Islamic world that it's not a closed club as far as non-Christians are concerned. Old Europe continues in its fantasy that it lives in a purely economic world, where security and political strategy should play no part in deciding questions of identity and integration. But even if you buy into that viewpoint, it can't last forever in a demographically moribund continent whose workforce is aging rapidly. Moreover, Europe can't occupy the high moral ground on both illegal Muslim immigrants from North Africa *and* Turkey's by-the-book admission request. Finally, because the EU has done so little to improve the security environment in the Middle East, where Turkey has long stood as the continent's bulwark against spreading instability, this is logically the EU's quid pro quo for NATO's effective no-show on America's long-term transformation effort in the Persian Gulf. And no, I'm not being too optimistic on this one, given Europe's profound racism toward Muslims, I just expect some very bad incidences of social and/or political violence inside Europe to eventually force its movement toward accommodation. So expect it to get uglier before it gets nicer.

2015

"Response to Adana Earthquake Proves Utility of Multinational Contingency Force"

Absent major wars between great powers, the main sources of mass casualties in the twenty-first century are going to be chronic internal conflicts and natural or man-made disasters that occur—by definition—inside the Gap. I say "by definition" because states cannot suffer mass outbreaks of internal conflict and remain part of the Core, and because Core status presumes a certain ability to take care of one's own—even in disaster (like India's response to the Asian tsunamis of 2004). Ultimately, the generation of a standing multinational contingency response force made up of elements—both military and civilian—across the Core is simply the recognition by the system's biggest powers of the utility of dealing with such potential downstream sources of instability and terrorism before those negative outcomes are allowed to unfold. Such a force, then, becomes the Core's equivalent of a Gap insurance policy—as in, "Pay now or shoot later."

"Taiwan Vote Clears Way for Political 'Road Map' Treaty with Mainland China"

As China rises economically, its political undertow pulls the rest of Asia into its sphere of political influence. Naturally, that's a dicier notion for the state that emerged out of the losing side of China's now distant but certainly not forgotten civil war. The problem, security-wise, is this: America's defense guarantee to Taiwan puts Taipei's leadership in the driver's seat regarding a possibly military confrontation between two nuclear powers with large standing militaries. If Taipei decides to move toward *perceived* independence from China (it could be something as trivial as a country name change), then the United States might get handed a war it cannot afford, one whose implications for the future of globalization could be profoundly negative. What we need instead is to lock in some sort of long-term confidence-building mechanism between island and mainland. In effect, Washington needs to put Taipei on a much shorter leash.

"Russia Begins Formal Membership Talks with EU; Energy Ties Result in 'Fast Track'"

Russia is the "Saudi Arabia of natural gas," and as the global economy moves inevitably toward the hydrogen age, that's not just a good thing, it's a great thing. If Turkey ends up being the EU's "this far and no farther" bridge to Islam, then Europe's great alternative on stable energy supplies becomes Russia, which, after all, is Christian. Europe will be less fussy over the Kremlin's state-heavy approach to economics, and Russia's aging demographics will dovetail with Europe's growing tendency toward political conservatism. Russia's prior full membership in NATO is probably required, but that's unlikely until the increasingly hard-line Putin leaves the scene.

"Caspian Coordination Group Finalizes Long-Term Pipeline Grid Construction Plan"

China had the Shanghai Cooperation Organization trying to run Central Asia's "great game" prior to 9/11, only to be subsequently pushed aside by the United States's Central Command without so much as a thank-you as America started dotting the landscape with "temporary" bases. China's interest in the region—along with the rest of Asia—obviously focuses on energy, and in natural gas in particular. Good pipelines require good neighbors, so expect both rising China and India to push for strong ties with any country that lies between them and the Caspian (like India's planned pipeline through Pakistan), which, not surprisingly, only reemphasizes Iran's strategic importance in the region.

"U.S.-Led Multinational Force Invades Northern Colombia; Bogotá in Flames"

Most of America's perceived security issues south of the border have to do with the flow of illegal drugs from Andean South America up through Central America and the Caribbean. America's societal dependency on foreign imports of cocaine from Colombia (roughly three-quarters of all we consume) dwarfs our alleged economic dependency on Persian Gulf oil (less than one-tenth of our total usage). For now, our military costs associated with the so-called war on drugs come nowhere near our direct expenditures in the global war on terrorism, but eventually our low-cost approach to prolonging but not quite ending South America's longest civil war will have to be ditched in favor of a more permanent solution. With Iraq settled and Korea united by this point, Colombia will inevitably rise to the top of the to-do list.

"Kyoto II Accord Goes into Effect When Indian Parliament Approves Pact"

The first Kyoto Protocol was a symbolic victory at best, since the United States opted out in large part because the treaty didn't include rising economic powers India and China. When it comes to per capita pollution generated, the United States has no peers, but Washington was right to argue that China would soon enough become the world's biggest producer of carbon dioxide. Expect the United States, India, and China to side against the Europeans, Russia, and Japan on Kyoto II, with the former arguing for high-enough caps to make sure they are not "kneecapped" in terms of economic competitiveness over the long haul.

"Thanks to NATO Effort, AU Peacemaking Force Proves Its Mettle in Central Africa"

The African Union's current military stabilization capabilities are both minuscule in size and essentially toothless in employment (they shoot photos, don't they?). Without logistical support, these forces can't really go anywhere or sustain themselves for any length of time in numbers worth mentioning. The impunity with which genocide has been repeatedly waged across the continent over the decades suggests that nothing less than a truly muscular military presence will rule the day. With the U.S. military tied down in the Middle East over the long term, the optimum solution is for NATO to take the lead in training and supporting a standing multinational peacemaking force for sub-Saharan Africa as a whole. The looming alternative is China's military, which has a tendency (displayed recently in Sudan) toward just selling arms to whatever authoritarian government can guarantee its access to raw materials.

"Brasilia Harmonization Talks Yield Draft Treaty for Free Trade Area of the Americas"

Geography drives trade deals more than anything else, so it only makes sense that a Free Trade Area of the Americas (FTAA) finally comes into being. As with China's rising economic clout in Asia, the United States gets its way on FTAA by first pursuing a series of NAFTA-like regionally specific free-trade agreements with Central American (the current hot-button issue of a Central American Free Trade Area, or CAFTA) and Andean South American (Andean Free Trade Area, or AFTA). The big holdout on all of this is clearly the Mercosur union, headed by Brazil, which has emerged as the New Core's most staunch and effective champion of the Gap's "little guys." Ultimately, making this deal work will require the United States's meeting Brazil's definition of fair trade. The best thing America has going for it in this regard is that China, our main competitor for Brazil's strategic affections, is now as ruthlessly capitalistic as we are.

"Korea's 'Four Powers' Served as Embryo for Pacific Rim Treaty Organization"

Military alliances begin with military victories, and although the toppling of Kim Jong Il's regime in North Korea is probably achieved with minimal force, the subsequent military occupation by the four involved external powers (China, United States, Japan, Russia) should constitute a strategic bonding experience that bodes well for long-term military-to-military ties. As China's explosive economic growth tapers off in coming years, Beijing's political leadership will be forced to spend more on the rural poor and less on the People's Liberation Army, tempering that institution's growing swagger. China will continue to spend on its navy, but that only means its foremost military capability in the region will be increasingly maritime in nature, just as with Japan and the United States. Once the Taiwan naval scenario is taken off the table, look for these three naval powers to increase their three-way naval cooperation dramatically. Navies are like dogs: they fundamentally desire—more than anything else—simply to spend time with one another, doing naval things. That's why the U.S. Navy has historically been the opening wedge in America's military-to-military ties with any state, and that's why Asia's version of NATO will be overwhelmingly maritime in character.

2020

"Spread of Religion Across China Alters Policies, Style of Sixth-Generation Leadership"

China's current generation of young people are, like any youth cohort in a rapidly modernizing country, instinctively turning away from the traditions of their parents, especially in terms of religion. But this overtly secular turn won't last, for as China's first truly modern generation grows into marriage and family, the tendency of all new parents to return to, or find new sources of, religion will naturally kick in. By 2020, China will be a surprisingly religious country, one whose diversity in faith is quite broad. Much like any revival of self-identity through increased nationalism, this largely youth-driven process will mark an accommodation with, or processing of, globalization's modernizing effects—not their rejection. China's sixth generation of leadership, much like the fifth generation that assumes power around 2010, will have been largely educated in the United States, so don't be surprised to see more leaders in China embrace their faith publicly as this generational effect works its way up the political ladder. Over time, demonstrating such connection with the masses will constitute a major source of regime legitimacy, along with—naturally—nationalism. Check out Chinese history. The merging of religion and rule is as old as that civilization.

"Islamic Opposition Parties Succeed in Loosening EU Restrictions on Immigration"

The Islamic population in Europe is derived largely from economic immigrants who came to the continent to take up relatively low-paying jobs. Significantly separated from the rest of society in terms of culture and clustered in Islamic enclaves, this "guest worker" society takes on all the classic characteristics of the Marxist proletariat. As such, one logical outcome is the rise of opposition-style parties whose ideologies echo those of Europe's Marxist parties of the twentieth century. As these forces gather political strength, expect them to push for and ultimately effect a loosening of the EU's restrictions on immigration from North Africa and the Middle East, thus altering Europe's cultural trajectory all the more.

"Persian Gulf Security Alliance Cements Role of India and Iran as Regional Pillars"

America remains militarily in the Middle East until that region transforms itself by opening up socially and economically to the world as a whole. As that broadband connectivity grows, local pillars naturally emerge to shape the region's permanent security rule set embodied in a NATO-like regional alliance. Iran will be the center of gravity for this alliance, with India the neighboring "elder brother." The United States's strategic connection to the alliance will remain, but over time will shift increasingly southward toward still troubled Africa.

"EU Pact with North Africa and Mideast States Completes Goal of Mediterranean Zone"

The corollary to America's economic dominance of the Western Hemisphere and China's economic dominance of Asia will be Europe's natural dominance of the Mediterranean. That fundamental rule set will be achieved not by force, but what Europe ultimately has to offer both North Africa and the Middle East: large markets for both commodity exports and the migration of youth seeking employment. Aging Europe naturally has to accommodate these demographic pressures (there are no such pressures from the east), and the best way to control that influx is to extend the EU's economic rule sets south.

"Hispanic Voters Emerge as Key Swing Vote in U.S. National Elections"

By 2020, Hispanics' share of the electorate will be approaching one out of every five votes, significantly outdistancing that of African-Americans (roughly one out of ten) or Asian-Americans (one out of twenty). Non-Hispanic whites will still constitute a majority, at roughly three out of every five citizens, but that share will continue to drop while that of Hispanics will continue to rise. And this growing voting power will be very unevenly distributed, with Hispanics significantly concentrated in the southern half of the United States—the states with the largest population growth and thus the growing balance of electoral votes in presidential elections. The salience of a "southern strategy" in capturing the White House will thus only increase with time, making inevitable the rise of Hispanic politicians to positions of national leadership and significantly reorienting our foreign policy southward.

"National Elections Complete Transition of Saudi Monarchy to Constitutional Status"

In the tribal Saudi Arabia, the House of Saud's dynastic monarchy has survived not simply because of oil wealth, but because it's a very large family (approximately 12,000) that is intricately linked to clans the country over. Unlike Saddam's authoritarian regime, this is not a "deck of cards" easily divorced from its ruling base, and yet, as the kingdom's per capita GDP plummets with each passing year, largely in response to the massive youth bulge working its way through the population, the political challenge of meeting all that growing demand for economic career opportunity will be profound. If met, and that's a big "if," it will get harder and harder for the Saudi royal family, whose own population is growing dramatically with time as well, to hold off calls for political pluralism. In effect, the royal family's future success in promoting broadband economic development is more likely to push it toward reform than America's external pressure to change politically in the short run.

"Online Game Triggers Dictator's Departure; Stunning Victory of 'People's Diplomacy'"

The complexity of planning postconflict stabilization operations in advance is daunting, simply because of the huge number of variables involved. It's not a matter of simply crunching numbers, but rather anticipating the free play of so many actors—your own military, allied civilians, enemy soldiers and insurgents, the local population, and so on. In many ways, this kind of complex simulation is well given over to massive multiplayer online games (MMOG), something I see both the military and the U.S. Government turning toward as a tool for predictive planning. Imagine if, months prior to the invasion, the Pentagon had started a MMOG that modeled Iraq immediately following the regime's collapse, allowing hundreds or even thousands of chosen experts (or even just enthusiastic gamers!) from the world over to fill out the multitude of possible characters involved on both sides. Imagine what insights could have been learned beforehand. Now jump ahead fifteen years and think about how sophisticated such MMOGs might be, and how they could be used to preplay—for obvious consumption by both the global community and the targeted state in question—a rogue-regime takedown and subsequent occupation, perhaps even to the effect of convincing the regime to abandon its untenable situation in advance of actual war being waged. Far-fetched? Not in a world where uncredentialed Internet bloggers can force Senate majority leaders and major network news anchors to resign in disgrace at lightning speed.

2025

"Final Section of Wall Dismantled as Peacekeepers Depart Palestine-Israel Border"

The two-state solution for Israel and Palestine will come about only when all the potential vetoes from neighboring regimes are accounted for, either through carrots or sticks. But achieving that success in prepping the larger diplomatic "battlefield" won't eliminate the need to keep long-warring parties on both sides physically separated for a period of time sufficient for generational change to occur. In short, we'll simply have to wait out all the unredeemable killers and crazies on both sides of that security fence Israel's been putting up between itself and the Gaza Strip and West Bank. The anesthetizing impact of that forced disconnectedness will seem cruel in the short run, but it will heal in the long run.

"Previously Strong Islamic Terror Network in Africa Now Described as 'Neutralized'"

As the United States and the rest of the Core succeed in connecting up the Middle East to the world, we'll end up driving out the violently radical Islamic response to globalization's creeping embrace of the region. As we do so, that fight will logically head south, into sub-Saharan Africa. Thus, progress in a global war on terrorism will be marked by its geographic shift deeper inside the Gap, meaning the last terrorist networks we destroy will probably be centered in the interior of Africa.

"In Historic Shift, Growing Hydrogen Economy Leads to Peaking of Global Oil Demand"

I know all we hear about is the "coming oil peak," referring to production, but that day will never actually arrive with any meaning, because it will be preceded by the peaking of global oil *demand* brought on by the Core's progressive shift toward fuel-cell vehicles to meet its transportation needs. We didn't leave the Stone Age because we were running out of stones, and we won't leave oil age because we're running out of oil. We'll leave because we've developed a better technology that puts less strain on the global environment.

"Cuba's 'Statehood Movement' Grows; Island Vote to Become 53rd State Seems Likely"

America will get back in the business of growing itself, not by any extension of "empire" or by any use of force whatsoever, but through the ballot box. It will happen because the increasing Latinization of our country will deeply alter our relationship with the Caribbean and Central and South America. Just as our—at the time—overwhelming cultural ties to Europe drew us into two world wars "over there," our growing cultural bonds with Latin America will naturally expand our definition of what these "united states" can actually encompass. Some will see the loss of America's essential character and roots in this development, but more will understand it simply as the continuing redefinition of our political "experiment" that's been going on—at this point—for over 250 years.

"Lunar Base Global Consortium Plans First Roundtrip of Space Elevator This Year"

Okay, so no flying cars. But you have to at least allow me one great reference to the "final frontier," if for no other reason than to remind us that globalization need not necessarily end with the final shrinking of the Gap. There will always be old debts to be paid, new challenges to be met, and new boundaries to be crossed.

If this extended "pointer scene" took you by surprise—good. If it forced you to reconsider your definition of optimism—even better.

Timelines are less important than a sense of progress and the inner desire for self-actualization. What I've just described doesn't have to happen, but I believe it will, and that I'll live to see it all. Convince enough of the world of this dream, and what you end up with is reality.

When Pablo Picasso showed Gertrude Stein his just-finished portrait of the famous author, she complained, "But it doesn't look like me."

Picasso replied, "It will."

ACKNOWLEDGMENTS

THIS BOOK WAS CONCEIVED as "volume II" in an effort to describe the current world system, propose a national plan of action for shaping its continued unfolding, and connect this ambitious global vision to the daily lives of individuals committed to creating that future worth imagining. I am under many illusions in this quest: that the past is eminently decipherable, the present ours to define, and the future always within our grasp if we choose to embrace its promises more than its fears.

I am far from alone in this. It is for my fellow travelers that this volume was designed, and many helping hands shaped that design with great care.

This book began with my wife Vonne's encouragement to write it, and our family's sacrifice in enduring its intense production schedule.

It came into play with my agent's great enthusiasm and graceful advice, and for both I thank Jennifer Gates of Zachary Shuster

Harmsworth, along with her colleagues Todd Shuster and Esmond Harmsworth.

This "volume II" found its direction with publisher Neil Nyren of G. P. Putnam's Sons. As with the first installment, Neil's strategic vision proved both accurate and powerful, propelling my manuscript in directions I had neither the experience nor courage to imagine without his wise words.

This book's content was provided in a manner I could have scarcely anticipated without the drive and ambition imparted to my life and career by my new partners of the New Rule Sets Project LLC, and its new parent company, Enterra Solutions. My webmaster and maven, Crittenden Jarvis, was the sole impetus behind the blog that brought me into contact with such an amazing array of readers, contributors, and sources of inspiration (e.g., Mark Safranski, T. M. Lutas, Michael Lotus, Sean Meade, and a host of equally energetic and passionate intellects). My business manager and connector, Steffany Hedenkemp, pushed me to reimagine my career trajectory in ways that deeply informed what I felt compelled to put on these pages. My newest partner in grand visions, Steve DiAngelis, has pushed me hardest to understand and realize the potential of my growing status as thought leader in my field.

But easily the greatest joy involved in creating this text came in being reunited so intensely with my editor, writing coach, and close friend Mark Warren. Our growing collaboration, both in these books and on the pages of *Esquire,* has made possible for me an entirely different career. Mark helped me discover what I could be as a writer, and it's hard to describe what a fantastic gift that's been, or how his incredible generosity as both editor and friend has improved my awareness of who I am and what I hope to accomplish as a grand strategist. Mark is simply one of the best minds I've ever had the pleasure of engaging.

There are others I must note in the journey from the "map" to the "blueprint," among them Steve Meussling, Jerry Barnett, Andy Barnett, Bradd Hayes, Art Cebrowski, Shane Deichman, Kevin Billings, Steve DeAngelis, Steve Oppenheim, Rob Holzer, Dave Ausiello, Hank

Gaffney, David Granger, Paul Davis, Dick O'Neill, Brian Lamb, Greg Jaffe, and David Ignatius.

I also acknowledge with great love two individuals who have kept me on an even keel over the last tumultuous year and a half, which began with the death of my father, John, just before *The Pentagon's New Map* was published. The great fortitude of my mother, Colleen, over the past months has provided me untold strength during a time of great transition for us all. My gratitude for her love knows no bounds. Along similar lines, I find myself—as always—greatly indebted to my mother-in-law Vonne for her wise counsel regarding my choices in life.

To all these individuals, but especially my family, I offer my great thanks for everything they've done to bring this book to life. I have never been more aware of what a hugely collaborative effort a vision such as this must necessarily be in its conceptualization, articulation, and delivery. I have done my best in these pages not to diminish anyone's faith in the future we all believe is worth creating.

This book ends one phase of my life and triggers another. As my family and I move back to "Big Ten" territory, we look forward to all the growth and connectivity I'm certain this volume will trigger in our lives, and so I thank you, the reader, in advance for all the interactions yet to come.

Find me at tom@thomaspmbarnett.com.

NOTES

Preface: A FUTURE WORTH CREATING

xi A grand strategy requires a grand vision . . . and Peace in the Twenty-first Century.
Thomas P.M. Barnett, The Pentagon's New Map: War and Peace in the Twenty-first Century (New York: G. P. Putnam's Sons, 2004).

Chapter One: WHAT THE WORLD NEEDS NOW

2 What was once just the high-tech waging . . . new challenge at hand: waging peace.
On this shift, see Greg Jaffe, "Rumsfeld's Gaze Is Trained Beyond Iraq: Defense Chief Focuses on Reshaping Military to Fight Unconventional Foes in Post-9/11 World," Wall Street Journal, 9 December 2004.

2 So instead of focusing on classified . . . shoulder the SysAdmin's many burdens.
Regarding the fiscal year 2006 budget priorities, see Jonathan Weisman and Renae Merle, "Pentagon Scales Back Arms Plans: Current Needs Outweigh Advances in Technology," Washington Post, 5 January 2005. On the talks with allies, see Thom Shanker, "Pentagon Invites Allies for First Time to Secret Talks Aimed at Sharing Burdens," New York Times, 18 March 2005.

2   Instead of sizing itself to fight two . . . of both warfare and what constitutes victory.

See Greg Jaffe and David S. Cloud, "Pentagon Intends to Refocus War-Planning Effort," *Wall Street Journal*, 25 October 2004; and Bradley Graham, "Pentagon Prepares to Rethink Focus on Conventional Warfare: New Emphasis on Insurgencies and Terrorism Is Planned," *Washington Post*, 26 January 2005.

2   The struggles over budgetary priorities . . . SysAdmin's well-trained counterinsurgency forces and military police).

On the budgetary fights, see Shailagh Murray, "Bush Faces Pentagon Gunfight: Proposed Weapons-System Cuts Stir Republican Opposition," *Wall Street Journal*, 1 February 2005; Greg Jaffe, "Rumsfeld's Push for Speed Fuels Pentagon Dissent: Billions Are Sought for Force to Fight Blitzkrieg War; Critics Cite Iraq Troubles; Who Will Repair the Sewers?" *Wall Street Journal*, 16 May 2005; and Tim Weiner, "Air Force Seeks Bush's Approval for Space Arms: Billions Have Been Spent; Opposition to Policy Shift Is Expected, and Many Hurdles Lie Ahead," *New York Times*, 18 May 2005.

3   And no, I'm not talking about some . . . enunciated by the Bush Administration.

For an overview of the classified planning document that identifies the U.S. military's core missions in years ahead, see Greg Jaffe, "Rumsfeld Details Big Military Shift in New Document: Drive for Pre-emptive Force, Wider Influence Will Trigger Changes in Strategy, Budget," *Wall Street Journal*, 11 March 2005.

4   Many established security experts condemned . . . to be that model's essential underpinnings.

See virtually all reviews of *The Pentagon's New Map* (I omit some of the weirder Web sources) at my site: www.thomaspmbarnett.com/reviews/reviews_index.htm.

UNDERSTANDING THE SEAM BETWEEN WAR AND PEACE

5   In many ways, the article was less a profile . . . the United States in the post-9/11 era.

Greg Jaffe, "At the Pentagon, Quirky PowerPoint Carries Big Punch: In a World of 'Gap' States, Mr. Barnett Urges Generals to Split Forces in Two; Austin Powers on Soundtrack," *Wall Street Journal*, 11 May 2004.

5   The first was by Colonel John Boyd . . . insurgency model) by William Lind and others.

The best biography on Colonel Boyd is Robert Coram's *Boyd: The Fighter Pilot Who Changed the Art of War* (New York: Back Bay Books, 2004).

5   This presentation, by legendary Pentagon . . . cover of *Time* magazine in 1983.

The cover of the 7 March 1983 *Time* sported the headline, "U.S. Defense Spending: Are Billions Being Wasted?" The cover story, "The Winds of Reform," was by Walter Isaacson.

6   The third brief was delivered . . . the "Yoda" or "rabbi" to today's high-tech military.

On Marshall's influence, read James Der Derian, "The Illusion of a Grand Strategy," *New York Times*, 25 May 2001.

10   In early 2005, I spent a week debating . . . 4GW standard *The Sling and the Stone*).

Colonel Thomas X. Hammes, USMC, *the Sling and the Stone: On War in the 21st Century* (St. Paul, MN: Zenith Press, 2004).

14   Neither regime-toppling exercise cost . . . local forces defending their homelands.

The best estimates are somewhere between 160 and 170 (166 is a frequently cited number) combat deaths in Afghanistan and between 130 and 140 (137 is most cited) in Iraq through the war's declared end in early May 2004 (President Bush's famous "mission accomplished" speech aboard the carrier).

15   In Iraq, this bureaucratic passive-aggressive . . . major combat operations ended."

Quoted in Thomas E. Ricks, "Army Historian Cites Lack of Postwar Plan: Major Calls Effort in Iraq 'Mediocre,'" *Washington Post*, 25 December 2004. See also Michael Moss, "Many Actions Tied to Delay in Armor for Troops in Iraq: Army Was Forced to Scramble as Reality of Insurgents' Effectiveness Set In," *New York Times*, 7 March 2005.

16   All will tell you that the looting . . . much of their initial efforts at re-building.

On this point, see Michael R. Gordon, "Faulty Intelligence Misled Troops at War's Start," *New York Times*, 20 October 2004.

17   We asked India for 17,000 peacekeepers . . . that likewise never materialized.

India's parliament said no to the Bush Administration's request in the summer of 2003; see John Kifner, "India Decides Not to Send Troops to Iraq Now: A Preference for Medical Aid; An Eye on Local Politics," *New York Times*, 15 July 2003. Stratfor (www.stratfor.com), an online source of global security intelligence, reported on 16 July 2004 ("Russia: Putin Considers Sending Troops to Iraq") that the White House had asked Russia's leader, Vladimir Putin, for approximately 40,000 troops and was likewise rebuffed.

18   In the end, the Bush White House . . . happened in Iraq: "catastrophic success."

Bush used this phrase (*catastrophic success*) in a 30 August 2004 interview with Associated Press on the eve of the Republican National Convention.

18   Not only is the Army needed now . . . ranks rapidly depleted by rotations into Iraq!

Last year, as a result of the stresses imposed by continuing operations in Iraq, Army recruiters began actively targeting Navy and Air Force personnel leaving their respective services for immediate reenlistment; see Eric Schmitt, "Army Looks for Airmen and Sailors," *New York Times*, 9 July 2004.

19   The big thinker here is William Lind . . . Face of War: Into the Fourth Generation."

William Lind; Colonel Keith Nightengale, USA; Captain John F. Schmitt, USMC; Colonel Joseph W. Sutton, USA; and Lieutenant Colonel Gary I. Wilson, USMCR, "The Changing Face of War: Into the Fourth Generation," *Marine Corps Gazette*, October 1989.

20   In his brilliant book *The Sling and the Stone* . . . of the Gaza Strip and West Bank.

Hammes, *The Sling and the Stone*, pp. 44–129 (Chapters 5 through 8).

21   We seek to create facts on the ground . . . the Internet for global consumption.

On the classified sewage plant in Iraq, see James Glanz, "It's a Dirty Job, But They Do It, Secretly, in Iraq," *New York Times,* 19 June 2004.

21   This strategic outlook dovetails with . . . or more recently Sudan's janjaweed).

The most expansive version Robert D. Kaplan offers of this vision is found in his book *The Ends of the Earth: From Togo to Turkmenistan, from Iran to Cambodia, a Journey to the Frontiers of Anarchy* (New York: Vintage, 1997).

21   Also, prior to 9/11, the 4GW crowd was . . . future opponent as was the NCO crowd.

See Hammes, *The Sling and the Stone,* p. 257, where he says "China is clearly our most dangerous opponent" among nation-states.

22   In the winter of 2005, I was asked by *Esquire* . . . post-9/11 international security environment.

Thomas P.M. Barnett, "Old Man in a Hurry: The inside story of how Donald H. Rumsfeld transformed the Pentagon, in which we learn about wire-brushing, deep diving, and a secret society called the Slurg," *Esquire,* July 2005.

22   As then-Chief of Naval Operations . . . we're going to create a whole new world here."

Barnett, "Old Man in a Hurry," p.142.

A DEPARTMENT FOR WHAT LIES BETWEEN WAR AND PEACE

23   One of the last sections I wrote for . . . postconflict stabilization and reconstruction . . .).

See "The System Administrator" in Barnett, *The Pentagon's New Map,* pp. 315–27.

25   The Bush Administration had promised . . . case of the "magic cloud" phenomenon.

See Neil King Jr., "Bush Has an Audacious Plan to Rebuild Iraq Within a Year," *Wall Street Journal,* 17 March 2003.

28   The Asian tsunamis generated right off . . . U.S. military has ever addressed.

Seventeen Navy ships and roughly 13,000 Marines and sailors were involved in the disaster response; see "Pentagon Spending $6M a Day on Asia Relief: Pentagon Says It Is Spending $6 Million a Day in Tsunami Relief Effort in South Asia," Associated Press, 6 January 2005.

29   Now, given the painful experience of the U.S. . . . (National Guard and Reserves).

On this subject see Greg Jaffe, "For Guidance in Iraq, Marines Rediscover a 1940s Manual: Small-War Secrets Include Tips on Nation-Building, The Care of Pack Mules," *Wall Street Journal,* 8 April 2004; Greg Jaffe, "Army Seeks Ways to Bolster Force in Iraq," *Wall Street Journal,* 26 April 2004; Daniel Williams, "Soldiers' Doubts Build as Duties Shift: For Many, Prolonged Stay and New Threat Have Eroded Early Optimism," *Washington Post,* 25 May 2004; Thomas E. Ricks, "U.S. Army Changed by Iraq, but for Better or Worse?: Some Military Experts See Value in Lessons Learned; Others Cite Toll on Personnel, Equipment," *Washington Post,* 6 July 2004; Greg Jaffe, "Intelligence Test: On Ground in Iraq, Soldier Uses Wits to Hunt Insurgents: Sgt. McCary, Fluent in Arabic, Improvises Tactics in Field; Not the War He Trained For," *Wall Street Journal,* 10 September 2004; Greg Jaffe, "On

Ground in Iraq, Capt. Ayers Writes His Own Playbook: Thrust into New Kind of War, Junior Officers Become Army's Leading Experts," *Wall Street Journal,* 22 September 2004; Greg Jaffe, "As Chaos Mounts in Iraq, U.S. Army Rethinks Its Future: Amid Signs Its Plan Fell Short, Service Sees Benefits of Big Tanks, Translators," *Wall Street Journal,* 9 December 2004; Bradley Graham, "General Says Army Reserve Is Becoming a 'Broken' Force," *Washington Post,* 6 January 2005; and Dan Baum, "Battle Lessons: What the Generals Don't Know," *The New Yorker,* 17 January 2005.

31 In *The Pentagon's New Map,* I described . . . often abetted by rogue regimes.

In the section, "The Rise of Asymmetrical War," in Barnett, *The Pentagon's New Map,* pp. 89–96.

31 The journalist Robert D. Kaplan likes to describe . . . settling of the American West.

See Robert D. Kaplan, "Indian Country: Our Military Has the Most Thankless Task of Any Military in the History of Warfare," *Wall Street Journal,* 21 September 2004. For a supporting notion, see James Glanz, "Truckers of Iraq's Pony Express Are Risking It All for a Paycheck," *New York Times,* 27 September 2004.

32 As described in a recent report . . . for any subsequent nation-building mission.

Hans Binnendijk and Stuart E. Johnson, eds., *Transforming for Stabilization and Reconstruction Operations* (Washington, D.C.: National Defense University Press, 2004), pp. 3–14.

32 Thus, our current ability to wage . . . SysAdmin force can barely get its act together.

Binnendijk and Johnson, *Transforming for Stabilization and Reconstruction Operations,* pp. xiii–xvi.

33 In terms of the additional costs imposed . . . and less than one-fifth on wars.

See Defense Science Board, *Transition To and From Hostilities* (2004 Summer Study, Office of the Secretary of Defense for Acquisition, Technology, and Logistics), p. 18.

34 During the Cold War, we took on nation-building . . . once every two years.

Binnendijk and Johnson, *Transforming for Stabilization and Reconstruction Operations,* p. 3.

34 Roughly 80 percent of all United Nations peacekeeping . . . the end of the Cold War.

Calculated from UN historical data found online at www.un.org.

34 As the recent definitive report from the Pentagon's . . . outbreak of mass violence.

Defense Science Board, *Transition To and From Hostilities,* p. 10.

35 But as we take on new nation-building . . . for waging peace will skyrocket.

Defense Science Board, *Transition To and From Hostilities,* p. 14.

38 If you think the Leviathan force promotes robotics . . . curve for such systems.

See Michael P. Regan, "Army Prepares 'Robo-Soldier' for Iraq," *Washington Post,* 24 January 2005; and Tim Weiner, "A New Model Army Soldier Rolls Closer to the Battlefield," *New York Times,* 16 February 2005.

40   Moreover, the recent move to create a czar-like office . . . capacity over time.

See Christopher Lee, "New State Dept. Office Aimed at Postwar Aid: Agency Would Lay Groundwork for Rebuilding Nations," *Washington Post,* 25 March 2005.

40   This process began in spades with the fiscal year 2006 . . . manpower needs.

See Greg Jaffe and Jonathan Karp, "Military Cuts Target Old Ways of War: Pentagon Budget Proposal Would Hit Navy, Air Force; Shipbuilders Face Squeeze," *Wall Street Journal,* 25 January 2005.

40   This is what has happened with Halliburton . . . burgeoning SysAdmin portfolio.

On this proposed development, see Russell Gold, "Halliburton's KBR May Be More Attractive in Pieces," *Wall Street Journal,* 14 May 2004. In August 2004, Halliburton held a meeting for investors and analysts in which a plan was presented to divest the Kellogg-Brown & Root division, either through a direct sale, spinning it off as a separate company, or through an initial public offering. The proposed company would be valued in the range of 2 to 3 billion dollars. A decision on the company's fate is expected sometime in 2005, according to industry analysts.

41   Well, the last time we actually declared war . . . in Europe during World War II.

On 5 June 1942, the U.S. Congress officially declared war collectively on Bulgaria, Hungary, and Romania. As the three were listed alphabetically, Romania was the very last nation ever to be named in a U.S. declaration of war!

42   As such, the U.S. lags behind virtually every . . . foreign aid as a percentage of GDP.

For details, see the editorial, "America, the Indifferent," *New York Times,* 23 December 2004; Robin Wright, "Aid to Poorest Nations Trails Global Goal," *Washington Post,* 15 January 2005; and Celia W. Dugger, "Discerning a New Course for World's Donor Nations," *New York Times,* 18 April 2005.

42   Of course, if we chose to count the roughly quarter-trillion . . . basis in recent years.

America has long been recognized as one of the world's most generous states when it comes to disaster relief. On average the advanced countries provide in the range of $60 to $80 billion a year in official development aid, according to statistics provided by the Organization for Economic Cooperation and Development (OECD).

42   In many ways, this phenomenon mirrors . . . of incomplete aid projects years later.

On this sad tendency, see Ginger Thompson and Nazila Fathi, "For Honduras and Iran, World's Aid Evaporated: Unfinished Work—Long-Term Fears for Tsunami Zone," *New York Times,* 11 January 2005.

BARNETT'S A-TO-Z RULE SET ON PROCESSING
POLITICALLY BANKRUPT STATES

43   The National Intelligence Council . . . agencies, including the well-known CIA.

The fifteen members of the intelligence agency are Air Force Intelligence, Army Intelligence, Central Intelligence Agency, Coast Guard Intelligence, Defense Intelligence Agency, Department of Energy, Department of Homeland Security, Department of State, Department of Treasury, Federal Bureau of Investigation, Marine Corps Intelligence, National Geospatial Intelligence Agency, National Reconnaissance Office, National Security Agency, and Navy Intelligence.

44   But to the public (and especially the Web community) . . . a good fifteen years or more.

The most recent reports are *Mapping the Global Future* (2004), *Global Trends 2015* (2000), and *Global Trends 2010* (1997). They are found online at the Council's Web site (www.cia.gov/nic).

44   I answered yes, and that this was a good thing . . . clashes between superpowers.

Thomas P.M. Barnett, "Does the U.S. Face a Future of Never-Ending Subnational and Transnational Violence?" (Conference paper, National Intelligence Council 2020 Project, May 2004), found online at www.thomaspmbarnett.com/published/NIC2020paper.htm.

49   Conversely, decrepitly authoritarian regimes . . . under the Taliban in Afghanistan).

If you explore the history of al Qaeda and the global Salafi jihadist movement, you find that most of its key players arise from either Egypt or Saudi Arabia. See Chapter 1 ("Origins of the Jihad") in Marc Sageman's *Understanding Terror Networks* (Philadelphia: University of Pennsylvania Press, 2004), pp. 1–24.

50   I once had a veteran of the U.S. Agency . . . networks would be thriving there.

The veteran employee was Tony Pryor, whom I first met in the Africa Bureau in the mid-1990s, when I did some contract work for USAID on "reengineering."

52   In its mature form, the SysAdmin . . . nation building, and economic development.

This breakdown is quite similar to that of the "Human Security Response Force" proposed by the European Union in a recent report entitled "A Human Security Doctrine for Europe," by the Study Group on Europe's Security Capabilities (18 November 2004), found online at www.lse.ac.uk/Depts/global/Human%20Security%20Report%20Full.pdf. In that report, the proposed SysAdmin-like force made up of 15,000 would be "at least" one-third civilian.

52   U.S. participation in all three aspects should . . . percent range of total personnel.

That percentage would correspond to the levels the United States maintained in the long-running Balkans peacekeeping efforts. For details, see James Dobbins et al., *America's Role in Nation-Building: From Germany to Iraq* (Santa Monica, CA: RAND, 2003), Chapters 6 and 7, on Bosnia and Kosovo, pp. 87–128.

52   Once stabilization operations yield to civilian security . . . Fund (IMF) and the World Bank.

Sebastian Mallaby, "The Lesson in MacArthur," *Washington Post,* 21 October 2002. See also his "For a 'New Imperialism,'" *Washington Post,* 10 May 2004.

53   As the IMF endeavors over time to codify . . . but hey, at least we *have* a process!

On this effort, see Martin Wolf, *Why Globalization Works* (New Haven, CT: Yale University Press, 2004), pp. 300–301.

53   So if you're Argentina and you default . . . is not so much required as expected.

On this wild tale, see Larry Rohter, "Economic Rally for Argentines Defies Forecasts: After Record '01 Default; Ignoring Orthodox Advice Results in 8% Growth for 2 Years Running," *New York Times,* 26 December 2004; Larry Rohter, "Argentina Announces Deal on Its Debt Default: Creditors to Get at Best 30 Cents on Dollar," *New York Times,* 4 March 2005; Paul Blustein, "Many View Argentina's Comeback with Skepticism: Some Financiers and Bondholders Say Offer to Settle Huge Debt Is Far Too Little," *Washington Post,* 4 March 2005; and Mary Anastasia O'Grady, "Argentina's Lessons for Global Creditors," *Wall Street Journal,* 4 March 2005.

53   I ginned up this six-part model in my brief . . . in a *Washington Post* op-ed.
Barnett, *The Pentagon's New Map,* p. 375.

54   Once I had presented the six-part model . . . Republic of Yugoslavia in the 1990s.
On this long process see Dobbins et al., *America's Role in Nation-Building,* Chapters 6 and 7, on Bosnia and Kosovo, pp. 87–128.

55   This tribunal, created by the Security Council . . . the International Criminal Court.
On this evolution, see Marlise Simons, "Court on Crimes in Former Yugoslavia Hits Its Stride: Suspects Charged with Atrocities Are Brought to Justice," *New York Times,* 15 May 2005.

55   The more important example? . . . Croatia in talks to join the European Union.
According to a NATO fact sheet (www.nato.int/issues/Afghanistan/040628-factsheet.htm), both the "former Yougoslov [sic] Republic of Macedonia" and Croatia were providing small numbers of peacekeepers to Afghanistan. On Croatia's talks with the EU: These talks were frozen by the EU in March 2005 because the Union felt Croatia was not forthcoming enough in its interactions with the UN war-crimes tribunal examining the multiple conflicts across the former Republic of Yugoslavia in the 1990s.

55   With Saddam Hussein's Iraq . . . the many years Iraq was subject to UN sanctions.
By *implicit villains,* a phrase I borrow from T. M. Lutas's online analysis of the long investigations of the UN Oil-for-Food scandal in Iraq, I mean those Core private-sector companies that long colluded with Saddam Hussein's regime to bypass the UN sanctions. Some were American, but the bulk of the money went to French and Russian companies. For details see T. M. Lutas, "Barnett's Implicit Villains," Flit, found online at www.snapping.turtle.net/jmc/tmblog/archives/004646.html; see also the profile of one American "implicit villain" in Simon Romero, "The Man Who Bought the Oil from Iraq: Inquiry into U.N. Program Puts Focus on Texas Deal Maker," *New York Times,* 19 October 2004; and finally David R. Sands, "Iraq War Opponents Fill Oil-for-Food 'Vouchers' List," *Washington Times,* 3 May 2004; and Justin Blum and Colum Lynch, "Oil-for-Food Benefited Russians, Report Says: Iraq Sought to Influence U.N. Through Moscow," *Washington Post,* 16 May 2005.

57   Similarly, the Coalition Provisional Authority . . . our top priorities were in reconstruction.
For a sampling of the multitude of criticisms leveled at the CPA, see Greg Jaffe,

"Winning the Peace: Early U.S. Decisions in Iraq Now Haunt American Efforts," *Wall Street Journal,* 19 April 2004; Rajiv Chandrasekaran, "Mistakes Loom Large as Handover Nears: Missed Opportunities Turned High Ideals to Harsh Realities," *Washington Post,* 20 June 2004; James Glanz and Erik Eckholm, "Reality Intrudes on Promises in Rebuilding of Iraq: 2,300 Projects Planned but Fewer Than 140 Are Under Way," *New York Times,* 30 June 2004; Erik Eckholm, "U.S. Seeks to Provide More Jobs and Speed Rebuilding in Iraq: A Focus on Large Projects Has Been Criticized as Wasteful," *New York Times,* 27 July 2004; Robin Wright and Thomas E. Ricks, "Bremer Criticizes Troop Levels in Iraq: Ex-Administrator Says Planning Failure Created 'Atmosphere of Lawlessness'," *Washington Post,* 5 October 2004; Greg Jaffe, "Rules Slow Rebuilding in Iraq: Spending Deadlines, Regulations to Fight Fraud Create Barriers," *Wall Street Journal,* 5 October 2004; and Erik Eckholm, "Rethinking Reconstruction: Grand U.S. Plan Fractures Again," *New York Times,* 17 April 2005.

58   Between the obvious corruption of the Oil-for-Food . . . change inside the Gap.
For a good critique of sanctions in general, with specific reference to Iraq during the 1990s, see John Mueller and Karl Mueller, "Sanctions of Mass Destruction," *Foreign Affairs,* May/June 1999.

58   As many critics point out with regard to the Balkans . . . and organizational capacity.
For a telling analysis of this problem, see Yaroslav Trofimov, "In Postwar Bosnia, Overruling Voters to Save Democracy: International Overseer Purges Elected Officials at Will; 'Why Me?' Gets No Reply," *Wall Street Journal,* 1 October 2004.

59   Taken together, these twenty entities capture . . . and over 90 percent of global GDP.
The members of the G-20 are: Argentina, Australia, Brazil, Canada, China, European Union, France, Germany, India, Indonesia, Italy, Japan, Mexico, Russia, Saudi Arabia, South Africa, South Korea, Turkey, United Kingdom, and the United States.

60   For example, when the Bush Administration . . . the goal of political reform there.
See Jackson Diehl, "An Opening for Arab Democrats," *Washington Post,* 11 October 2004.

61   But it's not just that the United States ends up . . . struggle with a vicious insurgency.
On the question of Saddam's trial and the issue of legitimacy, see Peter Landesman, "Who v. Saddam?: The U.S. Has Spent Years Preparing for Saddam Hussein's Trial. But It Is Not All That Certain Who Will Try Him or When—or Whose Ends That Trial Will Ultimately Serve," *New York Times Magazine,* 11 July 2004.

62   In contrast, the United States has pressured our NATO . . . in other sections of the country.
On this development, see staff report, "Germany Opposes US Plan in Afghanistan: NATO's Mandate Is to Stabilize Afghanistan, Not Fight Terrorism," *Deutsche Welle,* 13 October 2004. In effect, Germany demanded that NATO's SysAdmin role in Afghanistan not be merged with America's Leviathan-like efforts against terrorist networks.

62   As *U.S. News & World Report*'s Michael Barone ... our military forces."
Michael Barone, "The Pentagon's New Map," U.S. News.com, 20 May 2004,
found online at www.usnews.com/usnews/opinion/baroneweb/mb_040520.htm.

63   "Right now all we've got is a hammer and ... What we really need is a
screwdriver."
Jaffe, "At the Pentagon, Quirky PowerPoint Carries Big Punch."

64   So when the Bush Administration announced ... commitment in the right
direction.
David Morgan, "U.S. Plans Military Retraining for Terrorism War," Reuters, 12
October 2004.

64   The other great temptation is to outsource ... deal of such outsourcing
has happened in Iraq.
On the many travails of outsourcing security, see P. W. Singer, "Nation Builders
and Low Bidder in Iraq: After Abu Ghraib and Falluja, Why Are We Still Outsourcing?" *New York Times,* 15 June 2004; and Craig S. Smith, "The Intimidating
Face of America," *New York Times,* 13 October 2004.

64   Finally, as we've seen in Iraq, where at one ... yield unintended
consequences.
For the confusion on medals, see Ariana Eunjung Cha and Renae Merle, "Line
Increasingly Blurred Between Soldiers and Civilian Contractors," *Washington
Post,* 13 May 2004; for the flip-side argument about how civilian workers don't get
any respect despite the great danger of the jobs they undertake, see Jonathan Fig,
"Civilian Jobs in Iraq Pay Well but, Wives Find, Not in Respect: Halliburton,
Others Help Out, but Spouses Learn They Must Do for Themselves," *Wall Street
Journal,* 3 August 2004.

65   As for Sebastian Mallaby's brilliant proposal ... of leaders rises to the
challenge.
Mallaby's fuller treatment of the concept is found in his "The Reluctant Imperialist: Terrorism, Failed States, and the Case for American Empire," *Foreign Affairs,*
March/April 2002.

66   As Francis Fukuyama argues ... as the technological prowess of our
armed forces.
Francis Fukuyama, "The Art of Reconstruction," *Wall Street Journal,* 28 July 2004.

67   Moving on to the last of the six pieces in this A-to-Z ... and related war
crimes.
These "crimes of concern" are listed in Article 5 (Crimes within the jurisdiction
of the Court) in the Rome Statute of the International Criminal Court that established the ICC.

68   This fear began with the Clinton Administration ... countries throughout the Gap.
As of late 2004, the U.S. Government had concluded 93 such Article 98 agreements
(many awaiting ratification by the legislature of the country in question), and 91
of them involved Gap nations. I obtained this information directly from the Office
of the Secretary of Defense. For an example of how our opposition comes back to
haunt us, see Jess Bravin and Scot J. Paltrow, "Washington's Darfur Dilemma:
Genocide Investigation Could Land in International Criminal Court That U.S.
Opposes," *Wall Street Journal,* 17 January 2005.

Chapter Two: WINNING THE WAR
THROUGH CONNECTEDNESS

71   Reviewers either loved or hated the book.
See www.thomaspmbarnett.com/reviews/reviews_index.htm.

71   During the several weeks my wife . . . (Beijing University) for the Chinese edition.
Read my online diary of the entire trip at my blog: www.thomaspmbarnett.com/china/index.htm.

72   In a world where 20,000 people die every day . . . this year, this month, this week.
This figure is often cited by Jeffrey Sachs; see his *The End of Poverty: Economic Possibilities of Our Times* (New York: Penguin Press, 2005), p. 1.

73   The Bush Administration's decision to lay a Big Bang . . . of the occupation.
See the section "The Big Bang as Strategy" in Barnett, *The Pentagon's New Map*, pp. 278–94.

74   We have approached similar crossroads . . . divided against itself can not stand."
This phrase comes from Abraham Lincoln's speech to the Republican state convention in Springfield, Illinois, on 16 June 1858. During the convention he was nominated to run for the U.S. Senate against Democrat Stephen A. Douglas.

CONNECTING THE MIDDLE EAST TO THE WORLD

75   One thing I've learned in my years as a strategist . . . got to know his limitations."
Clint Eastwood delivering the line as "Dirty Harry" Callahan, San Francisco police detective in the movie, *Magnum Force* (1973).

76   "If the White House tells us to suck eggs . . . makes no sense to me whatsoever."
Quote from "one senior official close to the process" in "Navy Looks Set to Lose Fight Over Puerto Rico Island," Associated Press, 3 December 1999.

77   One of the best compliments I've ever received . . . shrink the Gap or make it worse?"
This quote was relayed to me by Greg Jaffe of the *Wall Street Journal* during his research on the article "At the Pentagon, Quirky PowerPoint Carries Big Punch." Mac Thornberry later reviewed *The Pentagon's New Map* in the article "Rethinking Strategy," *Washington Times*, 3 June 2004.

81   That connectivity comes in the form . . . retreat of al Qaeda and its subsidiaries.
For a good snapshot of this phenomenon, see Douglas Farah and Richard Shultz, "Al Qaeda's Growing Sanctuary," *Washington Post*, 14 July 2004.

82   This is why we haven't seen any major attacks . . . rim of Europe and Russia.
On this clear trend since 9/11, see Dana Priest and Spencer Hsu, "U.S. Sees Drop in Terrorist Threats: Al Qaeda Focusing Attacks in Iraq and Europe, Officials Say," *Washington Post*, 1 May 2005.

83   Of course, the extent of that reach still matters . . . Old Core allies from our coalition.

On Madrid and the linkages to al Qaeda, see Peter Ford, "Terrorism Web Emerges from Madrid Bombing: Links Across Europe Show al Qaeda Quick to Regroup and Combine Different Networks," *Christian Science Monitor,* 22 March 2004; and Keith Johnson and David Crawford, "Madrid Bombing Suspect Is Key al Qaeda Liaison," *Wall Street Journal,* 7 April 2004.

83   Likewise, as in the case of the Beslan school massacre . . . Chechen conflict).
For a good overview of the aftermath, see Sebastian Smith, "Top Chechen Commanders: Moscow Has Declared Top Chechen Rebel Leaders Shamil Basayev and Aslan Maskhadov Equally Culpable in the Beslan Tragedy," *BBC News,* 9 September 2004.

83   So when China and India, for example . . . our military goals in the region?
For examples of this coverage, see Andrew Browne et al., "Asian Rivals Put Pressure on Western Energy Giants: In a String of Recent Deals, China, India Display Clout, Funds and Stomach for Risk," *Wall Street Journal,* 10 January 2005; and Keith Bradsher, "2 Big Appetites Take Seats at the Oil Table: China and India Compete for Energy Resources in Places Others Shun," *New York Times,* 18 February 2005.

84   To answer those questions, you really need to step . . . markets and investment flows.
For a good overview on this, see Martin Wolf, "On the Move: Asia's Giants Take Different Routes in Pursuit of Economic Greatness," *Financial Times,* 23 February 2005; and Edward Luce and Richard McGregor, "A Share of Spoils: Beijing and New Delhi Get Mutual Benefits from Growing Trade," *Financial Times,* 24 February 2005.

84   So when *Washington Post* columnist David Ignatius . . . democratic political reform.
David Ignatius, "Winning a War for the Disconnected," *Washington Post,* 14 December 2004.

85   As defined by leading terrorism expert Marc Sageman: . . . share a large support base.
Sageman, *Understanding Terror Networks,* p. 1.

86   That is because, in the end, what Osama bin Laden . . . as the violent, corrupt "Gap."
Marc Sageman makes this similar distinction when he writes, "Traditional Islamic jurisprudence saw jihad as an obligation in a world divided into the land of Islam *(dar al-Islam)* and the land of conflict *(dar al-harb)."* See his *Understanding Terror Networks,* p. 2.

86   Until globalization began to encroach on the Middle East . . . of the whole of Islam.
As Islamic expert Olivier Roy writes, "Re-Islamisation is part of a process of deculturation (that is, of a crisis of pristine cultures giving way to westernization and reconstructed identities)"; and "Re-Islamisation means that Muslim identity, self-evident so long as it belonged to an inherited cultural legacy, has to express itself explicitly in a non-Muslim or Western context." See his *Globalized Islam: The Search for a New Ummah* (New York: Columbia University Press, 2004), pp. 22–23.

87   As noted Islamic expert Olivier Roy points . . . World Trade Center and the Pentagon.
Roy, *Globalized Islam,* p. 46.

88   So it is the argument of the 4GW crowd . . . replay of cowboys and Indians.
      See Robert D. Kaplan, *Warrior Politics: Why Leadership Demands a Pagan Ethos*
      (New York: Random House, 2001).

89   So the visionaries of this future-worth-avoiding . . . of African-American
      "gangstas."
      Two classics of this genre are Martin van Creveld's *The Transformation of War:
      The Most Radical Reinterpretation of Armed Conflict Since Clausewitz* (New
      York: Free Press, 1991), which is built substantially off experiences faced by Israel
      in the Middle East, and Robert D. Kaplan's *The Coming Anarchy: Shattering the
      Dream of the Post–Cold War* (New York: Random House, 2000), which leverages
      substantially from recent African history as well.

90   As this dark view argues, these people simply *love* war.
      As Hammes argues in his *The Sling and the Stone:* "A warrior society thrives on
      and exists for war. Often, the young warrior has everything to lose (except his life)
      if he stops fighting" (p. 41).

90   I know that may sound counterintuitive . . . its military retreat from the
      region.
      For examples of this analysis, see Dana Priest, "Iraq New Terror Breeding Ground:
      War Created Haven, CIA Advisers Report," *Washington Post,* 14 January 2005;
      and Dana Priest and Josh White, "War Helps Recruit Terrorists, Hill Told: Intelli-
      gence Officials Talk of Growing Insurgency," *Washington Post,* 17 February 2005.

90   First, while the region as a whole is enduring . . . remaining high relative to
      the Core.
      For an overview of this historical phenomenon, see Graham E. Fuller's brief
      paper, "The Youth Crisis in Middle Eastern Society" (Clinton, MI: Institute for
      Social Policy and Understanding, 2004).

90   In the wealthier oil states like Saudi Arabia . . . from foreigners to the
      native youth.
      For a description of this new policy, see Scott Wilson, "Saudis Fight Militancy
      with Jobs: Private Posts Formerly Held by Foreigners Are Offered to Locals,"
      Washington Post, 31 August 2004.

91   The most famous example of this was when . . . out its small military
      contingent.
      For details, see Carlos H. Conde, "Philippines Viewed as Being Forced to Yield on
      Hostage," *New York Times,* 16 July 2004; and "U.S. Rips Philippines for Pulling
      Out of Iraq," Associated Press, 24 July 2004. In the AP article, President Gloria
      Macapagal Arroyo "denied any break with the United States during a foreign pol-
      icy speech today, making clear that she felt she had to put the welfare of its 8 mil-
      lion citizens working overseas at the top of her priorities. The remittances power
      the Philippine economy."

91   While the House of Saud has long bragged . . . Asian laborers (roughly six
      million).
      As the Saudi oil minister declared, "There is a market illusion how much the king-
      dom is affected by foreign workers"; cited in Neil MacFarquhar, "Saudi Attack
      Spurs More U.S. Workers to Pull Up Stakes," *New York Times,* 3 June 2004. The
      figures on foreign workers come from Hugh Pope and Chip Cummins, "Saudis
      Suffer Fresh Terrorist Attack: Assault Takes Lives of 22; Some Westerners Leave,
      But Oil's Flow Still Steady," *Wall Street Journal,* 1 June 2004.

91   In June 2004, Saudi Arabia suffered its worst terrorist attack in over a year.
      For details, see Pope and Cummins, "Saudis Suffer Fresh Terrorist Attack"; and
      "Saudis Act to Ease Concerns After Terror Attack" (from staff and wire reports),
      USA Today, 1 June 2004.

91   Perhaps surprisingly, foreign direct investment . . . capital has begun.
      This data is provided in Glenn Yago and Don McCarthy, "The Post-Saddam
      Boom," *Wall Street Journal,* 13 January 2005. It is important to note, however,
      that the lack of foreign direct investment in postwar Iraq has hampered the recon-
      struction there to a huge degree. On this, see Ariana Eunjung Cha and Jackie
      Spinner, "U.S. Companies Put Little Capital into Iraq: Many Firms Interested, but
      Are Held Back by Security Concerns, Lack of Political Stability," *Washington
      Post,* 15 May 2004; and David J. Lynch, "Cash Crunch Curbs Rebuilding in Iraq:
      Jobless Rate Stuck Near 30% as Businesses Seek Capital," *USA Today,* 1 June
      2004.

92   Second, for most Muslims in the region . . . it is an attempted retreat into
      the past.
      As Olivier Roy argues, "Islamic revival may thus be experienced according to
      Western and modern paradigms of social and professional behavior, while
      embodying a way of internalizing such modernity. It is a common mistake to
      interpret any public expression of re-Islamisation as a traditionalist backlash or a
      sort of political statement; see his *Globalized Islam,* pp. 218–19.

93   As King Abdullah II of Jordan stated . . . trigger a process that you can't
      turn back."
      Quoted in Diehl, "An Opening for Arab Democrats."

93   This sense of reformist urgency is being reflected . . . terrorists beheading
      civilians.
      For an overview see Neil MacFarquhar, "As Terrorists Strike Arab Targets, Escala-
      tion Fears Arise," *New York Times,* 30 April 2004; Hugh Pope, "Iraq, Terrorism
      Strain Brittle Mideast Status Quo," *Wall Street Journal,* 5 May 2004; John Kifner,
      "Massacre Draws Self-Criticism in Muslim Press," *New York Times,* 9 September
      2004; and Neil MacFarquhar, "Muslim Scholars Increasingly Debate Unholy
      War," *New York Times,* 10 December 2004.

93   In Saudi Arabia, as militants emboldened . . . will suffer great instability
      as a result.
      On this growing awareness, see Neil MacFarquhar, "Saudis Support a Jihad in
      Iraq, Not Back Home: Riyadh Bombing Stirs Widespread Outrage," *New York
      Times,* 23 April 2004; Craig Whitlock, "Saudis Facing Return of Radicals: Young
      Iraq Veterans Join Underground," *Washington Post,* 11 July 2004; Joel Brinkley,
      "Saudis Blame U.S. and Its Role in Iraq for Rise of Terror," *New York Times,* 14
      October 2004; and "Saudi Cleric Faults Islamic Militants," Associated Press, 20
      January 2005.

94   As the events of early 2005 indicated . . . in over two decades of "emer-
      gency rule."
      For an overview see David Brooks, "Why Not Here? Bush Changes the Subject,
      Worldwide," *New York Times,* 26 February 2005; Neil MacFarquhar, "Mubarak
      Pushes Egypt to Allow Freer Elections: After 50 Years of One-Party Rule, Move to
      Amend the Constitution," *New York Times,* 27 February 2005; and Bill Spindle,

"How Lebanese Drive to Oust the Syrians Finally Caught Fire: Killing of Ex-Prime Minister Capped Events with a Link to U.S. Mideast Initiatives," *Wall Street Journal,* 28 February 2005.

94   Factor in Saudi Arabia's first local elections . . . at the hands of the United States–led coalition.

On Saudi Arabia's election, see Scott Wilson, "Saudis Get Civics Lessons in Advance of Local Vote: Democracy New to Most in First Ballot Since '63," *Washington Post,* 8 February 2005; and Neil MacFarquhar, "For Many Saudi Men, a Day to Cherish," *New York Times,* 11 February 2005. On the wider implications, see Steven R. Weisman, "Mideast Mix: New Promise of Democracy and Threat of Instability," *New York Times,* 1 March 2005; David Ignatius, "Full-Speed Ahead in Middle East," *Washington Post,* 2 March 2005; Roger Cohen, "What's in It for America?: In the Middle East, Democracy Takes on Its Biggest Task: Killing a Radical Ideology," *New York Times,* 6 March 2005; Peter Baker, "Mideast Strides Lift Bush, but Challenges Remain," *Washington Post,* 8 March 2005; Todd S. Purdum, "For Bush, a Taste of Vindication in Mideast," *New York Times,* 9 March 2005; and Scott Wilson and Daniel Williams, "A New Power Rises Across Mideast: Advocates for Democracy Begin to Taste Success After Years of Fruitless Effort," *Washington Post,* 17 April 2005; Fouad Ajami, "Bush Country: America's President Bears the Gift of Wilsonian Redemption," *Wall Street Journal,* 16 May 2005; and Hassan M. Fattah, "Kuwait Grants Political Rights to Its Women," *New York Times,* 17 May 2005.

95   As one Arab prime minister recently . . . train cannot run ahead of the other."

Quoted in Roger Cohen, "An Obsession the World Doesn't Share: On Other Continents, America Doesn't Even Get Credit for What's Going Right," *New York Times,* 5 December 2004.

95   This is why, for example, calls for America . . . military solutions over the long haul.

For two examples of this, see Thomas L. Friedman, "Fly Me to the Moon," *New York Times,* 5 December 2004; and Robert MacFarlane, "A Declaration of Energy Independence: We Can End Our Reliance on Foreign Oil by 2035," *Wall Street Journal,* 10 December 2004.

98   In my mind, the truly central independent variable . . . nor Saudi Arabia, but Iran.

I first expressed this notion in "Dear Mr. President, Here's How to Make Sense of Your Second Term, Secure Your Legacy, and, Oh Yeah, Create a Future Worth Living," *Esquire,* February 2005. For a related argument, see Robin Wright, "In Mideast, Shiites May Be Unlikely U.S. Allies," *Washington Post,* 16 March 2005.

99   And it is Iran, which, by virtue of being a top-five player . . . by India and China.

The Department of Energy, using the sources *Oil & Gas Journal* and *World Oil,* lists Iran as number 2 in gas reserves (after Russia), and number 5/6 in oil (*Oil & Gas Journal* recognizes Canada's huge oil shale and oil sands reserves, while *World Oil* does not, hence the latter journal lists Iran as number 6 in its global rankings. Ahead of Iran in both oil rankings are Saudi Arabia, Iraq, Kuwait, and United Arab Emirates.

99   Iran is not a source for, or a supporter of, the Salafi . . . embodied by al Qaeda.

See Sageman, *Understanding Terror Networks,* p. 73.

99   In many ways, the Shiite revolutionary spirit . . . the government pretends to reform.

For a good overview of this, see Tim Judah, "Iran's Sullen Majority," *New York Times Magazine,* 1 September 2002; Nicholas D. Kristof, "Overdosing on Islam," *New York Times,* 12 May 2004; Nicholas D. Kristof, "Nuts with Nukes," *New York Times,* 19 May 2004; and Robin Wright, "25 Years Later, a Different Type of Revolution: Western Culture Is Seeping into Iranian Society, Despite Lingering Restrictions," *Washington Post,* 12 December 2004.

100   However, as the presidential election of 2005 proved . . . the state's perpetual failure in Iran.

For analysis of the election, see Michael Slackman, "Victory Is Seen for Hard-Liner in Iranian Vote: Reformers Fear Sharp Shift on Freedoms," *New York Times,* 25 June 2005; and Michael Slackman, "For the Poor in Iran, Voting Was About Making Ends Meet," *New York Times,* 4 July 2005.

101   Our grand bargain with Iran . . . its removal from the axis of evil.

Can movement be had in this manner? Surely. The United States recently dropped its opposition to Iran negotiating for entry into the World Trade Organization. We alone had vetoed the negotiations since Iran first applied for membership in 1996. On this, see Elaine Sciolino, "Trade Group to Start Talks to Admit Iran," *New York Times,* 27 May 2005.

102   Meanwhile, offering Tehran's government-reform . . . an unworkable approach.

For some of the details of the negotiations as they have unfolded, see Elaine Sciolino, "Europeans Say Iran Agrees to Freeze Uranium Enrichment: An Accord Is Hailed in Europe, but Greeted Cautiously in the U.S.," *New York Times,* 16 November 2004; Nazila Fathi, "Nuclear Deal with Iranians Has Angered Hard-Liners," *New York Times,* 17 November 2004; Greg Jaffe, "Non-Proliferation Enforcement Dilemma: U.S. Has Few Good Military Choices for Getting Iran, North Korea to Curb Nuclear Efforts," *Wall Street Journal,* 28 February 2005; and David E. Sanger and Steven R. Weisman, "U.S. and Allies Agree on Steps in Iran Dispute: Incentives and Penalties on Nuclear Issue," *New York Times,* 11 March 2005.

103   The growth of that relationship . . . conflict between Islamabad and New Delhi.

For a review of how this thaw followed the close call with war in early 2002, see John Lancaster, "India, Pakistan to Set Up Hotline: Talks End with Agreement to Maintain Moratorium on Nuclear Testing," *Washington Post,* 21 June 2004; Amy Waldman, "India and Pakistan: Good Fences Make Good Neighbors," *New York Times,* 4 July 2004; and Manjeet Kripalani, "How a Thirst Led to a Thaw," *Business Week,* 15 November 2004. For Pakistan's linkages to Iran's drive for nuclear power/weapons, see Douglas Jehl, "C.I.A. Says Pakistan Gave Iran Nuclear Aid: An Illicit Network Passed Bomb-Making Designs in the 90's," *New York Times,* 24 November 2004.

103   China's emerging strategic partnership with Iran . . . in the Gulf and Central Asia.

On China, see Robin Wright, "Iran's New Alliance with China Could Cost U.S. Leverage," *Washington Post,* 17 November 2004; and Nayan Chanda, "Crouching Tiger, Swimming Dragon: Will China Play Nice in the Persian Gulf?" *New York Times,* 11 April 2005. On India's similarly growing ties, see John Larkin and Jay Solomon, "India's Ties with Iran Pose Challenge for U.S.," *Wall Street Journal,* 25 March 2005.

CREATING THE NEW RULE SET ON GLOBAL TERRORISM

109 During the presidential election campaign of 2004 . . . such threats a "nuisance."
Naturally, the Bush campaign jumped all over this quote, and for good reason. Kerry, while spelling out the long-term goal correctly, nonetheless called into question his commitment to the difficult short- and mid-term tasks involved in making that happen. In short, the quote came off as exceedingly naïve and idealistic, or too big of a reach at this point in time. For details, see "Bush Campaign to Base Ad on Kerry Terror Quote (Democrats: GOP Again Taking Senator's Words out of Context)," CNN.com's "Inside Politics," 11 October 2004, found online at http://www.cnn.com/2004/ALLPOLITICS/10/10/bush.kerry.terror/.

111 By relying so extensively on reservists . . . on demand, no matter how much it hurts").
For some good analysis of this phenomenon, see "Find the Deputies: They Could Be in Baghdad or Kabul," *The Economist,* 29 December 2004.

112 So when the presidential election campaign . . . Special Operations Command.
For details on this and other proposals Kerry made regarding the military, see Barbara Slavin and Jill Lawrence, "Follow-Through Is Critical," *USA Today,* 3 June 2004.

113 Why? I agree with Secretary Rumsfeld that what SOCOM . . . for killing bad guys.
As one Civil Affairs commander put it in a recent article over his plan to move Civil Affairs units from Special Operations Command in Tampa and give them back to the U.S. Army: Rumsfeld "wants the SOCOM guys to focus more on kinetic stuff"; see Thomas E. Ricks, "Army Contests Rumsfeld Bid on Occupation: Special Operations Would Lose Cadre of Nation-Building Civil Affairs Troops," *Washington Post,* 16 January 2005.

113 I want them to have the loosest rule sets possible . . . never-ending bodyguard jobs.
And that is just what Secretary Rumsfeld has ordered up. See David S. Cloud and Greg Jaffe, "U.S. Drafts Order for Special Forces: Troops Are Being Prepared for Clandestine Operations Against Terrorist Groups," *Wall Street Journal,* 24 November 2004.

116 The character of Kaiser Soze appeared in the 1995 crime film *The Usual Suspects.*
Kevin Spacey won the Oscar for Best Supporting Actor for his portrayal of the seemingly small-time hood Verbal Gint.

116 Is either bin Laden or al-Zarqawi the all-powerful figure . . . popular imagination?
For a fascinating example of this phenomenon in media coverage, see Craig

Whitlock, "Grisly Path to Power in Iraq's Insurgency: Zarqawi Emerges as Al Qaeda Rival, Ally," *Washington Post,* 27 September 2004. In the article, he is described as a one-legged Palestinian whose uncanny ability to avoid capture has led some people to doubt he really exists. Other intelligence officials say he has two legs and is real. But as one terrorism expert puts it in the article, "Certainly he's a real figure, but he's a myth-laden figure, and it's difficult to discern where the lines are."

117   The strategy of the Big Bang in the Middle East . . . killing to its logical conclusion.
"Speeding the killing" is a concept I drew from Bret Stephens's op-ed about harsh military responses used by Israel vis-à-vis the Palestinians. Here is what he wrote:

> Taken together, these measures [assassinating terrorist leaders, harsh re-prisals on suicide bombings] prove what a legion of diplomats, pundits and reporters have striven to deny: there is a military solution to the conflict. This is true in two senses. First, a sufficiently strong military response to terrorism does not simply feed a cycle of violence (although a weak military response does); rather, it speeds the killing to a conclusion. That makes it possible for Israelis and Palestinians to resume a semblance of normal life. Second, a military solution creates new practical realities, and new strategic understandings from which previously elusive political opportunities may emerge.

See Bret Stephens, "The Way We Live Now (in Israel)," *Wall Street Journal,* 14 October 2004.

118   We see this phenomenon at work . . . offers for our retreat from the field of battle.
For examples, see Douglas Jehl and David Johnston, "In Video Message, Bin Laden Issues Warning to U.S.," *New York Times,* 29 October 2004; and Don Van Natta, "Sizing Up the New Toned-Down Bin Laden: He Is Acting Like an Elder Statesman from a Borderless Muslim Nation," *New York Times,* 29 October 2004.

118   The danger in this for al Qaeda is that when it switches . . . seeing in Saudi society.
On this change, see Craig Whitlock, "Al Qaeda Shifts Its Strategy in Saudi Arabia: Focus Placed on U.S. and Other Western Targets in Bid to Bolster Network, Officials Say," *Washington Post,* 19 December 2004.

119   Bin Laden and his lieutenants have long . . . superpower is a 4GW-like insurgency.
As Colonel Hammes puts it in his *The Sling and the Stone*: "Not only is 4GW the only kind of war America has ever lost, we have done so three times: Vietnam, Lebanon, and Somalia" (p. 3).

119   But in reality, al Qaeda, and foreign fighters . . . in defeating the Soviets.
Sageman, *Understanding Terror Networks,* pp. 56–59.

120   Listen to Zarqawi himself . . . and our future looks more forbidding by the day.
Quoted in Fouad Ajami, "Iraq's New History: Only Iraqis Can Reclaim Their Country from the Purveyors of Terror," *Wall Street Journal,* 29 June 2004.

121   As one front-page *Wall Street Journal* . . . of footloose militants looking for work.

Andrew Higgins, Guy Chazan, and Gregory L. White, "How Russia's Chechen Quagmire Became Front for Radical Islam: Aligning with Arab Militants Gained Money, Fighters for Rebel Leader Basayev; Swapping 'Che' for Allah," *Wall Street Journal,* 16 September 2004.

121 A good example of this phenomenon is seen in . . . he of Beslan massacre fame.
Vladimir Isachenkov, "Chechens' Terror Links Drawing Attention," Associated Press, 26 September 2004.

121 Al Qaeda got a new franchise . . . strategy of preemptive war inside the Kremlin.
For both sides on this development see the editorial, "Preventive War: A Failed Doctrine," *New York Times,* 12 September 2004; and "Russia May Fight Terror Pre-Emptively," Associated Press, 13 September 2004.

121 According to our best estimates, al Qaeda's . . . network of Southeast Asian groups.
Sageman, *Understanding Terror Networks,* pp. 46–51 and 70–73 and Chapter 5 ("Social Networks and the Jihad"), pp. 137–74.

122 When we can't bag them, then we'll seek to tag them . . . chock-full of civilians.
Defense Science Board, *Transition To and From Hostilities,* pp. xvi–xvii and 163–73.

124 Good examples of this process can be seen . . . obviously centered inside the Gap.
On these developments see John Diamond, "CIA Plans Riskier, More Aggressive Espionage: Campaign Would Send Undercover Officers to Get 'Close-in Access' to Hostile Groups, Nations," *USA Today,* 18 November 2004; Barton Gellman, "Secret Unit Expands Rumsfeld's Domain: New Espionage Branch Delving into CIA Territory," *Washington Post,* 23 January 2005; and Eric Schmitt, "Pentagon Sends Its Spies to Join Fight on Terror," *New York Times,* 24 January 2005.

125 This is a vitally important rule set to create . . . CIA's secret "rendition" program.
For an overview of the "rendition" program, see Dana Priest, "Jet Is an Open Secret in Terror War," *Washington Post,* 27 December 2004; Dana Priest, "Long-Term Plan Sought for Terror Suspects," *Washington Post,* 2 January 2005; Bob Herbert, "Torture, American Style: Handing People Over to Brutal Regimes," *New York Times,* 11 February 2005; Douglas Jehl and David Johnston, "Within C.I.A., Growing Fears of Prosecution," *New York Times,* 27 February 2005; Douglas Jehl and David Johnston, "Rule Change Lets C.I.A. Freely Send Suspects Abroad: Interrogation at Issue; Official Defends Program as Being Helpful in Effort on Terror," *New York Times,* 6 March 2005; and Michael Scheuer, "A Fine Rendition: The C.I.A. Was Right to Ship Terror Suspects Abroad," *New York Times,* 11 March 2005.

125 This is clearly an emergent rule set . . . rationalized to our allies' content.
On this need, see Don Van Atta, "U.S. Recruits a Rough Ally to Be a Jailer," *New York Times,* 1 May 2005; Philip Shishkin, "Uzbek Crackdown Fuels Instability in Central Asia: As They Bury Their Fallen, Andijan Residents Say Innocents Were Killed; U.S. Ally Cites Terror Threat," *Wall Street Journal,* 19 May 2005; and Somini Sengupta and Salman Masood, "Guantanamo Comes to Define U.S. to

Muslims: A Champion of Rights Is Accused of Torture," *New York Times,* 21 May 2005.

126   For example, a two-man sniper team came close . . . for weeks on end in 2002.

John Malvo and his underage "partner" killed their first victim on 2 October 2002 in the suburbs of Washington, D.C. Both were finally apprehended on 24 October 2002, after nine more killings.

129   In sum, the Core needs a common definition . . . routes for achieving that prevention.

I first articulated these concepts in my article, "The New Magnum Force: What Dirty Harry Can Teach the New Geneva Conventions," *Wired,* February 2005.

130   The new rules need to define how this Core-within-the-Core . . . snatch or kill suspected terrorists.

On this issue, see "Italy Seeks 'CIA Kidnap Agents': Italian Authorities Have Issued Arrest Warrants for 13 People They Claim Are Agents 'Linked to the CIA,'" *BBC News,* 24 June 2005.

130   In a global body where Libya gets to chair . . . some punks really have gotten lucky.

Libya was elected to chair the UN's Human Rights Commission in 2003.

Chapter Three: GROWING THE CORE BY SECURING THE EAST

135   More than a few negative reviews . . . the Middle East) for quite some time."

See www.thomaspmbarnett.com/reviews/reviews_index.htm.

LOCKING IN CHINA AT TODAY'S PRICES

137   As we planned the first week of our lengthy adoption trip . . . official program began.

For my weblog diary of this trip, see www.thomaspmbarnett.com/china/index.htm.

138   I ended up lecturing at both Beijing University . . . Central Party School in Beijing.

For my description of these interactions, see the blog post entitled "Theory of a Peacefully Rising China," at http://www.thomaspmbarnett.com/weblog/archives/000764.html.

139   What the Beijing reformist researchers liked . . . not one that needed avoiding.

Niu Ke originally contacted me on the basis of an article written about *The Pentagon's New Map* in the Chinese newspaper *Nanfang Daily* by Yong Xue, a Ph.D. candidate at Yale University. Find a rough translation of that review, along with my commentary, online at http://www.thomaspmbarnett.com/weblog/archives2/000573.html.

143   This is why China, while accounting for roughly . . . of the world's steel production.

This details are drawn from Keith Bradsher, "The Two Faces of China: Giant Global Producer Is Expanding Its Role as a Consumer, Creating Threats and Opportunity," *New York Times,* 6 December 2005.

143 Guangzhou's skyline in southern China . . . all of it was built in the past fifteen years.

My wife Vonne and I took, along with our group of fellow adopting parents, an evening boat tour of the Pearl River in Guangzhou in late August 2004. As the boat chugged past dozens upon dozens of high-rise office and apartment buildings in a seemingly never-ending procession, I asked a local Chinese man what the skyline looked like at the beginning of the 1990s, and he replied that there was no skyline at the beginning of the 1990s.

144 For example, its space program places it somewhere . . . classic 1930s period.

China launched its first man in space in October 2003. For a sense of its film industry, see Howard W. French, "China Hurries to Animate Its Film Industry," *New York Times,* 1 December 2004; and Manohla Dargis, "Glamour's New Orientation: The Era of Lustrous Screen Sirens Lives On, Thousands of Miles from Hollywood," *New York Times,* 5 December 2004.

144 In sports, China's emergence on the Olympic stage . . . sensibilities of the 1970s.

China finished third in the overall medal count in the Athens Olympics of 2004 (second in gold medals) and will host the 2008 Summer Games in Beijing. See also Becky Dubin Jenkins, "Chinese Hurdler Lands a Smoking Deal," *USA Today,* 22 October 2004. Tell me that doesn't sound like 1950s America! On the burgeoning sexual revolution in China, see "China's Sexual Revolution," *China Daily,* 12 November 2003; Kathy Chen and Leslie T. Chang, "China Takes Aim at Racy, Violent TV Shows," *Wall Street Journal,* 24 May 2004.

144 China's construction and stock market booms . . . places it closer to our 1980s.

For examples, see David Murphy, "Chinese Construction Companies Go Global: Evolving Know-How and Low Costs Help Firms Score Contracts Abroad," *Wall Street Journal,* 12 May 2004; and Howard D. French, "New Boomtowns Change Path of China's Growth," *New York Times,* 28 July 2004. On the burgeoning financial markets, see Joel Baglole, "China's Listings Lose Steam: Several Big Stock Sales Are Put Off Amid Accounting Questions," *Wall Street Journal,* 26 April 2004; Peter Wonacott, "As Investors Rush into China, Cautionary Tales Start to Pile Up: China Life Says It's 'Gold Mine,' but Fails to Mention Probe by Government Auditors; Scandals as Sign of Progress," *Wall Street Journal,* 17 May 2004; Darren McDermott, Bruce Stanley, and Cris Prystay, "Derivatives Trade Goes Sour in China," *Wall Street Journal,* 2 December 2004; Gary Rivlin, "Talk of a Bubble as Venture Capitalists Flock to China: Investors Show a Willingness to Traverse 16 Time Zones in Search of the Next Start-Up Success," *New York Times,* 6 December 2004; and Jeff D. Opdyke and Laura Santini, "Emerging Ways to Invest in the Wild, Wild East: Some Pros Tout Buying Stocks Directly, but Risks Are Immense," *Wall Street Journal,* 9 March 2005.

144 The country's often brutal labor conditions . . . into industry recalls 1940s America.

For an overview (country, extractive, urban), see Joseph Kahn, "China Crushes Peasant Protest, Turning 3 Friends into Enemies," *New York Times,* 13 October 2004; Edward Cody, "About 150 Feared Dead in China Mine Blast," *Boston Globe,* 22 October 2004; and Charles Hutzler, "China's Workers Vent Anger:

Protests Grow Common as Privatizations Shatter Job Security," *Wall Street Journal*, 18 April 2005.

144 China's go-go capitalism is as frantic as our own . . . its robber barons and pervasive corruption.

For examples of such descriptions, see Kathy Chen, "China Faces Rash of Protests: Officials' Abuses of Power and Social Inequities Provoke Unrest," *Wall Street Journal*, 5 November 2004; and Charles Hutzler and Kathy Chen, "China Grapples with Social Ills: Leaders Fear Economic Boom's Inequities Imperil Stability, Growth," *Wall Street Journal*, 2 March 2005.

145 This is why current descriptions of China's emergence . . . more manageable pace.

See Robert J. Samuelson, "Great Wall of Unknowns," *Washington Post*, 26 May 2004; Kathy Chen and Constance Mitchell-Ford, "China Sees Success in Taming Growth: Senior Official Says Prices of Commodities Are Easing, Investment Is Toning Down," *Wall Street Journal*, 1 June 2004; and Andrew Browne et al., "China's Expansion May Be Easing: Soft Landing Could Stem Inflationary Pressures Threatening Global Stability," *Wall Street Journal*, 11 June 2004.

146 Right now one of the greatest migrations in human history . . . and head for the city.

On this, see Jim Yardley, "In a Tidal Wave, China's Masses Pour from Farm to City," *New York Times*, 12 September 2004; Leslie T. Chang, "At 18, Min Finds a Path to Success in Migration Wave: Like Millions of Others, She Left Country for the City, Ill-Prepared for Life There," *Wall Street Journal*, 8 November 2004; and Jim Yardley, "Rural Exodus for Work Fractures Chinese Family: The Great Divide (A Missing Generation)," *New York Times*, 21 December 2004.

146 By latest estimates, China will become a majority urban . . . the same tipping point.

Most population projects, including those by the UN, predict a total Chinese population of about 1.5 billion before 2020, and most predict an urban population in the range of 750 million by the 2015 to 2020 time frame. For a good comparison of these many projections and their inherent uncertainty, see Gerhard K. Heilig, "Can China Feed Itself: A System for Evaluation of Policy Options," International Institute for Applied Systems Analysis, found online at http://www.iiasa.ac.at/Research/LUC/ChinaFood/index_h.htm. The world will become majority urban in 2007, a serious tipping point for globalization; see Irwin Arieff, "Half World's People to Live in Cities by 2007," Reuters, 17 February 2005.

147 There is so much counterfeit paper money in China . . . and currency exchanges.

My estimate is based on numerous conversations with Chinese officials and businessmen and street vendors in August 2004. For an overview of global counterfeiting of U.S. currency, see Lee McIntyre, "Making Money Keeps Getting Easier," *Regional Review* (published by the Federal Reserve Bank of Boston), Quarter 2, 2000, found online at http://www.bos.frb.org/economic/nerr/rr2000/q2/money.htm.

147 Over time, such gross inefficiencies will be . . . squash these negative activities.

On such efforts, see Andrew Browne, "Zhou's Theories Clash with China's Realities: Scholarly Central Bank Head Finds Market-Based Tactics Hit Local Political Obstacles," *Wall Street Journal*, 15 November 2004; Howard W. French, "Whose

Patent Is It, Anyway?: Foreign Companies Confront China on Rights to Intellectual Property," *New York Times,* 5 March 2005; and James T. Areddy and Peter Wonacott, "As China Rises, Sinking Stocks Spark Middle-Class Protests: Investors Accuse Communists of Hyping Market Outlook; Dilemma of State Shares," *Wall Street Journal,* 21 April 2005.

147 For now, the Party allows a certain amount . . . their newfound wealth from fraud.
For a sense of how this unfolds in terms of Party leadership, see Howard W. French, "China Opens a Window on the Really Big Ideas: The Public Gets to Hear the Great Decisions of State Kicked Around," *New York Times,* 2 June 2004; and Keith Bradsher, "In Hong Kong, China Prefers Power to Law: The Party Promotes Legal Debate, but Only Up to a Point," *New York Times,* 20 March 2005.

147 The boom areas of local political activism in China . . . off their lands by developers.
See Jonathan Kaufman, "Tiananmen Square Now Draws Protestors with Housing Issues: It's All Very Middle Class—Apartment Owners Who Have Pool Problems," *Wall Street Journal,* 9 June 2004; Philip P. Pan, "China's Orphans Feel Brunt of Power: Party Thwarts AIDS Activist's Unofficial School," *Washington Post,* 14 September 2004; Edward Cody, "Workers in China Shed Passivity: Spate of Walkouts Shakes Factories," *Washington Post,* 27 November 2004; and Edward Cody, "System No Help to China's Laid-Off Workers: Couple Who Petitioned for Promised Benefits Get Jail Terms Instead," *Washington Post,* 24 January 2005. For how all that impacts Chinese industrial development, see Ginny Parker, "A Tricky Transition in China: Manufacturers Adapt to Lure More-Sophisticated Consumers," *Wall Street Journal,* 23 November 2004.

147 Probably the most impressive change has occurred . . . in response to these protests.
See Edward Cody, "Chinese Newspapers Put Spotlight on Polluters: Factory Shutdowns Follow Reports," *Washington Post,* 25 May 2004; and Peter Wonacott, "Beijing Invokes Environmentalism to Slow Projects: Watchdog Agency Takes Unusually Tough Stand Against Power Plants," *Wall Street Journal,* 19 January 2005.

148 This rule-set reset has allowed provincial governments . . . politics and economics."
Keith Bradsher, "Chinese Provinces Form Regional Economic Bloc: Beijing Backs Move to Lower Barriers," *New York Times,* 2 June 2004.

148 For example, China goes from having no one . . . certain politically sensitive sites.
For examples, see Joseph Kahn, "China Is Filtering Phone Text Messages to Regulate Criticism," *New York Times,* 3 July 2004; Tom Zeller, Jr., "Beijing Loves the Web Until the Web Talks Back: Economic Promise of Internet in China Brings New Restrictions on Speech," *New York Times,* 6 December 2004; Howard W. French, "Chinese Censors and Web Users Match Wits," *New York Times,* 4 March 2005; Jim Yardley, "A Hundred Cellphones Bloom, And Chinese Take to the Street," *New York Times,* 25 April 2005; and Nicholas D. Kristof, "Death by a Thousand Blogs: China's Leaders Have a New Watchdog," *New York Times,* 24 May 2005.

148   My favorite recent example of this futile censorship . . . a concert tour in China.
      K. Wilcox, "Pop Notes," *Washington Post*, 2 June 2004.

148   No single society has ever aged more quickly . . . to restrict population growth.
      For a quick overview, see Joseph Kahn, "The Most Populous Nation Faces a Population Crisis," *New York Times*, 30 May 2004.

149   This policy has been enormously successful . . . population total of 1.3 billion.
      So successful that the backlash has begun. See Charles Hutzler and Leslie T. Chang, "China Weighs Easing Its Harsh 'One Child' Rule: Family-Planning Policies Have Long Drawn Flak; Demographic Issues Loom," *Wall Street Journal*, 4 October 2004; and Howard W. French, "As Girls 'Vanish,' Chinese City Battles Tide of Abortions," *New York Times*, 17 February 2005.

149   The notion that China will be awash in males . . . burn off all those "excess males."
      See Valerie M. Hudson and Andrea M. den Boer, *Bare Branches: The Security Implications of Asia's Surplus Male Population* (Cambridge, MA: MIT Press, 2004). For the more general argument, see the report by Richard P. Cincotta, Robert Engelman, and Danielle Anastasion, *The Security Demographic: Population and Civil Conflict After the Cold War* (Washington D.C. Population Action International, 2003).

149   The problem with this theory, however . . . parents and *four* elderly grandparents.
      I heard this concept from a surprising number of Chinese, both on the street and in research centers.

149   With China opening up so much in terms of overseas tourism . . . *someone* to marry.
      For details, see James Brooke, "China Sees Chances for Fun and Profit Overseas: More Air Service, Tourism and Investment Flow from Mainland to the South Pacific," *New York Times*, 25 November 2004.

151   China's rising influence in the global economy . . . words" in global manufacturing.
      See Peter Engardio and Dexter Roberts, " 'The China Price': They Are the Three Scariest Words in U.S. Industry," *Business Week*, 6 December 2004.

151   But the surging protectionist sentiment of . . . strikes me as rather disingenuous.
      For examples, see Engardio and Roberts, " 'The China Price' "; and Michael J. Mandel, "Does It Matter If China Catches Up to the U.S.?: History Says It Won't—If Political Stability Allows Trade to Flow Freely," *Business Week*, 6 December 2004.

152   Whenever the United States starts making arguments . . . at the Olympics anymore.
      For an overview of this globalization process in the NBA, see Jonathan B. Weinbach, "The NBA's Foreign Exchange," *Wall Street Journal*, 28 January 2005.

152   But already we're seeing the unbelievable . . . nothing in terrible labor conditions.

See Jim Yardley and David Barboza, "Help Wanted: China Finds Itself with a Labor Shortage," *New York Times,* 3 April 2005.

152   We're already seeing the latter occur . . . have left China for neighboring Malaysia.

For an example, see Keith Bradsher, "Chinese Automaker Plans Assembly Line in Malaysia: Rivals Are Keeping an Eye on the Cars, Which They Say Too Closely Resemble Their Own," *New York Times,* 19 October 2004.

152   Having noted that long-term inevitability . . . economists call the "China Syndrome."

On this concept, see Peter S. Goodman, "Booming China Devouring Raw Materials: Producers and Suppliers Struggle to Feed a Voracious Appetite," *Washington Post,* 21 May 2004.

153   For example, China's demand for minerals . . . infrastructure as a result.

For details, see Nicole Itano, "To Supply China, South African Mines Want More Trains," *New York Times,* 21 December 2004. See also Arnaud Zajtman, "Chinese Demand Boosts DR Congo Mines," *BBC News,* 16 March 2005.

153   Likewise, it's not just commodity producers . . . in 2003 to China's market alone.

See Thomas L. Friedman, "Jumping Out of Sick Bay," *New York Times,* 29 April 2004; and Sebastian Moffett and Phred Dvorak, "As Japan Recovers, an Unlikely Source Gets Credit: China; After Long Seeing Jobs Flee, Tokyo Now Finds Benefits of Its Neighbor's Boom," *Wall Street Journal,* 4 May 2004.

153   China's demand for metal is so . . . still sitting around from the socialist past.

James Brooke, "Asian Scavengers Feed China's Hunger for Steel," *New York Times,* 11 June 2004.

153   Naturally, when China revives a country's key industry . . . between the two states.

Todd Benson, "China Fuels Brazil's Dream of Being a Steel Power," *New York Times,* 21 May 2004; and Geraldo Samor and Joel Millman, "Brazil Seeks to Broaden China Trade," *Wall Street Journal,* 21 May 2004. See also Simon Romero, "Canada's Oil: China in Line as U.S. Rival," *New York Times,* 23 December 2004; Chris Buckley, "Venezuela Agrees to Export Oil and Gas to China," *New York Times,* 28 December 2004; and Juan Forero, "China's Oil Diplomacy in Latin America: Deals with Venezuela Include Offers of Needed Development Aid," *New York Times,* 1 March 2005.

153   Anyway, the old-line manufacturing sector . . . from Asia—China in particular.

For details, see Elliot Blair Smith, "China Spreads Wealth: U.S. Firms Stands to Gain from Growth," *USA Today,* 18 January 2005.

154   The members of the Association . . . by China's powerful undertow.

See Jane Perlez, "Southeast Asia Urged to Form Economic Bloc," *New York Times,* 29 November 2004.

154   China's insatiable demand for raw materials . . . too much competition from China.

For details, see Patrick Barta, "Laos Is Looking Like a Gold Mine to Foreigners: Boom in Commodity Prices Draws Investments by Mining Companies Straining to Find New Deposits," *Wall Street Journal,* 16 September 2004; and James Brooke, "Finding a Mother Lode in Mongolia: Close to Mineral-Hungry China, Big Veins of Copper and Gold," *New York Times,* 14 October 2004.

154 So if China wants lots of foreign investment flows . . . community in general.
For examples, see Mary Kissel and Laura Santini, "Global Stock Exchanges Vie for a Slice of China's IPO Pie," *Wall Street Journal,* 2 December 2004; and "U.S. Regulators Formally Investigate China Life IPO," Reuters, 29 December 2004.

154 Moreover, if a private-sector company is big enough . . . the first time in its history).
For details, see Peter S. Goodman, "China's Revolutionary Tactic: Bailout," *Washington Post,* 26 August 2004.

154 If China wants to gain "market status" in the WTO . . . Avon enter its marketplace.
See Charles Hutzler and Qiu Haixu, "China Contesting 'Nonmarket Economy' Status," *Wall Street Journal,* 24 June 2004. See also Leslie T. Chang, "China Opens Retail to Foreign Investors," *Wall Street Journal,* 1 June 2004; Leslie T. Chang, "China Prepares Rules on Direct Sales," *Wall Street Journal,* 9 November 2004; and Jiang Jingjing, "Wal-Mart's China Inventory to Hit US$18B This Year," *Business Weekly,* 29 November 2004.

154 If China wants help in reducing its roughly half . . . Goldman Sachs just did).
On this transaction, see David Barboza, "Horse Trading for a Venture in China: Goldman to 'Donate' $67 Million to Cover Losses at a Failed Brokerage Firm," *New York Times,* 4 March 2004.

155 And if China wants to continue enjoying . . . needs to start purchasing U.S. companies.
On this natural development, see Greg Ip, "Unocal Sale Could Signal New Directions: Purchase of U.S. Company by Chinese Firm Is Seen as Shift in Investment Approach," *Wall Street Journal,* 24 June 2005; and Henry Sender, "Meet China Inc.: Topping Japan Inc. of 1980s; Corporate China Shows Muscle as Host of Global Bids Emerge, Marking Only Start of Deal Flow," *Wall Streeet Journal,* 24 June 2005.

155 This acquisition strategy, in turn . . . is their senior managerial talent.
The figure of seventy-five thousand executives is cited in Kevin Maney, "Chinese Companies Tap U.S. Firms for Management Training," *USA Today,* 29 June 2005. See also Geoffrey A. Fowler, "Buying Sprees by China Firms Is a Bet on Value of U.S. Brands," *Wall Street Journal,* 24 June 2005.

155 And so America needs to ask itself . . . at this point in its rapid embrace of both capitalism and globalization.
For a good summary of this debate, see Neil King, Jr., Greg Hitt, and Jeffrey Ball, "Oil Battle Sets Showdown Over China: CNOOC's Offer for Unocal Raises Stakes in Conflict Over Sino-U.S. Ties; Threat, Rival or Vast Market?" *Wall Street Journal,* 24 June 2005; and Greg Ip and Neil King, Jr., "Is China's Rapid Economic Development Good for the U.S.?" *Wall Street Journal,* 27 June 2005.

156 If the United States is committed to winning . . . locking China in at today's prices.
I first expressed this notion in my article, "Dear Mr. President, Here's How to

Make Sense of Your Second Term, Secure Your Legacy, and, Oh Yeah, Create a Future Worth Living," *Esquire,* February 2005.

157   That promise is still on the books . . . like some blue law from a by-gone era.

It is set forth in the 1979 Taiwan Relations Act, which obliges the United States to assist in Taiwan's self-defense, declaring any threat from China to be of "grave concern."

159   Did China complicate things with its in-Taiwan's-face . . . People's Congress session?

For details, see Philip P. Pan, "China Puts Threat to Taiwan into Law: Move Could Reverse Recent Warming in Cross-Strait Relations," *Washington Post,* 14 March 2005. See also Jason Dean, "Taiwan Straits' Political Gulf: An Island's Economy Turns to China, Independent Spirit Persists," *Wall Street Journal,* 23 March 2005. But also see China's moves to relax tensions in the aftermath in Edward Cody, "China Opens Travel to Taiwan: In a Bid to Ease Tensions, Tourists Allowed to Visit Island," *Washington Post,* 21 May 2005.

159   Hu had a hard time wringing that position . . . that said Hu was weak on Taiwan.

For analysis on this, see Joseph Kahn, "Former Leader Is Still a Power in China's Life: Repressive Effect Seen in Jiang's Long Reign," *New York Times,* 16 July 2004; Joseph Kahn, "Hu Takes Full Power in China as He Gains Control of Military: Orderly Transfer Gives Freedom to Maneuver," *New York Times,* 20 September 2004; and George Melloan, "Hu Faces Rising Distrust of the Communist Party," *Wall Street Journal,* 15 March 2005.

160   As Robert Wright has said . . . Don't fight the inevitable.

Robert Wright, *Nonzero: The Logic of Human Destiny* (New York: Vintage Books, 2000), p. 230.

160   In the run-up to the December 2004 national elections . . . the Republic of China.

For analysis of this close call, see Trevor Corson, "Strait-jacket: December Elections Could Edge Taiwan Closer to a Symbolic Declaration of Independence—and the United States Toward Military Conflict with China," *Atlantic Monthly,* December 2004.

IN THE FUTURE, AMERICA'S MOST IMPORTANT ALLIES WILL BE NEW CORE STATES

162   When the book came out . . . from Asian journalists but none from European media.

For example, I gave interviews to the *Nihon Keizai Shimbun,* the *Asahi Shimbun,* and the *Yomiuri Shimbun* from Japan.

163   When asked by a congressional commission . . . to that effect, I did so in late 2004.

My testimony, entitled "Testimony Submitted to the Overseas Basing Commission by Dr. Thomas P.M. Barnett, Professor, Naval War College [9 November 2004]," is found online at www.thomaspmbarnett.com/published/OBCTestimony/pdf.

164   The logic of the balance-of-power enthusiasts . . . much less involvement.

For examples, see Zbigniew Brzezinski, "How to Make New Enemies," *New York Times,* 25 October 2004; Charles Krauthammer, "Tomorrow's Threat," *Washing-*

ton Post, 21 January 2005; and Robert Kagan and William Kristol, eds., *Present Dangers: Crisis and Opportunity in American Foreign and Defense Policy* (Washington, D.C.: Encounter Books, 2000).

165 The new long-term military strategy of the United States . . . within failed states.
For a good description, see Jaffe, "Rumsfeld Details Big Military Shift in New Document."

167 First, the New Core is where the action is on new technology.
This is true for a variety of reasons, but especially because the New Core is where you'll find technologists willing to take the greatest risks in coming years. For a good example of this, see Andrew Pollack, "Cancer Therapy Dropped in U.S. Is Revived in China," *New York Times,* 25 February 2005.

167 When the German industrial giant Siemens AG . . . you know the worm has turned.
See Matthew Karnitschnig, "Vaunted German Engineers Face Competition from China: Siemens Taps Beijing for Help in Designing New Phone," *Wall Street Journal,* 15 July 2004.

167 The Old Core is somewhat saturated . . . places like Brazil, Russia, India, and China.
For an overview, see the special-issue article "Tech's Future," *Business Week,* 27 September 2004. For more specifics, see Chris Buckley, "Nokia Makes the Call: China Will Be No. 1; Chief Sees It Passing U.S. in Next 3 Years," *New York Times,* 24 February 2005; "The Real Digital Divide," *The Economist,* 10 March 2005; and Rebecca Buckman, "In China, Look Beyond Portals: Smartest Internet Plays May Have Mobile-Phone Connection," *Wall Street Journal,* 29 March 2005.

167 The next billion customers will come overwhelmingly from the New Core.
Ethan Zuckerman, of Harvard's Berkman Center for Internet and Society, makes basically the same point about Internet users; see his article on this subject, "Making Room for the Third World in the Second Superpower," found online at http://h2odev.law.harvard.edu/ezuckerman/sstw.html.

168 In the end, China will become the center . . . alliance-building process as well.
For a description of this fear, see Michael Lind, "How the U.S. Became the World's Dispensable Nation," *Financial Times,* 25 January 2005; and Francis Fukuyama, "All Quiet on the Eastern Front?," *New York Times,* 1 March 2005.

168 As such, both states can often display rather . . . a United States–dominated Old Core.
For details, see "Lula to Boost Brazil-China Alliance," *China Daily,* 22 May 2004; Erin E. Arvedlund, "Investors of the World, Here's the Word on Putin, Inc.," *New York Times,* 2 March 2005; and Gregory L. White, "Yukos Puts Putin in Quandary: Mixed Signals Raise Questions About Control Over Government," *Wall Street Journal,* 25 April 2005.

168 This is a crucial step for any rising power . . . giant is a very good sign in this regard.
See Todd Benson, "Brazil: Free Software's Biggest and Best Friend," *New York Times,* 29 March 2004.

169 In reality, of course, where America belongs . . . hydrogen-age energy).

For an example, see Joel Garreau, "Inventing Our Evolution: We're Almost Able to Build Better Human Beings. But Are We Ready?" *Washington Post*, 16 May 2005.

169   It's this sort of fear that pushes Japan to announce . . . of Imperial Japan, no less).

Anthony Faiola, "Japan to Join U.S. Policy on Taiwan: Growth of China Seen Behind Shift," *Washington Post*, 18 February 2005. See also Yong Xue, "Is the Empire Striking Back?: Keep Japan Out of the Taiwan Debate," *New York Times*, 16 March 2005. For coverage of the resulting tension, see Sebastian Moffett and Charles Hutzler, "Protests in China Against Japan Reflect Regional Power Struggle," *Wall Street Journal*, 20 April 2005; Raymond Bonner and Norimitsu Onishi, "Japan's Chief Apologizes for War Misdeeds: 'Deep Remorse' Voiced at an Asia-Africa Summit Meeting," *New York Times*, 23 April 2005; and Jim Yardley, "China Moves to Crack Down on Protests Against Japan," *New York Times*, 23 April 2005.

169   It's also what pushes Washington to pressure . . . its arms-trade embargo on China.

On the larger issues here, see Mark Landler, "Europeans See Pluses in Ending China Ban: Commercial Ties and Diplomacy Lead to Dispute with U.S.," *New York Times*, 24 February 2004; Raphael Minder, "China's Focus on Galileo Pinpoints U.S. Security Fears: Beijing's Involvement in Europe's Rival Navigation Service to GPS Has Washington Chiefs Worried," *Financial Times*, 24 February 2004; and Thom Shanker and David E. Sanger, "U.S. Lawmakers Warn Europe on Arms Sales to China," *New York Times*, 2 March 2005.

169   A more realistic way to look at it is to say . . . group is commensurately extended.

For a good example of this, look at how China has worked to discourage the world from considering Japan's elevation to the UN Security Council as a permanent member. For example, see Joseph Kahn, "If 22 Million Chinese Prevail at U.N., Japan Won't: A Grass-Roots Campaign to Block a Bid to Join the Security Council," *New York Times*, 1 April 2005.

170   China's significant push into Africa in recent years . . . investment packages galore.

For a great overview, see Karby Leggett, "China Flexes Economic Muscle Throughout Burgeoning Africa: Beijing Forges Deep Alliances with War-Torn Nations, Countering U.S. Influence; A Dam Gets Built on the Nile," *Wall Street Journal*, 29 March 2005. See also Peter S. Goodman, "China Invests Heavily in Sudan's Oil Industry: Beijing Supplies Arms Used on Villagers," *Washington Post*, 23 December 2004.

171   The Chinese Communist Party's ruling legitimacy is based . . . increasingly marketized conditions.

The estimate of 25 million new nonfarm jobs each year comes from various investment analysts on Wall Street. China has averaged roughly half that amount in recent years (12–13 million new nonfarm jobs created), suggesting that it's almost impossible for the economy to grow fast enough to meet the rising demand for urban jobs.

171   My consulting company, The New Rule Sets Project . . . Brazil (Seam States) and Iran (Gap).

For background and anlysis of this wargame, see the site www.newmapgame.com. For a press account, see Alec Russell, "War game gives Washington a lesson in power," *Daily Telegraph*, 4 June 2005.

173   **And then there's the defense-industrial complex . . . "near-peer competitor threat" that China represents.**
A recent Government Accounting Office report ("Assessment of Selected Major Weapons Programs," GAO-05-901, March 2005) describes 54 programs with a lifetime cost of approximately $800 billion. Extrapolating from that total, which is roughly two-thirds the current pool of programs, one can estimate a total Pentagon programs-in-the-works lifetime cost approaching $1.4 trillion.

174   **When China "builds strategic relationships . . . U.S. and regional security."**
For examples of such coverage, see Amy Waldman, "City of Fisherman in Pakistan Becomes Strategic Port," *New York Times*, 28 September 2004; and for an example of truly breathless reporting, see Bill Gertz, "China Builds Up Strategic Sea Lanes," *Washington Times*, 18 January 2005; and Bill Gertz, "Analysts Missed Chinese Buildup," *Washington Times*, 9 June 2005.
But also see Howard W. French, "China's Splurge on Resources May Not Be a Sign of Strength," *New York Times*, 12 December 2004.

174   **And when China asks Russia to join it . . . their conspiracy for global domination!**
"Beijing, Moscow Plan Joint Military Exercise," *Los Angeles Times*, 14 December 2004.

175   **Probably the worst sort of these self-projecting fears . . . Chinese, and U.S. navies.**
Some good recent examples (some quite alarmist, others fairly reasonable) include Anthony Faiola, "Exercise Display's Japan's Ambitions: Seeking New International Stature, Government Steps Away from Pacifist Past," *Washington Post*, 7 November 2004; David Lague, "China's Growing Undersea Fleet Presents Challenges to Its Neighbors," *Wall Street Journal*, 29 November 2004; Mark Valencia, "Pouring Oil on the East China Sea," *New York Times*, 24 February 2005; James Brooke, "Drawing the Line on Energy: China and Japan Wrangle over Oil and Gas Projects in Disputed Waters," *New York Times*, 29 March 2005; Jim Yardley and Thom Shanker, "Chinese Navy Buildup Gives Pentagon New Worries," *New York Times*, 8 April 2005; and Edward Cody, "China Builds a Smaller, Stronger Military: Modernization Could Alter Regional Balance of Power, Raising Stakes for U.S.," *Washington Post*, 12 April 2005.

176   **Strategic deconfliction across the Core . . . about the peace (and the contracts too)!"**
See my interview, along with others, in Amanda Griscom, "What Next?: Rolling Stone Convenes a Panel of Experts to Discuss What Went Wrong in Iraq—and Where We Can Go from Here," *Rolling Stone*, 8–22 July 2004.

178   **The saddest aspect of our current inability . . . the New Core and vice versa.**
I first explored this concept in my article, "Forget Europe. How About These Allies?," *Washington Post*, 11 April 2004.

180   **It tends to win those cases . . . a Core member to court over its agricultural subsidies.**

For details, see Elizabeth Becker and Todd Benson, "Brazil's Road to Victory Over U.S. Cotton," *New York Times,* 4 May 2004.

180   In the fall of 2004, when most Old Core . . . contingent there from 159 to 850.

Irakli Jgenti, "Georgia Bolsters Iraq Troop Commitment; Country Increases Forces Five-Fold," Georgian Embassy press release, 8 November 2004.

183   Remember, the economic destinies of China . . . how this should all go down.

I first expressed this notion in my article, "Dear Mr. President, Here's How to Make Sense of Your Second Term." On this subject, see also Howard W. French, "China Uneasy in Korea Role, Wary of U.S.," *New York Times,* 19 February 2005; and Joseph Kahn and David E. Sanger, "China Rules Out Using Sanctions on North Korea: Undercuts U.S. Strategy; Intelligence Appears to Be Inconclusive on Signs of Nuclear Test Plans," *New York Times,* 11 May 2005.

183   Kim Jong Il has checked all the boxes . . . narcotics and counterfeit American currency.

For details, see Jay Solomon and Hae Won Choi, "In North Korea, Secret Cash Hoard Props Up Regime: Defectors, Intelligence Sources Say Division 39 Supplies Billions to Kim Jong Il; Ginseng and Counterfeit Bills," *Wall Street Journal,* 14 July 2003; Victor Cha and Chris Hoffmeister, "North Korea's Drug Habit," *New York Times,* 3 June 2004; David E. Sanger and William J. Broad, "Uranium Testing Said to Indicate Libya-Korea Link: Fears of Possible Sales; Questions over Whether North Has Given Fuel to Other Countries," *New York Times,* 2 February 2005; Anthony Faiola and Philip P. Pan, "N. Korea Declaration Draws World Concern: Nuclear Arms Assertion Spurs Calls to Revive Talks," *Washington Post,* 11 February 2005; and Howard W. French, "Glimpse of World Shatters North Koreans' Illusions: About 200,000 North Koreans Have Entered China Secretly and Live Near the Border," *New York Times,* 24 March 2005.

183   He once kidnapped two of South Korea's biggest movie stars . . . own pathetic films.

For all the crazy details, see John Gorenfeld, "The Dictator Who Snagged Me," *Salon,* 12 March 2003.

183   But if that doesn't do it for you . . . are double that, but why quibble with statistics?).

For analysis, see "Asia-Pacific: '3.5m North Koreans Starved to Death,'" *BBC News,* 30 August 1999, found online at http://news.bbc.co.uk/1/hi/world/asia-pacific/433641.stm.

184   Over the years, we've seen this scenario . . . Haiti's leaders leave any other way?).

The Shah of Iran left the country for Egypt in 1979. Idi Amin lived in Libya for years after his ouster in 1979 from Uganda. Charles Taylor fled to Nigeria from Liberia in 2003. In early 2005, Togo's Faure Gnassingbé was shouted out of the presidency after illegally trying to assume it following his father's death. He remained in the country, later running for the office in a legitimate election in late April. Gnassingbé prevailed in this election, despite widespread cries of voting fraud. Upon his victory, state security forces immediatley began a heavy crackdown on the strongman's political opponents, forcing thousands to leave Togo

as political refugees. Besides "Baby Doc" Duvalier's engineered departure, the
United States did similarly for Jean-Bertrand Aristide in 2004.

186   Star Wars has probably been the single worst boondoggle . . . Tang to
show for it.
Since 1985, the United States has spent more than $80 billion on missile defense,
and the Pentagon is planning to spend another $50 billion over the next five years.
See David Stout and John H. Cushman, Jr., "Defense Missile for U.S. System Fails
to Launch: Setback for Interceptor," *New York Times,* 16 December 2004; and
David Stout, "Rocket Fails to Launch in Test Run: Third Straight Error for Missile
Defense," *New York Times,* 15 February 2005.

186   Bush is the "blink president."
President Bush is a man who goes with his instincts, in the manner trumpeted by
Malcolm Gladwell in his book *Blink: The Power of Thinking Without Thinking*
(New York: Little Brown, 2005). I got this idea from Joe Klein, "The Blink Presi-
dency," *Time,* 28 February 2005.

THE TRAIN'S ENGINE CAN TRAVEL NO FASTER
THAN ITS CABOOSE

192   Rather, as historian Mark Safranski writes . . . to access choices for themselves."
Safranski offered this definition in his review of *The Pentagon's New Map,* entitled "Why Some Are Calling Thomas P.M. Barnett Our Age's George F. Kennan,"
History News Network, 27 December 2004.

195   It's only when the bulk of a society's economic development . . . and open-
ness from its government.
For analysis of this phenomenon, see Fareed Zakaria, *The Future of Freedom:
Liberal Democracy at Home and Abroad* (New York: Norton, 2003), pp. 69–70.

196   Nothing is more crucial for improving a family's . . . improved an entire
family).
Quoted in Irshad Manji, "Remaking Iraq Without Guns," *New York Times,*
5 June 2004.

196   Early development typically focuses on extractive . . . labor with little regard.
For a good presentation of this sort of historical analysis, see Jared Diamond,
Collapse: How Societies Choose to Fail or Succeed (New York: Viking, 2005).

197   Europe prefers to offer substantial safety nets to . . . expanding the pool of
winners.
For this argument, see Jeremy Rifkin, *The European Dream: How Europe's Vision
of the Future Is Quietly Eclipsing the American Dream* (New York: Tarcher,
2004); Katrin Bennhold, "Love of Leisure, and Europe's Reasons," *New York
Times,* 29 July 2004; and Alan Cowell, "Demographic Time Bomb Threatens Pen-
sions in Europe: Saving More, Paying Higher Taxes and Working Longer for
Retirement Benefits," *New York Times,* 26 November 2004.

198   Check out the countries with the highest inflows . . . experiencing negative
growth.
The development economist William Easterly makes this interesting observation;
I quote his presentation at an 18 October 2004 workshop held in northern Virginia for the intelligence community. For an example of this excellent analysis, see

his "The Cartel of Good Intentions: The Problem of Bureaucracy in Foreign Aid," *Policy Reform,* March 2003.

199 I think these emerging (or, in the case of Russia . . . Bhagwati calls "optimal speed."

Jagdish Bhagwati, *In Defense of Globalization* (Oxford: Oxford University Press, 2004), pp. 34–35. For a more general argument, see Carl Honore, *In Praise of Slowness: How a Worldwide Movement Is Challenging the Cult of Speed* (San Francisco: HarperSanFrancisco, 2004); for a specific example, see Karen Mazurkewich, "In Bhutan, Happiness Is King: Society Values Well-Being Over GDP—and Economists Take Note," *Wall Street Journal,* 13 October 2005.

201 Brazil's own Gap spoke in the election of . . . previously more rapid globalizing pace.

For analysis of the election, see Peter Collins, "Make or Break: Under Its New Leader, Luiz Inácio Lula da Silva, Brazil Could Take a Leap into Prosperity—or Slide Back Towards Poverty," *The Economist,* 20 March 2003.

201 India's own Gap triggered the return of the Congress . . . belong in "Shining India."

For analysis of the election, see Saritha Rai, "Indian Voters Turn a Cold Shoulder to High Technology," *New York Times,* 12 May 2004.

201 Ukraine's contested election of 2004 . . . western half turned toward Europe.

For analysis of the election and its aftermath, see Steven Lee Myers, "A Tug of War over Ukraine: In Cold War–Like Rift, It's Putin vs. the West," *New York Times,* 24 November 2004; Steven Lee Myers, "Contagion: Popular Risings in Ex-Soviet Zone: Democracy Is in the Air, and Even Moscow Feels the Breeze," *New York Times,* 25 March 2005; and Elisabeth Bumiller, "Bush Tells Putin Not to Interfere with Democracy in Former Soviet Republics," *New York Times,* 8 May 2005.

201 In Russia, Vladimir Putin's recent turn . . . G-8 inviting China to a summit meeting).

On Putin's policies, see Peter Baker, "Bush Says He Wants to Keep Ties with Putin: Relationship Called 'Good' Despite Policy Concerns," *Washington Post,* 21 December 2004; and C. J. Chivers, "Getting Personal, Putin Voices Defiance of Critics Abroad: Heated Words About an Oil Giant's Sale and Post-Soviet Elections," *New York Times,* 24 December 2004. For analysis of the first time China met with the G-8, see Elizabeth Becker, "Guess Who's Invited to Dinner: Group of 7 Nations to Meet with China," *New York Times,* 23 September 2004.

201 Putin's crudely staged renationalization of the oil giant . . . conflict in Chechnya.

For a good international view, see Erin E. Arvedlund and Jad Mouawad, "Yukos Auction Deepens Doubts of Investors," *New York Times,* 21 December 2004. For the best internal critique of this approach, see Gregory L. White, "Insider Chides Kremlin Over Policies: Government Adviser Warns of Venezuela-Style Trouble Amid Dismantling of Yukos," *Wall Street Journal,* 8 April 2005. Also see the report "Russia Bars Foreign Bidders from Big Mineral Auctions," Associated Press, 10 February 2005; and Gregory L. White and Guy Chazan, "BP Russia Venture Faces More Taxes: Bill for $790 Million Comes After a Pledge by Putin to Rein In Revenue Officials," *Wall Street Journal,* 12 April 2005.

201 Internally, Putin has likewise displayed a greater reticence . . . pensioner generation.

On this issue, see Guy Chazan, "Putin's Opponents Wake Up: Pensioners' Protests Provide Rare Chance to Tap Sour Mood," *Wall Street Journal,* 25 January 2005.

Chapter Four: SHRINKING THE GAP BY ENDING DISCONNECTEDNESS

203 When C-Span broadcast my PowerPoint briefing . . . begins to hurt after a while!

I posted a selection of the letters on my blog at www.thomaspmbarnett.com/weblog/archives2/000816.html.

THE COMING CHOICES

207 But what the U.S. Government doesn't spend . . . war to peace, and you know what?

I base this judgment on years of interacting with both the Defense Department and the U.S. Agency for International Development. Why is this so? War games end up being focused on the movement of stuff more than policy decisions. It's the logistics that give the game a coherent substance, either by moving war matériel to the battlefield or moving relief supplies to the postwar situation. The thing about the transition from war to peace is that it doesn't have a separate requirement for stuff to be moved per se, but rather the transition from one skill set to another. This is really hard to game, hence this intellectual territory has gone unexplored for far too long. I will note that this is changing. When you talk to exercise planners on both sides today, everyone is getting more interested in, and amenable to, gaming the "hump" that marks the peaking of conflict and the tipping point on the path to postwar peace. Positions are being created or have been created on both sides of the Potomac to explore this transition territory, and inside the Defense Department, in particular, there are a host of new research and pilot programs to explore this "undiscovered country." For examples, see Defense Science Board, *Transition To and From Hostilities,* p. 22.

211 First, we wouldn't be able to afford that force . . . with this more conflicted scenario.

For examples of the economic logic that would drive such a scenario, see Greg Ip, "Could Overseas Financing Hurt the U.S.?," *Wall Street Journal,* 26 April 2004; Hal R. Varian, "Currency Exchange Rates Matter and Will Play a Prominent Role in Determining the Kind of Recovery the U.S. Economy Experiences," *New York Times,* 3 June 2004; Jill Dutt, "China Unlikely to Float Currency Soon, Official Says," *Washington Post,* 17 November 2004; Edmund L. Andrews, "Foreign Interest Appears to Flag as Dollar Falls," *New York Times,* 27 November 2004; David Wessell, "Behind Big Drop in Currency: Imbalance in Global Economy: U.S. Soaks Up Asia's Output by Going Deep into Debt; Something Has to Give," *Wall Street Journal,* 2 December 2004; James Brooke and Keith Bradsher, "Dollar's Fall Tests Nerve of Asia's Central Bankers," *New York Times,* 4 December 2004; Fred Kaplan, "China Expands. Europe Rises. And the United States . . . : As the Dollar Falls and Debt Grows, America No Longer Seems Indispensable," *New York*

Times, 26 December 2004; Keith Bradsher, "China Says It Won't Sell Dollars," *New York Times,* 7 March 2005; and Jonathan Fuerbringer, "Talk in Japan About the Dollar Stirs Up Markets," *New York Times,* 11 March 2005.

213 What happens when the United States seeks . . . like China's growing ties to Iran?"

For analysis of Iran's approach on this, see Jad Mouawad, "Facing Sanctions, Iran Uses Oil to Seek Allies," *New York Times,* 19 April 2004.

215 If we stipulate that the only way one can describe . . . are the most likely pathways?

My consultancy explored the notion of such pathways in a unique war game we designed and conducted with Alidade Incorporated in Newport, Rhode Island, in the spring of 2005. For details on the event, see the site www.newmapgame.com.

217 I'll explore each sequence in turn now . . . imagine being attached to each strategy.

For the first version of this analysis, see my conference paper entitled "Does the U.S. Face a Future of Never-Ending Subnational and Transnational Violence?," presented to the National Intelligence Council as part of their 2020 Project in May 2004. Find it online at http://www.thomaspmbarnett.com/published/NIC2020paper.htm.

219 Additionally, this scenario would place a premium . . . the Gulf to Developing Asia.

On this, see some interesting analysis in Jim Bencivenga, "Footsteps Heard at Sea: As Indians and Pakistanis Cross Kashmir 'Peace Bridge,' US and Chinese Admirals Take Note," *Christian Science Monitor,* 8 April 2005.

219 This scenario would see the Core's . . . Challenge project of the United Nations.

For an overview of the first group of nations to receive aid in this manner, see Michael Schroeder, "Sixteen Nations to Get Initial Millennium Aid," *Wall Street Journal,* 7 May 2004.

219 As such, the U.S. military's evolution toward the . . . economic interests there.

The United States agreed to regular high-level talks with the Chinese in April 2005; see Glenn Kessler, "U.S., China Agree to Regular Talks: Senior-Level Meetings to Focus on Politics, Security, Possibly Economics," *Washington Post,* 8 April 2005. See also Murray Hiebert et al., "U.S.-China Tensions Resurface: Beijing Legislation on Taiwan, Defense Buildup Fuel Criticism," *Wall Street Journal,* 25 February 2005.

224 Statistically speaking, the most likely sequence . . . Core's sense of security priorities.

For an example of this possibility, see James Hookway, "In Rural Cambodia, Avian Influenza Finds a Weak Spot: Human Cases Escape Notice Amid Ignorance, Poverty as a Pandemic Threatens," *Wall Street Journal,* 4 March 2005.

224 The second most likely geographic source would be . . . isolate Africa even further.

For an example of this possibility, see Sharon LaFraniere and Denise Grady, "A Daunting Search: Tracking a Deadly Virus in Angola," *New York Times,* 12 April 2005.

TIPPING POINTS IN THE JOURNEY FROM THE GAP TO THE CORE
226 Since the terrorist attacks of 9/11 . . . have identified the problem and we can fix it."

The preeminent expression of this mindset has been the widely publicized report of the 9/11 Commission, although there has been a plethora of like-minded volumes, the two biggest being Richard Clarke's *Against All Enemies: Inside America's War on Terror* (New York: Free Press, 2004) and Michael Scheuer's *Imperial Hubris: Why the West Is Losing the War on Terror* (Washington, D.C.: Potomac Books, 2004).

227   In ten years' time, no one with a decent . . . American plot to rule the world.
I first explored this notion in my op-ed "Not in America's Image," *Baltimore Sun,* 3 January 2005.

228   All Europe really has to do is simply move beyond . . . you plan to win the peace.
For a great example of this kind of strategic thinking, see Henrik Breitenbauch, "Bold Continuity: A Transatlantic Analysis of the 2002 National Security Strategy with a Suggestion for Europe," Institute for Statskundskab (Denmark), Arbejdspapir 2004/01.

228   If it's suddenly a lot more hip to be Asian . . . Japan is the big reason why.
For a brilliant article on this subject, see Douglas McGray, "Japan's Gross National Cool," *Foreign Policy,* May/June 2002.

230   India has not only remade the face of both . . . several times more in the Old Core).
For an overview of India's emergence, see P. Chidambaram, "A Passage to Prosperity," *Wall Street Journal,* 4 March 2005. On the medical tourism, see John Lancaster, "Surgeries, Side Trips for India's 'Tourists': Cheap Health Care Draws Foreigners," *Washington Post,* 21 October 2004; and Saritha Rai, "Low Costs Lure Foreigners to India for Medical Care," *New York Times,* 7 April 2005.

230   Then there's Bollywood's rising profile in global cinema.
On India's cinema exports, see Todd G. Bucholz, "G-rated Exports," *New York Times,* 19 October 2004. Bollywood's overseas box office has doubled in the past few years.

230   Between Russia and the Caspian Basin states . . . there that Saudi Arabia does in oil.
For an interesting projection of this possibility, see Artem Agoulnik, "A New OPEC in the Pipeline?," *Washington Post,* 20 October 2004.

230   South Africa, as long predicted . . . technology adoption and network construction.
On this trend, see Marc Lacey, "Accent on Africa: A New Continent for Outsourcers," *New York Times,* 1 February 2005; and "Mobile Growth 'Fastest in Africa,'" *BBC News,* 9 March 2005.

230   South American New Core powers Argentina . . . the world's largest beef exporter.
For a great overview of this development, see Larry Rohter, "South America Seeks to Fill the World's Table," *New York Times,* 12 December 2004.

230   Along with India, Brazil has also . . . Doha Development Round of the WTO.
For details on how the G-22 (first known as the "Group of 20"), or the group of predominantly New Core (with some Gap) states, came together spontaneously as an apparent voting bloc in the Cancun meeting of the World Trade Organization's Doha Round negotiations, see Patrick Smith, "Poor Nations Keep Heat on Trade:

After WTO Talks, the 'G-22' Group of Developing Nations Focuses on More-Open Agricultural Markets," *Christian Science Monitor,* 30 September 2003.

231   Brazilians also represent a rapidly growing . . . open-source software movement.

See Benson, "Brazil: Free Software's Biggest and Best Friend."

231   In his classic description of globalization . . . we all have to become Americans?"

Thomas L. Friedman, *The Lexus and the Olive Tree: Understanding Globalization* (New York: Farrar, Straus & Giroux, 1999), p. 326.

231   Second, we should abandon efforts to create . . . to be at risk for becoming terrorists.

For an example of such arguments, see Defense Science Board, *Transition To and From Hostilities,* pp. x–xii.

232   What's the difference between an LDC . . . and an LCC, a low-cost country?

On this terminology, see Paul Blustein, "Implored to 'Offshore' More: U.S. Firms Are Too Reluctant to Outsource Jobs, Report Says," *Washington Post,* 2 July 2004.

233   Today's Gap company may just be an OEM . . . and China and India did in the 1990s.

For an example of this in the information technology sector, see Lee Gomes, "PCs Aren't Just Made in Asia Now: Many Are Designed There," *Wall Street Journal,* 19 July 2004; and Keith Bradsher, "China Looms as the World's Next Leading Auto Exporter," *New York Times,* 22 April 2005.

233   Eventually, that unknown firm becomes an ODM . . . own proprietary technologies.

For a historical example of this pathway, see Anthony Faiola, "Luxury Electronics Power Japan's Recovery: New Factories Reflect High-End Focus," *Washington Post,* 6 April 2004.

233   And such journeys from the Gap to the Core . . . India to natural-gas giant Iran.

On the challenges of this development, see Alan Friedman and Frederick Kempe, "Pakistan to Push Pipeline Plan with India, Iran: Aziz Vision Must Overcome Political, Security Risks; Ramifications for the U.S.," *Wall Street Journal,* 26 January 2005.

233   India is itself a wonderful source of such "inconceivable" . . . high-tech Bangalore.

On the prayer issue, see Saritha Rai, "Short on Priests, U.S. Catholics Outsource Prayers to Indian Clergy," *New York Times,* 13 June 2004. On Kolkata's revival, see Joanna Slater, "Influx of Tech Jobs Ushers in Malls, Modernity to Calcutta," *Wall Street Journal,* 28 April 2004.

234   One of the first will be a dramatic ramping up . . . pollution, especially air pollution.

For analysis of global research on this subject, see Martin Wolf, *Why Globalization Works,* pp. 188–89. For an example of this dynamic at work, see Stan Sesser, "Air Pollution Is a Big Concern in Asia," *Wall Street Journal,* 24 November 2004.

234   Cities will be transformed from . . . of huge blocks of new high-rise developments.

China's rapid development is absolutely amazing in this regard. See Kathy Chen,

"China Sees Rise of a New Middle-Class Profession: Landlord," *Wall Street Journal,* 3 November 2004. Regarding similar dynamics in India, see Rama Lakshmi, "Bombay Moves to Push Out the Poor: Slums Are Razed as Plans Envisage Reinvented City," *Washington Post,* 8 May 2005; and Somini Sengupta, "Dispute Tears at Mumbai: House the Rich, or the Poor? Plan for Wasteland Ends Up in Court," *New York Times,* 17 May 2005.

234   Many lower-class people will get priced out . . . and burst with painful regularity.

For an overview of these issues, see Joseph Kahn, "China Worries About Economic Surge That Skips the Poor," *New York Times,* 4 March 2005; and David Barboza, "China Acts to Curtail Property Specualtion: With Shanghai Prices Up 70% in Two Years, Beijing is Worried About a Bubble," *New York Times,* 13 May 2005.

234   Young people will simultaneously display . . . tendency toward rabid nationalism.

On these contradictory trends, see James Hookway, "Now, It's Hip to Be Chinese: Many Asians Flaunt Roots to China as Nation Gains Cachet," *Wall Street Journal,* 16 March 2004; and Charles Hutzler, "Yuppies in China Protest Via the Web—And Get Away with It: Nationalistic Dissidents Press for Hard-Hitting Policies on Japan, Taiwan, U.S.," *Wall Street Journal,* 19 March 2004.

234   But a youth-tilted culture will also just want . . . Latin America, Southeast Asia).

MTV currently has programming that covers the entire world, but its full-fledged networks are centered in the Old and New Core regions. For details, see "Launch of MTV Base in Africa to Mark the Final Frontier in MTVN's Global Footprint," Viacom press release, 15 November 2004.

234   They'll come back because it's not only a place . . . a family compared with the West.

For examples of this fascinating phenomenon, see Amy Waldman, "Indians Go Home, but Don't Leave U.S. Behind," *New York Times,* 24 July 2004; John Markoff, "Have Supercomputer, Will Travel: A Technology Pioneer Leaves the U.S. for Opportunities in China," *New York Times,* 1 November 2004; and Jason Dean, "Entrepreneurs Bet on Chip Designing in China: Nationals Educated Abroad Return Home to Help Build a True High-Tech Industry," *Wall Street Journal,* 2 December 2004.

235   You'll know you've really made it when . . . your nation because they feel the same.

A story too cool to be true! See Amy Waldman, "A Young American Outsources Himself to India," *New York Times,* 17 July 2004. See also Erin White, "For M.B.A. Students, a Good Career Move Means a Job in Asia," *Wall Street Journal,* 10 May 2005.

235   Moreover, expect more than a few Western retirees . . . last career adventure.

For an example of this trend, see James T. Areddy, "Older Workers From U.S. Take Jobs in China," *Wall Street Journal,* 22 June 2004.

235   You become a place where Olympics . . . by feng shui considerations, of course).

All the Summer Games of the modern Olympics have occurred in countries that fall into my definition of Old or New Core (no sense of looking at the Winter

Games, because that's geographically limited by definition). None has ever occurred in a country currently inside the Gap. The list of countries is Athens (1896), Paris (1900), St. Louis (1904), London (1908), Stockholm (1912), Antwerp (1920), Paris (1924), Amsterdam (1928), Los Angeles (1932), Berlin (1936), London (1948), Helsinki (1952), Melbourne (1956), Rome (1960), Tokyo (1964), Mexico City (1968), Munich (1972), Montreal (1976), Moscow (1980), Los Angeles (1984), Seoul (1988), Barcelona (1992), Atlanta (1996), Sydney (2000), Athens (2004), Beijing (to host 2008). The only truly "counter-Core" to host the games was the Soviet Union in 1980, but there you can argue it was the lead member of the "alternative Core" of that era—the Soviet bloc.

235 Your country thus becomes a new hot spot . . . accidentally lost for many centuries.

This is both good and bad. For an example of the bad, see Karen Mazurkewich, "To Stop the Pillage of Its Historic Art, China Turns to U.S.: Hot Antiquities Market Girds for Crackdown as Beijing Pushes Trade Restrictions," *Wall Street Journal,* 2 March 2005.

235 Your public starts becoming a major market . . . acts start touring in your major cities.

The Rolling Stones, for example, finally toured China on their fortieth-anniversary tour in 2003. See also Blythe Yee and James Inverne, "Give My Regards to Shanghai: Big Musicals Arrive in China, as Broadway Looks East; The 'Edelweiss' Sing-along," *Wall Street Journal,* 29 April 2005.

235 Eventually, you become a media content exporter . . . bigger than the country itself.

The growing global clout of China's movie industry is a good example; on this see David Barboza, "Hollywood Movie Studios See the Chinese Film Market as Their Next Rising Star," *New York Times,* 4 July 2005. Then there is the juggernaut that is Japanese anime, whose influence is so profound in the United States that the publishers of Nancy Drew recently came out with a very manga-inspired graphic-novel version of her books; see Carol Memmott, " 'Nancy Drew' Finds Clues in Graphic Novel," *USA Today,* 19 April 2005.

235 Plus, it starts becoming a big deal for Westerners . . . to be made in that achievement.

Just check the overseas box office amounts for Hollywood films in any issue of *Variety,* and you'll see that our movie stars are now typically more "bankable" overseas than in the United States. And the overseas markets where they make the most money are inevitably Core states, both Old and New.

235 By 2020, China will provide the global travel industry . . . customers annually.

See James Brooke, "In Pacific, a Red Carpet for China's Rich Tourists," *New York Times,* 13 May 2004.

235 China, for example, is opening 150 major airports . . . the Pentagon for its profits.

For details, see Sara Kehaulani Goo, "Chinese Airlines Agree to Buy 60 Boeing 7E7s," *Washington Post,* 28 January 2005.

235 Meanwhile, India just got its first budget-fare airline . . . many as 70 million by 2010.

See Saritha Rai, "Budget Fares Change Face of Air Travel for Indians," *New York Times,* 10 September 2004; and "India's First Airline Offering Is Scooped Up in Minutes," 25 February 2005.

236 This wasn't a big deal in the past . . . it as both a threat and an unfair trade practice.

This development will inevitably unfold between the United States and China, just as it did between Japan and the United States at the end of the 1980s; for analysis of this rising sentiment, see Keith Bradsher and David Barboza, "Made in China. Bought Everywhere: As Trade Surplus Balloons, So Does Talk of Protectionism," *New York Times,* 9 April 2005.

236 And so you slowly but surely accede to these demands . . . patent protectionists.

For examples of this shift, see Ted C. Fishman, "Manufaketure: Counterfeiting and Pirating (That Is, Making Knockoffs of What Developed Nations Have Created) Are at the Heart of the Chinese Economic Boom," *New York Times Magazine,* 9 January 2005; Alex Ortolani, "China's Game College Seeks to Foster Innovation," *Wall Street Journal,* 3 March 2005; Alex Ortolani, "China Moves from Piracy to Patents: More Companies Are Trying to Be Product Innovators Rather Than Just Imitators," *Wall Street Journal,* 7 April 2005; Eric Bellman, "India Senses Patent Appeal: Local Companies Envision Benefits in Stronger Protections," *Wall Street Journal,* 11 April 2005; Pat Choate, "The Pirate Kingdom: Make the W.T.O. Get Tough on China," *New York Times,* 12 May 2005; and Guy Chazan, "In Russia, Politicians Protect Movie, Music Pirates," *Wall Street Journal,* 12 May 2005.

236 But while pluralism is always on the rise . . . the rural poor aren't left too far behind.

For examples of this fear, see Amy Waldman, "Premier of India Is Forced to Quit After Vote Upset: Party of Gandhis in Lead; Poorest Seem Angry with Uneven Gain—A Family Returns," *New York Times,* 14 May 2004; Andrew Browne, "Asia Shifts Focus to Rural Development," *Wall Street Journal,* 20 July 2004; John Lancaster, "Indian Economy Leaves Workers Behind," *Washington Post,* 3 November 2004; Joseph Kahn, "China to Cut Taxes on Farmers and Raise Their Subsidies: An Effort by Beijing to Make a Dent in Rural Poverty," *New York Times,* 3 February 2005; Jim Yardley, "China Plans to Cut School Fees for Its Poorest Rural Students: A New Policy Seeks to Redress Inequities in the Education System," *New York Times,* 13 March 2005; Andrew Browne, "China Wrestles Rich-Poor Gap: As Divide Threatens Unrest, Beijing Turns to Rural Development," *Wall Street Journal,* 4 April 2005; and Anthony Faiola, "Anti-Japanese Hostilities Move to the Internet: Chinese and South Korean Hackers Blamed for Digital Barrage Designed to Cripple Web Sites," *Washington Post,* 10 May 2005.

237 As your nation moves into membership . . . tomorrow they start taking *our* rules."

This is basically what the Chinese told themselves, by all accounts, in their quest for membership in the World Trade Organization; see Hutzler and Haixu, "China Contesting 'Nonmarket Economy' Status."

238 As you become more interdependent with the Core . . . from outside influences.

For a great example of this, see Joseph Kahn, "China Pushing and Scripting Japan

Protests," *New York Times,* 15 April 2005; and Jason Dean, "Living the Chinese Dream: Success Stories from the Poor Hinterland Help Share the Wealth," *Wall Street Journal,* 26 April 2005.

239   Turkey, for example, has been important . . . EU for being too culturally "different."

For some great analysis of this situation, see Robert D. Kaplan, "At the Gates of Brussels: If Recep Tayyip Erdogan Gets His Way, Turkey Will Be More Islamic and Europe Will Be More Turkish. Both Would Be Good," *Atlantic Monthly,* December 2004.

239   Meanwhile, Pakistan has been . . . it have to show economically for all that effort?

For the promise and the peril that is Pakistan right now, see Jay Solomon, Zahid Hussain, and Saeed Azhar, "As Growth Returns to Pakistan, Hopes Rise on Terror Front: Exports, Malls Enjoy Boom, as West Ramps Up Aid; But Will Militants Notice?; 'Economies Isn't Everything,'" *Wall Street Journal,* 9 November 2005.

239   If a country is important enough for the United States . . . advance of globalization itself.

For some examples of the United States's rather mixed record on this score in the Middle East, see Paul Blustein, "U.S. Free-Trade Deals Include Few Muslim Countries," *Washington Post,* 3 December 2004; Neil MacFarquhar, "Melting Icy Egypt-Israel Relations Through a Trade Pact: The Inseparability of Politics and Economics Leads Pragmatists to Join Forces," *New York Times,* 16 December 2004; Michelle Wallin, "U.S.-Bahrain Accord Stirs Persian Gulf Trade Partners," *New York Times,* 24 December 2004; and Neil King, Jr., "Democracy Drive by America Meets Reality in Egypt: U.S. Funds Mideast Activists, but in Cairo, Strong Ties to Regime Limit the Effort," *Wall Street Journal,* 11 April 2005.

240   So as far as we're concerned . . . Guantánamo prisoner-abuse scandals.

For examples on each, see Senator Kay Bailey Hutchison, "Truth About the Drug War," *Washington Post,* March 9, 1999; Tim McGirk, "Hiding in Plain Sight: Why Pakistan Still Isn't Aggressively Pursuing the ex-Taliban Leaders Living Inside the Country," *Time,* 29 November 2004; and Shawn W. Crispin, "U.S. Ally in Asia May Have Crossed Line in Terror Fight: Thailand Admits Its Police Abducted Muslim Suspects in Wake of Brutal Attacks," *Wall Street Journal,* 21 April 2004.

241   That's what gets you a Vietnam . . . own program of internal economic integration.

For details, see Keith Bradsher, "Outsourcing Finds Vietnam: Loyalty (and Cheap Labor)," *New York Times,* 30 September 2004; and Jane Perlez, "Chinese Premier Signs Trade Pact at Southeast Asian Summit," *New York Times,* 30 November 2004.

241   When Russia agreed to ratify the Kyoto Protocol . . . Moscow's bid to join the WTO.

See Erin E. Arvedlund, "Europe Backs Russian Entry into W.T.O.: Moscow Agrees to Support the Kyoto Protocol in Exchange for a Trade Deal," *New York Times,* 21 May 2004; and Christopher Cooper and Gregory L. White, "Bush, Putin Take Cooperative Tack as WTO Beckons," *Wall Street Journal,* 25 February 2005.

241   But what has Washington done in exchange for . . . Soviet republics of Central Asia?

See Eugene B. Rumer, "Why 'Contain' Russia?," *Washington Post,* 17 December 2004; Gregory L. White, "Moscow Tends to Its Backyard: Russia Strives for Regional Clout as Former Soviet States Tilt to West," *Wall Street Journal,* 2 February 2005; and Elisabeth Bumiller and David E. Sanger, "Bush and Putin Exhibit Tension Over Democracy: An Awkward Appearance; Two Sides Announce Deal to Reduce Threat of Nuclear Terrorism," *New York Times,* 25 February 2005; Philip Shishkin, "In Putin's Backyard, Democracy Stirs—With U.S. Help: Before Kyrgyzstan Elections, Western-Backed Groups Offer Aid to Opposition," *Wall Street Journal,* 25 February 2005; and Steven R. Weisman, "Rice Tells Putin U.S. Is No Threat in Region: Mixing Pressure on Moscow with Words of Mutual Respect," *New York Times,* 21 April 2005.

241 The EU wants to lift its self-imposed ban . . . in our global war on terrorism?

See Matthew L. Wald, "U.S. to Make Deep Cuts in Stockpile of A-Arms," *New York Times,* 4 June 2004; and Joseph Kahn, "Europe's Shift on Embargo Places Taiwan at Center Stage," *New York Times,* 23 March 2005.

241 If the Core hasn't moved beyond great-power . . . one-third of their Cold War highs?

Details found in Robert Samuelson, "Nuclear Nightmare," *Washington Post,* 20 October 2004.

243 The poor soil quality that afflicts much of the Gap . . . simply can't feed themselves.

I was alerted to this fundamental geographic reality by Walter E. Parham, who, upon seeing my brief on C-Span sent me his paper (dated 1975) entitled "Geological Controls on Environmental Problems of Developing Countries of the Humid Tropics," Department of Geology and Geophysics, University of Minnesota.

243 The recent effort by the world's best scientists . . . beyond sustenance farming.

For a great summary of the Copenhagen Consensus's findings on agriculture, see "Economic Focus: Feeding the Hungry (in the Fourth of a Series of Articles on the Copenhagen Consensus Project, We Look at Hunger and Malnutrition)," *The Economist,* 8 May 2004.

243 If we want to start building the next contingent . . . argues for sub-Saharan Africa.

For a good summary of his vision, see Daphne Eviatar, "Spend $150 Billion Per Year to Cure World Poverty," *New York Times Magazine,* 7 November 2004.

244 The Core likewise needs to rethink its foreign aid . . . practice, holds much promise.

For good analysis of how the first grant came about in this program, see Michael M. Phillips, "New Bush Strategy on Aid Faces Test in Madagascar: U.S. Lets African Nation Pick Ways to Use $110 Million; Corruption Remains Issue," *Wall Street Journal,* 18 April 2005.

244 Most of what the Gap suffers is not the . . . expertise but access to foreign capital.

As Brink Lindsey puts it, "Without access to financing from abroad, poor countries would be forced to fund their economic development exclusively from domestic savings"; see his masterful *Against the Dead Hand: The Uncertain Struggle for Global Capitalism* (New York: John Wiley, 2002), p. 195.

244 When a country develops to the point of shedding . . . the production-value chain.

On this migration up the production chain, see Bhagwati, *In Defense of Globalization*. As he puts it, "The fear that the 'yellow peril' (as the phenomenon of rapidly expanding exports from Japan was described in the 1930s) would be joined by the 'brown peril' and eventually by the 'black peril' as poor countries emerged as exporters of labor-intensive manufactures is belied by the fact that the 'yellow peril' is *replaced* by the 'brown peril,' and so forth. International economists have long understood this phenomenon empirically, calling it the phenomenon of ladders of comparative advantage" (pp. 124–125). On the more general challenge faced by the Old Core in terms of moving on up the ladder, see Daniel H. Pink, "Revenge of the Right Brain: Logical and Precise, Left-Brain Thinking Gave Us the Information Age. Now Comes the Conceptual Age—Ruled by Artistry, Empathy, and Emotion," *Wired,* February 2005.

245 On the migration of labor, here's the progression . . . (the ability to move up in jobs).

Hormats presented these ideas at a Highlands Forum (XXV, December 2004) that featured *The Pentagon's New Map* as its baseline scenario in creating alternative global futures. The Highlands Forum is a special series of conferences held to benefit long-range thinking in the Office of the Secretary of Defense. The next forum (XXVI, May 2005) explored the SysAdmin Force concept in conjunction with the Defense Science Board's report, *Transition To and From Hostilities.*

245 A good example of this is when Africans tear down . . . eating your own seed corn.

See Michael Wines, "Cable Thievery Is Darkening Daily Life in Mozambique," *New York Times,* 15 June 2004.

245 Otherwise, you typically end up with control-freak . . . in the telephone industry.

For a good sense of the difference in approach between a New Core and a truly Gap state in encouraging the growth of the telephone industry as part of a development strategy, see "Mobile Phones Take Over in India: Indian Mobile Phone Users Have Outnumbered Fixed-Line Customers for the First Time, According to the Telecom Regulatory Authority of India," *BBC News,* 9 November 2004; and "No Bids for Algeria Phone Permits: Algerian Regulators Say There Have Been No Bids for Two Fixed-Line Telephone Permits Which Required $1bn-Worth of Investment," *BBC News,* 9 November 2004.

246 Meanwhile, as history has amply demonstrated . . . of declining national wealth.

On this trend, see Bjorn Lomborg, *The Skeptical Environmentalist: Measuring the Real State of the World* (Cambridge: Cambridge University Press, 2001), p. 137. Lomborg's book is a magisterial demonstration of the utility of meta-analysis, or the analysis of analyses. In this book, Lomborg applies his statistical skills to analyze hundreds and hundreds of empirical studies on the state of the world, examining both past trends and its current situation, and making reasonable projections into the future—always emphasizing humanity's ingenuity.

247 America has long had the capacity . . . of the world's most impressive thirty-year-olds.
    See Michael Barone, *Hard America, Soft America: Competition vs. Coddling and the Battle for the Nation's Future* (New York: Crown Forum, 2004).

248 He makes the argument that "what you are . . . lasting way, centering them in time.
    Morris Massey, *What You Are Is Where You Were When,* Program 1 of The Massey Triad, found online at www.enterprisemedia.com/massey.html#anchor968546.

249 India passed this test, displaying a private-sector . . . that was highly professional.
    See John Lancaster, "India Takes Major Role in Sri Lanka Relief Effort: Aid Is Sign of Nation's Emergence as Regional Power," *Washington Post,* 20 January 2005.

249 Indonesia faltered at moments politically . . . even in the politically volatile Aceh region.
    See Alan Sipress and Noor Huda Ismail, "Relief Transcends U.S-Indonesia Divide: Rights Concerns Sidestepped as Militaries Respond Jointly to Disaster," *Washington Post,* 4 January 2005; and Agence France-Presse, "U.S. to Resume Training of Some in Indonesia Military," *New York Times,* 27 February 2005.

249 China, however, was really missing in action.
    See Anthony Faiola and Philip P. Pan, "As Asians Offer Much Aid, Chinese Role Is Limited," *Washington Post,* 5 January 2005; and Martin Fackler and Charles Hutzler, "China Is Small Player in Tsunami Aid," *Wall Street Journal,* 10 January 2005.

249 Yes, its private-sector giving was unprecedented . . . great goodwill in the process.
    See Ginny Parker and Leslie T. Chang, "Japan, China Enter New Era of Giving," *Wall Street Journal,* 11 January 2005. On the U.S. side, see Rama Lakshmi, "Private Citizens Outdo Officials in Aid Efforts: Affluent Urbanites Organize Quickly for Direct Deliveries," *Washington Post,* 1 January 2005.

249 A lot of strategic analysts in the West . . . misses the larger strategic opportunity.
    For examples, see Greg Sheridan, "The Year of Living Diplomatically: America Must Seize the Moment in Indonesia," *Wall Street Journal,* 10 January 2005; and Jim Hoagland, "Bush's Asian Opportunity," *Washington Post,* 16 January 2005. For analysis of how the U.S. military did take advantage of previous military-to-military ties to improve America's standing in the region, see Matt Pottinger and Barry Wain, "Military Ties Speeded Tsunami Relief," *Wall Street Journal,* 19 January 2005.

ESSENTIAL BUILDING BLOCKS FOR SHRINKING THE GAP FROM WITHIN

250 So the taglines for the most reflexive reviews . . . and "war only leads to more war."
    For examples, see www.thomaspmbarnett.com/reviews/reviews_index.htm.

251 Good markets need good governments.
    This title comes from Wolf, *Why Globalization Works,* p. 73.

252 As the global economy has spread . . . absolute poverty in human history.
    See Lomborg, *Skeptical Environmentalist,* p. 72; and Wolf, *Why Globalization Works,* pp. 158–59.

252   Whatever perceived strength those organizations . . . connectivity, not the cause of it.

On this, see Lindsey's excellent analysis in *Against the Dead Hand,* pp. 260–65.

252   The United States doesn't enjoy a magnificently . . . arising over the years.

This observation comes from Wolf, *Why Globalization Works,* p. 3.

253   You might think the last place you'd find . . . and yet that's where you find most of it.

For an excellent dissection of these criticisms, see Bhagwati, *In Defense of Globalization,* pp. 13–27.

253   Far more widespread and damaging . . . oppression and decreases wealth worldwide.

On this and a host of related criticisms, see Wolf's magisterial exploration of these topics in *Why Globalization Works,* Part IV, "Why the Critics Are Wrong," pp. 137–305.

253   Tell me which is worse: the alteration . . . and primitive forms of impoverishment?

On this point, see Bhagwati, *In Defense of Globalization,* pp. 114–15.

254   It goes to the countries with the highest . . . labor regulations and social safety nets.

On this issue, see Wolf, *Why Globalization Works,* pp. 232–35.

254   The data here is overwhelming . . . than other workers can achieve in that country.

See Bhagwati, *In Defense of Globalization,* pp. 172–73; and Wolf, *Why Globalization Works,* p. 235.

254   So globalization doesn't increase child labor . . . higher expectations for their kids.

See Bhagwati, *In Defense of Globalization,* pp. 172–73; and Wolf, *Why Globalization Works,* p. 235.

254   As international economists love to point . . . nation stems from a definition of place.

See Wolf, *Why Globalization Works,* p. 187, on child labor. On a "definition of place," see Gillian Rose, "Place and Identity: A Sense of Place," in Doreen Massey and Pat Jess, eds., *A Place in the World?: Places, Cultures and Globalization* (Oxford: Oxford University Press, 1996), pp. 87–132.

254   Throughout human history, we've consistently . . . now in a very globalized manner.

This is the underlying theme of Robert Wright's brilliant book *Nonzero.*

255   The difference today is that the ideology . . . than it has ever been in history.

This is the underlying theme of Brook Lindsey's excellent book *Against the Dead Hand.*

255   If there's a race, it's not to the bottom but to the top . . . direct investment and trade.

This is the underlying theme of Martin Wolf's superb book *Why Globalization Works,* and Jagdish Bhagwati's well-argued volume *In Defense of Globalization.*

256   There is an old African saying that goes "The world moves on a woman's hips."

This was first brought to my attention by its use in a song by the rock band Talking Heads ("The Great Curve" on the album *Remain in Light,* 1980).

256   At that point it is likely that you're living . . . likely that your economy is globalized.

On this issue, see Isobel Coleman's very powerful article, "The Payoff from Women's Rights," *Foreign Affairs,* May/June 2004.

256   In many parts of the Gap, the notion of empowering . . . subversive proposition.

See Coleman, "Payoff from Women's Rights," pp. 88–91.

257   The benefit from educating girls is very . . . transmitted diseases (reducing both).

Coleman offers a brilliant argument on this subject; see her "Payoff from Women's Rights," pp. 82–86.

257   Show me a democracy . . . state that does not marginalize its females.

See Coleman, "Payoff from Women's Rights," p. 84.

257   Women's rights should be the Core's leading agenda . . . is so high and so permanent.

For this argument, see Coleman, "Payoff from Women's Rights," pp. 91–94; Barbara Ehrenreich, "The New Macho: Feminism," *New York Times,* 29 July 2004; and Warren Hoge, "Panel Backs Women's Rights After U.S. Drops Abortion Issue," *New York Times,* 5 March 2005.

257   There is also little doubt that the population that . . . most inside the Gap is female.

For examples, see Judith D. Auerbach, "The Overlooked Victims of AIDS," *New York Times,* 14 October 2004; Somini Sengupta, "Attacks on Women in West Sudan Draw an Outcry," *New York Times,* 26 October 2004; Mary Jordan, "A Harsh Price to Pay in Pursuit of a Dream: For Central American Women, Sexual Coercion Is Hazard on Route to U.S.," *Washington Post,* 6 December 2004; and Marc Lacey, "For Africa's Poor, Pregnancy Is Often Life Threatening," *New York Times,* 12 December 2004.

258   So, too, many traditional Gap societies hold the line . . . and human rights in general.

Coleman makes this point in her "Payoff from Women's Rights," p. 89.

258   And yet nothing signifies victories in the global war . . . actually assume office.

For good examples, see Carlotta Gall, "Out of Sight, Afghan Women Still Register to Vote," *New York Times,* 26 June 2004; Carlotta Gall, "Blast Kills 2 Afghan Women on Election Workers' Bus," *New York Times,* 27 June 2004; Amy Waldman, "Fearful Choice for Afghan Women: To Vote or Not to Vote; Shame If 'Something Should Happen,'" *New York Times,* 5 October 2004; Molly Moore, "Democracy's New Face: Radical and Female; Palestinian Mayor Embodies Both Tradition and Change in Middle East," *Washington Post,* 29 January 2005; and Marc Lacey, "Women's Voices Rise as Rwanda Reinvents Itself: But Numbers in Office Do Not Mean an End to Their Suffering," *New York Times,* 26 February 2005.

258   As one elderly Iraqi woman declared on her way . . . the booth, I will do as I wish."

Quoted in James Glanz, "In Culture Dominated by Men, Questions About Women's Vote: Not Just a Decision How to Cast a Ballot, but Whether to At All," *New York Times,* 30 January 2005.

258   While men tend to vote according to religion . . . who represent law and order.
      See Glanz, "In a Culture Dominated by Men, Questions About Women's Vote."

258   Women tend to dominate in microfinance . . . been starved for such access to capital.
      On this subject, see Manji, "Remaking Iraq Without Guns"; and Cris Prystay, "With Loans, Poor South Asian Women Turn Entrepreneurial," *Wall Street Journal*, 25 May 2005.

258   And women should welcome globalization's embrace . . . advancement transformed.
      Wolf makes this point in *Why Globalization Works,* p. 186.

259   No capital, no capitalism.
      The title is inspired by Hernando de Soto's *The Mystery of Capital: Why Capitalism Triumphs in the West and Fails Everywhere Else* (New York: Basic Books, 2000).

259   As Francis Fukuyama argues . . . "despite the best intentions of the donors."
      Francis Fukuyama, *State-Building: Governance and World Order in the 21st Century* (Ithaca, NY: Cornell University Press, 2004), p. 39.

259   The problem is that the development . . . construction but not for maintenance.
      This observation comes from William Easterly. For an example of this phenomenon, see Celia W. Dugger, "Roads Lead to a New Way of Life for Ethiopia," *New York Times,* 8 November 2004.

260   But by and large I don't like to see development . . . of government institutions there.
      For analysis on this problem, see Susan Rose-Ackerman, "Governance and Corruption," in Bjorn Lomborg, ed., *Global Crises, Global Solutions* (Cambridge: Cambridge University Press, 2004), pp. 301–44.

260   Those higher transaction rates demand a more . . . property rights and contract law.
      See Fukuyama, *State-Building,* pp. 35–37.

260   But as the noted Peruvian economist Hernando . . . segments of the population.
      See Hernando de Soto, *The Other Path: The Invisible Revolution in the Third World* (New York: Harper & Row, 1989), Chapter 7, "The Parallel with Mercantilism," pp. 201–30.

261   In such governments (of which there are many . . . de Soto calls the "legal tangle."
      For a brief description, see Mario Vargas Llosa's Foreword to *The Other Path,* pp. xviii–xix. See also James Hookway, "A Paradox for Poor Nations: Inventors Face Big Barriers Where Entrepreneurs Are Most Needed," *Wall Street Journal,* 9 May 2005; and Matt Moffett and Geraldo Samor, "In Brazil, Thicket of Red Tape Spoils Recipe for Growth: Former Emerging-Market Star Loses Ground to Asia, EU; Lufthansa's 24-Year Fight; Waiting All Night at Tax Office," *Wall Street Journal,* 24 May 2005.

261   As de Soto's pioneering research on Peru's economy . . . out over many months.
      See Hernando de Soto, *The Other Path,* p. 135.

261 It's what some call the "black market" but what de Soto . . . any legal standing.
For a quick summary, see Llosa's Foreword to *The Other Path,* pp. viii–xv.

261 It's the economic equivalent of America's Wild West . . . population lived outside it.
On this concept, see de Soto, *The Mystery of Capital,* p. 106.

262 Over the course of development, government will . . . in strength is not the issue.
On the concepts of "strength" and "scope" of government, see Fukuyama, *State-Building,* pp. 6–14.

Chapter Five: WE HAVE MET THE ENEMY . . .

265 In *The Pentagon's New Map* I argued . . . *required* it shrink the Gap over time.
Pentagon's New Map, Chapter 4 ("The Core and the Gap"), pp. 191–245.

267 In my "global transaction strategy," . . . successful expansion in the current era.
Pentagon's New Map, Chapter 6 ("The Global Transaction Strategy"), pp. 295–339.

THE RESUMPTION OF HISTORY AND THE LATEST ENEMY
271 On it was displayed the migration of humans . . . Africa, roughly 100,000 years ago.
A variation of this map is found in Doreen Massey and Pat Jess, "Introduction," in Massey and Jess, eds., *A Place in the World?,* p. 9.

274 After that period of blocked expansion . . . (Globalization III, from 1980 to 2001).
I basically follow the dating of globalization eras as presented in Paul Collier and David Dollar, *Globalization, Growth and Poverty* (New York: Oxford University and World Bank, 2002).

275 Meanwhile, with the fall of the Portuguese empire . . . Mozambique, Ethiopia).
On this subject, you can find my first great attempt to figure out how the world works in *Romanian and East German Policies in the Third World: Comparing the Strategies of Ceausescu and Honecker* (Westport, CT: Praeger Publishing, 1992).

276 It was at this point in history that . . . (the subject of my Ph.D. dissertation as well).
See Francis Fukuyama, *The End of History and the Last Man* (New York: Free Press, 1992).

276 Yet, despite this retreat into the past . . . similar to its defunct, secular cousins."
Lindsey, *Against the Dead Hand,* p. 271.

276 For like all the Lenins and Maos before it . . . of the Industrial Counter-revolution."
Lindsey, *Against the Dead Hand,* p. 272.

277 But, unlike previous versions of ideological . . . their most like-minded coreligionists.
Lindsey, *Against the Dead Hand,* p. 273.

277 Martin Wolf, longtime writer . . . became an excuse for grubby tyranny."
     Wolf, *Why Globalization Works,* p. 38.
277 As Ian Buruma and Avishai Margalit point out . . . of a machinelike soci-
     ety without a human soul."
     Ian Buruma and Avishai Margalit, *Occidentalism: The West in the Eyes of Its Ene-
     mies* (New York: Penguin Press, 2004), p. 102 ("idolatry") and p. 9 ("machinelike").
278 Occidentalism, as the authors note, is neither a left- nor right-wing phe-
     nomenon.
     Buruma and Margalit, *Occidentalism,* pp. 5 and 12.
278 Occidentalism actually began in the West . . . of people from the country
     to the city.
     Buruma and Margalit, *Occidentalism,* p. 6.
279 Such wars against "sin city," the West . . . State Shinto, communism and
     Islam."
     Buruma and Margalit, *Occidentalism,* pp. 16–19 and 105.
279 In his book *The End of History* . . . What is the best political order for
     societies?
     Fukuyama, *The End of History and the Last Man,* pp. xiv–xxi.
280 These "wars of the spirit," as Fukuyama . . . one's sense of unique self-
     worth.
     Fukuyama, *The End of History and the Last Man,* pp. 328–29.
282 In this way, our current main enemies . . . will bring about worldwide
     revolution.
     Olivier Roy makes this connection in *Globalized Islam,* p. 57.

THE CONVERGENCE OF CIVILIZATIONS
     My thanks to Mark Safranski for this phrase as it applies to my vision.
283 It is quite ironic to me that the man best known . . . of college and gradu-
     ate studies.
     Samuel P. Huntington, *The Clash of Civilizations and the Remaking of World
     Order* (New York: Simon & Schuster, 1996).
283 In his latest book on the changing character . . . universalist, economic,
     and moralist.
     Samuel P. Huntington, *Who Are We? The Challenges to America's National Iden-
     tity* (New York: Simon & Schuster, 2004), pp. 264–71.
285 As the EU's periodic national "no" votes prove . . . higher authority—the
     union.
     For analysis of these votes, see Richard Bernstein, "2 'No' Votes in Europe: The
     Anger Spreads; As Ruling Elites Falter, Union Suffers the Pain," *Wall Street Jour-
     nal,* 2 June 2005; and Marc Champion, Dan Bilefsky, and John Carregrou, "A
     French 'No' Reminds Europe of Many Woes: Behind Constitution Vote Lies an
     Economic Malaise EU Leaders Haven't Cured," *New York Times,* 2 June 2005.
287 Unlike Francis Fukuyama . . . the "many Non-West" against the American-
     led West).
     See Huntington's chapter "The Global Politics of Civilizations," pp. 207–45.
290 Huntington is absolutely correct in noting . . . no geographic component
     whatsoever.
     Huntington, *Who Are We?* pp. 38–39 and 49–52.

291 There are strong differences between the types . . . with those flowing into Europe.

For analysis of these differences, see Roy, *Globalized Islam*, pp. 100–01.

292 As Islamic expert Olivier Roy notes . . . For a rebel, to convert is to find a cause.

Roy, *Globalized Islam*, pp. 48–49. On the general political trend, see Craig S. Smith, "Europe's Muslims May Be Headed Where the Marxists Went Before," *New York Times*, 26 December 2004; and Lizette Alvarez, "Britain's Mainstream Muslims Find Voice," *New York Times*, 6 March 2005.

293 As in the case of their elders in the political . . . goal of adolescents everywhere.

See Roy's brilliant analysis on these youth trends in *Globalized Islam*, pp. 139–45.

293 Watching France's rather idiotic efforts to ban head . . . this comes over generations.

For examples of this struggle in both France and the U.K., see Elaine Sciolino, "France Turns to Tough Policy on Student's Religious Garb," *New York Times*, 22 October 2004; and Dilpazier Aslam, "British Girl Wins Battle over Muslim Clothing: 'I'm happy that I did this. I feel that I have given hope and strength to other Muslim women,'" *The Globe and Mail*, 3 March 2005. For a more reasonable and defensible choice, see Elaine Sciolino, "A New French Headache: When Is Hate on TV Illegal?," *New York Times*, 9 December 2004.

294 These "progressive Muslims" . . . or must we force confrontations and showdowns?

Some examples include Laurie Goodstein, "Muslim Women Seeking a Place in the Mosque: More Are Challenging Segregated Roles in American Services," *New York Times*, 22 July 2004; Laurie Goodstein, "Woman's Mosque Protest Brings Furor in the U.S.: Challenging Rules and Traditions, and Paying a Price," *New York Times*, 22 July 2004; and Andrea Elliott, "Muslim Group Is Urging Women to Lead Prayers: Stirring Debate About the Role of Women in Islamic Worship," *New York Times*, 18 March 2005.

294 The counterintuitive reality of people migrations . . . call a "revival of ethnicity."

On this, see Stuart Hall, "New Cultures for Old," in Massey and Jess, eds., *A Place in the World?*, p. 200.

295 Malaysia, in particular . . . despite the country's 60 percent Muslim population.

Quoted in Paul Wiseman, "In Malaysia, 'Islamic Civilization' Is Promoted: Tolerance One of the Tenets," *USA Today*, 5 November 2004. For related reasons, see John Krich, "Malaysia Draws New Tourists: Middle Easterners Wary of U.S. Find Appealing Alternative," *Wall Street Journal*, 23 April 2004.

296 Despite popular perceptions, radical fundamentalism . . . the New Core and Gap.

For this rather stunning prognosis, see Laurie Goodstein, "More Religion, but Not the Old-Time Kind," *New York Times*, 9 January 2005.

296 Evangelical Christian faiths . . . profound attention toward the suffering of others.

On this interpretation, see Goodstein, "More Religion, but Not the Old-Time

Kind"; and Allen D. Hertzke, *Freeing God's Children: The Unlikely Alliance for Global Human Rights* (New York: Rowman and Littlefield, 2004), pp. 335–39.

296 This is why the strongest internationalists in America . . . a source of isolationist sentiment.

On this development, see Hertzke, *Freeing God's Children,* pp. 302–35; and Nicholas Kristof, "Following God Abroad," *New York Times,* 21 May 2002; Peter Waldman, "Evangelicals Give U.S. Foreign Policy an Activist Tinge: A Campaign to Export Values Makes Legislative Headway Even As It Arouses Critics," *Wall Street Journal,* 26 May 2004; Murray Hiebert, "Christian Right Focuses on North Korea: Human-Rights Policy Tops Agenda as Evangelicals Look to Broaden Mission," *Wall Street Journal,* 13 May 2005; and David Brooks, "A Natural Alliance: Coming Together to Fight Poverty," *New York Times,* 26 May 2005.

296 Look at the groups arguing for stronger . . . Kansas a leading figure of the movement.

Nicholas Kristof, "When the Right Is Right," *New York Times,* 22 December 2004.

296 Look who's pushing for stronger environmental . . . resolution throughout the Gap.

On the issue of environmentalism in particular, see Blaine Harden, "The Greening of Evangelicals: Christian Right Turns, Sometimes Warily, to Environmentalism," *Washington Post,* 6 February 2005; and Laurie Goodstein, "Evangelical Leaders Swing Influence Behind Effort to Combat Global Warming," *New York Times,* 10 March 2005.

297 Consider these rather fantastic facts . . . Today that percentage is below 40 percent.

Hertzke, *Freeing God's Children,* pp. 16–19.

297 Moreover, if the Republicans . . . *as a foreign policy conscience of conservatism."*

Hertzke, *Freeing God's Children,* p. 341.

298 Yesterday's Protestant work ethic . . . the Core to similar ones inside the Gap.

These concepts of "social capital" are presented and explored at length in Robert Putnam, *Bowling Alone: The Collapse and Revival of American Community* (New York: Simon & Schuster, 2000). I had the great privilege of taking a comparative politics graduate survey class at Harvard that featured both Professor Putnam (then chairman of the Government Department) *and* Professor Samuel Huntington! It was one of the great highlights of my education.

A WORLD MADE ONE . . . OR JUST NONZERO
299 The oft-cited estimate by environmentalists . . . that currently enjoyed by Americans.

Edward O. Wilson wrote famously, "For every person in the world to reach present U.S. levels of consumption with existing technology would require four more planet Earths"; see his "The Bottleneck," *Scientific American,* September 2002.

299 There's a famous quote from a New York City financier . . . needed to switch cable."

Quote located online at the site known as "Strowger Net: devoted to trailing-edge telecommunications" (a subset of the SIGETEL.COM site), on page entitled "Quotes on the phone" (www.sigtel.com/tel_quotes.html).

300 Sure, Jared Diamond, in his book *Collapse* . . . ending their existence in the process.
Jared Diamond, *Collapse: How Societies Choose to Fail or Succeed* (New York: Viking, 2005).

301 Too many celebrated writers in history . . . of such political orders by the year 1984.
Classic books for each include *The Time Machine* (Wells), *We* (Zamyatin), *Brave New World* (Huxley), *Do Androids Dream of Electric Sheep?* (Dick), and *Nineteen Eighty-Four: A Novel* (Orwell).

301 Current Orwell aspirants . . . frightening extrapolations that narrow the mind.
Classic books/essays for each include *The Coming Anarchy* (Kaplan), *The War in 2020* (Peters), *The End of Work* (Rifkin), and "Why the Future Doesn't Need Us" (Joy).

302 As Robert Wright argues in his book . . . years of unfolding non-zero-sum logic.
Wright, *Nonzero*, p. 7.

303 At the beginning of the nineteenth century . . . an estimated 1.1 billion in the year 2001).
Data derived from a chart in Wolf, *Why Globalization Works*, p. 158.

303 If the only categories that make sense . . . Ditto for living standards.
For a detailed examination, see Wolf, *Why Globalization Works*, Chapter 9 ("Incensed About Inequality"), pp. 137–72.

303 Inequality among individuals has not increased . . . of roughly 400 million people.
For good summaries, see Wolf, *Why Globalization Works*, p. 171; and Lomborg, *The Skeptical Environmentalist*, p. 72.

304 When the UN says that more has been done . . . to the rise of the global economy.
Cited in Andrew S. Natsios, Administrator of the U.S. Agency for International Development, in "Alleviating Poverty and Hunger in the 21st Century" (March 2002), found online at usinfo.state.gov/journals/ites/0901/ijee/natsios.htm; and Lomborg, *The Skeptical Environmentalist*, p. 4.

304 Life expectancy is up dramatically . . . mortality rates have decreased significantly.
For a very concise summary of these positive trends, see Lomborg, *The Skeptical Environmentalist*, p. 4.

304 Fertility rates have plummeted, as have child labor rates.
Lomborg, *The Skeptical Environmentalist*, pp. 50–59.

304 At the beginning of the twentieth century . . . are still approximately double those of males.
This data is summarized in Lomborg, *The Skeptical Environmentalist*, p. 81.

304 Manufacturing's share of American . . . manufacturing has declined dramatically.
This development mirrors that of farm labor across the twentieth century; see Lindsey, *Against the Dead Hand*, p. 221.

304 As part of this progression, China will end up buying . . . manufacturing arm in 2005.

On this sale, see Greg Hitt, "Lenovo Deal Elevates China Fears: Proposal to Buy IBM Unit Raises Security, Competitive Issues," *Wall Street Journal,* 10 February 2005; and Steve Lohr, "Sale of I.B.M. Unit to China Passes U.S. Security Muster," *New York Times,* 10 March 2005.

305 As for the notion that China's "inexhaustible" . . . inadequate purchasing power."

Wolf, *Why Globalization Works,* p. 183.

305 Swedish environmentalist Bjorn Lomborg . . . life at least as good as ours, *all in all.*

Lomborg, *The Skeptical Environmentalist,* p. 119.

306 There is more food today . . . it is expected to drop to fewer than 700 million by 2010.

Lomborg, *The Skeptical Environmentalist,* pp. 108–9.

306 Check out any number of "environmental sustainability" . . . in the worst ways.

On the 2005 index of environmental sustainability, generated by the Yale Center for Environmental Law and Policy (the lead author is director Daniel C. Esty) in cooperation with the World Economic Forum, see Felicity Barringer, "Nations Ranked as Protectors of the Environment," *New York Times,* 24 January 2005. Of the 141 countries listed, Gap states tend to be largely concentrated in the lower rankings. For example, of the bottom 71 countries, 61 are Gap, 9 are New Core, and only 1 is Old Core. Of the top 40 states, 25 are Core (18 Old Core and 7 New Core), and 15 are Gap. The complete index is available online at www.yale.edu/envirocenter/esi/.

307 No surprise on this one, as basically every named "hot spot" . . . or along its Seam.

On this debate, see Lomborg, *The Skeptical Environmentalist,* pp. 149–52. For an example of this burgeoning and overwhelmingly alarmist analysis, see Michael T. Klare, *Resource Wars: The New Landscape of Global Conflict* (New York: Henry Holt, 2001). For lists of "at-risk" states, see Lomborg, p. 152, and Klare, pp. 213–31.

307 Humanity has increased its use of water . . . to draw upon fresh-water supplies.

Lomborg, *The Skeptical Environmentalist,* p. 149.

308 On the latter point . . . *been a war fought primarily over water in human history.*

Lomborg, *The Skeptical Environmentalist,* p. 156, citing research using international databases of crises in general and water-related treaties in particular.

308 Again, the record here, as Lomborg . . . portion of the current forest cover.

Lomborg, *The Skeptical Environmentalist,* p. 117.

309 In terms of human deaths from disasters . . . reflecting a decline of over 90 percent.

Lomborg, *The Skeptical Environmentalist,* p. 85; and Bill Marsh, "The Vulnerable Become More Vulnerable," *New York Times,* 2 January 2005.

309 As Lomborg argues so effectively . . . and energy resources is high prices.

Lomborg, *The Skeptical Environmentalist,* p. 125.

310   Lomborg's best point is this . . . assuming that you'll run out of food after three days.
Lomborg, *The Skeptical Environmentalist,* p. 125.

310   Some experts would have you believe . . . oil production is just around the corner.
For a good overview of the doomsayer position, including exposition of the "dreaded" Hubbert Curve (!), see Jeffrey Ball, "As Prices Soar, Doomsayers Provoke Debate on Oil's Future: In a 1970s Echo, Dr. Campbell Warns Supply Is Drying Up, but Industry Isn't Worried; Charges of 'Malthusian Bias,'" *Wall Street Journal,* 21 September 2004. See also Jad Mouawad, "Irrelevant? OPEC Is Sitting Pretty: The Greater the World's Thirst for Oil, the Sooner OPEC May Have All That's Left," *New York Times,* 3 October 2004.

310   These national oil companies tend to keep . . . levels are much lower than realized.
The single most persuasive argument on this subject is found in an op-ed by J. Robinson West. The key numbers are that the national oil companies, or NOCs, control only 60 percent of the production (the traditional oil companies account for the bulk of the rest) but own almost 90 percent of the reserves. The key passage is worth including:

> The capabilities of the national oil companies vary widely. Some are as competent as the international firms. Others are deeply corrupt and lack the capital and skill to meet the sophisticated requirements of portfolio and reservoir management. Furthermore, exploration for new reserves can involve massive risks, which most governments are unwilling to underwrite, whereas the internationals, with huge balance sheets and diversified portfolios, are quite comfortable with these risks.
>
> The thesis of the Hubbert curve is correct, but the conclusion that a fall in global oil production has inevitably begun is not. The Hubbert curve analysis applies where full commercial exploitation has taken place, but in many areas, other factors, including politics and policy, weigh in. It is true that production in most of the United States, Canada and the North Sea is in decline—there, exploration and production have been exhaustive. But the most oil-rich areas, notably Mexico, Venezuela, Russia and the Middle East, have not been fully explored.

See J. Robinson West, "Paying the Pumper," *Washington Post,* 23 July 2004.

310   This has just happened with Russia . . . example, have never been seriously explored.
On Russia, see Gregory L. White, "As Westerners Move into Russia, Its Vast Oil Wealth Keeps Growing: BP, Others Boost Production with Basic Tools of Trade; Reserve Estimates Surge," *Wall Street Journal,* 30 September 2004. On Libya, see Simon Romero, "From Pariah to Belle of the Oil Ball: For Energy Companies, Libya Is Suddenly the Hottest Date Around," *New York Times,* 20 July 2004.

311   For similar reasons in the area of electricity . . . nuclear power in coming years.
For an overview, see Peter Schwartz and Spencer Reiss, "Nuclear Power: How Clean, Green Atomic Energy Can Stop Global Warming," *Wired,* February 2005. For more specific trends, see the example of Patrick Barta, "Uranium Becomes the

New Hot Commodity: Concerns About High Oil Prices, Greenhouse Gases Revive Interest, but Assessing Supply May Be Hard," *Wall Street Journal*, 18 March 2005.

311   For example, to reduce U.S. carbon . . . production as we currently have.
Data provided in Schwartz and Reiss, "Nuclear Power."

311   So as the Chinese increase their car . . . pebble-bed modular nuclear reactors.
On China's strong push for nukes, see the following two articles by Mure Dickie in the *Financial Times:* "China Pioneers 'Cheap, Safe' Nuclear Reactors" and "China to Pioneer 'Pebble Bed' N-Reactor," both dated 7 February 2005. India's right behind China on both measures, as their own car culture and rising energy requirements will trigger many of the same internal dynamics and demands from the outside world. For an example, see Eric Bellman, "Indian Oil Firms Scour Globe: Surging Demand Compels World-wide Quest for Energy Supplies," *Wall Street Journal*, 18 June 2004; Saritha Rai, "Gridlock on India's New Paths to Prosperity," *New York Times,* 12 February 2005; and John Larkin, "India Takes On the World: State-Owned Oil Firm Joins Global Fight for Energy Security," *Wall Street Journal*, 19 May 2005.

312   History shows that local air pollution . . . measured by a rise in GDP per capita.
Lomborg, *The Skeptical Environmentalist,* pp. 175–77.

312   But here's the hitch . . . air pollution—for example, carbon dioxide (CO_2)—tends to worsen.
Daniel C. Esty, director of the Yale Center for Environmental Law and Policy, made this argument in his presentation to Highlands Forum XXV, December 2004. Martin Wolf also offer this analysis in his *Why Globalization Works,* pp. 188–89.

313   When that labor makes its way to the Core . . . Core in Official Developmental Aid.
A recent study of Latinos in the United States demonstrates the profound nature of this financial flow. Seventeen million Latinos work in the United States, earning almost a half-trillion dollars every year. Ninety-three percent of that $450 billion is spent here, with the remaining 7 percent (approximately $30 billion!) being remitted back to the various home countries. How much does that add up to be? Latinos in six American states (California, New York, Texas, Florida, Illinois, and New Jersey) manage to send back more than a billion dollars each. Taken together, that total of $6-plus billion is roughly equal to what the United States sent annually—on average—to the Gap as a whole in Official Developmental Aid (nonmilitary) in the post–Cold War period. The total flow of remittances is thus many times more than the flow of U.S. foreign aid to Latin America. For details, see Joel Millman, "Immigrants Spend Earnings in U.S.: Latin American Workers Send Most Money Home? Not According to Study," *Wall Street Journal*, 17 May 2004.

314   For example, the vaccine that prevents . . . care burden that results from the disease.
The Copenhagen Consensus offers the following analysis: In 2002 there were 57 million deaths, with 20 percent occurring to children under the age of five, with virtually all of those (98 percent) occurring in developing countries, or what I'd call Gap and New Core. Communicable diseases account for almost two-thirds of

those early deaths, and almost 90 percent of those are easily preventable, with vaccines playing a key role in several instances (measles, malaria, and tetanus, for
example). Preventable childhood illness has a hugely negative ripple effect in an
economy, leading to child malnutrition, less schooling, impaired cognitive ability,
higher fertility (to replace lost kids), and—obviously—higher child mortality. All
of these negative outcomes lower per capita income and reduce labor productivity.
For an excellent article on the subject, see Anne Mills and Sam Shillcutt, "Communicable Diseases," in Lomborg, ed., *Global Crises, Global Solutions*, pp. 62–114.
On future possibilities, see Marilyn Chase, "Malaria Trial Could Set a Model for
Financing of Costly Vaccines," *Wall Street Journal*, 26 April 2005.

314   As we've seen with the spread of the worldwide disease . . . cheaper than
      treatment.
      The best global analysis I've seen on AIDS within a global security context comes
      from the National Intelligence Council. See David F. Gordon, *The Next Wave of
      HIV/AIDS: Nigeria, Ethiopia, Russia, India, and China* (National Intelligence
      Council/Intelligence Community Assessment 2002–04D, September 2002). See
      also the following recent articles: Lawrence K. Altman, "Spread of Polio in West
      and Central Africa Makes U.N. Officials Fear Major Epidemic," *New York
      Times*, 23 June 2004; Sebastian Mallaby, "How Africa Subsidizes U.S. Health
      Care: By Poaching the Poor World's Medical Workers, We're Siphoning Doctors
      from Places Where They Are Needed," *Washington Post*, 29 November 2004;
      David Brown, "AIDS in India, China and Russia Nears 'Tipping Point,'" *Wash-
      ington Post*, 1 December 2004; Craig Timberg, "In Rural Zimbabwe, AIDS
      Still Means Death: Politics and Poverty Deprive Many of Relief as New Drugs
      Stem Disease Across Africa," *Washington Post*, 20 April 2005; and Donald G.
      McNeil, Jr., "Polio Back in Yemen After 6-Year Absence," *New York Times*, 22
      April 2005.

314   Toss in, if you will, what we end up paying . . . agricultural development
      in the Gap.
      On the question of farm subsidies, see Wolf, *Why Globalization Works*, pp.
      212–13, where he notes that among high-income countries the tariffs on agricul-
      tural imports are twice that of manufactured goods. Sebastian Mallaby notes that
      Europe spends $2 a day on each cow within the Union, while Japan's government
      spends $4 a day. The average African income is roughly $1 a day. See his "Easy
      Ways to Aid Africa," *Washington Post*, 21 March 2005. For more details, see Eliz-
      abeth Becker, "Farm Subsidies Again Take Front Seat at the W.T.O.," *New York
      Times*, 28 July 2004; Scott Miller, "WTO Farm Pact Wouldn't Be Panacea," *Wall
      Street Journal*, 29 July 2004; Scott Miller, "Why Not to Cut Farm Aid: Many Poor
      Nations Fight Europe's Bid to Lower Barriers," *Wall Street Journal*, 16 December
      2004; and Dan Morgan, "An End to Days of High Cotton?: GOP Constituents
      Caught in Battle Over Subsidies," *Washington Post*, 8 March 2005. The U.S. Gov-
      ernment spends about $1 billion a year in counterdrug operations and aid (Inter-
      national Narcotic Control and Law Enforcement and Andean Counterdrug
      Initiative in the "150 account—International Affairs" of the U.S. federal budget).
      For details on jump-starting agricultural development inside the Gap, see Jeffrey
      Sachs et al., "Investing in Development: A Practical Plan to Achieve the Millen-
      nium Development Goals," Report to the UN Secretary-General by the Mil-
      lennium Project, 2005).

314 There is no mystery to any of this . . . agricultural development inside
the Gap.

The U.S. National Academy of Science released its authoritative report in 2004
stating that "genetically engineered crops do not pose health risks that cannot
also arise from crops created by other techniques, including conventional breed-
ing"; see Andrew Pollack, "Panel Sees No Unique Risk from Genetic Engineer-
ing," *Wall Street Journal,* 28 July 2004.

315 Think of all the military spending inside the Core . . . there against one
another.

The world as a whole spends close to a trillion dollars a year on defense ($956 bil-
lion in 2003, according to the Stockholm International Peace Research Institute).
A fair assessment would be that at least half of that spending is directed at protecting Core states from one another, or roughly $500 billion a year.

315 Then think of all the money Core . . . military aid to states inside the Gap.

According to the U.S. federal budget, the United States spends about $5 billion in
military aid to Gap states every year (training plus financing for arms purchases).
If the United States accounts for roughly one-half of global defense spending,
then it's reasonable to estimate that it accounts for one-half of total Core military
aid to the Gap, suggesting an annual flow in the range of $10 billion.

315 Then think of all the money Gap nations spend on purchases . . . the
United States.

The Core sells about $25 billion of arms to the Gap every year (down from Cold
War highs in the low to mid-40s), according to the Congressional Research Service
in its annual report, "Conventional Arms Transfers to Developing Nations."

315 Then think of all the money spent inside the Gap on these conflicts
and wars.

The average Gap country increases its defense spending by the equivalent of 2 percent of national GDP for the period of the conflict and for several years following
its conclusion. You can add additional costs relating to arms races triggered
among that country's neighbors (roughly equivalent in magnitude), plus all the
related costs triggered by refugees, the spread of disease, and so on. For details on
such estimates, see Paul Collier and Anke Hoeffler, "Conflicts," in Lomborg, ed.
Global Crises, Global Solutions, pp. 131–36.

315 Then think of all the money spent by Core militaries . . . to these conflicts
and wars.

According to the Defense Department's Defense Science Board, the U.S. military
has averaged in the post–Cold War period approximately $3 billion a year in com-
bined major combat operations inside the Gap. Again, applying the rule of thumb
that when it comes to defense spending, if the United States spends roughly half
of that spent by the world as a whole, then the total Core effort might be viewed in
the range of $4 billion a year. For the U.S. estimates, see Defense Science Board,
Transition To and From Hostilities, p. 18, and Appendix D supporting data,
pp. 193–96.

316 Then think of all the money spent by Core . . . following all their conflicts
and wars.

Using the same approach as in the previous note, the United States has spent
approximately $10 billion a year on postconflict stabilization and reconstruction
operations since the end of the Cold War. If the rule of thumb holds on our

spending—on average—what the rest of the Core's powers spend on such things, then we could be talking about upwards of $20 billion a year in flows. For the U.S. estimates, see Defense Science Board, *Transition To and From Hostilities*, p. 18, and Appendix D supporting data, pp. 193–96.

316   Then think of the economic losses by all . . . economies in these conflicts and wars.

The average civil war runs about seven years and costs the country in question approximately $65 billion for the total war (in lost economic output). If twelve such wars are raging inside the Gap on an average annual basis, and each one costs close to $10 billion a year, that's more than $100 billion of lost output each year due to civil wars inside the Gap; see Collier and Hoeffler, "Conflicts," in Lomborg, ed., *Global Crises, Global Solutions*, pp. 129–50. For an interesting analysis of what conflicts such as these generate in nonviolent deaths (malnutrition, respiratory disease, diarrhea, anemia, measles, meningitis, accidents, tuberculosis, fever, and other causes), see Marc Lacey, "Beyond the Bullets and Blades: How a Society Breaks Apart When Africans Flee the Onslaught," *New York Times*, 20 March 2005. In another article, Lacey cites estimates by relief organizations that, of the millions who perished in Africa's many civil wars of the last decade "less than 2 percent of the deaths were caused by violence"; see his "In Africa, Guns Aren't the Only Killers," *New York Times*, 25 April 2005.

316   Then think of the economic opportunities lost . . . suffer these conflicts and wars.

If the Gap "costs" around $100 billion in lost output every year due to civil wars, we might consider the cost to the global economy as being a multiple of that amount, because all that lost income could have been spent on goods and services from the Core and fellow Gap economies. Typically, when an individual working overseas sends back remittances to his or her country of origin, the one "dollar" sent home generates typically three dollars' worth of additional transactions in the local economy—the multiplier effect. You get the idea. Whatever it costs the world to suffer all these civil wars in the Gap is a whole lot more than just *their* lost GDP. We lose out simply by missing out on all that potential economic connectivity (we buy their stuff, they buy ours, and the world goes around).

316   Because at that point I will tell you this . . . on its own, it slips back into conflict.

Collier and Hoeffler, "Conflicts," in Lomborg, ed., *Global Crises, Global Solutions*, pp. 145–47.

316   The Copenhagen Consensus project . . . force in the manner that I just described.

Collier and Hoeffler compare five methods of reducing the incidence and length of civil wars inside the Gap. Of the five (foreign aid to prevent wars, postconflict aid to prevent relapses into war, postconflict peacekeeping to do the same, and two forms of international control over extractive industries that typically account for much of the frequency and length of such wars), the best outcomes (by far) were estimated to be achieved through international peacekeeping efforts in the first several years following a civil war, followed by well-timed foreign aid in the first decade following conflict. The reason the best payoffs were found in postconflict situations was that most civil wars start in countries that are recovering from previous civil wars, or a ten-to-fifteen-year period they identify as the "conflict trap."

316 By the Copenhagen Consensus's best estimates . . . is roughly $10 billion.
     Collier and Hoeffler, "Conflicts," in Lomborg, ed., *Global Crises, Global Solutions,* pp. 134–36. Note that these estimates accounted for only the recouped earnings for the state in question and did not calculate the additional multiplier effects on the global economy of having that country operating its economy in peacetime conditions versus in war.

317 Once a state exits a civil war situation . . . back into civil war decrease dramatically.
     Collier and Hoeffler, "Conflicts," in Lomborg, ed., *Global Crises, Global Solutions,* pp. 135–36.

317 The Consensus's best estimate . . . for each civil war shortened by one year's time.
     Collier and Hoeffler, "Conflicts," in Lomborg, ed., *Global Crises, Global Solutions,* pp. 147–50.

Conclusion: HEROES YET DISCOVERED

321 The Echo Boomers, or the huge 80-million-plus . . . our economy and political scene.
     For a great overview, see the transcript of the *60 Minutes* segment "The Echo Boomers," found online at www.cbsnews.com/stories/2004/10/01/60minutes/main646890.shtml.

322 As *60 Minutes* correspondent Steve Kroft . . . in a cafeteria that serves peanut butter."
     See "The Echo Boomers," *60 Minutes* online transcript.

322 As a result, they are naturally team-oriented . . . emulate their parents instinctively.
     See "The Echo Boomers," *60 Minutes* online transcript.

322 They distrust slick packaging . . . themselves to a degree never witnessed before.
     On this, see Tobi Elkin, "Echo Effect: A New Generation of Media Users, Ad Distrusters," *Media Daily News,* 17 February 2004.

322 Natural multitaskers because . . . plugged-in citizens of a worldwide community."
     See "The Echo Boomers," *60 Minutes* online transcript.

322 As such, they know multiculturalism not as something . . . third of this generation is nonwhite.
     See "The Echo Boomers," *60 Minutes* online transcript.

322 Probably the least "churched" generation in U.S. history . . . the world a better place.
     This is an analysis you can run into on almost any religious-oriented site offering opinions on the Echo Boomers. They are consistently portrayed as a "lost generation" that needs to be converted or invited into formal religious settings. Watching mainstream churches fret over this generation is like watching the National Football League fret over a generation of soccer kids growing up into their expected fan-base age range: they feel instinctively that they should be able to connect with them but worry that they never will.

322   As historian Neil Howe describes Echo Boomers . . . up than tearing them down."
      See "The Echo Boomers," *60 Minutes* online transcript.
323   The establishment of official diplomatic relations . . . Vatican will constitute an important early milestone.
      On this imminent possibility, see Elizabeth Rosenthal, "Hints of Thaw Between China and Vatican," *International Herald Tribune,* 22 May 2005.
337   To the surprise . . . a German.
      For coverage, see "Larry Rohter, "In Selection of New Pope, Third World Loses Out: Some Disappointment in Latin America, Less in Africa and Asia," *New York Times,* 20 April 2005.
339   George Bernard Shaw once said . . . therefore, depends on unreasonable people."
      Source is BrainyQuote.com, page entry for George Bernard Shaw, found online at www.brainyquote.com/quotes/authors/g/george_bernard_shaw.html.

Afterword: BLOGGING THE FUTURE

341   The filmmaker George Lucas describes . . . was going to destroy the Death Star.
      Audio commentary track by George Lucas et al., *Star Wars Episode VI: Return of the Jedi* (2004 *Star Wars Trilogy* edition).
349   Not surprisingly, nineteen of the twenty-five most polluted cities . . . in Asia, with nine in China alone.
      Sources for this are the World Resources Institute, the World Health Organization, and the National Intelligence Council. For a summary slide, see my *NewRuleSets.Project* summary briefing of the "Asian Environmental Solutions" Economic Security Exercise conducted by the Naval War College with Cantor Fitzgerald atop World Trade Center 1, 4 June 2001, found online at www.thomaspmbarnett.com/projects/newrulesset/Asian%20Energy%20Solutions%20roadshow%20brief.htm.
350   In December 2004, South America's two . . . at only a fraction of the GDP power).
      For details of the original declaration of intent, see "S. America Launches Trading Bloc: Representatives from 12 South American Countries Have Signed an Agreement to Create a Political and Economic Bloc Modeled on the European Union," *BBC News,* 9 December 2004.
354   America's societal dependency on . . . one-tenth of our total usage).
      According to various estimates (e.g., White House fact sheets, major news programs), Colombia accounts for anywhere between 75 and 90 percent of the cocaine in the U.S. market, along with upwards of two-thirds of the heroin. For an example of such data, see "White House Fact Sheet on U.S.-Colombia Counterdrug Cooperation," August 30, 2000, found online at ciponline.org/Colombia/083003.htm.
354   When it comes to per capita pollution . . . biggest producer of carbon dioxide.
      On this subject, see my "Asian Environmental Solutions" briefing.

358   By 2020, Hispanics' share of the electorate . . . or Asian-Americans (one out of twenty).

Date drawn from U.S. Census Bureau, 2004, "U.S. Interim Projections by Age, Sex, Race, and Hispanic Origin," available online at www.census.gov/ipo/www. usinterimproj/. On the more general subject of growing political clout, see Ginger Thompson, "Latin Migrants Gain Political Clout in U.S.," *New York Times,* 24 February 2005.

358   In the tribal Saudi Arabia . . . that is intricately linked to clans the country over.

For an excellent overview, see Robert Baer, "The Fall of the House of Saud," *Atlantic Monthly,* May 2003.

362   When Pablo Picasso showed his just-finished portrait . . . replied, "It will."

As described in Stein's book *The Autobiography of Alice B. Toklas,* Picasso had a very difficult time painting her, preferring, as usual, his own particular vision to any empirical reality. For details on the painting, see the Metropolitan Museum of Art's entry, "Pablo Picasso (Spanish, 1881–1973); Gertrude Stein, 1906; Oil on canvas; Bequest of Gertrude Stein, 1946," found online at www.metmuseum. org/Works_of_Art/ViewOne.asp?item=47.106&dep=21.

INDEX

military. *See also* Leviathan force;
    Pentagon; SysAdmin (System
    Administrators) force
  base realignment, 162–164
  for counterinsurgency, 64
  future heroes in, 324–326
  -market nexus, definition, *xvii*
  transformation of, 2, 3, 22–23, 28,
    123–124, 165
  use of, to enable globalization, 52,
    61–62, 113, 250–251, 315–319
Military Operations Other Than War
    (MOOTW), *xix*, 13
Milosevic, Slobodan, 55, 114
Mubarak, Hosni, 94
Muslims. *See also* al Qaeda; Salafi
    jihadists
  in Asia, 295
  balance of globalization with
    retention of identity, 87–88
  in Europe, 86, 291–294, 330, 357
  in Gap-shrinking scenarios, 217–222
  religious revivalism, 86, 92, 270, 294,
    297
  women, 92, 293, 336
  youth, 292–293

National Defense University (NDU), 32
National Intelligence Council (NIC),
    43–46
natural resources, 246, 261, 305, 306–310
Network-Centric Operations (NCO).
    See also Leviathan force
  and Fourth-Generation Warfare, as
    opposing visions of war, 8–11,
    18, 20–21
  premises and concepts of, 8, 9, 12–15
  in transformation of military, 47–48,
    61
New Core. *See also specific countries in
    New Core*
  countries constituting, *xvi*
  global economy, requisites for
    inclusion in, 232–233

globalization, pace of, 199–202
globalization rule set, 229–230
security strategies, deconfliction of,
    176–181
U.S. security partnerships in economic
    competition, 167–168
  need for, 164–166, 186–187
  perceived threats to Old Core,
    168–175
in U.S. military strategy, 3
Nichols, David, 84
9/11 attacks, changes engendered by
    Department of Homeland
    Security, 24, 27, 327
  G-8 agenda, 59
  nature of mass violence, 31
  need for Core-wide security strategy,
    49–50
  transformation of Pentagon, 3, 22
  U.S. globalization policies, 74, 94–95,
    190–191, 226–227, 231–232
  U.S. relations with China, 21, 127, 141
Niu Ke, 138
Non-Integrating Gap. *See* Gap, Non-
    Integrating; Gap, shrinking of
North Korea. *See* Korea

Old Core. *See* Core, Functioning

Pakistan
  China, alliance with, 103
  globalization, response to, 86
  inability to assume regional role,
    98–99
  India, tensions with, 163, 224
  Indian pipeline through, 103, 233, 353
  nuclear bomb proliferation, 349
  as Seam State, 239
  terrorists in, 177–178, 223, 240, 349
Palestinian-Israeli conflict, 98, 102–103,
    109, 336, 360
Pentagon. *See also* Leviathan force;
    SysAdmin (System
    Administrators) force